TALK IT OUT!

No More Gay Shame!

Dr. Vincent Pellegrino "Dr. Vince"

OPENING QUOTES:

"I'm a gay man, but I don't like to associate myself with the gay community, simply because I can't stand the way they treat one another! (Leonard L. - NYC)

"I don't like women and ugly men!" (A quote from a tragic hustler in the movie *Circuit*)

"I see no difference between the viciousness in which some *queens verbally attack one another and the behavior of *homophobes who are the first ones to yell "FAG" to their so-called "straight" friends whenever they see a gay man on a city sidewalk. (Rick Barton of Dallas, Texas & Tulsa, Oklahoma).

ALL MEN ARE BEASTS! SO JUST IMAGINE TWO BEASTS GETTING TOGETHER? NO WONDER YOU FELLAS HAVE A PROBLEM WITH COMMUNICATION!!!!
*(The late Cassandra Danz – from NYC and the *Regis and Kathie Lee Show*, was a wife, mother, and professional comedienne who played the character "Mrs. Greenthumb")

Gay men and women have often felt guilty for his/her actions; sadder still, is that many have often also felt shameful for who they are and they often take that shame out on their fellow gays! (Dr. Vince)

* Queens – not to be confused with the ruler of a country, although, some of them would like to believe they possess that kind of power.
* Homophobes – mostly shameful men, who can't deal with their homosexual urges and are notorious for physically attacking gay men when in packs.

ACKNOWLEDGEMENTS

I would like to thank all those who participated in making this book a reality: My long-time friends Tim Rogers and his former lover, the late Bob Dobson, and my dear friend and manager, Wayne Scherzer for his years of dedication and belief in this book, My kind and considerate interviewees: David Pevsner, Aaron Tanner and his friend Eric, Rob Ordonez, Brian Kent, Ira Smith, Brad Carpenter & Chris Aruda, Ray Dunbar-Smith, Brian Gleason, Ron Ben Israel, and all my wonderful friends at the David Barton Gym in NYC.

I would also like to express my gratitude to those friends who chose to remain anonymous for their own reasons, and to my very talented friend, Chris Silva for his excellent artistic skills in designing both the front and back covers of my book. In addition, I wish to give a special thank you to Mike Fusco for his helpful editing skills and Christian Ladigoski for his computer skills and social media expertise.

Most importantly, I wish to give special gratitude to my eternally young mother, Mary Pellegrino, my beautiful sister Maryanne Juresich, and to my brother, Dr. Dennis Pellegrino, for their unwavering support and encouragement in assisting me toward completing this work.

I hereby dedicate this book in loving memory to my father, Salvatore Pellegrino, and to all my friends and partners who have left this world much too soon due to AIDS and especially, to those who lost their lives as a direct result of Gay Shame.

It is my sincere hope that this book and the very personal stories shared here will give those who are still struggling with their true sexuality the same level of comfort and support that so many of us need in these uncertain times in this ever changing world.

Also, I will refer to the gay community as both the LGBT and GLBT communities as it is referred to with both designations – perhaps this is indicative of the difficulties in defining ourselves as a culture and as a people.

TABLE OF CONTENTS

CHAPTER ONE – THE GAY COMMUNICATION GAME

A VERY PERSONAL STORY"

Having moved to a rural part of Connecticut in the beginning months of the nineties, I fully expected big changes to happen. With my partner in tow, I left a one-bedroom apartment on the Upper West Side of Manhattan to move into a picturesque stone house with three bedrooms and two acres of land. Images of a more settled "married life" in this countrified community of manicured lawns and quiet dinners with friends came to my mind.

Unfortunately, my "married life" ended up lasting less than a year. My lover and I were totally unable to communicate. He was always expressing a fervent desire to leave and giving me a major guilt complex! According to him, it was, "all my fault that the relationship was not working out."

So, the Christmas holidays came and went with my being left alone in my beautiful house with four dogs and not knowing a single soul in the area. That was until I found a local gay travel, Aldis from Latvia, who soon introduced me to other gay men and women in the community. I was saved, or, so I thought!

In time, I became aware of the difficulties in being gay and living in Connecticut. I no longer had the large gay community of New York City to draw back upon. One could easily find himself alone in an area where the gay community is very much in the minority and all too spread out. A feeling of isolation was not uncommon. And yet, when I went to parties and functions where gay men were plentiful, I noticed an interesting dynamic of non-communication or selective communication occurring. It was as if I was back in the "cruise bars" of New York City, but this time, in more suburban surroundings.

Most puzzling to me, were observing attractive gay men in cliques talking negatively about other men around them with whom they were clearly attracted to, but instead, failed to introduce themselves or, express their true interest to them. In fact, the entire night would pass and not one man would take the initiative to say "hello," but, to comment critically of others. It was as if I was back in the "cruise bars" of New York City where few men work up the courage to talk to one another but, now I was in a completely different setting but, with more "attitude" than NYC!

This type of communication immediately brought up painful childhood memories for me where I was either the object of other children's cruel comments or, would purposefully chose to avoid their comments by any means possible.

At an early age I knew that I was different from most of the other boys and girls in school. I tended to either keep to myself or act up like the "class clown" to get approval. My parents and my brother perceived my behavior as less than "man-like," more like a "sissy, and at the tender age twelve, I was sent to a military school in Miami, Florida to "make more of a man out of me!" I lasted all of three months! Needless to say, my parents were very disappointed knowing their plan failed but, I was never the same; my innocence was gone!

Although our family dynamics have drastically changed over the years, at that time, I felt alone in the world where I would often feel the need to appease my family by either avoiding them or placating their needs. The thought of "acting up" like my little nephew often does, was something I would rarely do.

Instead, I often felt like a little, fat boy with a smiling mask or facade. I would often cry and say "I'm sorry," for no good reason. As an adult, I realized that I allowed myself to become an easy victim for abusive boyfriends, because for some inane reason, I felt I deserved the abuse. But in time, I found my refuge in the theater and Al-Anon, where I found others just like me.

As you will see from most of the individuals interviewed, there are a significant number involved in the theater. This decision stems from my own involvement with the theater during the age of my "coming out." The theater was the one place where I felt I belonged. It was also where my "sensitivity" was accepted and channeled into a creative venue. Of course, there was still some competition and an attitude of superiority between the actors and actresses at my school, nevertheless, I loved being in thirteen plays in a two year period.

At my college was also where I made my official "coming out." I vividly recall going to the Catholic Center one evening and meeting a gay priest and a group of gay women who decided to take me with them to Albany that weekend in 1972 for my first Gay Pride March. It was one of the most terrifying and thrilling times of my life!

My own personal history and my expertise as a teacher of communication, has led me to write this book that has such as direct correlation to my life. In addition, my years as a certified therapist have provided me with the ability to analyze human behavior when examining the communication of gay men in social settings. This analysis will be present throughout the "Life Stories" chapters in significant points while describing various events in each gay man's life. Analysis will be most evident whenever a subject's comments or actions pointedly relate to communication and on how each subject views himself or other gay men in a negative way.

*I do want to make it perfectly clear that I am not suggesting that every gay man interacts in a dysfunctional manner when communicating with one another. However, there is a large enough number of us for whom I believe this book IS important. Important, for not only providing a tool for obtaining more awareness as to how we speak and interact with other gay men but, to learn where most of our dysfunctional behaviors possibly originated from in the first place. All of which has led to this Gay Communication Game becoming so prevalent in our lives and culture.

WHY CALL THIS TYPE OF COMMUNICATION A GAME?

Okay, so why do I choose to call the communication patterns between gay men a game? Just what is a game? The dictionary definition is: A **game** - (noun) diversion, pastime; jest; contest for amusement; A scheme, strategy; animals or birds hunted, adjective) brave, or willing to gamble. (Collins, 1987)

All the above definitions can easily be associated with the "game" that frequently occurs between gay men in their social interactions. "Animals or birds hunted," brings to my mind the popular term of "being on the hunt" for potential sex partners within the gay scene of "cruising."

The game itself can often be an unconscious one. After all, there isn't always a conscious desire on the part of the initiator to play a "game" with their communication partner. But, as a gay man, I have frequently experienced this game being played as both observer and a participant and, I have also seen the results. That through this dysfunctional behavior, a number of outcomes have occurred, chiefly, that the self-esteem of those in the losing end of this game are the ones who truly suffer.

For with any "game playing," where someone is being dishonest or uncaring of their partner's feelings, not only are feelings hurt but, one's own self-esteem is injured by the actions of others. For that specific reason, I have chosen to write this book for you.

As my ex would often comment to me in reference to this book: "it's called it a game because if you get the boy – you win!" (Barton, 2007)

Also, in this "game," there are many ways in which this game can be acted out. Some through certain language and references to "win" the game or, would be acted out non-verbally by either facial expressions or body language.

The following are all examples of gay male interaction including some *common thoughts* among many gay men with regards to their desire to communicate and the barriers that prevent us from doing so: Enjoy the following stories and see if there is something you can identify with:

REJECTION OR ACCEPTANCE

Story #1: Walking into his best friend Carlos's annual Christmas party, Anthony observes several attractive men interacting with one another. Immediately his inner dialogue goes into overdrive and he hears a familiar voice in his head that has not always served him well but doesn't know how to voice off:

"I don't know who to talk to? "Why do I want to talk to?" I'm really attracted to that guy over there on the sofa but can I summon the courage to approach him?" "I know I 'm attractive but, if he rejects me, I'll die of embarrassment in the middle of this party!" And, so on and so on....

Fortunately for Anthony, Carlos performs his hosting duties beautifully, and soon takes Anthony by the hand and introduces him to all the men, including the "hottie" on the sofa... Within a short period of time, the two men find many common interests and are increasingly attracted to one another. By the time the party comes to an end, the two are a couple making plans for the rest of the evening and future dates. Problem solved for Anthony for now but, what about for the rest of us?

SEXUAL OR PURELY FRIENDLY

Story # 2: Craig is in the middle of his workout at the gym and notices for the hundredth time the man of his dreams working out on the workout bench next to his, His thoughts begin to race as he nonchalantly glances over in his idol's direction as the man pumps the barbells with clear determination. As soon as the *man* finishes his set, Craig considers "making his move" but these cautionary voices soon become louder in his head:

"I want to meet him, but I'm afraid to approach him. I won't allow him to snub me!" "I know I should smile more, but I'm afraid." "Why do I always perceive a sexual innuendo whenever I meet another gay man for the first time? Can't we just talk to one another without that feeling coming up for me? Am I alone in feeling this way?" And, so on and so on.......

As it happily turns out, the man of his dreams completes his set and is soon asking Craig if he had finished with the dumbbells he was using? With a new found courage, Craig jokes to the man about the intensity of his workout and how he admired his focus and determinism. (What a line!) The man smiles widely recognizing a "line" and quickly introduces himself as John and even compliments him on his own workout routine. As the men begin to converse, Craig admits to John his previous hesitation in meeting him feeling a bit intimidated by John's attractiveness.

Without missing a beat, John comments of hearing that line all too often but, of also having noticed Craig on the workout floor and was unsure himself of whether to talk to him as well. After much relieved laughter, the two men decide to continue their workouts together and make plans for lunch after the gym. Perhaps the beginning of a beautiful friendship and more if they can just get "out of their heads" and be honest and more sincere with their feelings.

Story # 3:- David has agreed to meet with his friends Brad and his boyfriend Tom at the bar close to David's gym for drinks and dinner at a popular restaurant. Unbeknownst to David, Brad and Tom have brought a friend for David to meet for a prospective love match. As David grapples his way through the throng of men at the bar, he notices another man talking to his friends. Knowing how his friends operate, David correctly suspects that the guy is someone his friends are looking to "fix him up with." The man himself is attractive but, not really David's "type." His inner dialogue goes into overdrive: "Why do I always perceive a sexual innuendo whenever I meet another gay man for the first time? Can't we just talk to one another without that feeling coming up for me? "I really don't want people I'm not attracted to thinking I'm "coming onto them"; then what will I do?" "I want more friends in my life, but everyone I meet just wants to fuck me!"

After being introduced to Mark, the prospective love match, David soon begins to warm up to this charming and intelligent man who is clearly attracted to David by his enthusiastic responses and strong eye contact. As the evening progresses, the group decide to leave the bar and go to a restaurant for dinner. Both Mark and David become so engrossed into their conversation that Brad and Tom begin to feel a little neglected but pleased at the positive outcome of their plan to get these two together. The result of the love matchmaking ends with David and Mark deciding to date the next night and subsequent nights in the following weeks.

PLEASE DON'T INVADE MY SPACE!

Story # 4: James is someone that tends to command considerable attention from men with his good looks and impressive physique. When he works out in the gym, he does not want to talk to anyone unless it is to ask if they are finished using the equipment so he can quickly work in and complete his set. Often while working out, he notices men looking in his direction or working out in close proximity to him which he hates!

His thought process goes as follows: "I want that guy to stay the fuck away from me so I'll just give him a quick scowl and hope he goes away?" "Will you please leave me along; can't you see I'm busy working out?" "The people in this gym are just too annoying, I wish I could afford to change gyms but unfortunately, I can't! What can I do?"

But instead of voicing his angry thoughts, James continues his workout displaying his usual grim facial expressions and intent toward finishing his workout as soon as possible without sacrificing his routine. Unfortunately, as a result of Eric's all-too-frequent unpleasant facial expressions, he has gained the reputation at the gym of being a "walking god with the personality of a fish!"

MEAN BOYS AT THE PARTY

Story # 5: Eric loves the beach and the group of attractive and popular friends he has acquired over the years, much to his satisfaction. Eric and his clique rarely go out in public without being in their own company. With the comfort and support of his "inner circle," Eric will often feel empowered to share his thoughts with his friends about other gay men he has observed, knowing full well they will enthusiastically agree with him.

At one very "A List" house party at the Hamptons, Eric freely shares to his friends about some of the more attractive and well-dressed men at the party with the exception of one: "I know that guy from my gym and I really don't want to **encourage** him so don't look in his direction and maybe he will get the hint and walk away?"

"Even though he is a nice guy, I know he just wouldn't fit in with our group. Maybe if he lost some weight I would consider him but, not for now!"

As a result of the behavior of Eric and his group, not one member of the group meets anyone new at the party despite some wonderful people present and interested in them. Their discriminatory behavior toward others resulted with only themselves to keep one another company; while the rejected guy from the gym meets someone wonderful to spend the weekend with.

Sadly, Eric and his group with their poor choices if not changed, will end up becoming a group of bitter gay men who will continu1lly bemoan their unsatisfactory love lives.

* QUESTIONS TO ASK YOURSELVES:

- With how many of the statements from all the stories listed above would you tend to relate or identify?
- Ask yourself what occurs in your body whenever you are experiencing those situations in your life either as the abuser or the abused? Does your body tense up in any way or, do you feel the opposite; relaxed and confident?
- Do you feel that you suffer in any way when you can't be honest and upfront with someone who may just want to converse and interact with you? Are you concerned that if you say hello to them, you are in a sense, inviting them to your bed?
- Is it simply too difficult to reject someone who is attracted to you so instead, you ignore them?
- Are you too afraid of doing something that may be deemed "not cool" so you do your usual nothing instead?
- Finally, do you find gay men gathering in cliques for the purpose of safety and support eventually end up looking and acting like one another? An image similar to the "clone look of the seventies," comes to mind where so many guys sported trimmed mustaches, white t-shirts and flannel?
- Do you believe that the group dynamic of displaying a similar appearance and behavior is similar to that of teenagers trying to stand out as special in a crowd?

Now, I'm not saying that this "game" doesn't also occur in the heterosexual world. The "straight" bar scene is well known for first encounters based primarily on physical attraction, but this book is primarily an exploration of the communication patterns occurring between gay men in various social interactions. I will, of necessity, include comparisons to heterosexual communication and dating rituals in various parts of this book in order to promote clarity and identification for the reader.

A second basis to the game analogy comes directly from one of the textbooks that I use the classes for my <u>Oral Communication</u> courses at Hofstra University. The following describes the pragmatic model of communication which focuses on patterns of our behavior. The focus of this model is all about our actions when we meet and interact, and how similar they are to the "moves" people make in playing a game such as chess.

"In the pragmatic model, communication is seen as a game of sequential, interlocking moves between independent partners. Each player responds to the partner's moves in light of his own strategy in and anticipation of future actions. Some moves are specific to this game, and others are common gambits and strategies. Moves make sense only in context of the game." (Trenholm, 1995)

Trenholm explains further that the game most resembles the game of chess, since the game is one of strategy and skill. Through this analogy, it is my conviction that those who excel in playing the game may feel a sense of control in their lives simply because they hold onto the belief that they have the ability to "out-think" their opponents or partners.

Perhaps by learning certain "tricks of the trade" in achieving objectives through game playing, the achievement of certain goals may be more easily achieved, but at what price? Does the game of Life or Monopoly ever consider the human aspect of hurting others through one's quest for self-esteem and personal gain?

Here's a narrative example to further illustrate a particular type of communication game that often occurs between gay men. I'm positive that the following narrative will provide several familiar experiences with not only the gay reader, but to everyone.

"WHEN TWO GAY WORLDS COLLIDE!"
(A Selective Communication Scenario)

SETTINGS: A popular gym in New York City and a restaurant in East Hampton.

On the large workout floor, Nick loves the social interaction with his "gym buddies." The camaraderie helps to add some welcome respite during his workouts.

There is one especially attractive and personable man named Tom whom Nick loves chatting with. The frequent topic of those talks concerned Tom's frustrations with his boyfriend Paul. Nick has often observed the "hot" boyfriend. Paul is young, handsome, and intelligent but, smiles infrequently. Nick suggested to Tom that he be honest with his feelings toward his boyfriend and tell him what upsets him with his behavior. In subsequent interactions with both men, Nick noticed that Paul smiles more and Tom says that he is more satisfied with their relationship. In the following weeks, Tom and Nick continue to chat and gossip, and both appear to enjoy the playfulness with one another in the gym.

Now outside the gym, Nick sees Tom and Paul in various gay "circuit" parties to which Tom has clearly told Nick that he cares not to participate. Last month, Nick and his new lover met Tom and Paul at an East Hampton political fundraiser. Both men were cordial, but neither attempted to include either Nick or his lover in their group's conversation. There were more than seven people with them at the time, so Nick overlooked the slight.

That same evening, Nick and lover were looking for a good restaurant in town. They found this charming place and were soon escorted to our table by the hostess. Almost immediately, Nick noticed Tom and Paul and greeted them with their names and a comment, "Wow, what a small world!" Tom simply smiled tightly and nodded his head; Paul did the same. They provided no opportunity to say more or allow Nick the opportunity to introduce his lover. There was a third gentleman at their table who looked up, yet said nothing.

The hostess seated our boys at a table near the threesome, but neither Tom nor Paul turned to say anything more to the couple. Nick and lover ate their entire meal without either Tom or Paul saying a word to them, choosing only to speak to their dinner companion. The three of them finished their meal and left the restaurant without even saying goodbye. In fact, Tom forgot something at the table and had to come back to retrieve it. Again, he did not say goodbye, or acknowledge Nick and his lover with a nod or a smile.

Nick was upset after they departed, and his boyfriend was clear in his desire NOT to meet either of them, and suggested that Nick ignore them when he next came in contact with the pair. That, "those jerks are not worthy of your friendship because of their stupid behavior." And yet, Nick continued to try to rationalize their actions by making excuses for them; that despite the third person appearing to be gay, perhaps the situation was too uncomfortable to make introductions.

Nick's boyfriend continued to argue his point. "They still could have greeted us more warmly or simply introduced us to their friend, and then continued their dinner conversation. That by not greeting us, they were communicating something shameful about acknowledging you."

Nick eventually agreed to his lover's more logical points and decided not to dwell on the clear snub and enjoy his lover's attention. But, in secret, Nick couldn't wait to confront Tom at the gym or, snub him in return.

As the reader, you would probably ask yourself the following questions with regards to this story and the communication dynamics that transpired between all the parties involved such as:

"What would prompt Tom and Paul to treat Nick and his new lover like that?" "Why did Nick get so hurt by Tom and Paul's actions?" "Why was Nick's lover so angry and defensive? "Could this happen to me and what would I do if it did?" Could I have hurt someone as Tom did to Nick and not realize it?"

Specifically, we need to ask ourselves why do we "fear" the hurt of rejection so much that it often incapacitates us from taking any action, as if we anticipate being hurt or, being rejected?

Returning to the players in this story, when back in their comfortable gym setting, Tom quickly attempted to be his usual playful self with Nick but this time, Nick was still upset from the insult at the Hampton and quickly rebuffed Tom and walked away. After doing so, Nick turned to see Tom looking stunned as if he received a body blow or had walked into an invisible force field! He had! At that moment, Nick wondered if Tom was completely unaware of his previous behavior to act so surprised at Nick's choice to walk away from him.

In retrospect, wasn't Nick imitating Tom's dismissive behavior by walking away? Should he instead have confronted Tom about his behavior at the Hamptons to find out the reason for the perceived snub? As a result of both their actions, neither man has spoken to the other but still see one another in public functions. At one time, Nick expressed to his lover a desire to re-establish communication, but his lover quickly restated, "Why bother, he was an elitist pig?"

What do you think? Should Nick try to re-establish contact with Tom or simply let it go and move on? How would you have acted if a similar situation arose in your life?

But the above-mentioned case is just one example of the type of behavior that started me thinking. I knew that all this disrespect was not an isolated incident of our culture. Gay men in groups frequently behave in selective, hurtful, and "gossipy" ways similar to teenagers in cliques. So, let's ask ourselves, "Why do so many men in our gay community display such disrespectful manners toward one another?" Because in doing so, that type of dismissive behavior only serves to demean us as individuals and detract from our power as a community.

WHY DO WE ACT THE WAY WE DO?

I started speaking with my friends about this type of communication and they all agreed that they also had similar experiences on both sides of the fence, ("do-err" and do-ee"). So I asked myself and them, "Why do we; outsiders to many, act with such adolescent behavior? Where does this behavior come from? Did this type of behavior originate in our childhood when we first started to notice our feelings for our own sex wasn't "normal" or comments from others that it isn't normal as well?"

I know for many of us, the "not normal' comment enrages us but, I have heard from our political and spiritual leaders that we have to begin to move away from those detractors and not sink to their level of ignorance. That most of us have experienced shame and guilt as a result of being gay at some time in our lives and we have to try to take a more direct action whenever confronted by such adversity. Otherwise, the shame could manifest itself by experiencing the compulsion to hide one's true sexuality from others and force us to make dishonest and often fearful choices that simply do not allow us to enjoy true happiness as a self-assured gay man. Sadly, many gay men have chosen to either marrying women for fear of exposure or, simply refuse to "come out" to family, friends or even themselves; an all too common occurrence.

More significantly with regards to this book, the desire to "mask" or hide our true sexuality could possibly cause a regression in our adolescent development specifically in terms of communicating well with others. An example of this regressed behavior can manifest itself by being quick to dismiss or devalue others simply because they don't exhibit our idealized image of our skewed desires such as depicted in the movie *Mean Girls*.

So, how can we get rid ourselves of engaging in this potentially hurtful behavior where we become unfairly critical of ourselves and others? How can we learn to treat ourselves and each other with more respect? Otherwise, we are living the shameful lives that those who demean us say we deserve.

In OUT Magazine(May,1998) there was an article on the gay circuit party scene called "Dirty Dancing" written by Jesse McKinley." The author focused upon the different aspects of the popular scene, and the different types of gay men who frequent them. One particular section of the article called "Night Moves-An Encyclopedia of Circuit Life," presented a glossary of popular jargon known within the "circuit scene."

What stood out most significantly to me, was the term, "whatever," which was quoted by McKinley as meaning an, "All-purpose response to everything from: If you take another personal day, you're fired" to "I think we should just be friends."

It is this type of indifferent response that concerns me most with regards to negative gay male communication. It demonstrates a disregard for another human being in order to preserve one's fragile ego. It reminds me of the "bitchy" woman or the callous "womanizer" from television soap operas and reality shows who is very self-focused and quick to demean or dismiss others.

*The following questions may assist you toward finding some of those answers?

I. ASK YOURSELF

1. Have you been going to the same gym for years and NOT spoken at length with more than three or four people there? *(Gyms in the gay culture are known for being major social "hot spots" for most gay men to cruise, socialize and compete with one another).

2. Has a recent "trick" ever passed you by in the street without saying a word to you?

3. What do you really think of the way many gay men act toward one another at the Pines, Cherry Grove, Castro Street, South Beach, P-Town, West Hollywood, Atlanta, Chicago, or any city where gay men congregate for fun and good times?

4. How is your life going in Oklahoma City? Dallas? New Orleans? You name it? Does each city or area promote a certain image for you? Is it "'hot or not" for you?

5. Do you think you're "HOT?" If so, does that feeling predominate your communication with other gay men who either fit or don't fit that category?

6. Are you habitually late for appointments with friends? Do you confirm plans with friends prior to traveling to the agreed-upon destination or, rarely do? Are you ever late for a "hot date, if not, are you frequently late when meeting with friends?"

II. NOW THINK, AND BE HONEST

1. Do you feel invisible in most gay circuit parties or, are you the life of the party?

2. Is your dog your most trusted friend or, only friend?

3. Do you wish you weren't gay? Would life be easier if you weren't? Could you be more open with others if you weren't?

4. How do you feel about women? Do you like them? Do you wish to make love to them? Do you believe that your feelings about women have had any impact on how you feel toward other gay men with regards to "acting out" toward your sex or love partners with

14

frustration for the fact that you are not attracted to women?

5. If you saw a beautiful woman sitting alone in a cafe looking lonely, what images would come to your mind? What feelings come up for you?

6. Do you envy heterosexual men; are you often uncomfortable around them?

7. Do you feel that you'll never be part of the "A List?" If you are part of the "in group," how does it make you feel? How do you relate and interact with men outside of your special group status?"

8. If you think you're "hot," does this belief cause you to become more discriminating or selective in your choice of friends?
9. Do you want a long-term lover? What is on your lover "wish list?" Does your wish list prioritize physical attributes, financial and social status, instead of their intellectual abilities or their emotional depths?

III. SO, NOW WHAT?

1.   Have we lost the ability to smile? STOP SCOWLING! IT'S NOT HOT!!!! (*quoted from David Pevsner- LA/NYC*)

2. Relationships; are for more than just sex? Are they too much hard work? Do you really want one or do you just think that you do?

3. If you answered, "yes" to the wish to be heterosexual, would your life be easier and more fulfilling? If not, what would make your present life feel more self-satisfying?

4. Do you believe your communication skills are a problem? Do you find it to be more difficult to communicate with someone you are attracted to?

5. Where's my sense of adventure? Can't I make decisions for myself instead of following the actions of my "pack?" Does the "pack mentality" honestly represent me?

6. If I feel insecure about myself and my communication with others, then what can I do differently?

7. In what situations do I wish I was more assertive and confident in my interactions with others?

8. What steps can I take toward feeling more "powerful" in my interactions with others?

CHAPTER II

WHY TALK IT OUT?

"Talking it OUT" is my way of saying that gay men not only need to "come out of the closet" in order to have a more honest and open relationships with their friends and family but, to be more open and honest with one another as well.

By "Talking it OUT" we can allow more people into our lives by being more honest and upfront about who we are, instead of choosing to deny ourselves the potential joy and peace of mind that comes from living our lives more fully rather than in the shame and denial.

Denial is the refusal to accept the reality of our lives most commonly associated with addictive behavior such as alcohol, drug or sex addiction but with regards to this book, the denial of our God given sexuality and the pain caused by denying who we truly are to ourselves and others.

I personally found a great deal of comfort and support from the Al-Anon (family and friends of Alcoholics) meetings that I attended weekly when my now ex-lover's behavior was out of control and created havoc in our home. Recognizing that I was denying his alcoholism and my dependency on keeping the "emotional mess" under control was the first step toward my own recovery.

Unfortunately within the GLBT community, substance abuse and unsafe sexual practices continue to be a serious problem primarily due a plethora of reasons but made more prevalent due to feelings of gay shame and other feelings of negative self-worth. Alcoholism, drug and sex addiction can become of means of "escapism" where the drug of choice becomes the focus and not making healthier choices until the addict chooses sobriety rather than the drug.

I propose that by conducting interviews with both gay men and women on the subject of gay male communication, they will yield many interesting anecdotes, as well as, unexpected comparisons, identifiable observations and insights. By investigating some of the roots of these often demeaning and devaluing communication patterns, perhaps we may together find a way to promote a more positive change.

It is quite interesting that as gay men, we continuously demand more respect from the heterosexual world. But why should the heterosexual world show more respect for us when so frequently, we often don't respect one another? So for that reason, I'm writing this book, because I'm a part of this group; experiencing and acting in this often dismissive and devaluing behavior and I'm not alone.

"MY STORY"

I knew that I was different from most of the other boys and girls in school at a very early age. I tended to either keep to myself or act up like the "class clown" to get approval. My parents and my brother perceived my behavior as less than "man-like," more like a "sissy." At age twelve, I was sent to a military school in Miami, Florida to "make more of a man out of me!" I lasted all of two months!

Needless to say, my parents were very disappointed. My brother was equally "pissed off" for again being forced to share his room with me. My father was pleased that I lost thirty pounds but it was because I had no appetite and knew my being overweight was an object of contention for him so I chose not to overeat. Years afterward, I struggled with body image issues as a result.

Although our family dynamics have drastically changed since that time, in those years past, I felt alone in the world with no friends who truly understood me. I often felt the need to appease those unhappy family members by either avoiding them or placating their needs. The thought of "acting up" like my little nephew often does, is something I would rarely do. Instead, I often felt like a little, fat boy with a smiling mask, or facade.

I would often cry and say "I'm sorry," for no good reason. As an adult, I realized that I allowed myself to become an easy victim for abusive boyfriends, because for some inane reason, I felt I deserved the abuse.

In time, I found myself in a relationship with a wonderful man. In September of 1996, we had a commitment ceremony to publicly recognize the strength of our bonds to one another. Unfortunately, our marriage ended in October of 2001 but, we are still friends and I will always remember my marriage celebration as one of the most joyous moments of my life.

For the past twenty two years, I have been a Professor of Communication & Rhetorical Studies at Hofstra University. I have also practiced for some thirty years as a psychotherapist/drama therapist in several psychiatric facilities in New York, New Jersey, and Connecticut. I enjoy a wide variety of close friends, and my relationship with my family, as with anyone, is mostly loving and nurturing but challenging at times.

As you'll see from the individuals interviewed, there is a significant number involved in the theater. My choice to interview friends from the theatrical world stems from my own involvement with the theater during the age of my "coming out." The theater was the one place where I felt I belonged. It was where my "sensitivity" was accepted and channeled into a creative venue. Of course, there was still some competition and an attitude of superiority between the actors and actresses at my school and I felt the struggle.

Nevertheless, I loved being in thirteen plays in a two year period from Sophocles to Genet but, it was there where I made my official "coming out." I recall going to the Catholic Center at my college and meeting a gay priest and a group of women who took me to Albany in 1972 for my first Gay Pride March. I was one of the most terrifying and thrilling times of my life!

My own history and my expertise as a teacher of Communication, has led me to write this book for you. In addition to teaching Communication courses, my years as a registered drama therapist and certified psychotherapist has also provided me with the significant insight and ability to analyze human behavior when exploring communication within group and paired situations.

For the purpose of this book I intend to examine how gay men communicate with one another within a predominantly social environment. I am not including the professional or relational contexts in this book, but if there are similarities to the social context, then well and good.

I personally believe that as a result of years of shame and guilt of being gay for many men has attributed to a "delayed adolescence," within a large percentage of gay men between the ages of 20 and 45 who often interact on the social level of teenage girls between the ages of 13 and 17."

The following are a list of some of the causes which results in dismissive and devaluing behavior among gay men toward others like themselves due to gay shame and personal discomfort with their sexuality. This shame can lead potentially lead to an "arrested development" in their level of maturity and their openness to communicate effectively with other gays:

THE GAY GAME DYNAMIC

1. This "developmental arrest" has led to the continual use of gossip and devaluation and the need to promote oneself at the expense of others.
2. Cliques, "strength in numbers," "mob psychology," whatever you wish to call it, as a means of exclusion. A mob mentality predominates wherein membership within these cliques becomes a sign of status.
3. A predominance of guilt and shame which I believe precipitates this type of devaluing behavior.
4. The fear and anxiety regarding one's true sexuality prevents these men from "coming out" to friends and family members. This "double life" is lacking in a positive self-worth, as well as, an inability to live a truly honest life.
5. The lack of value in which many gay men feel they possess due to developing in a "less than nurturing environment, could lead to an attitude of superiority toward others which masks one's more honest feelings of inadequacy.

"Attitudes are based on values and more specific applications of those values to the events of the world around you. An attitude can be defined as "primarily a way of being "set" toward or against certain things." (Zeuschner, 1997)

And it is this attitude which attempts to separate oneself from others that will often present itself in such social places as: bars, clubs, parties (including circuit parties), gyms, grocery stores (especially in Los Angeles), charity fund-raising events, the theater, and any other areas where gay men congregate and socialize with the potential of sex or more.

I plan to interview a diversified number of gay men with a variety of ethnic backgrounds from several geographical locations in the U.S., but with a predominance of those from the New York

City area. I will also send questionnaires to some fifty anonymous respondents throughout the United States to gather their views and experiences of gay male communication and interactions.

There will also be a thorough investigation of psychological evidence further supporting my claim. By examining both the social behavior of teenage girls and gay men, I will attempt to demonstrate differences and commonalities between the two groups. For example," *We were considered the "Models" because my friends and I were so concerned with our looks.*" (former Hofstra student of mine at age nineteen, Season M., April, 2008).

A respected colleague within the Drama Therapy community, Dr. David Read Johnson, stated in Dramascope that, *"there is growing interest in the study of shame and its impact on psychological conditions. Shame is usually differentiated from guilt in that, in guilt, one is deficient for what one has done and, in shame, and one is deficient for who one is."* (Johnson, 1996).

Johnson went further in explaining the shame theory by terming *"Heightened Interpersonal Boundaries* as: *"The shamed individual tries to protect the self from intrusion by others and exhibits marked guardedness and a strong need for control over situations. The ability to compromise becomes impaired because ambiguity or gray areas are avoided. *Organizations of shamed individuals therefore tend to fragment easily."(Ibid).*

The gay community is a culture frequently focused on socializing, therefore group orientated. If so, it has little need, in fact, stays away from intimate friendships or relationships when there is this vast, gay social network to draw upon. If there is strong disagreement on the above statement, then simply peruse the increasing number of gay-marketed magazines such as *Next Magazine* and *Metrosource* in the New York area alone and the predominance of ads with beautiful and well-muscled men for social events, bars, dance clubs, sex room ads. With all this fun and frivolity, when does one have time for serious relationships?

Eric Marcus in his book, The Male Couple's Guide (1992) provides a wonderfully in-depth look on how gay men can find one another, make a home, and build a life together. Issues of monogamy vs. no monogamy and learning to make the relationship between two men work by keeping open good lines of communication, is strongly emphasized.
Marcus felt that the setting of clear boundaries where one partner can or can't go need to be clearly set, otherwise, blame or fault-finding become the primary part of the relationship. "*Now that the physical passion has cooled, it doesn't seem like much else has been holding the relationship together. Or you and your lover may compete with each other in a destructive way.*" (Marcus 1992).

This competition between lovers takes us back to the need to promote ourselves above others and the "blame/shame syndrome." Returning to Johnson's depiction of the shame component in our behavior, the following statement further emphasizes our tendency to place the blame on others when it is too difficult to acknowledge it, more correctly, within ourselves.

Transfer of Shame to Others: "Shame is so intolerable that the individual attempts to redirect it to others. This defense leads to the development of judgmental attitudes, overly rigid standards, fault-finding and, even, contempt as a personality style." (Johnson, 1992.).

This judgmental attitude of contempt toward others both results in erecting invisible emotional boundaries that often deny emotional comfort to the individual and the group. *"Shamed individuals will often strive for perfection, hoping that by being perfect, no one will make fun of them. Attitudes of false pride develop in which one's achievements are overly valued. Often a compensatory fantasy evolves in which people perceive themselves as misunderstood and underappreciated but, secretly, unique and creative." (Ibid.)*

Evidence of this type of behavior can often become the focus for many gay men upon seeking for themselves or their desire love match, the "perfect body type", as exemplified by the Calvin Klein model with the sculpted abdominal muscles. With this type of mindset, it is too often believed that by obtaining this desired body will produce fewer problems in life. Additionally, someone who obtains that ideal body type through rigorous workouts and eating like a bird can often gain close to "celebrity status" within the community.

As a result of such externalized views, a false ego can be formed based primarily on heightened physical appearance and not upon solid, emotional or spiritual security. It's almost as if there has been a "trade-off with the devil" wherein the "person" becomes traded for the "look." A strong statement, sure, but sometimes one has to be strong in opinion in order to facilitate a change, or at least, prompt some positive insight into one's potentially self-destructive behavior.

Repetition Compulsion: Unfortunately, all of these defenses against shame fail to relieve the self from the original pain and lead the person to endlessly repeat similar situations in which they are shamed again. The result is the development of a shame-prone personality." (Ibid.).

It is this type of personality that this book will attempt to illustrate further through the detailed stories provided by my interviews as they examine their own lives within the gay culture. Perhaps by citing examples of this "shame-prone behavior," we as a population can become more aware and sensitive to the problem before us and learn to recognize it when it occurs.
*"**PAIN:** the effort required to cling to old ideas and old behaviors"* 12 Step Program slogan

A FEW MORE ANECDOTAL STORIES FOR YOU

I was shopping at a local farmer's market in Connecticut browsing through the produce section when I came upon three teenage girls giggling and commenting on a cute boy that just walked by them. It was quite obvious that those girls liked the boy, a point that he was well aware of, but instead, they simply smiled sweetly as he walked past them. I'm sure they'll see him again at school.

Last week, I was at a popular New York City bar called G Lounge. I was sharing a drink with two friends and noticed three very attractive young men conversing next to me. One particular man was being greeted by another male acquaintances as they walked by him. Each time someone passed this fellow, he would make funny faces and laugh to his friends commenting on each acquaintance who passed. I reflected upon the three girls at the market and compared them to those three young men. NOT MUCH DIFFERENCE, but the teenage girls were most definitely, young enough to change while the boy at the bar, I question?

"For the most part, I do believe that we live a sort of 'retarded adolescence.' I know there are exceptions to everything, but in my personal estimation, my adolescence was not a normal adolescence for me. Because, if I had a normal adolescence, I would have dated the boys that I was attracted to and, I couldn't! I had to stop those feelings; otherwise, I would have been called a "fag" when I was six years old! (David Pevsner, N.Y., 2007)

*A SPECIAL NOTE FROM THE AUTHOR

I want it to be very clear that I <u>do not </u>perceive being gay as a shameful experience, but as a prideful experience. Feelings of shame and guilt are only two of the many aspects of the gay experience, as it is for the entire human experience. Love, anger, pride, joy, sensuality, intelligence, compassion, friendship, intuition, strength, empathy, and a rich spirituality, are only a few of the aspects of the human experience that is open to us all. Learning to accept oneself and one other is all I seek here.

•   The following chapters will provide in-depth stories of those people who have been interviewed for this book. Each subject willingly volunteered to discuss their life stories with a special emphasis on the topic of gay male communication and gay shame and how both dynamics have affected their lives and their relationships with other gay men.

TIM ROGERS   **BOB DOBSON**

CHAPTER III – TIM ROGERS

"I JUST WANT TO LOVE BOB!"

My first interviewee is Tim Rogers in June of 1998, a Floridian in his mid-thirties who is a gay man who exudes a sexual energy that attracts men easily. As he sits in a comfortable chair, his body language especially, his direct eye contact exudes confidence, sexuality, and air of masculinity. In this observer's view, it is easy to see how Tim and Bob together are an unstoppable force in meeting men. Here is his story:

Childhood & "Coming Out" Experiences

It was as early as 10 years old, when I first realized that I was attracted to men and not women. I always wanted to be around men and boys, but I never took part in the "gay scene" or, a gay relationship, until I joined the army. The truth be said, I never allowed myself to be gay or have a sexual relationship with another male till then. I used to fantasize about males a lot, but I was in a situation where it was not conducive to having a gay relationship. It even got to the point where I almost got married when I was very young, thinking that it was the right thing to do. Thankfully, I never took that extra step back then.

I know it would have been a mistake if I had gotten married in my teen years. I would have still been gay, and been married to a woman. It would have complicated matters a lot more. I did have a marriage of convenience when I was in the army that lasted for a total of four years but we were both gay. We basically did it for financial reasons.

At nineteen was when I had my first sexual experience with another man. It happened when I was stationed in Germany. I met some people who I thought were fun and attractive and in the "In Crowd" so, I decided to "come out of the closet" to them. Being born in Ohio and raised in Florida, Germany was like being on another planet! A perfect place to explore the urge!

It was very difficult being gay where I was raised in a more rural part of Florida. It was very difficult to be effeminate or different. You always had to be on the alert, or always be aware if someone was going to call you a "fag." In fact, one of my brothers used to call me a "girl" all the time. I used to get so angry with him.

I would hide who I truly was with him all the time. Not that I was a girl! I wasn't an effeminate person even growing up. It seems that my brother could pick up on my true feelings. I remember him always trying to act "cool." Trying to show everybody he was "Mr. Macho," where he could say or do anything he wanted to and people would listen. In my opinion, he was just this "Big Ole Redneck."

At this point in the interview, Tim has basically admitted the need to hide his true sexuality for the sole purpose of survival and self-preservation. It appears that Tim's brother clearly suspects

Tim's true sexuality and that the brother is attempting to separate himself from Tim by acting overly "macho" in order to protect himself from any suspicion of being gay as well.

The brother's behavior toward Tim must have been very difficult for Tim to have to deal with on a daily basis. Also, the brother's "machismo" attitude is teaching Tim that acting in an overly masculine manner is the more appropriate way to act in order to divert suspicion of being gay. Both the brother's attitude and behavior were clearly instilling feelings of gay shame in Tim.

At present, my relationship with that brother is excellent. As I think about it, my relationship with my brothers and sisters when I was growing up was not so great. And it's funny, because now, I don't think it could ever be better. I get along so well with all of them. They confide in me and I confide with them. We just get along so well! All seven brothers and two sisters! They love me and I love them. They look up to me.

It is interesting that the abusive relationship with the brother appears to be a thing of the past... Is Tim being completely honest here or is he already attempting to mask the truth regarding his relationship with his family? If that is true, then Tim's communication with others is already distorted in order to present a happy, more acceptable picture of what should be, rather than what is actually true. This type of dishonest behavior is called "masking" where one lives behind an imaginary mask similar to smiling when you are really depressed.

Parents

All my brothers and sisters realized that as we were growing up, we didn't have anybody but each other. We had a really rough family life, as far as our parents were concerned.

My parents divorced when I was four. My mother was an alcoholic. She was just a mess, a complete mess. She was in and out of mental institutions as long as I can remember. We realized pretty early, that we only had one other. I think that lack of having a mother made our relationship with one another a whole lot stronger. Even up till today, that's what we base our relationship on. We just know that we have each other and that we'll <u>always </u>have each other.

My father was a caretaker only. He was always working and was never there, except (*pause*) for discipline. My stepmother would say (*longer pause*) "Such and such did this," and my father would react. He was really funny in a strange kind of way; because if you told him something that you did wrong and then managed to stay away from him for the first hour after he found out, you were fine. But if you were there when he first found out, forget it!

This parental history of having an alcoholic and emotionally disturbed mother and a distant and angry father where the children had to basically care for one another are both sad and disturbing. Also, with these parents being Tim's primary caretakers and role models, what kind of lessons of life does it teach Tim on how to treat others and vice versa?

Most importantly, the fact that Tim's mom was an alcoholic and distant from her children places

Tim and his siblings as lifelong members of ACOA or Adult Children of Alcoholics. In addition, parental histories like Tim's, will most certainly lead to the strong possibility that more than a few of the children will inherit the same alcoholic or addictive tendencies of the parent or parents. The familiar adage: "The apple doesn't fall far from the tree," comes to my mind here.

Today, I still see my father as an odd kind of guy. My relationship with him is better that it's ever been! He and I get along so well. We're making up for a lot of lost time on both ends; my end and his. When I think about it, as I was growing up, I felt ashamed that I was gay; that I had let him down. As I'm growing older, and hopefully wiser, I 'm realizing that he never looked at me in that way. It was only my perception of what he felt of me and not what he actually felt.

Tim is clearly trying to come to terms with the "reality" of his childhood relationship with his father by questioning his own perception of it at the time. He takes the "blame" for thinking that he had "let his father down" by being gay and then says he now believes his father never felt that way. Given the family background, where he grew up, and the childhood he describes, it can be a reasonable assumption to make, or is it just another example of Tim trying to mask the truth and 'insulate' or shield himself from painful childhood memories?

I believe he felt that he couldn't communicate with me because, I wouldn't let him. I always felt I had let him down by being gay, and it was hard for me to get over that feeling. But now, I realize that he loved me as much as he loved them; the rest of my siblings. And he was always there and I wouldn't participate in his giving, because I was always beating up on myself. He's funny acting at time; hard to explain. He calls me all the time now and I'll say "Dad, is that you?" Sometimes I think it's weird that he calls me and asks for my advice.

For today, he lets me participate as much as I want to. He just wants me to be part of the family, which I am now grateful because I used to really beat up on myself so much for being different. I sadly used to think my siblings (*pause*) It's weird. (*becoming visibly emotional*) I used to think my siblings would hate me if they knew my secret.

I used to be afraid to be alone with their children because I would be afraid that they'd think I was molesting their children. (*pause*) But, they never thought that way. I discussed my feelings with them and they would say, "What are you talking about?" They are all comfortable with me.

This desire to present a loving picture with the father is a similar pattern to Tim's relationship with his brother. It is difficult to tell if Tim is being completely honest or wants me to feel that everything is okay in his life. I also question whether Tim has a pattern for hiding the truth from others; and if that is true, what is his communication with other gay men likely to be?

About Shame

I believe a lot of my negative thoughts about myself stemmed from that old shame of being gay. Growing up in a small town, I felt as if everybody was talking, pointing the finger, saying, "Oh, he's a fag, he's sick!" There was always a negative connotation associated with homosexuality.

And as I was growing up, you certainly didn't want to be that type of person. That was definitely a "No-no!" Especially in my hometown where it was very small and very anti-gay.

My town was also very anti-black. They were a very racist and prejudiced people! The black people in my hometown, a suburb of Orlando, lived on the outskirts of the town. They weren't allowed to live in the city, or in the town itself! The town's attitude was racially constricted, very backwards in having any racial consciousness. What I would call a very "country- type" place.

Jewish people were unheard of; in fact, I never knew what a Jewish person was until I moved to South Florida. I never had a clue! I had heard the term, "Jew," but I never associated it with a type of person. When somebody said, "Oh, he's a Jew," all I would think is, "So, what's a Jew?" Jewish people were never in my town. It was mostly a black and white issue!

In some ways you could say that I had to hide who I was, just like a Jewish person in my town would have to hide who he was, but I hid my secret very well. I was very good at hiding my feelings. A black in my part of town would also have to keep his mouth shut and not start any trouble. Blacks were always being referred to as "niggers." We're talking about people who burn crosses on people's yards and stuff! Therefore, being gay was definitely something you would want to hide!

Tim admits that hiding the truth in order to survive bigotry and hatred which is understandable. But, if someone has a long history with hiding the truth from others, when does the lying stop; both to oneself and others? A black man or woman cannot hide their skin color and a Jewish man or woman may not want to hide their faith and their heritage as in the film Driving Miss Daisy, but a gay man can feel compelled to hide his sexuality. For if Tim felt that hiding served a clear purpose, then why stop? And, how would that pattern for lying and hiding one's true feelings become enacted when communicating with other gay men? Can he be trusted?

My Sexual Preferences

I always remember wanting to spend time with men or boys rather than girls. I wanted to be around men for as long as I can remember; always wanting to see certain attractive men naked…definitely, naked! That was really something that I fantasized about all the time. I hoped someday to be with a man sexually, but I was just too afraid.

I remember being "turned on" by my brother-in-law. I thought he was gorgeous! I always used to be looking at his body. He always had his shirt off! He was a big show-off. He knew that people were always checking him out. Being that he was a construction worker, he always liked to work out in the gym. He was a big construction worker who exuded sexuality!

The brother-in-law also appeared to play the role of the 'hot guy' who knew people were always "checking him out". Perhaps it was this man also provided Tim with a powerful role model for getting the attention of other men. A model which Tim clearly has copied, since he is also a sexy man who attracts other men easily and gained sexual and ego-boosting rewards as a result of his physical and sexual prowess.

An Official "Coming out"

I "came out" in 1977. I was hanging around with a group of people in the army. It was typical…it's so typical that it's not even funny. We all went out, got drunk, and I of course, ended up in bed with this guy. I must have passed out, and ended up waking up with his lips on mine. I remember the first time I kissed a man, it was like (*smiling*) I'll never forget (*long pause*), the feeling that it was. It's so weird how wonderful it felt.

He must have initiated the kissing and yeah, I responded! I remember feeling, "Oh, this is so weird," but it felt nice. It was weird because it was like a release. It was just like opening a closed door and saying," I'm out, I'm here!" We later became boyfriends for about two to three months. Then he it was so typical, he suddenly didn't want anything to do with me, and I was heartbroken, because he was my first love. So, I retaliated by going to the gym and becoming the best looking, best dressed, and best everything that I could be. Then all of a sudden, he started to pay attention to me, and I didn't have the time for him! I was desired by so many others! It was very strange but, so typical. I see that happening all the time. Seeing how gay men build up their bodies to make a rejected lover jealous and end up rejecting him in revenge.

This last statement by Tim clearly represents the most crucial aspect of what the "Gay Communication Game" chapter is all about, because it is as if Tim is saying: "Now that I have built up my body to a point where it becomes the object of desire and lust by other men, I won't have to concern myself with feelings of rejection and disapproval. Now, this new body and my new-found sexuality will fill up all the emotional holes others may have caused. Not only that, but now this new body, it will allow me to be more in control and I can hurt others in the present as I have been hurt in the past." The following questions put to Tim will help elaborate this point further:

Interviewer question: **"Are you saying that gay men feel compelled to: build up their bodies, be in the "hottest" clique, become the best they can be both physically and socially, simply to make others jealous of them?"**

Right! That's exactly the way it happened! It's so funny. Because, all of a sudden, he didn't want anything to do with me and I was heartbroken. I remember that I cried, and cried, and cried, and I kept thinking," What's wrong with me?" Then, all of a sudden I said, "I'll show you!" So, I went shopping! I got all the best clothes and started looking really sexy and wonderful. Then, all of a sudden, he wanted me back. So, I said, "Honey (*pause*), I don't want it anymore."

I think he rejected me at first, because I was so in love with him, so quickly. In hindsight, I think he had a problem with intimacy. I can see now that it probably was just that; especially, if you were a gay man who had as many relationships as he had, and seeing this eighteen-year-old clinging to him, wanting to always be with him. He was a good deal older than me, probably at least twenty two or twenty three.

My second question: (with a smile on my face) "You think that's a big age difference? Okay, so it was this rejection by him that prompted you into action. You built up your body, bought the best clothes, only to make yourself more desirable to others, not just him. Is that the way you perceive the situation?"

Oh, definitely. I was the "Belle of the Ball" in Germany from then on.

The Gay Armed Forces

The Army <u>is</u>, one, big, gay bar! I've never in my life ever seen a bigger gay community than I experienced in the Army. All the armed services! The Air Force, the Navy (*smiling*). It's all one, big, gay Mecca!

It's also common knowledge among everyone in the military that, if you're in the Army, you know everybody is gay. Wherever you go, everyone is gay. It's really amusing to be an outsider looking in, with all the controversy that surrounds the service now, and knowing the: "Don't ask, don't tell thing." It's the funniest thing in the world because, it's all gay! Especially in the woman's forces! There's a big lesbian community in the Army. In all the armed services!

The military provided Tim with a dual purpose: instilling a feeling of machismo by being seen as a warrior for his country, and offering Tim the opportunity of having many men to provide him with attention he needed to elevate the self-esteem he lacked following a sad childhood and the rejection of his first lover's attention.

3rd question: "It sounds as if you had a blast in the military but, if you had the choice today, would you still choose to be gay?" (To be clear; I do not believe being gay is a choice, it's simply a hypothetical question to Tim)

Being Gay Today

If I had to choose, I'd probably (pause) that's a hard question. I'd probably still choose to be gay but, there are a lot of things that I still don't like about it. There's a lot more openness involved in being gay today and, not as much of a stigma associated with being gay today as there was in the past. But, there still is a considerable amount of stigma today, as exemplified by the Christian Right Movement and their desire to suppress, but not as much as there was in the past.

Being gay today, you don't generally hear, "OH my God, you're gay! Even with HIV/AIDS? Now, it's changed a lot! Maybe people have become more sensitive to gays because of HIV/AIDS? I just don't know.

As far as the misconception of choosing to be gay, that seriously needs to change. I believe that "straight" people still have this false idea that we just sat down one day and said, "Oh, I think I'm going to be gay today." That just doesn't happen! It just doesn't happen that way! It's not a decision you just wake up with. It's not a social thing. I personally believe it's genetic!

There may be social conditions involved that nurtured my gayness or homosexuality. But, you can't tell me I just woke up with this idea and decided I'll be gay today. I'll never believe that! I will believe that the same genetic factors that cause one to have brown hair or blue eyes, also contributed to us being gay and I'll never be convinced otherwise!

Tim's reactions to the 'straight world's confusion and derision with regards to the causes of homosexuality are understandable. Many gay men struggle with their own identity and their 'coming out' process as they seek self-acceptance as well as acceptance from significant others in their lives. Many religious groups' condemnation of homosexuals only serves to fuel distrust and misunderstandings leading to feelings of hatred and division on both sides. Even the onslaught on AIDS has not lessened this polarization but times are fortunately, changing.

Self-Acceptance for Being Gay

I believe now, at this point in my life, it's more positive than it is negative, to be gay. There are still negative feelings attached to being gay. You still have to be "on your guard." I don't believe in being flamboyantly gay in a "straight situation." I don't believe that that's necessary. I don't believe you have to put on a dress just because you want to show somebody you're gay. I don't think that being gay is about that!

Some people feel the need to be loud and flamboyant in expressing their gayness in public. They believe "straight" people need to be shocked by those young men screaming for their freedom to do as they please. It's not always necessary to be so loud or flamboyant. Like, Gay Pride Parades and Gay Fests, although they can be a lot of fun, there are a lot of things that go on during them that give a particular perception to the "straight" world. For example, during the Boston Pride Parade, there was this guy parading down the street in a skirt, and he would be lifting his skirt and he had nothing on underneath! Not a "cool" thing to do with kids watching!

Was that necessary? I don't think so. That is not what the gay world, or being gay, is all about! To the bigots, that's all they see! And, it gives the impression that that's all we're about! And, we're not, obviously! We're normal. Aren't we?

At this point in the interview, Tim is clearly questioning what gay is supposed to look like. He has developed clearly negative attitudes with regards to effeminate or flamboyant gay men. This belief appears based on a desire to separate himself from a negative stereotype that may be perpetuated by many in the heterosexual world, many of who are unaware of the diversity within the GLBT community. Of primary concern to this interviewer, would be how Tim would speak and interact with other gay men who may act in effeminate or flamboyant ways.

The Big Breakthrough

The biggest breakthrough in my "coming out" process" was in letting my family know that I was gay, and if it was a problem, then it wasn't mine; it was their problem. I think that not disclosing who we truly are to family is a tragedy, because a lot of gay people live their entire lives not letting their families in on what's going on…what their lives are about…not letting them be a part of whatever it is they're going through because, they are gay.

Being gay is a big difference from living the heterosexual lifestyle and it makes a huge difference not letting your loved ones know who you are! Therefore, I definitely advocate "coming out" to one's family. One day I just got up and said, "My family has to know! I have to be truthful with my family!" I was in a relationship at the time, so that might have prompted me to "come out." I thought it might have helped the relationship grow to let my family know and learn to accept us.

I decided right then, to let my family know basically all at the same time. I accomplished my goal all within a couple of months, or so. I remember talking with each and every one of them. And what was great, was that I talked with them personally! It wasn't something where they told each other, "Oh, Tim is gay!" I had the opportunity to tell them all in my own words, that I was gay and this is how things are, and it was good. It wasn't a gossip thing. I simply needed to be truthful with my family.

You know, whenever I visited my parents, I had a man with me! So, I felt like, maybe they knew already…which in fact, they did! But, I still had to be open with them and tell them directly. Perhaps in time, they would not only see him as a friend, but as a lover. Perhaps I did it for myself as well. Now, I could come to their house, be comfortable, and feel a part of a family without secrets.

Tim's decision to "come out" and be honest with his family was a very positive step toward self-acceptance and communicating authentically with others. 'Coming out' in general, is intrinsically a very positive step in accepting and loving ourselves for who we truly are, and whenever we take those conscious steps toward self-love, that self-love will be communicated to others as well. Tim's honesty with his family about who he truly is, communicates to them that he accepts who he is and opens the door to letting his loved ones into his life.

Now that I think about it, there are a few of them, like my Mom and Dad, where I don't think it would have made a big difference by "coming out" to them because they would still love me.

<u>My Two Moms</u>

Fortunately for me, my mother is still around. But, I don't view her as a mother figure. I look at her; I don't know. It's a strange relationship; very strange. I almost look at her as if she's my child. It's weird. I always feel this need to take care of her. With my stepmother it's different. She and I have a good relationship. We're both honest and open with each other, actually, brutally honest with each other!

With my step-mom, I know that if I have to ask for something, she'll tell me straight out what I need to hear. She won't "sugarcoat" anything, she'll just tell me! It's good that I have an alter-ego like that! That if you ask her for advice, you don't want to hear "sugarcoat!" If you want to hear the truth, you'll get it!

Tim's stepmother is clearly being described as a good role model for honest communication. Perhaps she will also be able to play the stronger maternal role for Tim since his biological mother has been unable to do so. Unfortunately, having had an inadequate maternal role model in his life, Tim has become emotionally disadvantaged and is suffering the consequences in his personal life, specifically in forming healthy relationships with others.

Bob, the Ex-Boyfriend and the Love of My Life

4th question: Tim, what are your family's feelings about Bob? Do they know of the relationship you have with him?
My family all have accepted Bob as another kid! They love Bob. Everybody loves Bob! I guess it's because they don't really know about the dynamics of our relationship. It's hard for anybody to understand! The only important thing is that I can understand it. *(Bob and Tim have been lovers for years but for now, they are only roommates and close friends with separate boyfriends; not of Tim's choosing).*
Being here in Cape Cod with Bob every year is my most satisfying gay experience. I love coming here to the Cape with him. It's not sexual between us anymore, but it can be. It's mostly here with Bob, where I feel the most comfortable in my life!

There's a certain tranquility attached to my summer vacations up here that I look forward to and yearn for, every year. It's also a time when Bob and I "click" a lot. A lot! It's like we're on the same wavelength and we think alike. It's a very bonding thing for both Bob and me.

I can easily say that my relationship with Bob is the highlight of my life and he definitely knows that! And, I believe he feels the same. At least I'd like to believe he does. (Soft laughter).

It doesn't sound as if Tim feels very secure in his relationship with Bob and I doubt whether a vacation home in a tranquil setting will help change that or, fulfill Tim's unspoken wish to be back in a romantic relationship with Bob.

Our present relationship is really complicated. There are those people who **do** understand it; and those are the people I want to be around. Mine and Bob's relationship has changed a lot! It's weird. It's like we're life partners. Just not in a sexual sense as much anymore; not like we used to. We just know that when all else fails, we have each other.

Bob's last boyfriend appealed to Bob's paternal instincts, because Julio was like a child. With my boyfriend, it's very spiritual. He understands my relationship with Bob. He understands there are a lot of years between Bob and I; that we are like brothers. Yes, like brothers! I know that I have plenty of brothers, Bob doesn't! My boyfriend understands my relationship with Bob is like a brother.

I refuse to believe that Tim's boyfriends are EVER understanding or, accepting of Tim's relationship with Bob, since it appears apparent that Tim will NEVER let go of Bob.

I'm aware that no boyfriend is going to replace Bob for me. I believe my lover is just looking for what I can give him, and what he can offer me. At present, I'm just not sure. Our relationship is too early to figure out. I know he's special in a way. He's certainly not a trick, or someone I just picked up! He's a boyfriend. He's very genuine. It's nice when you find someone whom you can really relate all the dynamics between Bob and me. It's very important that no boyfriend throw any shame or guilt at my loving relationship with Bob, very important!

The dynamics of Tim's relationship with Bob are almost predictable as a result of Tim's lack of a primary maternal role model. As previously discussed in the "Two Moms" section of this interview, this kind of dysfunctional relationship often results in forming unhealthy love relationships with men or women.
*I believe Bob to be emotionally unavailable to Tim. The fact that Tim has a tendency to draw lines or emotional boundaries with potential boyfriends because of his feelings for Bob, prevents Tim from having true intimacy with other men...including Bob. For example, why should any man **have to accept** Tim's relationship with Bob in order to have a relationship with Tim? Tim is in a sense, starting each potential relationship with clear conditions and restrictions, which I believe is unfair to others who want to be the primary relationship in Tim's life.*

Shame and Guilt about Being Gay

To be honest with you, at this point of my life, I don't feel any shame or guilt associated with my homosexuality. Years ago perhaps, in a business situation, you may have felt shame when people generalize you with being part of their negative connotation of homosexuals, and you're immediately being grouped with them. But, I really don't have a lot of shame or guilt. I can't really pinpoint any time when I felt my homosexuality was a bad thing in my life!

Yet, in any type of work situation where people associate gayness with the job especially, in retail where you might hear: "Oh, you're all fags; you're all fags that work here!" Then, you don't want to be associated as being gay in that situation. I can get really upset when I find out that someone, with whom I originally respected, had negative feelings about gays. It's as if you thought you had a higher position with them than you actually did. Suddenly, you realize that they looked at you more favorably only because they associated you as being as "straight" as them.

I know that it is only my perception that they will look unfavorably at me if they know I'm gay. It's difficult to let go of that belief. And yet, I do believe my perceptions with that work environment were correct although, I did the make mistakes with my family.

Tim is expressing strong feelings with regards to having his gay identity being exposed at work or, being made uncomfortable upon hearing derogatory comments about gays. This attitude does suggest an inner struggle with who he is and how he is perceived by others, which is common for most gay men. His anger at bigots is clearly justifiable, the question here has more to do with how he will act if confronted by a bigot, and whether he will be honest about his true sexuality?

And yet, knowing Tim, I am positive if the situation ever arose, he would choose to speak up for other gay men who may be on the receiving end of gay bigotry. As far as his family is concerned, Tim is honest about misinterpreting his original thoughts about his family's potential reactions with regards to their acceptance of his homosexuality and that was most fortunate for him.

The Origins of My Shame and Guilt

Society as a whole when I grew up, contributed to my feeling shame and guilt about being gay. How people looked at homosexuality as a bad thing…that you had a choice and you made the wrong choice similar to my small town of closed minds. But for today, I simply don't care anymore. I simply don't catch that attitude anymore! I think as the older you get, the less likely you are to put yourself in a situation where you'll be judged. You learn what kinds of situations not to put yourself in.

For example, the prevalent gay attitude of: "let's get out of Straights-Ville!" But, I think places like P-town are an extreme! Just as Key West, South Beach or Fire Island being only a few of the places where gay people can be comfortable. There are all these nice "gay meccas" to go to, but I don't think it's necessary to saturate yourself in gayness! There has to be a happy medium. I know it's nice to go to P-town to "party" and have fun, but I don't think it's a necessary part of being gay to go to a "gay Mecca." What does letting yourself be as flamboyant as you want to be, have to do with being homosexual?

Again, Tim is making strong connections between homosexuality with flamboyance and gay shame. There appears to be some clear conflict with regards to associating his homosexuality with flamboyant behavior. Tim falls into a large, decades-old group of gay men who struggle with society's negative view of the gay community and desire to be accepted and approved of for who we are and not with whom we sleep.

I know that there are a lot of people who don't have the opportunity to be themselves that often. They feel they <u>have </u>to go to places like P-Town, Key West, Ogunquit, or, the Pines, which they believe are the few places where they can have their sexual freedom or feel comfortable just being themselves. That's not necessary! I think the older you get, the more you don't feel you need all that! I mean, its fun, it's a "party," but if you look at it as the only place I can go to be gay, then, that's a problem!

Tim's last comment clearly affirms the need for all gay men to learn and accept that we can be comfortable being ourselves in other physical environments than just in the gay vacation places or sanctuaries such as the San Francisco, P-Town, West Hollywood, Fort Lauderdale, Russian River, as well as, the vacation destinations mentioned by Tim.

South Yarmouth, Cape Cod – the "New P-Town!"

Being comfortably gay can be as easy in South Yarmouth, Cape Cod as it can be in P-Town, or even in West Palm Beach, or wherever! It's where you "hang your hat and let your hair down." For me, personally, the reason I can do that is because I know that I'm not going to put on a dress and march through the streets of Mannish! I am comfortable with my own sexuality, so, it doesn't matter to me what others think. I don't feel any different from any of them.

I fit in wherever I go. I am someone who is comfortable in my own skin. Now, more than ever! I think that's something that a lot of people don't get. Don't you? I think a lot of people go through their lives not "being comfortable in their own skin." I find it's particularly true in the gay world! People are simply not comfortable with themselves due to a lack of self-esteem. It's a basic feeling around gay people that you can't be gay! It all has to do with social limitations and social conditioning. It's almost a form of brainwashing!

I am in complete agreement with Tim with regards to many gay men feeling "uncomfortable in their own skins". I also perceive Tim to be someone who does enjoy being gay, since it affords him many prizes with regards to feeling included within a group; and the success he sustains in meeting men; a clear boost to his ego. The "brainwashing" statement clearly relates to society's conditions for what a man is supposed to act like and the rituals he is supposed to follow, such as marrying and having a family, and in so doing, conforming to what the general society deems as normal and more acceptable behavior.

Attitudes of Superiority & "Clique" Behavior

Shame and guilt did not have an adverse effect on me. Again, the longer you live, the less you tolerate those behaviors! You're purposefully choosing not to tolerate the banality of most of the cliques. But then, aren't you creating your own clique? Do you know what I'm saying? I'm saying that you choose your surroundings! You choose who you want to be around! I believe we choose a group of people to surround us to whom we feel safe and comfortable with.

Tim is contradicting his previous statement with regards to "shame and guilt not having an adverse effect on me." It is clear that shame and guilt has had a profound effect on him as it has on most gay men. In fact, it is almost impossible for gay men not to have shame and guilt with all the messages thrown at us by society and the media. With regards to his own shame and guilt, Tim stated earlier the effect that racism enacted by people in his birthplace toward minorities caused him to hide his gay sexuality. This behavior is a clear result of feeling shameful for who he is and feeling guilty for his sexual thoughts towards men.

Tim does make a good point with regards to cliques being formed by those who group together with a common purpose, even if that purpose is to criticize other cliques. Cliques can, and do, serve an intrinsic purpose of providing some comfort and support during moments of fear and uncertainty in the personality-forming, developmental years. My primary concern is when cliques are formed to purposefully promote oneself by demeaning and ostracizing others.

For some of us, our own families provide us with that "safe place." For others, we make our friends become another sort of family. You'd like to think that your group of friends is like your family, in the respect, that you can be yourself and let them be themselves as well. You can't judge them. You have to try to love them and help them when they need it.

Tim's statement does confirm the tendency for many gay men and women to form a family of friends as a consequence of not having supportive and accepting members in their own families. Every human being needs to derive feelings of comfort and support from others, and if their family does not provide that comfort and support, then they must seek it somewhere else. For example, I find it to be sad whenever I hear of a friend who is alone at the holidays because they are no longer welcomed in their parent's or sibling's homes primarily because they are gay.

It's so important to feel comfortable in your surroundings. The primary or a principal relationship cannot be a superficial thing. You need to feel comfortable with the people you choose and simply know that your friendship will be there no matter what happens, or where you may go or, become, even "through thick or thin and through the good times and bad times.'

But, there are only a limited number of people you can do that with. I've always considered myself lucky that I can have a relationship with more than one person at a time. Not necessarily sexual. I know that I can give to each person what they want and need, and still, get what I want from them! Not in a "using" standpoint but, from a "friendship" standpoint. I just feel I have a lot of love to share and that people can get whatever out of it!

At this point in the interview I am a little confused as to what Tim means by "having a relationship with more than one person at a time"? Is this relationship a friendship or another intimate, romantic relationship? My assumption is that Tim feels that he can sustain two romantic and intimate relationships at the same time, as long as he keeps one of those relationships nonsexual. This type of 'mindset' clearly appears to be potentially explosive and somewhat unrealistic. The principal question here is why does Tim need to place himself in the middle of a potentially explosive and clearly dramatic situation? Is it a desire to keep his early dysfunctional family dynamic alive by recreating it with lovers?

Loving Two Men at the Same Time.

I know that many gay men wouldn't want to jeopardize a present relationship by introducing another partner; and yet, gay men are simply not "comfortable in their own skins." They are not comfortable with who they are. I feel lucky to be emotionally bonded with Bob, and sexually and spiritually connected with Richard. I desire only to be with those individuals who can understand and accept my relationship with Bob. I'm comfortable with gay men who do understand.

Tim has clearly drawn the lines here and equates being "comfortable in one's own skin", with being able to accept a complicated and potentially unworkable situation that one partner demands the other to accept. *What are your responses to Tim's conditions? Would you accept them from the outset of the relationship if you felt the potential partner was worth the effort? I, for one, would have to step back from the relationship and seriously consider what I was potentially getting myself involved in by pursuing a relationship with Tim.*

Competition on the Beach or at the Gym

It's a predominant factor in gay life. The way gay people act has a lot to do with guilt and shame. That they grew up not being comfortable with themselves or others. The way gay people act has a lot to do with their psychological and sociological backgrounds.

Tim's statements clearly reflect some truth with regard to gay men having feelings of guilt or shame about being gay and how those feelings result in them "acting out" in their relationships with others. Could this guilt and shame also have something to do with the conditions Tim places on potential boyfriends in requiring that they accept Bob as Tim's significant other? If someone is filled with gay shame and guilt, how can they sustain healthy intimate relationships with other gay men?

I know that "straight" men are constantly commenting on "tits and asses;" wanting to "fuck them." Heterosexual women are very blunt nowadays about men's butts and their physiques. Women often say that they're more interested in the emotional relationship but, we see the popularity of the male strip joints with women. They're acting just as sexually aggressive as men.

I do believe though, that the pursuit of sex is more predominant in the gay world. That's how we develop relationships in the gay world; the emphasis is on physical attraction. You'd like to think it's not how you look but, what's in here (pointing to his heart) inside. What attracts you first is their looks, but you want there to be something inside that keeps you stimulated, and not necessarily a "big dick" or a "bubble butt!"

Sexual attraction and conquests provide immediate gratification and ego stroking but, the sexual act often leaves the pursuer with feelings of emptiness once the sex act is completed and the sex partner leaves. Tim's comments, that heterosexual's focus on sexual behavior is similar to gay's, simply reflect the predominance in which both cultures value sexuality over the formation of more stable emotional bonds. Sexual gratification is important but not as self-affirming as forming and maintaining loving intimate relationships. Gay male's sexual communication is at the center of the way gay male culture is perceived. This phenomenon continues to be emphasized in such television shows as Queer as Folk, but as Tim stated, sexual conquests have a short shelf life and we must learn to look past sexual "wins" and focus upon more loving and stable interpersonal connections.

Relations with the 'Straight World?'

There are a lot of gay people you don't interact with a lot of people in the 'straight world'. You tend to be, always on your guard, for fear of some type of fallout that being gay will affect your relationships with heterosexuals. I don't fear being physically attacked as much now as I did in the past. I simply don't feel it's necessary to expose yourself to people who don't need to know you're gay.

It is sad that many gay men often choose not to interact socially with heterosexual men and women for fear of potential non-acceptance and discomfort. Unfortunately, many men such as myself, do recall personal instances of verbal, emotional, and physical abuse by "so-called" heterosexual men and "straight" women. But then again, I often question how heterosexual those men truly were, since many acts of violence toward suspected gay men are often the acts of closeted and terrified homosexual men who can't deal with their own suspected homosexual feelings. This despicable behavior by abusive men is not what I would classify as a game but, instead, as a crime!

I was lucky…luckier than most! I'm comfortable with all my siblings, but sometimes, I wonder why there isn't another one like me. I mean, don't the statistics state one out of ten are gay or bisexual? But, it still isn't that important because I feel comfortable with all of them, gay, straight, or bisexual.

It would be neat if one of my siblings were gay. It would be a really neat thing! But, I don't feel alone being the only gay one. I just think it would be "cool" if one of my brothers was gay, though I never longed for an incestuous relationship with one of my brothers! (laughs) The thought kind of turns my stomach, although all my brothers are gorgeous! It's funny, because Bob has wanted to "jump my brother's bones" before. (Smiling) He'd say like, "Why don't you ask him to come down and visit. He can sleep with me!" My usual response was an unequivocal, "No!"

Tim conveys a strong impression of being unusually at ease with his feelings toward his brothers and Bob, so much so, that he feels strong enough to even discuss the possibility of Bob having sexual relations with one of his brothers. Tim's own sexual feelings towards his brothers and the possibility of having a sexual and intimate relationship with a potentially gay brother are most curious. Also, the fact that Bob has made such provocative statements about Tim's brother, causes me to question Bob's sensitivity for Tim and his own sexual compulsiveness. Tim and Bob appear to have a most interesting relationship. Specifically, with regards to the ways Bob is playing a mind game with Tim that could have potentially serious consequences.

I am glad to have a lot of heterosexual friends in my life today and I do believe they relate to me just as normally as they relate to their heterosexual friends. I don't believe it's any different. I surround myself with heterosexual friends who are open-minded. It's funny with heterosexuals, because they often look at homosexuals as having only sexual relationships. They don't look at us on the level of social interaction. They seem to believe that the only reason we're homosexuals, is because of this sex thing, and it's not! Sometimes, that idea really upsets me! It does bother me that they think it's all about sex! But in fact, it's no different from their relationship with each other; which is probably all about sex as well!

Tim is basically reinforcing the misconception heterosexuals have about homosexuals by saying that both groups form relationships based mainly on sex. And yet, Tim, within the next sentence, seems to reject this misconception by saying that we're homosexual for reasons other than sex. Tim's inner conflict with regards to understanding his sexual identity is shared by the majority of the gay community who struggle to understand and accept their true sexuality.

I think the older you get the more you surround yourself with only people you feel comfortable with. You certainly don't want to surround yourself with people who have a problem with you, or, with what you're thinking! Being gay is not about only sex! So, don't go asking me, "Why do you do this, and why do you do that?" I choose not to surround myself with those people, asking those questions.

Tim is clearly drawing another line between himself and others by stating he wants nothing to do with bigoted or self-righteous people. My question is, "When does Tim stop drawing lines and begin to examine why he feels the need to draw lines between himself and others?" People ask questions because they're curious and want answers to perhaps correct their misconceptions. For how can we bring about change in ignorant people's attitudes, if we don't try to talk about our lives openly, and hopefully establish an honest dialog and help educate the world at large?

"Coming Out" - A Step Toward Acceptance?

"Coming out of the closet" was most definitely, a very important step for me. Throughout my life in fact, I've never really had to fight the fact that I was a homosexual. I know a lot of homosexuals deal with that question: "Am I gay, or, am I not gay"? Or, "I know I'm gay but, I can't be gay!" I don't think I've ever had to deal with any of that before. I feel really lucky about that! I've never felt the need to question who I am. I always knew what I was! Being a heterosexual simply "wasn't in the cards." I just always knew that I was a homosexual.

I quickly began to welcome my true sexuality. I embraced it! (Pause) It's funny how we perceive ourselves, and how others perceive us, and the difference between the two. I've always perceived myself as not being…just normal…always being, a little bit off center. I'd like to think that people see me as not your "Average Joe" but also, not being too off the average!

Tim is presenting a much healthier attitude here, even with a good sense of humor that is very attractive. Being able to joke about oneself is very important because it suggests a sense of comfort and inner security.

Most Significant Role Model during the "Coming Out" Process

(Pause) I believe the most significant person I met when I was "coming out," would not be just one particular person but, this group of people I knew when I was in the Army. This group of men and women were older than me and I would look at them and see this comfort level that they associated with being gay. I think that substantially propelled me to "come out." I would look at them and say to myself, "Oh, wow! These people are living comfortably and they look happy, and that's how I want to be myself!" So, to this day, I continue to look toward older people who are gay, and learn from them, essentially by the examples they set and the choices they make.

Being an older gay man, I appreciate Tim's comments about older gay men being role models for younger gay men, because I believe it is our duty to be mentors for other gay men to follow our example. I recall my "coming out" experience, and I wish I had someone to mentor me or show me the way. Gay men have had an important role in the shaping of our world history and every important lesson learned, should be shared with others in order to promote a decrease in ignorance and fear.

Advice to Younger Gay Men on "Coming Out"

I would tell them that it isn't easy to be gay. I mean, it can be easy if you let yourself be yourself. But, if you choose to hide behind a facade or a mask, or try to be somebody different from who you are or, that it isn't necessary to be outrageously flamboyant! I think that as a group, we need to be more focused as a group of gay men that have a common agenda, rather than each individual having their own personal agenda! In the gay world, there's simply too much scattering with no actual bonding.

Tim's statements reinforce Johnson's and my earlier comments regarding "shamed individuals" and their tendency to fragment and not bond as a community with a common agenda. Unfortunately, many people who wear masks, fake smiles, or even scowls, are unaware of their behavior, and subconsciously believe that they are being served by the facades they create.

Being overly 'butch' or 'flamboyant' can also be viewed as a mask or facade if it is behavior or a lifestyle we choose to engage in, in order to be part of a "gang' or group. Primarily, for the purpose of gaining comfort and support from others with similar behaviors, basically, a strength in numbers or, "clique mentality."

For today it's so important to be yourself! Being "real" with other people and not putting so much emphasis upon what I have, and what you don't have! That's what keeps us scattered!

Best Pick-Up Line

(Laughs) My best "pick-up line" is really funny, but it works every time! If I meet somebody in a bar that I like the look of, I use this line. It's my best line but corny, and yet, it works every time!

I'm basically a shy person when meeting someone for the first time. In fact, most people are intimidated by me and don't view me as a shy person. But, if I see someone I like, I walk up to them and say (*pausing in thought then laughs*) This is a classic! I'll say, "Don't I know you from somewhere?" It works every time! Every single time, I swear! And usually, it is someone that I have met somewhere, like Miami or New York. It's funny, but I have another line when I see someone in the bar that is really pretty. I'll go up and say, "You're too pretty for this room!"

They always like that. It's funny.

Of course it doesn't hurt if you are handsome and self-confident yourself and exude that self-confidence when you approach that sexy guy across that crowded room. Tim's self-confidence with meeting and capturing the attentions of many men was never a problem for him following his ego-stroking military experiences, but his ability to sustain a loving and healthy long-term relationship has most definitely been, a big problem.

I met my boyfriend with the "Didn't I know you from somewhere" line. I remember he responded, "Yeah, I think I do know you from somewhere?" I just think it's an okay way to "break the ice" despite the fact, that it's so corny. Actually, the homosexual community or specifically, the "gay circuit" is relatively small when you consider those guys who go out a lot to parties or the clubs. You always seem to be running into the same group of guys over and over. Like, when Bob and I go to Boston Pride every year, we always see the same group of guys every time! I mean, the homosexual community may be large but, it's still small in several ways.

Yes, because the gay community that Bob and Tim tend to connect with and attract, are mostly very attractive and personable young men who enjoy the company of men who look and act as they do. This behavioral pattern reinforces the tendency of many of these men to accept only certain groups of men and excluding others who do not fit the appearance and attitude that they find physically attractive and emotionally satisfying. This behavior of exclusive selection is very similar to someone choosing steak instead of chicken or, wine instead of beer, and refusing to try other foods or drink. But then, the behavior can change if and when the individual begins to realize that their choices don't really work for them.

Attractive Physical Attributes

I like a gay man who is not necessarily big, but that he takes care of himself. He cares enough about himself to dress nice or dress decent. It's a look. It's not necessarily huge and muscular or whatever. It's a look! If they have that look, it's evident that they care about themselves.

Fifth question posed: "Okay then, what non-physical behavior impresses you?

Can We Talk?

Conversation! Conversation is very important especially, when you first meet someone. Stimulating conversation is probably the first thing I find most attractive! Also, sloppiness! I can't stand a messy guy at all! But, the ability to converse is still the most attractive attribute. I don't believe there's anyone out there who's boring. Everyone has something to say, if we will only take the time to listen.

This last statement appears to be more open and inclusive for Tim, since it appears based more on intellectual and emotional stimulation and less, on physical or sexual attraction. I would not say that Tim tends to not include people of all types and appearances from being his friend or acquaintance. Whether he would rebuff their advances if they chose to pursue him on another level comes into question here; but I believe that most gay men such as Tim would naturally tend to place a good deal of importance upon an attractive physical appearance before pursuing a more intimate physical and emotional relationship with someone. Then again, don't most people feel a physical and emotional attraction is essential before pursuing a relationship beyond the initiation stage to deeper levels of intimacy? After all, doesn't physical appearance come first?

Unattractive Attitudes

Oh, that's easy. There are many superior attitudes in the gay world! The one attitude that I find most disturbing is those people who think that they are "the set," the "jet set" or, the "A List." I don't even want to be a part of whatever they're all about, because they're not about anything!

    1. People will look at you and ask, "Did you go to so and so's party last week? Oh, weren't you invited? (*Tim is making a sour face at this moment*) I say, "Who cares?" I find it so unattractive in people. It makes them shallow and very unattractive. I don't care how good looking they are!

    2. Femininity in a big, butch man is a big turn-off! (*Tim is making a disgusted face*). I can't stand a big, butch man dressing up like a girl. I don't find that attractive at all!

    3. People who are out only for themselves. Selfish, egotistical queens!

    4. People who abuse drugs on a daily basis. It's fine to "party" with but, there's a time and a place for drugs.

    5. What really "gets me," are people who think they are better than everybody else.

Tim's negativity about feminine and flamboyant men is no surprise to me, since he mentioned those feelings several times during this interview. It could be that his "macho" brother was influential in instilling these feelings in him from his boyhood? But, his more contemptuous feelings toward snobbish behavior and drug abuse are important for this study. In fact, the attitudes and behaviors that he has elaborated upon are those behaviors that are my principal concern with regards to how gay men speak and interact with one another in social settings. Many of the dismissive and/or self-destructive behaviors that Tim noted in others are often the result of feelings of low self-esteem and low self-worth. What is most disturbing by those exhibiting those behaviors can often result in an individual or group, only selecting others who conform to their list of specifications, and slight or, ignore others who don't have the attributes they require. To conjure an extreme example, this judgmental behavior reminds me of those exhibited by the French aristocracy during the time of Marie Antoinette and King Louis XVI, and we all know what happened to them!

Attractive Behaviors

Basically, I am attracted to the opposite: people who have a positive attitude and can't be so close-minded to think that just because you're not as attractive as they are, you have nothing to offer them! So many people have so much to offer you and me; heterosexual or homosexual, just listen to them! These close-minded people don't bother to listen to what people are saying, and it's a shame, because you can learn so much from so many others.

Future Gay Life

For my future, I simply want what everybody else wants to achieve: financial stability, not necessarily in a gay world but, in the world itself; religious comfort (*pause*). I want to feel that we are all here for a purpose, and our interactions with other people is not just chance but, that it's predetermined guide that is set forth for you. You just want to be happy. I don't have any goals that I think have been unfulfilled. If I were to die tomorrow, I think I would feel comfortable with where I've gone and where I've been. Who knows, if I may die tomorrow?

HIV/AIDS

I do feel that because of AIDS, a lot of gay men view themselves as short term and that AIDS has had a definite impact on the community. It has simply changed the way we think about certain choices we make in our lives, and has had a prevalent role in our thinking, more so than ever! To be perfectly blunt, AIDS is not a good thing!

The only positive effect of HIV/AIDS is in bonding our "scattered gay community" but, I do believe that we still have a long way to go. For example, the AIDS RIDE that I recently participated in with Bob was the most bonding thing I've ever done in my life! AIDS definitely changes your thinking. I've watched seventeen of my friends die so far and, I know that number plus, who are sick right now. Some of my closest, best friends have all died. It's weird, because each one that has passed away (*Overcome with emotion*). I can still feel them in here. (*Points to his heart*) They're all here! Sometimes, I'll be walking down the street and I'll say, "Oh, there's David," or, I'll say, "Oh, there's Mark." I say that to myself when I see someone doing something that was so like them. It's a weird thing, AIDS, in that it's just changed our community so much. *I agree completely with Tim's heartfelt sentiments since I have lost many friends to AIDS as well; the fact that many of us have suffered due to AIDS, makes it more important to live our lives more lovingly and honestly.*

There are some positive things that have come out of it. People seem to be a little more introspective. I think that it's a good point that you brought up in that it has bonded us a little bit more, but it's still not a good thing! Some days, I just wish I could just erase it, because it has hurt so many people who you've loved.

Closing Comments

I want to say, "Stop AIDS now!" You know, telling my story was fun. It was really fun. It helped me to think about a lot of things. For instance, when Bob and I first came down to Boston, we met a guy that we later "picked up" who was HIV-positive. One of the first things that he said to us was, "I'm HIV-positive." I'll never forget the impact that had on Bob and I; that this person had thought enough to say that, when people don't normally say, "I'm HIV-positive." But, the impact he made on us and he's been a really good friend of ours to this day! It was weird, because you could tell that people had shunned away from him because of his HIV status.

Today, he is still alive and gorgeous! He was really beautiful then, and still is! He helped set the standard of telling up front, "I'm HIV-positive and if you have a problem with it, tell me now!" That's powerful! He is the model of the type of gay man that really impresses me today.

Tim reinforces my premise that being honest and caring toward others can truly make someone be perceived as being more powerful and beautiful in the eyes of observers. Tim's closing statement that "Michael set the standard" proves the importance of being genuine and caring toward others. Tim's reaction to Michael's candor should inspire all of us to strive to live our lives as positive role models for the world at large.

END OF CHAPTER THREE

*Following my interview with Tim, Bob sat down in the chair Tim vacated with the same ease and confidence exuded by Tim but with a magnetic smile that would charm anyone male or female. His body is tall, muscular, defined, and relaxed. In fact, my friend Wayne (with whom I interview later in this book) described Bob as a "god spending time here on Earth." Bob has been patiently waiting to be interviewed following his partner Tim and has listened too much of the interview and is thereby anxious and raring to tell his story.

CHAPTER IV – THE BOB DOBSON STORY

"JUST TOO HOT TO HANDLE ME"

PERSONAL HISTORY

I'm a thirty-seven years old detective-sergeant down in Florida. I was raised as an only child. Both of my parents are deceased. I lost my mother in 1976, a week before my high school graduation of a sudden illness. My father passed away at age sixty five back in 1992 in one week! Both of my parents we sick only for one week prior to their deaths!

When my mother passed away it was a shock. It was very traumatic because it was a week before my high school graduation where everything was planned. There was no indication that she was ill; none, whatsoever!

I knew my father was going to die from the first couple of days he was in the hospital. He died three days after he found out he had cancer. I have no siblings, only a lot of cousins who all reside in Connecticut.

Bob's story clearly suggests a tragic childhood, and as a young child dealing with such tragedy, one has to learn how to cope with events out of one's control. As a result, the adult will try to overcompensate with feelings of control by attempting to control his present environment. In meeting Bob for the first time, the casual observer will notice a man in impressive physical condition with a quick smile and an easy charm that could easily disarm another man's defenses; and that is how I believe Bob would want it to be viewed. But, under the impressive exterior there must still be that lonely boy still trying to come to terms with the loss of his parents.

Today, I feel very independent. After my mother died, I became extremely independent. Because, my mother was more of a "go-getter," and my father was more the person that needed to be taken care of. So, I ended up taking care of my father until the day he died. (Sarcastically) And taking care of someone's daddy is a great character builder!

Bob's tone appears sad and it was almost as if he was emphasizing the sad tone in order to convey the dramatic affect. As a drama therapist, it is very common for children who suffer from early parental loss to have a difficult time separating themselves from their tragic story and have a tendency to make that story an integral part of their adult lives.

A Significant Childhood Trauma

I was molested at fourteen by my next door neighbor. I don't really remember how it all began. I do recall that he used to "blow me" all the time! He was an older guy who was married and had three kids. Subsequently, he served some jail time. But, he wasn't arrested for molesting me. He was arrested for molesting other boys. I guess you could call him a child molester!

Within only a few minutes of this interview, Bob tells of a second potentially significant childhood trauma where he has clearly learned to build up early coping mechanisms. From knowing of Bob's self-disclosed sexual prowess, he has apparently learned to cope by constructing emotional walls through sex as a means of protecting oneself from further harm.

When I think on it, I don't think this changed anything in my life about being gay. I had a girlfriend at the time. I had a series of girlfriends up until I was twenty.

Here we see the common gay male defensive stat where if "I have a girlfriend," or "I like girls", therefore, "I am not really gay." This shame-prone communication does not serve us as gay men, nor, as human beings, because it keeps us from being honest and true as to who we authentically want to be.

"How I Live My Life"

Actually, I had two sexual experiences with high school buddies at a camping trip. We experimented then, and it was like a "one time deal; one time shot!" I didn't have sex with them both at the same time, on two separate occasions on the same camping trip.

They were basically, "jerk-off sessions!" I never had "real sex" until I was much older. With women, it was more sexual? That all started when I was sixteen. I had one girlfriend from age sixteen to age twenty. We were going to get married and then I had gone to this gay bar in Springfield, Massachusetts.

I soon began to realize that I wasn't happy with women. Men simply "turned me on" more than women! I can't exactly remember that there was just nothing there for me with women. No sparks! I was eighteen when I started having sex with guys. But those experiences were far and few between.

I was beginning to feel that Bob was having a good time telling of his sexual history so quickly after sharing the loss of his parents and being molested by the neighbor. This quick switch from the telling of his family history and talking about early sexual experiences could be his unconscious attempt to emotionally distance himself from emotional pain.

What do you recall being your first serious experience with a guy?

His name was Peter. He was from Springfield, Massachusetts. His mother was a lesbian and she had a lesbian mother. Peter and I immediately "hit if off!" He was very young, sixteen, and we met in a gay bar. He got in at such a young age because of his lesbian mother.
Can you tell us more about Peter?

He was very cute. We went up to Boston; to the Parker House and spent the entire weekend there. That's when I did the whole thing! It was incredible and we had a great time. I was very nervous being with a guy. I didn't know how to act. Didn't know what Boston was all about, especially since Peter said he," fell in love" with me when the weekend had come to an end.

Thank goodness, I had a good friend in Boston named Diane who helped though my identity crisis. She was very open with me.

This significant first experience appears to have laid the groundwork for Bob's "meet and flee" routine. A routine that provides a very exciting sexual and emotionally gratifying tryst with a sexy and desirable young man but, causes Bob to feel the need to mentally obsess and justify his need to flee when the intimacy becomes too uncomfortable or painful. The reason for such behavior can easily be attributed to having been molested as a teenager and where Bob is still holding onto feelings of shame and guilt that will forever build up emotional walls. These walls will continue to prevent him from having a mature and mutually satisfying relationship with another man unless he is treated therapeutically for these early childhood stressors.

Diane is straight woman in her late forties who has a child now, but, she was in her early thirties then, and her boyfriend was in his teens! They are together to this day! They have an incredible relationship even though the baby was not his!

So, you "came out of the closet" at age eighteen, and the principal reason you did, was because you were unhappy having sex with women?

Yes. I was very unhappy with women.

But, you continued in this relationship with your girlfriend until you were twenty despite being sexually unsatisfied with her?

Yes. She used to "blow me" all the time but, it was very boring. We were still going to get married prior to my moving down to Florida. I recall that we went down together to see mutual friends; another couple. Later, I returned to Florida to look for a job as a policeman during a vacation, and it was then, that I realized getting married wasn't the right thing to do. I had a change of heart. I realized I was more influenced by my family to get married. I was being pressured!

This shame-inducing phenomenon is not uncommon for many gay men when having to deal with their family pressuring them to get married and follow the correct path in life, according to their own ideals. Bob at least had the sense of mind to follow his own path as far as being honest with regards to being gay.

So, how close were you to getting married?

Very close. The date for the wedding was set. No rings had been bought yet. We had said we'd be married in the springtime. But, I didn't have to make the decision to end the relationship! When I returned from Florida, I found out that she was seeing another guy! A next-door neighbor! She told me that she also wanted to break up with me. That she felt things just weren't going to work out with me!

Did she sense you were no longer interested in her sexually?

Probably, but to this day I continue to keep in touch with her every couple of years or so. She has five kids! She's still married to the same guy so I don't have any hard feelings.

Was it to the next-door neighbor?

Yes. She ended up marrying him.

"Coming out of the Closet"

Would you consider that time with Peter to be your most significant "turning point" or was there another more dramatic "coming out" experience?

Oh, yes! There was another experience even more dramatic! I recall another time going to Springfield. I had met this guy named Chris. Chris was very sweet, hot, and passionate. He made me feel very good. There was a real "spark in my heart" for him.

What happened with Peter?

Peter was too young for me. It was too confusing for me with his lesbian mother and her girlfriend, and everything. It was just too much of a scene for me to take!

This behavior reinforces my earlier impression that Bob is a "meet and flee" type of guy similar to an emotional "hit and run" driver. This new love interest will also take the same pattern as what occurred with Peter but Bob is unaware of this tendency to flee intimacy. And as long as Bob continues to be the "hot man in town" he can continue to gather his list of sycophants for quick trysts but without true emotional commitment.

Was Peter heartbroken when you split up with him being that you were his first love and all?

(Bob spoke as if he hadn't really given Peter much importance). Probably true. He wanted to explore more with me and I wanted to explore more with others.

Feeling it was better to move onto someone Bob was more comfortable talking about, and, not wanting to "push Bob too hard "so soon in the interview, I decided to return to a more comfortable subject.

So, let's go back to Chris.

(Bob was clearly happy to be back on the subject of Chris and not feeling guilty about Peter).

Yes. Chris and I "hit it off" very well! His parents knew everything! He had a "very open relationship" with his brother and sister as well. I felt very much "at home" with them. So, knowing that maybe I moving a little too fast, I asked Chris if he would consider moving down to Florida with me? He agreed to do it! So, we packed up and moved down to Florida together.

Chris and I lived together in Florida and we had a lot of great times! We met a lot of nice people in Florida. Of course, I was on the police force down there so, I was very nervous about my relationship with Chris being a police officer and having a lover as well.

Bob must have been under considerable mental pressure, being both a police officer and gay at a time when being gay was illegal in the state of Florida. I wondered how Bob was able to conceal his relationship from others but, my question was quickly answered by Bob's next response. It was a response that I already expected, since Bob is clearly afraid of intimacy.

I became a police officer around the age of twenty two or twenty three. Unfortunately, my relationship with Chris ended soon after I became a police officer, because Chris was a very susceptible kind of guy. He wasn't a strong willed person. He had a lot of friends who did cocaine all the time! So, he got addicted to cocaine. I got very nervous about his habit because of my job.

I used to come home from working the midnight shift and there would be pieces of furniture missing; lamps and stuff like that! You see, what he used to do was pawn those things just to get money for cocaine. We fought for many months after that. Finally, I said, "You have to leave" but he wouldn't leave! So, I left, and then I met Tim. Tim was going through the same thing! His lover had basically left him for another guy who lived down in Miami.

Bob is demonstrating two other habits as a result of being a child of alcoholics and having been sexually molested; an attraction to addictive partners and a tendency to replace one lover quickly with another. These avoidant type behaviors will provide Bob with the opportunity to put his focus upon the actions of others and not upon his own actions or behaviors.

Tim and I were both breaking up with lovers. He was an emotional mess because he couldn't understand why his lover was always going down to Miami to be with their best friend who was HIV positive, who subsequently died. He felt that his lover was spending way too much time in Miami, and eventually found out the truth. Of course, I had left my lover Chris, with whom I had bought a house with.

So Chris moved out and Tim moved in?

No. Chris wouldn't leave the house because his name was still on the deed. So, I moved out and lived with Tim and his then, ex-lover, and that situation continued for two or three months.

Didn't you experience any conflicts living under the same roof as the ex-lover? Did the ex-lover ever try come between Tim and you or sabotage your relationship?

No. We were not attracted to one another and there were few problems other than the bonds that were established between Tim and his ex-lover. But, we were able to get along okay until the ex-lover eventually moved out.

This three-way relationship is just the beginning for Bob and his multitude of boyfriends, sex partners, intimate friends, and these odd but, dramatic configurations of men. All of which, only serve to prolong Bob's unwillingness and surprising naiveté with regards to the lengths he will go to avoid true intimacy with another man.

"ALL ABOUT SEX"

My first relationship began in 1980, and to this day, I feel great about being gay! I feel more at ease, more comfortable with being gay. I think the older you get, the more you really have to do things for yourself. You can't worry about what people think about you.

So that's your philosophy learned from your experiences of being gay?

Yeah. You have to think for yourself. No matter what the consequences of your actions are, you can't be overly concerned about what other people think about whom you are and your sexuality. To me, being gay is no longer a concern of mine. I'm not going to jump up and down and say, "I'm gay", but then again, I don't ask a heterosexual person, "are you straight," so why should someone ask me, "are you gay?"

Are you talking about self-esteem and that it doesn't matter if you're gay or straight?

I am who I am! I am simply being who I am, which is being gay.

How do you demonstrate your gay pride within your community?

I support all the gay causes, all the benefits. I do whatever I possibly can to support the gay community without putting myself on a billboard but, behind the scenes. Of course, I plan to do more as the year's progress. As I said, the older I get, the more I've become prouder ever year of my sexuality.

"The Stud at Work"

At this point in the interview, I felt it was important to question Bob on his flirting behavior that he clearly exhibited the night before at a club in New York City which clearly demonstrated his amazing self confidence in his ability to approach and seduce men.

Last night, I observed you interacting with a very attractive bartender at Splash. You clearly have a certain confidence about yourself which is demonstrated by the way you walk and carry yourself in public. I also observed, that you had no difficulty, whatsoever, interacting with that "hot" bartender, when others may have been intimidated by the possibility of being rejected by that type; the type of handsome man with the "attitude of superiority." What's your secret? Is your behavior the result of feeling somewhat superior yourself?

(*Smiling*) You smile. You smile and be pleasant, and people will accept you. If you just stand there as if you are made of stone, no one will approach you. No one will talk to you.

People want to be around "fun people." People want to be around positive "vibes," not negative "vibes." So, I can talk to the ugliest person in the bar, and can carry on a conversation for as long as it takes. I can also talk to the most beautiful person in the bar, and carry on a conversation with that person. If that person is arrogant and so forth, I can "turn that person around" in a matter of minutes! I can "loosen him up," because they all put up this shield at first! You have to break up that shield, and I can break that shield in a matter of minutes!

So, you're the "shield breaker"?

Yeah. I can "break the ice" with them! It's the smile.

But, you're a handsome man. Isn't it easier for you to get your way with these guys because of your looks?

Yes. But, a smile is very important. You should smile more, and just get along with other people, regardless, of what they look like. I know some people who would say to me, "Why are you talking to that guy? He's ugly!" I simply respond, "Why not? He's a human being, just like you or I!" I don't care whom I'm seen with!

Bob is clearly "in his element" when in a bar with men looking for a mostly sexual connection with another man. He knows that he has the "power" to charm and drop another gay man's defenses very quickly with his sexual "power" and charm. Unfortunately, that "power" cannot stay strong as one gets older and less physically desirable to others unless it is supported by a strong ego and self-confidence based on emotional stability.

Yes, but there are certain perceptions in the gay community that are firmly entrenched. For example, if one talks for a long period of time with a guy in a bar, it is perceived that you are sexually attracted to him.

Yes. But, that's not what I'm about! If I want to talk to someone first, I don't care what they look like. That makes a difference of course! Oh sure, sometimes I like having a pretty boy by my side. But for today, I simply want to have an interaction with someone who simply knows how to "hold up his end" of the conversation! I don't always go out looking to get someone into my bed!

I know that I have a history of pursuing and "bedding" the pretty boys with my ex-lover, but now, I want to know them on a personal level before pursuing them in a sexual way. Being alone with someone, there has to be some feeling there. I just can't go "wham-bam, see ya later." There has to be something there. I have to be either interested in their personality; their attitude. There has to be something more than their looks!

This comment by Bob appears to suggest a willingness to be approached by someone at a bar for the sole purpose of conversation. As a result, Bob is removing the pressure of having a sexual conquest for the night taking precedence over the interaction. But, that may not be the "hidden agenda" for the person approaching Bob and engaging him in conversation.

I would then tend to question Bob's willingness to approach someone with whom he does not have a physical attraction toward? Is Bob really saying that physical attraction is not of primary importance to him when meeting someone for the first time at a bar or club? Or, is he simply stating that he is available to anyone who is a decent conversationalist despite their physical appearance? What do you think? What attribute of a potential communication partner holds more importance to you, physical attraction or stimulating conversation? And, if you answer is the first choice, then how many men have you pushed away from your life as a result?

When I go to bars, I'm not always looking for sex, sometimes I want more! With Chris, and with most of my ex-lovers, we always became friends. We've always kept in touch, and we get along great! With my relationship with Tim, we every so often, introduce a third party to our bed.

Everyone thinks that we have a very unusual relationship because we often introduce a third party to our relationship. But the in the gay world, it's more normal to introduce a third party into their relationship, than it is in the heterosexual world.

Bob is attempting to justify his sexual behavior by stating that it is "normal" for gay men to introduce a third party into their bedroom. The only feeling that is being served by introducing a third person for sex is to add a new stimulation to their sexual interactions but in the meantime, this conscious choice by one or more partners directly results in a reduction of intimacy between the primary partners.

If someone thinks that gay men should model themselves after the heterosexual community, than they are sadly mistaken. They are completely "out of the ballpark!" It just does not work! That is my belief.

So, you're saying if gay men are attempting to mimic the heterosexual relationship, they are wrong for doing so?

Yes. That if they are attempting to mimic the heterosexual relationship, then what they are doing is totally absurd! It's just not going to happen! Number one, we can't be legally married in all fifty states. But, if Congress should pass the legislation that will help toward legitimizing our lifestyle, that may help gay men feel more accepted by our society. But still, men are men!

What does that mean?

It means that men are very promiscuous people. Men like variety!

Are all men promiscuous or, just gay men?

Making such general statements regarding promiscuity in all men gives legitimacy to Bob's actions and in the same respect, allows him to deny his addictive behavior. It is becoming clear to this observer that Bob is being rigid in his excuses and even feels somewhat justified with regards to his sexual behavior. His denial of their being a problem will cause him to repeat this behavior continuously in his life with the same results; hot and emotionally "empty" sexual trysts without true intimacy. *(This interview took place some years before gay marriage legislation and changes in laws came into effect).

I believe it refers to all men in general. I also believe that the majority of heterosexual men, who are presently in a heterosexual relationship, have had a gay experience at one time or another and that the only reason that the majority of these men are married is due primarily to peer pressure. The stigma of not being married goes impinges on many gay men's lifestyle.

For example, I have this married friend down in Florida, he's twenty eight, married, and he loves to come over and have sex with me every now and then. He loves having sex with his wife, but he also likes having sex with men.

Does he have sex only with you or does it include Tim as well?

No. He has sex with both of us. (Big smile) And, he loves to get fucked! He loves getting fucked because it is obviously a sexual act that his wife can't provide him with. Not unless, she's willing to shove a dildo up his ass every once and a while!

Does this kind of sexual behavior happen often or is it rare?
(Laughs) Very rare, but some women are kinky like that! I know of some couples who go to gay bars to "pick up" men for both partners. Most likely, she enjoys watch other men fuck her husband, and vice versa.

Did you ever participate in a situation like that?

Oh, yes! I was with this one couple several times who were just like that! I would primarily fuck her and he would watch. But, one time, I fucked him too and he liked it! But this scene no longer exists because they ended up getting a divorce.

What a surprise. So, now he's pursuing a gay lifestyle?

Yes, he is gay. In fact, I see his car constantly parked in front of an adult bookstore on Southern Boulevard!

That type of behavior suggests that he's feeling quite a bit of shame with his choice to "hang out" at adult bookstores so he can pick up other men like himself looking for that quick "hook-up" or "fix."

"About Shame"

Cruising bookstores for anonymous sex demonstrates a compulsion to find mostly anonymous sex partners for a quick sexual interaction without any type of emotional connection or commitment. This avoidance of a potentially intimate relationship and the conscious choice to pursue only sexually satisfying "trysts" will only prolong feelings of loneliness and feelings of shame and guilt for being gay.

So, what do you attribute to your more positive gay identity than your friend or, are you still struggling with your gay identity? To be specific, do you feel more positive or negative regarding your identity?

Mostly positive, in fact now, it's all positive. I'm not afraid to be seen in public holding another man's hand or arm-in-arm with another man. I've even been on television with the Florida AIDS Ride. I was seen down in Miami on Channel 10, escorting the "Riderless Bike" in the Gay Pride Parade.

What does the "Riderless Bike" stand for?
It represents all the people who died of AIDS. They have a ceremony for those who died of AIDS and can no longer be with us on that special day. I walked the bike up to the podium while the speaker made his presentation. It was very emotional, and the entire ceremony was televised on Channel 10. There were some five thousand people there! I personally, looked into the camera two times, so I knew I was being seen by thousands of people. My fellow officers at the station house even saw the footage and were okay with it.

The entire day was a very touching experience, and we raised a considerable amount of money for a good cause.

Would you say that experience was your most positive gay experience? Was it a "breakthrough" toward your acceptance of your gay identity? Or, was there one momentous occasion or a series of events that most affected your decision to "come out of the closet"?

I would say it was the death of my father in 1992. I always wanted to tell him, but I never had an opportunity to tell him. That kind of saddens me, that I never had the opportunity to tell him. I think he would have accepted my being gay. We both really loved each other, and it would have been nice. (*Pause*) I was going to tell him that year, and then he died. I had it in my mind that I would have sat him down and said, "Hey, look. I'm gay, and you're not going to have any grandchildren unless I adopt, and that's how I want to live my life!" I knew what his answer would have been. It would have been, "Well, I love you anyway." (*Another pause, difficulty finding words*).

So, after that, after he had passed away, I got it into my mind to "come out". I knew that all of my relatives already knew I was gay but the question never came up yet. I remember even getting a little paranoid when I was around them. I perceived that they believed it's was all going to go away with time, a phase, even though I had been with Tim for some twelve years. They always invited him to weddings and other family gatherings with me. They already knew what was going on. No big surprise!

As a drama therapist, Bob's comments regarding his missed opportunity to have that significant conversation with his father would provide for an excellent opportunity for a role play dramatization. In the role play work. Bob would then have the opportunity to talk to his father through my playing the role of his father using the words the Bob would give to me to say. In doing so, Bob could potentially experience some of the feelings that may have occurred, if he had the actual conversation with his father.

Unfortunately, since Bob never did have that conversation, there will always be some uncertainty as to how Bob's father would have reacted? And, with that conversation, Bob may have had a closer relationship with his dad and his life may have significantly benefited from it. Instead, it appears as if Bob had to substitute those feelings for his dad to other loves in his life. Two ways for replacing that lost love could be to either find a boyfriend, even a series of boyfriends to fulfill that need or, by self-medicating oneself as a means for temporary self-fulfillment. Examples of how that self-medicating can be experienced, are through sexual compulsion, and a dependency on alcohol and, or, drugs. Of course, none of these attempts to self-medicate can be anything more than "quick fixes" and fix nothing.

Another incident that occurred that same day as the interview that supported my impression that Bob still feels shame over being gay among his family members was when his father's brother came by the house for a visit and Bob appeared visibly uncomfortable at his presence. This just Bob's visible discomfort at that moment prompted me to ask the following question:

When your uncle came by the house I had a feeling of you being uncomfortable around him. Was it because the house was filled with men? Tim was right beside you when you greeted him. You also chose not to introduce me or my lover to him when he entered the room. Were you afraid that we might have said something that would have embarrassed you? Frank, your best friend and our host, did mention some timidity on your part toward introducing us. Your uncle did enter the house with another man his age so, he could be gay for all you know?

No. They have been best friends for years! Frank feels it is my obligation to say something to my uncle. That it is something that I have to deal with, but not Frank! Frank says, "Tell him, tell him, tell him!" He has a different perception about that. It's my feeling that if I meet a guy to play racquetball with, why should I tell him about my being gay? What is the significance? I just think that we are all human beings, and to me there is no difference! We all love people!

It's not going to make me feel any better by telling him that I'm gay! So, if it's not going to make me feel any better, then why should I do it? But, I can hear people saying, "Well, it's going to make you feel better; it's going to make me feel better." Everybody's different! Everybody has a different philosophy about whether you have to tell people about your sexual preference. It's something personal. That's the problem with society.

What is the problem with society?

Society needs to label gays, and why do we have to be labeled? Very rarely do you hear any other terms about heterosexuals other than "straights". But for homosexuals, you hear, "fags, homos, dykes, lesbians, carpet-munchers!" Everybody has all these nicknames for gays!

What about the derogatory term for "straights" spoken by many gay men: "breeders."

(Big sigh) I know of that term, it's just another label! Why do we need these labels?

Bob appears visibly agitated as he expresses his frustration with society's need to label minority groups that upset many because of their lifestyle. It is clear that Bob hates being "labeled" in any way. His feelings are easily understandable since society's treatment history of homosexuals has been rife with verbal and physical abuse. Having my own history of abuse by society, I can relate and identify with Bob's anger. But the question of shame over being who we are and guilt over our actions may also add fuel to this type of self-righteous anger.

Do you feel shame with regards to your gay identity? For example, I find the term, "breeders" when spoken by a gay man, signifies shame or guilt on the gay man's part. I believe that if a gay man or heterosexual man is comfortable with their own sexuality, they wouldn't necessarily care about other peoples' sexual orientation. Do you agree or disagree?

I feel that we ALL joke around. I believe that we get accustomed to using certain words over and over through the ages. It becomes almost habitual to label others; in both the gay and straight worlds! It is very rarely to not find others participating in the labeling those they don't agree or relate well with. Not everyone is well meaning or altruistic. Even with political fundraisers or charitable events, you simply don't find the majority of those attending for charitable reasons.

You mean people are attending "to see or to be seen"?

Yeah. These "circuit parties" are not about, "how much money did we make?" It's about, "did you have a good time; did you get laid?"

So, you question gay society's true altruism. Do you feel that gay men tend to be more self-centered and immature and if so, did you always feel that way about being gay? For instance, what was high school like for you? Was sex gratification always your goal in your interaction with others?

Well, I remember being the jock. I had girlfriends all the time. I was very popular in school. But, when I did fool around with a guy, I remember saying to myself, "I hope he doesn't tell someone else that I fooled around with him." Then I thought, "He's probably thinking the same thing about me," hoping that he won't tell anybody else! The truth is, I know that it was wrong to be sexual with another boy and that it was wrong to be doing so much "fucking around" in general.

Did you feel shameful?

I was thinking with my "dick" because it felt good, versus anything else! I even fucked around with my neighbor. At fourteen years old (sighed), you don't necessarily have it "all together" Course, it felt good! So, anytime he wanted to do it, he would just wave me over, and I would come over, and we would "go to town!" I do remember one time when we were down in the cellar of his house, and his wife came home! She was upstairs, and she began to come down the stairs to the cellar while we were down there! I remember having to hide behind the furnace!

How did you feel about that moment, and did she see anything?

I was scared to death! Scared to death! But no, she didn't see anything, she never suspected because he said he was working hard at his workbench and she believed him, so, she went back upstairs. Shit, I was only some five feet away; it was so close!

Did you feel guilty or shameful?

Oh, very guilty! I felt very guilty to her and at the time. I was sincerely ashamed for what I did. I couldn't understand it. I felt a lot of anger toward HIM, but instead of dealing with my anger in an appropriate way, I released my anger at him onto his son!

What? You chose to take your anger out on his and her son? How?

He was a couple of years younger than me so what I did was to "get together" with his son, and we fooled around. (Pause) The guy's a very prominent doctor now, in Boston.

So, you feel you expressed your anger toward the father by having sex with his son?

Yes. I did.

Do you recall if you purposefully went after the son because of the father, or did you honestly desire the son?

He was very cute, and I think it just happened.

What did you do with him sexually?

I fucked him!

What did it feel like to fuck him?

It was very unusual. Because I was young; he was young. We used to go into the back- woods and fuck all the time

How old were you then?

Fourteen!

Earlier in this interview you failed to mention him as one of your earlier sex partners and specifically, he was not even mentioned as one of your "jerk-off" partners!

(Surprised) Oh, right! I forgot about him!

You forgot to mention fucking the son of the man who molested you?
Wow! I forgot about that! (*Loud laughter*) But you see we only had sex on several occasions.

So, because the sex only occurred on several occasions, you forgot to mention having sex with this young man until now? In fact, you "fucked" the son of our molester more than once?

Yes. *(Bob continued his story without fully grasping the significance of what he was describing)* So after a while, he didn't want anything to do with me anymore.

Who didn't want anything to do with you, the son or the father?

The son didn't want anything to do with me.

The son no longer wanted to have a sexual relationship with you?

Right! That's how I interpreted his avoidance of me, to be.

What about his dad, did he choose to avoid you as well?

(*Fumbling for words realizing his actions*) Well, they eventually moved. I don't think that he ever found out about it, and, I eventually cut off the sex with him.

What was the father's reaction to your choice to cut off sex with him?

He couldn't understand why I wouldn't come over? In fact, one night he was caught scratching on my window screen with a rake. My father was in the bedroom at the time and saw him. He asked me, "What the fuck is he doing?" I got really, really nervous, and said, "I don't know? What's his problem?" My dad just blew it off, but I think at that time he knew something was going on with this guy, and decided not to pursue it! That was the end of it! But, I was so nervous at that point that I decided to stop seeing him completely! After that I was only with Chris and then Tim.

At this point in the interview, I chose not to pursue this very significant information and recommended that Bob seek some counseling to deal more specifically with these traumatic events that have directly affected his past and present actions. It appears as if Bob is in denial of his true feelings as a direct result of this early molestation by the neighbor and his choice to have aggressive sex with the son of his molester. It was intriguing that Bob forgot to mention his neighbor's son as one of his first sexual partners, especially since this was someone with whom he had anal sex with, and was clearly NOT one of his "jerk-off buddies; "neither was the dad.

Bob, these dramatic events that you admitted having will continue to significantly affect your relationships with gay men, especially with your relationship with lovers such as Tim.

No. No. I have a very hard time talking about my experiences with anyone!
So, this is the first time you've shared this story with anyone?

No. I've shared it with Tim and with only close, personal friends.

People need to read about these stories. Relating these stories to others does help to educate and inform those with a lack of understanding of gay men and their issues. Many gay men, even myself, have had similar events of molestation at an early age as you've had. These experiences can often lead to feelings of guilt and shame about being gay.

These men, who like to molest boys, must have viewed you and I as potential sex partners because we were immature and vulnerable. These feelings can eventually transform to hate toward the molester who took advantage of our vulnerability, and shamed us.

We need to focus on the origins or history of your feelings of shame and guilt with regards to your gay identity. Do you feel the origin of your shameful feelings began with the sexual encounters with the neighbor or, with his son?

The sex with both men did help bring about my feelings of being gay! I sometimes wonder if that hadn't occurred, would I be gay today. That's why the anger comes into play, because someone made that decision for me. I simply did not get the opportunity to make that decision for myself. That the sexual gratification I received from this guy sort of swayed me in the direction of becoming gay. Whether or not I would have followed that path anyway, I don't know? But, had it not happened, I sometimes wonder if I would have been gay now, or, would I be married with a wife and children.

(Disbelieving what I'm hearing) ***You still believe that you could be married to a woman? It sounds as if you still question whether or not you're gay. Do you doubt whether you are gay?***

Oh, yeah! There's no doubt about it! I know I'm gay!

(Pursuing this point further) ***But, you said that you feel as if this guy forced your decision upon you sooner than you would have made one?***

Yes! I didn't meet this guy and say, "C'mon let's get together!" He's the one who seduced me!

That's where the anger comes from.

You feel as if he made you become gay? That if he didn't have sex with you and the fact that you enjoyed it, made you gay?
Right!

But you feel that you would have "come out of the closet" eventually?

Yes! But with that happening, my trust in people was affected. My "giving of myself" to someone, makes me very tentative! But, I also feel that my hesitancy stems from my mother's death. I loved her very much, and I lost her. I can't help but think that if I ever love someone else again, they'll either die or hurt me tremendously! So, then, I have a tendency not to express myself more openly with anyone!

The loss of his mother plus the early sexual molestation have all contributed in building up those "emotional walls" for Bob that were constructed in order to protect him from additional harm. Unfortunately, those walls become more effective in keeping others out, rather than protecting ourselves from additional harm. Plus, those types of defense mechanisms make it impossible to learn and adapt to new experiences, since those walls are built on fear and distrust.

I know that I'm making progress toward "letting down" my defenses. Perhaps some sort of counseling or therapy may help me to move closer to that goal.

Yes, I agree that therapy will be helpful for you, since all the experiences you related have had a direct impact on your difficulty with being intimate with another man. Therapy would help you in exploring those conflicts. Your conflict with Tim is evidence of your problems with intimacy and how you are blocking the relationship from flowing more easily. It's obvious that he loves you. Can't you see that?

I don't know what's going to happen with Tim. I can't predict the future. We just live day by day and take it from there. I'm not going to regret any of my decisions.

I don't blame you. Whatever happened to you in the past was not your fault! That's how a therapist can help you get "off the hook" The neighbor was the bastard! He was the shameful one. He simply transferred his shame to you through making you feel guilty for feeling good about the sex.

Yes, that's true.

Do you feel that the shame and guilt you have expressed about being gay, have had an adverse effect on how you relate with other gay men?

Oh, definitely!

How?

In what we already talked about with regards to my sexual behavior. I believe that many gay men "act out" our sexuality in the wrong places. Parks, public restrooms, sex clubs, bookstores, become convenient places to go to "act out". And every time I go to those places for sexual gratification, I felt guilty.

So every time you go to one of these places you feel guilty for going?

Used to, I don't go to those places anymore!

When did you stop going to these places?

We stopped about two years ago.

When you say "we" you mean both you and Tim?

Oh yeah. Yeah. And, we would always say afterward, that we weren't going to go to these places anymore. (Pause) I mean, nowadays, you really have to think, "Do I want to live a long and prosperous life, or do I want to have five minutes of sexual gratification!

Did AIDS have any effect on that decision? I also want to know whether you feel the AIDS epidemic is a result of gay shame. You mentioned the "sexual acting out places" that have dramatically caused the spread the virus so easily to so many, when you went to those places, that fact must have been on both your minds.

Yes, and in a way, I feel bad for those people.

But both of us could easily have become one of those people!

Yes, easily. It's that need for self-gratification which arose from my lack of self-esteem. That I allowed someone to "go down on me" without even saying," hello", saddens me.

But, that's all you wanted at that time.
-
Yes, that's all I wanted.

So, like others, gay men were only objects for sexual gratification?

Yes. But, as I re-evaluate that whole scene, that's not where I want to be in life! I want to rise above that! I want to have fun, but I know I have my responsibilities. I think I'm very kind person. I love people, regardless, of who they are or what color they are. That's why I became a policeman. I enjoy helping people who are just "down and out." On many occasions, police officers are very rough with the people they arrest. These guys give policemen a bad name. They're the same guys who are anti-gay and make comments about other gay police officers.

I've escaped that type of derision being that I'm a supervisor.

They know you are gay and still make comments about other gay officers in front of you?

Oh, they would. That's just their mentality! I can stop them from getting "carried away" because of my position as a supervisor. I just won't put up with that! I've been in the police force for some fifteen years. I'll go as far as I have to go to stop any harassment in the job!

Your gay pride is evident in your statement, but I also hear your anger.

Yes, but it works on the job!

Gay Communication Game at Work

My next question is related to your last comments with how gay men interact with both the gay and straight communities. For instance, do you feel that some gay men act superior to others, perhaps subliminally (without purposeful thought), as a means of "acting out" their shame? For example, by being abusive or simply ignoring other gay men, what do you believe they are communicating to one another? I'm especially interested in the way gay men interact in cliques. Do you believe that most gay men desire being in a popular clique to feel safe?

I don't! I don't want to be part of a clique. (Bob audibly sighs) For instance, it's got nothing to do with wanting to have a pretty boy by your side. I don't go out saying, "All I want to do is hang out with pretty people." I don't give a shit!

I, for one, do not believe that last statement from Bob because I have observed him on several social occasions surrounding himself with beautiful young men.

Okay. You had made a similar statement earlier, but don't you see others doing this?

Oh yeah. Yeah! And that's their choice and I have to respect that, because I fit in with them and their cliques.

Yes, and I see you going home with a lot of pretty boys too. In fact, I've never seen, or, heard of you going home with an overweight man or physically unattractive man.

No. But, I talk to them. I don't mind talking to them. They come up to me. "How are you doing? Where are you from?" I don't mind carrying on a conversation, but I'm not attracted.
So, if one of these guys then, "put the moves on you?"

Then, I'll say, "I'm simply not interested. I'm sorry." And, I've done that many times. I look at people's eyes, and I can see if something's there. Just by speaking with them for five or ten minutes, I can tell if there's something good between us. I look for that "sparkle in their eyes." I learn a lot by simply looking into someone's eyes.

Are we talking about sex or just good conversation?
Sexually, yes, but good conversation too! I know that there's something that they can get out of me and I can get out of them. Not everyone gets along or, have the same likes and dislikes.

Returning to the topic of feelings of indifference and superiority based on physical attractiveness, wealth, fame, etc. Do you feel they are or, are not, associated with feelings of shame and guilt? Or, do you feel these attitudes are basic, human attitudes that come with feeling one has more advantages in life than others?

I feel that one does not have to be attractive, wealthy, or tremendously gifted, in order to have a positive attitude about oneself. For example, I have this boyfriend in Miami named Julio, who isn't what one would call a "hunk," or a "pretty boy." But, he's one of the sweetest guys I've ever met! We've shared a lot and I didn't want to break that bond. But, he's young and very immature

I decided to end the relationship and he said that he never wanted to see me again. That, "I tore out his heart!" I know I hurt him, but I know he'll recover soon. He has lots of friends to comfort him. But, he was simply, much, much too young for me. I would want to keep him as a friend.

So, sex with him in the future would be out of the question?

Maybe, but the sex between Julio and I was really great, it simply was not enough to sustain a relationship!

True. Then let's return to this topic of shame and guilt and its effect on the way gay men communicate or don't communicate? We discussed how they communicate within their own but, how do you feel we communicate with our heterosexual counterparts?

Well, for one, you just can't really be yourself! The stigma that is still attached to the gay community, with AIDS, the promiscuity, the "kinky" sex that they think we all have, can be a problem so, yeah, it can be hard to interact with straight people. And, I have a hard time doing that now. Unless, it's in a business type relationship or with friends I've had for years. It's hard for me to want to call one of my straight friends up and to ask them if they want to go water-skiing. Even though they're friends, and we used to do the same things, it's different now. I just can't say to them, "Oh, look at that hot water skier over there!" It's always, "Oh, man! Look at the tits on that one over there!" I just can't say, "Well, he's got a nice ass." (*Bob laughs*)

I understand. But, I think we're still talking about sexual topics. What about last night when Rick and I came in, and Tim's ex sister-in-law was here? You appeared very comfortable and at ease with them. What's the difference?

I'm very comfortable with them, because they know I'm gay and with Tim!

So, you're comfortable when people know you're gay and are accepting of your lifestyle?

Yes. I'm very comfortable when people know the situation. They don't question me or the comments I may make in their presence. But, nobody else knows.....

(Deciding to pursue this line of questioning with Bob) **Let's return to talking about your uncle. Now, you assume that he does know about you so, you choose not to discuss it?**

That's why I'm beginning to feel it's a good idea to tell him, so I can act as myself with him.

That would be fantastic. But, I can assure you that everyone who knows about my upcoming commitment ceremony will come because they care about me and are accepting of my sexuality and my relationship. We need to get our families out of these rooms of denial, but if we're in denial, then how can we possibly let them out?

I agree.

What if I came out of the bedroom when your uncle was here and absent-mindedly said to Rick, "Honey, I forgot my toothbrush, do you have one," what would your response has been?

(Pause) I would probably have said nothing.

Bob may have said nothing out of fear but, I am sure in his mind that he would have visualized in his mind pushing me off a cliff!

Would you uncle's eyes have bulged with shock and disbelief?

(Sighs) You see, the truth is, I don't want to embarrass him of what other people in his hometown might say. For example, "How's your gay nephew?"

Where does that negative comment come from? Why would they not ask, "How's your handsome nephew, the policeman?"

Because of the stigma that's attached to being gay. People just don't understand.
Okay, but if your family was comfortable with who you are, and had accepted you, they would.

(Trying to interrupt and challenge me) Different people are raised in different parts of the country. I'm Irish Catholic, very Catholic, and in my hometown, viewed gay as? *(Bob sighs)*.

Where is your hometown?

Stafford Springs, Connecticut.

So, what was going on in Stafford Springs about being gay?

Nothing was, but every other word was, "You're a fag" or, "That one is a fag!"

So then, being gay is a shameful act?

Oh, yes! Being gay in Stafford Springs is very shameful.

* (author's note) This interview took place some years before Connecticut became one of the first states to pass gay marriage legislation and strong anti-gay bias laws.

And a gay teen would feel guilty over having homosexual fantasies?

Yes, very! So, those people who were brought up thinking like that!

(Interrupting) But, we're talking about your uncle who obviously cares about you! Also, he came into your house with another man! They looked very cute together. Obviously, he has a very close friendship with this other man.

He does! They've been friends since college!

Then, do you think he perceives your relationship with Tim as another buddy, or do you think he knows the truth?

You see, I'm not sure. They're very ignorant up here. They're very ignorant of what goes on in the gay scene. For example, I had an uncle who was very bigoted. He hated blacks and fags!

He was a shameful man. If he has to hate fags, and hate Blacks – who else? Does he hate Jews too? The ones who hate are often filled with inner shame and it's easier to hate than cry!

My boyfriend Julio has an uncle similar to mine. His uncle called his mother, who is his sister, after she informed him that Julio was working for the Florida AIDS Ride. She was very proud that his son, who is a medical technician, helped to raise a lot of money for AIDS. But instead of being proud, his uncle said to his sister, "he's probably got fucking AIDS, and he's probably dying, so, that's why he's doing it!"

That's only his own shame and guilt talking. For him, it's easier to hate than love.

But, you see what I mean? It's impossible to try to convince these people!

But, would the uncle that I met, make a comment like that? That was Julio's stupid uncle! Your uncle seemed like a really nice guy! Would he say something like that to you?

Yes, he is. He's a very nice guy.

So, why don't you just tell him?
You are probably right. The next time that I get another opportunity like I did today, I will sit him down and tell him! That will be very hard for me to do.

It would only improve the closeness of your relationship with him. I'm positive that he already knows, and has fully accepted you and your relationship! That's what happened for me and many others, so, take the chance! What do you have to lose? Certainly not your uncle's love, because he clearly loves you.

I know. I have friends who have told their families, and they've all responded with, "he's my son and I still love him."

Someone who hates blacks, gays, Jews, etc., is basically, a hateful person who's full of shame! It's a shame that Julio has an uncle like that, but it may be true that Julio's uncle may be homosexual and has a ton of shame about it!

Well, this is where the ironic part comes in with Julio's uncle.

Okay, so you're going to prove me right?

His uncle molested him.

Part of me feels sorry for both Julio and his uncle, but this new information that Bob is telling me is only proving my main point that gay shame often leads to hateful acts which only demean and devalue us. Therefore, "coming out of the closet" serves to stop all the bullshit and can save many of us a world of misery and making innocent others miserable in the process.

Okay, so here's my case in point about the guilt and the shame. He probably thinks that he made Julio this way, and now Julio might die for his sins!

Oh, yes! He must feel shameful for molesting Julio and may be responsible for his being gay.

He probably even wants Julio to die in order to continue keeping his gayness a dirty secret!

Yes!

Just like the son-of-a-bitch who molested you!

Yes, and I wish he was dead.

Yes, I know! But, he probably wishes you dead for leaving him or, for you bringing out his own sexuality, which he viewed as a shameful act. He then transferred his own feelings of guilt and shame to you! Whereupon, you took your own shame out on his son!

Yes, I am guilty for what I did to his son and what you say makes perfect sense.

Bob, it is because of that hateful shame and guilt that I am writing this book. I want to help those individuals who view homosexuality as a shameful act. These examples that you have cited are perfect examples, because they demonstrate history repeating itself. The molester or fag hater is not only the shameful one, but he also transfers his shame to others like you and Julio! So despite your history, you're comfortable with heterosexual people if they know and accept your sexuality?

(Pause) I'm comfortable with everybody! But, I enjoy being in the company of people whom I can be raunchy! I don't want to hear about wanting "tits and pussy." I want to talk about "hot ass and cock!" I want to be comfortable saying, "He's got a hot ass and body, I'd like to fuck him."

Finally, "Coming OUT of the Closet"

Do you feel then by "coming out of the closet" added to your acceptance and comfort-ability about being gay? You came out pretty recently didn't you?

Yes. I "came out" in 1992 after my father died. There's really nobody there for me right now, except my friends. I have to take care of myself. I'm a very proud person so, if it came down to the wire and I was confronted at work, I would admit to being gay. Of course, I'd immediately reply, "If you have a problem with that, tell me now! Because, I'm going to continue working here and if I get harassed in any way, shape or form, I'm going to slap you with the biggest lawsuit you've ever seen in your life!"

You see, I have a chief of police who's a "Born Again Christian." He belongs to this all male Christian group called the "Promise Keepers." They view the woman as being subservient to the man. He has all these articles about the "Promise Keepers" stapled on his office wall. That is really offensive to me.

Why is it offensive to you? Their premise appears more insulting to women?

He's displaying this literature in the workplace! Why should I be subjected to that type of literature in my workplace? Should I have gay publications stapled on my wall? Should I have a cross on my wall if I'm a Catholic and a good Christian? That might insult someone else. Why do we have to display what we do in life? In fact, I'm still evaluating that situation with regards to my sergeant. Every time I have to go into his office and see all that "shit" on the wall, it makes me feel that they would be adamantly against everyone unlike themselves.
The truth is that they can't stand homosexuals! They think it's a sin; it's evil! And here I am, a gay man entering his office, and I have to see that literature on the wall!

It makes you feel more angry than shameful?

Yes! It makes me feel only anger! And like I said, I'm still evaluating the situation. I'm considering contacting his boss, who's the city manager. If she doesn't remove it from the wall, what does it say about her? His literature does not only target gays but, women!

Absolutely true but let's change the subject and talk about who would you consider to be the most significant person in your life when you decided to "come out of the closet?" What did they do that propelled you to take that step? Was it a positive or negative experience?

I would say more positive. I think it began with Tim. He made me feel more comfortable with my identity. He played a big part in my life.

What did he do?

Tim just made me feel real comfortable about being myself. My comfort level was there with him. I think it's very important in a relationship, that the other person makes you feel comfortable most of the time.

Not all the time, because everybody has their "ups and downs." But the majority of the time, if you're really comfortable with each other, you don't have to worry about almost anything! If I wanted to fart in front of him, I can fart in front of him! If I wanted to pick my nose, I can pick my nose! Anything! We can just interact and take care of one another. We're not embarrassed or "grossed out" by one another. We're just joined together! You know how it is when you first start going out with someone and you wonder," Should I do this, am I going to offend them?"
The truth is, nothing offends them!

Knowing Tim helped propel you to "come out?" Did you feel he was a positive role model to follow or, was it you comfort level living with him that motivated you to "come out?"

Yes. The relationship felt so comfortable, that I felt less resistance to being seen in public with him! I feel totally accepted and respected being a gay man in my community today.

Considering the gay community, what advice would you give to other gay men who read this book about the way they interact and relate with one another?

Get to know people! Even if things don't work out well between you, try to still be friends. Life is too short. We all have to interact with one another, especially with AIDS being in the picture! I remember years ago going out and seeing guys who were visibly sick. I would say, "Oh my God, he used to be so beautiful!" Beauty is transitory, but friendship and love can be long-lasting! Just "cut the attitude" and treat each other with the respect we all deserve!

Thank you Bob for taking the time to give this interview and it was really a pleasure interviewing you.
Thank you. I enjoyed myself immensely.

End of interview

Sadly, Bob passed away some years ago due to an overdose of prescription medication in his sleep while in bed with his boyfriend. This sad event came not long after losing his job at the police department in Florida due an earlier arrest for internet pornography. At Bob's funeral, all his family members were there including his uncle.

His family admitted to me of always being aware of Bob's true sexuality and acknowledged to me at the funeral that they were always worried about him. In fact, a cousin of Bob, who looked like he could be his brother, visibly expressed his rage and sadness over Bob's passing and his self-destructive behavior by yelling at Bob in his casket and even hitting the casket.

Gay shame takes another victim. Also, on an equal sobering note, Tim within the past year has lost touch with both myself and our mutual friend Frank and we are very worried about his present state. Tim took Bob's passing very badly and has had many personal setbacks which has caused his life to take a downward spiral.

Rest in peace Bob and wishing you to be safe and well Tim.

CHAPTER FIVE

"I'M JUST A NICE JEWISH BOY"

The following interviewee and dear friend expressed a wish to remain anonymous due to his ongoing work for the Catholic Church. This interview took place in his apartment in Brooklyn, NYC, July 30, 2006

(In his kitchen following a little lunch) My friend appeared excited to tell his story and knowing his extensive background in film and theater, I was looking forward to this interview.

I was unaware at this time that he would later ask not to be identified as gay in this book but am happy to honor his request.

Unlike my previous interviewees, my friend is thin; almost bony, but with a cheerful exuberance and an intelligent wit.

GAYS AND THE CINEMA

You made a statement earlier, about the way the "straight" world portrays the "gay" world, specifically, how gay men are portrayed in the cinema, and what you'd like to do to change that. Would you care to elaborate being a playwright and screenwriter yourself?

Yes. As everybody knows, it's all about suffering. As in Vito Russo's *Celluloid Closet*, where he showed the outcome for most gay cinematic characters with a montage of all these gays either killing themselves or, being killed in the end or, during the films. That still goes on. I loved the movie, *Independence Day*, but the one major character out of all the other lovable characters that gets killed early on, is the gay character played by Harvey Firestein.

As I recall, the First Lady is also killed?

Yes, but she gets to suffer and say her goodbyes to everyone in the end. But returning to my point of gay characters dying in movies, it even continues to be the case even in foreign films.

Although, I recently saw a film in Rome where the gays win and the straights lose called, *Come, Me Voi*, meaning, "As You Want Me," or, "As You Desire Me." It was very funny and the gay characters are three dimensional with real lives!

There's a split not only in movies, but also in stage plays on what is really gay and what is really straight. For example, *Suddenly Last Summer* is a gay movie! Even though, the character turns out to be gay in the end. Let's use another example, *Cat on a Hot Tin Roof* or, *The Women*, even, *Whatever Happened to Baby Jane*, there's nothing ostensibly gay in those films, but those are absolutely gay films; as is *All About Eve*!
Yet, if you look at something like, *Too Wong Fu* or, *The Birdcage,* those are "straight" movies!

The straight audience goes to see those. The gay characters are portrayed as alien creatures that are two dimensional, and played just for laughs! They're rendered sexless and plastic, and quote on quote, "safe!"

Too Wong Fu was a rip-off of a gay film, *Priscilla, Queen of the Desert*, and *The Birdcage,* was a rip-off of a gay film, *La Cage Aux Folles.* I think it's all about sensibilities and respect for gays. If we are really laughing at ourselves and we're portrayed as human beings, it tends to be a gay sensibility; a piece of art! If we're rendered stereotyped and two dimensional, and we're to be laughed at or, pitied, then it's probably a "straight" sensibility!

Listening to that last statement, reminds me of Barbara Streisand in <u>Funny Girl</u>, where she defies Ziegfeld by saying, "I don't care if they laugh with me, I just don't want them to laugh at me!" That is my own personal credo! I don't want them to laugh at me, but they can laugh with me!

Yes, exactly! And that's a gay movie, because of statements just like that! Every gay man in the universe hears that, and nods his head.

I agree with you about films like <u>Birdcage</u> and <u>Too Wong Fu.</u> I found them both to be boring and played for laughs; very exaggerated performances!

And insulting! With regards to Nathan Lane in *Birdcage*, we see gay influences in Walt Disney films like *The Lion King* and *Beauty and the Beast*. It was Howard Ashman who was very comfortable with his gayness and a lot of gay wit comes out in his work. There are also all the icon movies like the Joan Crawford, Bette Davis, and Katherine Hepburn films. They are all so "over the top," or "campy." Where you have people suffering or, being treated unfairly, which we as gay men can identify with. I don't know much about the lesbian sensibility and what the lesbian icon movies would be.

MY COMING OUT" STORY

Perhaps I can get some of those answers when I interview lesbians for this book and my radio show? But for now, I'd like to ask you some questions as to your history of being gay or feeling different from other children?

I'm from New England. Nobody is gay in New England! (*laughter*) You have to leave New England to be gay!

Very funny. I have a home in Connecticut.
Sorry, but seriously, when I was growing up, if anyone was perceived as different, they weren't called "gay." There was no word for "gay" back then! The insults were, "Mo," short for "Homo," or "Queea," no "R," that was very New England. Or, "Guhl," which was New England for "Girl." If you were "gay," obviously you had a lisp and minced, and wanted to carry a purse and be a "Guhl "or be a "Queea!"

I certainly didn't feel like that! I didn't want to wear a dress. I had no urges to put on Angora mink or anything. I didn't know what I was, so, I was basically asexual!

I had one or two experimental experiences in high school but, nothing in college. So, when I came to New York City and saw the variety of people in show business; and people were not being stereotyped, shocked me.

Back in New England, the only thing I did to explore my sexuality, was to go to the library and look under the letter "H," which is what a lot of people did! But, any information about homosexuality was very repressed. Even now, when I return to New England for a visit, I sense a real difference between the gay communities there when compared with New York City.

How and when did you "come out of the closet?"

Therapy helped a lot. I went through the phase of saying, "This is just a passing phase for growing boys." "We all soon grow out of it," After all, that was what the encyclopedia said. Thank God I never did!

I remember reading that horrible book by Dr. David Rueben, *Everything You Want to Know About Sex, But Were Afraid to Ask.* That guy should have been shot for what he said about gays! It was horrifying what that fool said. If you were gay and read his book, you would have said, "Oh, No! I don't want to be like that! I don't want to shove light bulbs up my ass!"

He said that?

Yes! The whole section about homosexuality described how it was a "horrible sickness, and if anyone was homosexual, they would be "doomed to a terrible life and die in a horrible way!"

And this book was accepted as the truth?

Writers such as Dr. Reuben should have been shot for promoting his dismissive and devaluing views on gays and lesbians, and perpetuating the stereotype of gays as sick individuals doomed to live their lives alone and tragically. Unfortunately, there are many ignorant people who seek out this type of information to confirm their own hate and fear of gays. But, my personal concern is for those young and impressionable gay men unlike Roy, who accepted this "expert's" views as truth, and suffered as a result of that ignorance and incompetent research.

Sadly, that fool's book was totally accepted and was an enormous bestseller for a very long time! Reading that book and other crap, put me off schedule from "coming out" until I was twenty-two. That was when I was doing theater in New York City. Doing therapy assisted me toward "coming out." In fact, I made my "coming out," in a gay musical; so, I came out in a big way!

I vividly recall the first gay bar that I visited was the Ninth Circle, which was a notorious hustler bar. I was so naive. I didn't know how to act! There were lots of drugs going on and was quite "seedy." I didn't know of other gay bars in the neighborhood, so I was terribly depressed, because I hated that bar and didn't know where to go? So, I just kept going to that one place and hated it!

You didn't know about Uncle Charlie's, Ty's, or, the Eagle? (Those bars were all popular gay bars in the late seventies and early eighties).

I didn't know about those places. I knew absolutely nothing about gay life! Nothing! Julius's was only a block away and I knew nothing about that! But, when I did a musical for John Glines, I soon discovered gay piano bars. That type of place was much more interesting to me, rather than going to bars where everyone poses and says nothing to you. I didn't drink, smoke, or, enjoy disco music. So, I was really unhappy in the regular bars and discos. But, piano bars were my salvation! Soon after, I got involved in the gay and lesbian synagogue and eventually found other venues. I think it's very important that gay people today to do things that interests them.

After all, if you're not thrilled with "hanging out" in a bar or club, you're not going to be attractive! I believe you're only attractive when you're doing things that make you happy. Yet, most gay people don't do that! It's a very unfortunate rule of the gay community, that if you go to a healthy gay group or event, such as a religious group, social organization, ethnic club, or, community fund-raising event, you're "out of touch with the gay scene!

I know I'm going to get into trouble for saying this, but gay men who usually attend these meetings are mostly unattractive men who don't do well in the gay club scene. I like men who take care of themselves, know how to dress and are socially adept, but, they don't seem to want to go to healthy, gay events. So, this is a problem. I've made wonderful friends though a lot of the gay organizations, but almost no dates! The men I've met who are attractive to me, I've met though private parties or friends.

<u>Finding Attractive Men Who are Attracted to Me too!</u>

I hear what you're saying about "healthy gay events." I notice a considerable number of gay men who tend to spend many hours in the gym, wear tight workout clothes, and cruise the bars in their social time away from work and the gym.

(Interrupting) I'm not even talking about that! I'm talking about a guy who stays in decent shape, takes decent care of himself, and can dress in natural fibers and, match his socks! A man who knows how to hold a decent conversation with you is rare. Unfortunately, that does not predominate in many gay organizations and, that's a shame.

What does predominate?

What predominates is the GLBT community is people who have very limited forms of self-identification. For example, most of the people who attend a specific religious organization that becomes their ONE form of self-identification. I used to be very negative about the looks of the men in the gay synagogue and then, I went with friends from other religious backgrounds to their gay and lesbian groups, and they had the same complaint! They said, "How come there are so many gorgeous gay men in New York City and when I go to MCC or to Dignity, I simply do not t find anybody that I'm attracted to?" At least, I felt that is was not just me who felt the same way and it wasn't me being totally judgmental, which I can be.

Yes, you are. But the more physically attractive men tend to be more interested in doing the club scene or the gym, working on increasing their physical attractiveness. After all, our community promotes a continued emphasis on being more physically attractive.

Yes. It's what most gay guys feel more comfortable being. As for me. I was raised in an environment where it wasn't safe to be emotional, where it wasn't safe to have feelings. So, I lived from the neck up and I developed my brains! Just like when somebody feels that all he has to offer is his looks and his body. That guy will "pump up" his body and "look down his nose" at people who don't do that. Or, at least, he's not attracted to people who don't do that. He will work on himself so he can be validated by somebody else he feels is on his level of "hotness."

You're making really good points and know with which group you fit in best.

Yes, and people tend to do that! For example, if you are working on a spiritual path, you want to surround yourself with people like that and that's great! But, if you do that at the exclusion of any other interest or any other facet of your life, it doesn't make you a well- rounded person; or, somebody who's going to be attractive to a large group of people. The good side of these organizations, is that those who have joined them, usually, have a very rigid, limited, self-identification hoping to meet other people of the same "ilk, "so to find long-term, steady relationships! So, God bless them if it works for them, it just doesn't work for me!

From your perspective, it sounds as if many gay men are choosing to limit themselves, and are not expanding their potential for choosing friends or partners different from themselves, as a result, there is a lack of variety in personalities.

That touches off the whole "clone" situation. Many people believe that since we've spent our entire formative years not "fitting in," not belonging, that once we find out that there's a gay community, we want desperately to really belong. It reminds me of the movie, *Is Paris Burning,* where there is this line, "What's your drag?" "Are you into muscles?" You go to the gym, so you wear this "dress of muscles!"

Or, are you "preppy," so, you dress "preppy." Are you into "Wall Street Power," then you dress in a business suit with red suspenders! Are you into Birkenstock sandals and ecological outfits? Are you into East Village "buzz tops," body piercings and tattoos? Are you into leather?

In our community, gays ask one another, "what group do you want to belong to? Don't you want to feel that connection with a group of people like you? But, what ends up happening, is that people work too hard trying to make that connection and end up getting immersed in it! Their pendulum swings the other way from us! Cause, if you have a lot of different interests and you don't have that one" end-all" form of self- identification, it's hard to fit into these groups where everybody has just one.

Finding Strength in the Gay Community

Focus?

Yes, focus! That's a good word for it! Thanks. Personally, I think that's one big problem in the gay community and I believe that the more people who "come out" earlier and earlier, that attitude will tend to fade. But so far, that remains to be seen.

How do you feel about being gay?

I'm very happy with it. I recall that question which tends to come up in therapy, "If you had a magic pill that you could take to turn you straight, what would you do?" I said, "I'd find the nearest toilet I could find and flush it!" No, I'm very content with the way God made me. I'd prefer to have a life partner. But, I think I'd have the same problems whether I was gay, straight or bisexual. The thing that I like about being gay is also, what I like about being Jewish! With both groups, you feel like you're in some sort of inner circle.

In fact, it's good to have been gay in New York City in the seventies through the new Millennium, you're "in" on a lot of things. You know which celebrities are gay. You're "in" on fashions and trends earlier than anybody else. Things like that! So, it's like being in the "inner circle" of a private club. You meet much more interesting people and have much more interesting friends. I think if I was straight, I'd still have mostly lesbian and gay friends!

What was the progression toward your acceptance of being gay? Do you ever find yourself struggling with your gay identity? For example, was your introduction to your gay awareness a positive or negative experience?

What happened for me was very fortunate. My parents were surprisingly ashamed of being Jewish! So, they attempted to raise me and my older brother as "Yankees," not Jewish!

Shame comes in many forms; being gay, Black, a woman, as well as, being Jewish.

When I got really involved with my Judaism and my spiritual and cultural path, there was a real "schism" between my family and myself. I had to overcome a lot of objections. There were a lot of their fears and self-doubts. There were many fights with my family because of my faith. I had to go through a lot of introspection and therapy. I worked very hard to get really comfortable with the Jewish part of my identity!

After working so hard on that part of me for such a long time, when I also found out I was gay during that same introspection and therapy, I said, "Oh, that's just like being Jewish! I'm still a minority!" So, I grew to accept and love that part of me. I realized the two aspects of myself were surprisingly, very similar. When I knew I was gay, I also knew that most of the hard work had been done already in dealing with my shame of being Jewish.

Being gay was simply another part of me to love and accept. There was literally, no problem, because the whole process had been done in another area. Several years later, a lesbian friend of mine told me she had gone through the very same process! She had no problem telling herself and others that she was gay, because she had already struggled with her Judaism at an earlier time. It would be interesting to hear what it would be like for gays in other minorities. Because, according to mainstream society, you got a "double whammo!"

Are you referring to African-Americans who are gay?

Yes, and Asian-Americans, Latin-Americans, etc. I'd be very curious to hear what other people had gone through, because it's like a double "coming out." I recall that being said in an anthology of lesbian and gay, Jewish writers called, *Twice Blessed.* That's what I feel too. But, you have to go through a lot of self-work before you feel what society calls "curses," are in reality, blessings!

Gays as a whole, appear to be the new minority where every other minority or, majority groups can all join in and criticize or, disparage, the GLBT community. In doing so, taking the negative focus off themselves and onto another more negatively viewed social group. Therefore, it is wonderful that my friend and others like him, view being gay and Jewish, Black, Asian, or Latin as a more positive, rather than, negative classification.

When did you experience a "breakthrough" toward your acceptance of your gayness? What transpired during that occasion or occasions?

The answer is the same as I just related. As soon as I realized I was gay, it was okay! Everything just "clicked into place."

Can you give us some details as to your most satisfying gay experience? Was it during a specific gay event or in a more private moment?
Wow! You mean I have to restrict myself to only one that I can talk about? *(laughter)* I'm just kidding.*(Pausing and smiling)* There's been a lot. I guess, my very first Gay Pride March. That was overwhelming for someone who thought that the Ninth Circle was the only gay bar that New York City could support, to now see tens of thousands of people in the streets dancing; it was amazing! The Gay Games and Stonewall Twenty Five were also significant, because I had friends visiting me from Italy, and seeing it all through their eyes, was a "rush!"

Also, when I am traveling to different places here in the United States and Europe, these visits have brought me into an inner circle of friendships with gay men and women throughout the world. It's wonderful to know that we have that special connection with one another.

Gays and the Theater

Of course, as far as being in the theater, three incredibly important experiences for me in the theater, were seeing Harvey Firestein in *Torch Song Trilogy*, Lily Tomlin in *Search for Intelligent Life in the Universe* and Pat Carroll in *Gertrude Stein, Gertrude Stein, Gertrude Stein*. If you saw those performances, you walked out of the theater feeling proud being gay.

It's clear that you are proud being a gay man who loves the theater.

I am.

Roy is the first of several actors I interviewed who were also involved in theater – a place I consider to be a refuge or sanctuary for many gay teens and adults where there is generally, more acceptance for gays and promotion of their creative abilities as exemplified in the popular television show, Glee.

Finding Your Gay Identity

I would now like to change direction of this interview and ask you when you feel shame and guilt with regards to your gay identity. Specifically, what effects did both feelings have on your behavior? Being Jewish, you may have very clear ideas of what the effects of shame and guilt can have on one's behavior.

(Laughter) Yes, I do! Because I went through my whole process early on in therapy, I don't have too much shame and guilt being Jewish and, I don't have any shame and guilt about being gay. I had shame about sex and physicality! My family was very non-expressive. They did not touch! The other thing was growing up in New England! (*Snickering*) Surprisingly, what I found out about myself, was that my shame was not just about gay sex or physicality, it was about my shame with sex or physicality, in general!

I was uncomfortable even hugging or touching friends! So, I had to start from "square one," and learn to touch friends. You still see this behavior in a lot of gay men. Especially, with those men who are involved with a lot of casual sex or anonymous sex. They're very comfortable with doing incredibly intimate sexual acts, but very uncomfortable with hugging or kissing! So, people have different ideas of what intimacy is. For example, "I'd be very happy to perform an act of penetration with you, but I'll be damned if I'll rest my head on your shoulder!"

Wow, that is so incredibly true!

(*Continuing on his point*) When I lived in Los Angeles, I noticed a lack of intimacy among the gay men I slept with, which was very much the case there. People just wanted very fast, very anonymous sex, with absolutely no intimacy.

True and I look forward to interviewing men from L. A., and hearing . .

(Quickly interrupting) And, they'll probably say the same thing about New York! *(laughter)*

When I lived in Los Angeles, I also felt it was very similar to New York but, there seemed to be a greater focus on the body in LA; not to say NYC isn't that far behind. How you looked was very important to guys there; everyone competed to be "the hot guy" in the gym.

It reminds me of your earlier statement on how we want a guy who's going to validate my hard work. "I pump up at the gym, and I have a washboard stomach so, I want someone who looks just like that! So basically, I'm making love to myself!"

When you hear statements like that, and you're seeking a more meaningful type of relationship? Do you ever feel that you may never meet the right guy?

Well, I can certainly scare myself. Put myself on that negative cycle that we all do so well! "Oh, well this hasn't happened and it never will!" What I used to do was blame the entire gay community for my single hood. But, I learned some time ago, to take responsibility for my own attitudes and actions. Since working on myself a lot, I've been meeting a lot more men. So, I think it's something we all tend to do; put the blame on the community and not on ourselves. I know that I've spent many years going after inappropriate people and "hanging out" in places that were inappropriate for me! Places where I was not happy to be.

I even went through a period of several years, where I called myself a "Sexual Anorectic!" Even though, it was my choice not to have sex! I felt at the end of nine or ten months, very unattractive and unwanted. So, I have stopped that behavior! As I've got more in touch with my own physicality, I've allowed myself to have a more healthy sex life.

Would you put shame and guilt about being gay in the same "emotional baggage" here? My view of guilt with gay men is that your acts make you feel guilty; while with shame, the shame is with who you are!
Yes, I'd agree with that. I don't have any shame because I'm shameless! I've been told that many times. There are actions that I have done, that I would have preferred not to have done. There is such a thing as making amends. Once you've made amends to those you might have harmed, hopefully, you won't have that guilt anymore.

But, after fixing a situation, and agreed not doing the same actions again and yet, still feel guilty; then that's shame! Because, you already resolved the action but, you're still feeling bad about yourself, it's what you said, you just feel bad about you, not your actions!

On the same point, do you feel that feelings of shame and guilt have had an adverse effect on how you relate or interact with other gay men? You touched on that question earlier when you felt that attitudes of superiority and indifference toward one another in the gay community are the result of shame and guilt about being gay?

Well, you can't get inside other people's heads. There is a psychological term called "grandiosity," which I've gone through. A lot of people who were made to feel inferior or, less than, it's a reaction against that insecurity or, feelings of inferiority and shame. Grandiosity! This is why gay men love drag queens, because they're so grand!

We all bemoan going to areas like Chelsea, West Hollywood, South Beach, where there are a lot of gorgeously buffed, gay men "throwing" attitude! We all complain about attitude. Attitude is a defense! It's grandiosity! "Turning up my nose" on others before the world rejects me.

Rejecting the world before the world gets a chance to reject me right?

Roy's point is one of the principal premises of my research on gay male communication as being selective communication where, the one who rejects others so quickly without clear reason is demonstrating a superior attitude based primarily on their own insecurity and poor self-esteem.

Yes. The best defense is to be as offensive as possible! (*Laughter*)

Now, that's a great quote to remember!

Thank you.

THE "ABUSE CHAIN"

The best defense is to be as offensive as possible? But by the offense, you mean how some people offend other people with airs of superiority or attitudes of indifference?

Yes, it's of the above, but it's also the mentality of: "I've been hurt, so now, I'm going to hurt everybody else first before I get hurt again!" Just as, we'd all rather quit than be fired! People are so afraid of being intimate, that they make sure they're never intimate! Now, that's a big problem. But, I think that's just endemic within our society "at large" and not solely owned by the gay and lesbian communities.

Yes. I would like to talk to a cross section of men and get their impressions of how men in general tend to oppress everyone, including women, and other minorities. The superiority and indifference is similar to the gay world. They often present an "I'm better than you" attitude.

It's the "abuse chain."

What is the "abuse chain? I have never heard of it before.

Yes. If you're from a group of people who have been abused, you are going to "mirror" your oppressors. Look at how Hasidic Jews behave. Those outdated, black outfits that they wear are surprisingly from the Eastern European, anti-Semitic, feudal lords who oppressed them two and three centuries ago. Now, they get to dress just like them!

You mean that the feudal lords who oppressed them dressed like that?

Yes! That's where the fur trimmed black caps and long, black cloaks come from. Those were historically, the garments worn by the lords of the manor when they were oppressing the Jews! In America, when you have four hundred years of Black oppression and suffering here in the United States, you are going to have a lot of oppression and abuse "mirrored" in the home.

A similar dynamic occurs under any oppressed minority. What happens in the gay and lesbian world where there is considerable oppression by society, has resulted in an enormously high rate of substance abuse. I think it's some thirty percent of the lesbians and gays have drinking or drug problems!

Roy is correct with regards to substance abuse, in fact, according to recent studies on comparing gay men with their heterosexual counterparts, gay men were 2.5 times more likely to suffer from feelings of anxiety, substance abuse and depression. *(Find recent stats here)

Thirty percent is a pretty high number. Do you feel that this statistic is a direct result of their shame about being gay?

I'm sure it is.

These feelings of shame are similar to what the Jewish and African-American communities have been striving to deal with for centuries, and yet, we're still the "new kids on the block."

Yes, but it's also that people were not categorized as gay or lesbian until the last hundred and fifty years!
How were we categorized?

Well, there were "sissy boys" or "Nancy boys" for men and "tough girls for more masculine acting women!" People were categorized like this somewhere in the 1840's, or 1850's but, I don't know the exact date?

But, they were officially placed in this very strict categorization of people into different sexual identities. Julius Caesar, was known to have had enemy generals that he had conquered spend the night with him in his tent. But, people weren't sitting around saying," Well, is he heterosexual or homosexual?" He was just their leader.

Why would he do that? Why would he have those generals sleep with him? Was it an honor or something to that effect?

It was more like subjection. That's where we get the word, "subjection" from. It comes from, "subjogo" which means "under the yoke."

So, basically, he raped these men?

That depends. There was respect between the leaders of opposing sides in battle. In Europe, in the eighteenth and nineteenth centuries, generals of opposing armies would go to an inn in the demilitarized zone, and carouse all night!

Would they have sex with their soldiers, or with one another?

They would have sex with each other; the officers and such. In Shakespeare's *Troilus and Cressida*, there was this whole scene about that. The night before the big battle, where the Greeks and the Trojans were carousing together, then the next day, they slaughtered each other! Alexander the Great had a Persian lover for many years, people were not worried whether he was gay or not. They cared more whether he was going to lead them successfully through the next battle.

There are many historical stories with regards to man/boy love being accepted within that society. In fact, my lover and I were married years ago by a priest who spoke from liturgy from before 400 AD when same sex marriage was acceptable in the Christian church.

I *recall Mary Renault's* <u>Persian Boy</u> *and her depiction of the life of Alexander the Great. But with regards to present day, do you feel that those feelings of shame have had an effect on how you relate and interact with heterosexual men and women?*

I think that comes from a place of confusion in not fitting in back in New England. If you did anything effeminate, you were immediately harassed. So when I was growing up, I was very careful about the way I talked, walked, and all of that nonsense. Just like in the play, *Tea and Sympathy* where the schoolboy under suspect for being homosexual was being harassed by the other boys.

Since "coming out" and "clicking into place," within the gay community as I mentioned earlier, I haven't worried about whether I "pass" or not. I can't stand all these gay personal ads that say, "straight-acting!" You don't see ads in *Ebony* magazine that say, "white-acting."

However, from having grown up and in a certain way, I was always aware of training myself to "pass" before I came out, because I was worried about possibly being gay. I don't try to "pass" now. I don't try to act "straight;" whatever that means?

Some of the most effeminate men I've ever known were totally heterosexual! A lot of "straight" people tell me if they have not had experiences with gay people, or at least, knew, they were having experiences with gay people before, but were comfortable with me. Because to them, I don't fit their stereotype of what gay people are. They may mean well, but in a way, it's insulting. I remember one person telling me that he was happy I was a "Jew" and not a "Kike!"

I've heard people say, "That person's okay, he's Black, he's not a nigger!" They have no idea how ignorant or prejudiced they sound. So, when "straight" people tell me they feel comfortable with me because I don't fit their stereotype of an effeminate gay man, I make sure they hear a lot about my gayness and about gay life in general.

So, perhaps that's one thing that colors my feelings with heterosexuals. But on the whole, I'm very comfortable with heterosexuals, and I would say, I have as many "straight" friends as I have gay friends; we're all very close, and we share all the same secrets and issues.

Let's go back to earlier in this interview, where you discussed how gay men are portrayed in films, television and the theater. Does it make you angry to see how many gay characters meet an unjust end in so many gay themed films?

Just recently, I saw a film where the young gay lead throws himself down a flight of stairs when his love for his best friend is cruelly rejected but, the double feature included another film with Christian Slater and Mary Stuart Master son, where the story revolves around a woman who is resistant to intimacy, but in the end, she survives and finds love.

Somehow, I knew that the gay film would end as it did, and the straight film would have a happy ending. Instead, I would have rather seen the gay film end happily, with the two boys finding love with each other. Instead, the best friend beats him up, and the boy goes insane and kills himself.

So, you were surprised that it was the same, old ending?
Yes, I was. I somehow expected the Dutch, who produced the film, would have been more progressive in their thinking. I know that they were trying to teach others to be more sympathetic toward the gay character. However, I'm sick of seeing that type of ending!

Yes. People can approve of gays, as long as they can feel sorry for us.

Exactly! So, how does that make you feel about the "straight world" and their thinking? How they attempt to feed the audience's perceptions to suit their own limited thinking?

Having worked in Hollywood, you'll see **gay people** "buying into" these perceptions left and right! So many of these horrible, disgusting, beliefs and attitudes that come out of Hollywood! Far from how gay men and women truly are! And yet, gay men and women are "buying into" these belief systems and propagating these stereotypes!

I'm not talking solely about the gay audience "buying into" the Hollywood system, but also, the many gay men and women who work in the film business and don't fight the stereotypes depicted on the screen. They simply allow these stereotypes to continue as they pick up their paychecks to pay for their car and condo bills.

So, you're basically saying that they're "selling off" their own people for the big bucks?

Yes! There were a lot of gay people involved in producing *The Birdcage*. There were a lot of gay people involved in that horrible movie, *It's My Party*! Where the only response to AIDS, is to kill yourself before it starts to affect your hairdo!

I just saw that movie despite knowing how was going to end but, I like Eric Robert's portrayal of a gay man in love.

I hated it! It's terrible.

That's a great line. "Kill yourself before it starts to affect your hairdo!"

I know I'm exaggerating a bit but, that's how I see it.

No, you're right. It's all about killing yourself before you lose your looks!

Yeah. In this case, the guy had Toxoplasmosis. He wasn't going to lose his looks, as much as he was going to slowly lose his brains! But, they don't show one alternative in the whole movie. Everybody who has AIDS kills themselves in the movie while they still have their looks and their money.

Yes, I recall others gay characters killing themselves before the lead does?
Yes! They show other people killing themselves within their little West Hollywood clique before the lead does. Also, his family who has been really out of his life for years are the ones who get to stay with him at the end. All his gay friends, who have been "there for him" through most of his life, get kicked out in the end! Only his blood family is allowed to stay with him as he dies!

Doesn't he have a boyfriend who stays with him in the end?

His boyfriend is really disgusting! He leaves as soon as the lover gets sick. He's "out of touch" with him for years, and when hearing his ex-lover is going to kill himself, he shows up and pushes his way into the party! He's not any nicer to anyone except the family members; he doesn't have to change himself one bit! But, because he's a Hollywood director, it makes it a good thing that he comes back in the end.

And he stays with the ex-lover till the end.

Yes, and he helps the ex-boyfriend to kill himself. And tragically, that film is where so many gay people are viewing as these jerks as role models who supposedly, "have it all together!"

I recall seeing the film and found it to be quite endearing with the exception of some of his obnoxious friends but I can relate to Roy's rage about the superficiality about some of the family members and the boyfriend's behavior.

In finishing this question, is there anything else you wish to say about heterosexuals and their relations with gay men?

I'm thrilled about heterosexuals. They should continue to make gay babies!

Roy would never miss out on a good punch-line being that he has enjoyed a career as a comedian, actor, and screenwriter.

Did you feel that "coming out" to your family and friends, was an important step toward your acceptance of your gayness?

I feel it's just very important to "come out of the closet," not only for self-acceptance, but for mainstream society's acceptance! If they see all of us, from all these different walks of life, presenting different images of what it is like to be openly lesbian and gay; than that, is the strongest political act that we can make as a community.

Not only being "open" about our gayness but, being comfortable enough with ourselves living as gay men and women. The only way to get respect is to respect yourself first and then demand respect from others!

The Importance of "Coming Out!"

So, you're advocating "coming out" as an important step toward acceptance?

Oh, absolutely!

What advice would you give to other gay men about "coming out?" For me, I chose to write loving but, truthful letters to all my immediate family members. As a result, I received overwhelming support and love from each one of them, despite their difficulty understanding and accepting my sexuality.

Now, there are more physical demonstrations of love from them with hugging and kissing, even from the men! What advice would you give on "coming out?" How did you do it?

Well, my parents finally "put one and one together" and when my then-lover moved in with me. Then, they realized it was not just a roommate situation. My father "went nuts!" Calling us with screaming phone calls at all hours of the day and night! I finally told him to stop! That he was forbidden to contact me until he read a letter that I going to write to him.

So, I wrote a very, long letter. My mother got it, and I give them credit. I didn't expect to hear from them for at least a year or two, but they called me in two weeks! They accepted it! But, they knew the only alternative to not accepting my gayness, was to lose a son all together!

What did you say in the letter?

I was very strong with them. I told them that there were a lot of books that I could send them about what to do if your child was gay and what it means to be gay. I told them, "If you really care at all, you'll do the work yourselves, and that I am not going to do the work for you!"

That," I've had to work a good deal toward respecting myself and accept who I am." I wasn't going to do that work for them! My parents were always very frightened people who always told me to, "be careful."

In the letter, I ended it saying, "You made me a very nervous and frightened little boy, because you were always telling me to be careful." I told them, "For once, you can tell me to be happy."

Now, that they've accepted my gayness, they prefer not to talk about it. But at least, it's in the open! I will discuss some things with them, but since I am not close with them, I choose to discuss more intimate details of my life with my "chosen" family of dear friends; both straight and gay.

Both of my friend's parents have passed away but I know that he was happy to have had that conversation with them for both his, and their benefit. But, it's sad that he appears to not have had the type of relationship he truly wanted with them.

One thing I'd like to add on this topic, is that EVERY, SINGLE, PARENT KNOWS! It doesn't matter if you are a "butch marine," a policeman, or whatever! Your parents gave birth to you. They know if you are lesbian or gay. It's only a question of whether or not, they want to discuss it or face it! As long as we avoid discussing it or facing it, we're sending out a message that it's something to be ashamed of.

You're saying that if we avoid talking about it or facing it, we're making a shameful statement.

Yes. We're reinforcing what society says, "Don't talk about it and don't scare the horses!"

You "crack me up!" Where did that statement come from?

It's a century-old saying, somebody once said, "I don't care about homosexuals, as long as they don't frighten the horses."

Is that saying about homosexuals? It sounds like whoever said it, had some pretty wild fantasies.

Most likely, it totally reminds me of Catherine the Great.

Yes, I remember the stories about her and her horses. But on a more serious note, by not coming out of the closet, you are only perpetuating the internalized gay shame?

Yes, most definitely.

Was there someone special in your life prior to your decision to "come out of the closet," and if there was, what did they do to propel you to take that important step?

I don't know if I had anybody really close to help me. I did have this very dear, straight friend that I had a "crush" on. He was very important in my life. As I recall, it did take a lot of pressure off my shoulders, to tell him, "Yes, I am gay, and the feelings I have for you are gay feelings." It helped to clear up the situation at that time but, I didn't have a gay uncle, friend, or, otherwise, to help me to move "out of the closet." I wish that I had.

It sounds like this guy did prompt you toward acknowledging your love for him. In whatever way you see it, he did you a big favor.

My own way of "coming out," was to go to the Newman Center on my college campus one night, and knock loudly on that door! To me, it was a moment of liberation! My actions resulted in attending my first gay meeting and being invited to a glorious weekend in Albany with this large group of lesbians. I marched in a Gay Pride Parade, attended a dinner dance with all these handsome men, and found love with the blonde bouncer at the local gay bar! I recall saying to my friends, "I like this!"

But with your story, how did the man you love respond to your confession?

He was very sweet, supportive and loving. Today, he's an attorney! I recall a period prior to my "coming out," of pursuing straight men because I wasn't comfortable with my gay physicality. What better a group of people to be attracted to than men who were not into gay physicality!

Did you ever think that these men were gay, but not acknowledging their gayness?

Perhaps, but I don't think so.

They were not the type of straight men, who were okay with getting a "blow job," but nothing else more intimate?

No, I think that would have happened! We were very close and loving to each other. I think these were just very straight men who were comfortable with having very intimate male relationships. By that, I mean, very non-sexual, male, relationships.

One that note, would you encourage heterosexual men to allow themselves to have very close, male bonding relationships? I perceive heterosexual men as being afraid to pursue close, male relationships, for fear of being perceived as a homosexual.

I think the only difference between gay and straight men, are that gay men are not worried about being gay, while heterosexual men for the most part, are terrified of doing, or, saying anything that might be perceived as latent homosexuality. Straight men are much more self-conscious about how they stand, walk, sit, and talk, because society "drums" this fear into them! It affects constantly upon how they relate and interact with one another in this country.

Yes, I see this behavior constantly with my college-age, male students. They write about their relationships with close friends in their journals, which is a required assignment. My female students frequently comment on the "careful" interactions that they observe between the young men on campus.

Yes, exactly! Look at how European men show affection to one another, and compare that to how American men show affection; this fear of being intimate.

You're referring to our resistance to hug and kiss one another?
Yes. If you watch a lot of music videos, you'll see that there's a whole, codified, syntax of acceptable, masculine motions.

What are you referring to with regards to this body language?

Things you can do with your hands and your body that make you a "macho man."

Can you give a clear example of this non-verbal gesturing?

For one, having a completely "splayed" open hand and then placing that hand on your chest or stretching your arms out wide when you're making a point.

Sounds like the movements I've seen on "rap music" performers.

Yes. A lot of "rap" moves are meant to exaggerate masculinity. Also, if you go to Wall Street, there's a very different code of motion for the same purpose. Every move is meant to say, "Yes, I'm a man and I'm straight. This is how I'm going to stand; this is how I will sit. This is the stance I'm going to take when I talk to another man. This is the amount of physical distance I can maintain. I won't stand too close to you. I won't touch you too often. If we hug, then I've got to smack you hard on the back as we hug."

Or, I'm going to beat you up a little bit!"

Yeah, it is as if they're saying, "if I rub your back while we're hugging it, that's effeminate! If I clap you on the shoulder, that's acceptably machismo."

Roy's analysis of body language among African-American rap singers was fascinating and indicative of the ways in which heterosexual need to cover up or, disguise intimate feelings for their same sex, even if those feeling are basically those of friendship.

But as a gay man, I love physicality with my lovers. I remember enjoying wrestling with several of them; all this "macho" roughness. Is this behavior a "throwback" to the heterosexual male's affectionate communication or, is it just our "little boys having fun" behavior?

Yes, I think it is all about playfulness and having fun! But, if you aren't worried about how you are going to look when you touch another man on the street, then this is what I mean about how we view as acceptable and non-acceptable shows of affection in our society.

Yes! Even in the gay world, I get looks from other gay men when I am being playful with men, even on Christopher Street! Even when we are simply holding hands!
Sometimes, I have to remind myself, "Where the Hell am I? I'm in the middle of a gay enclave!" But, if I'm afraid of making a statement, then, everything we do is making a statement!

That makes perfect sense.

I recall on those walks on Christopher Street, where a straight couple is holding hands while inquisitively looking at us holding hands. I want to shout at them and say, "Hey, this is our street, get over it!

I know. It's not fair.

I also remember this story of a gay man kissing his lover "goodbye" on the Pines' pier, and this straight guy with a family, went up to him and slapped him on the face and said, "Don't do that in front of my family!"

The gay man then slapped the guy right back and said, "Don't you know where the fuck you are?" This story may have become exaggerated, but I also heard that it nearly caused a riot!

Wow, I never heard that story. I probably would have pushed the guy off the pier!

So would I. Violence also reminds me of when I and my lover were attacked by this group of "straight" surfers on Santa Monica Beach in California in 1979. One of them had kicked my lover David in the back, the next thing I knew, we were involved in the large melee. I eventually escaped with a bloody nose and mouth.

But ironically, I believe to this day, that several of those kids were in truth, gay, but, terrified of letting it be known. Why else would they be harassing gay men and women? If they were comfortable in their heterosexuality, they wouldn't care how others lived their lives in private or, within their communities. But, you're saying that the straight man will be playful with one another but, are more concerned about the way they appear to others than gay men are?

Yes. The straight man is going to be more self-conscious about his physical interactions with other men than a gay man is for sure.

But, many gay men are also self-conscious about how they are perceived by others.

Yes, we are, but in a **very** different way. I'm not worried that I might be latently gay; I'm openly gay. I'll never have that worry for the rest of my life. There's a thesis of mine that the most self-conscious people in society today, are the "closeted homosexuals!" They must be "sweating bullets" over every move they make! I've known some "closeted" gay men, and their movements and behavior are so exaggeratedly masculine, that everyone knows they're gay because of it.

What advice would you like to give gay men reading this book as to the way they interact and relate to one another? What attitudes or behaviors you would encourage?

There is a lot of advice I would give them. First, I'd encourage them to have intimate, platonic, male friends, both gay and straight. Many gay men can only relate to other men sexually. They divide the world into two groups: the men they want to go to bed with, and the men they want nothing to do with! They lose out on a lot of good, old-fashioned friendships and support as a result. Another thing is, "Come out, come out, wherever you are!"

Besides working towards "coming out of the closet," gay men need to find close, platonic, friends, both gay and straight. That too many gay men choose only to relate to other men sexually, and that to you, is not self-affirming.

Yes. I also advocate loving, monogamous relationships.

Okay, then, as for meeting those men, what would you consider your best technique for meeting other gay men in a gay bar or social events? I know you don't advocate going to gay bars to meet prospective lovers, because that is a place more likely for "one-night stands."

That's not true. I know people who've had long-term relationships through meeting in gay clubs and bars.

Okay, but other than clubs and bars, where would you recommend they go to meet that special someone?

I recommend being comfortable with yourself. I know it's a "very tall order.

How does one get comfortable with himself as a gay man?

Therapy helps, as well as, having a strong support system. "Coming out of the closet," is basically taking a spiritual path toward self-discovery. Also, work towards having a career that you enjoy and having a fully rounded life!

That sounds like a desire shared by almost everyone I know.

Maybe so, but so often I hear, "I have a job I don't like, but it pays the rent. I go to the gym, and then I go to the bar." That sums up their lives! If that's truly your only interests in the world, God bless you, I hope you find somebody else in the world who shares that same limited outlook.

<u>Closing Comments</u>

Returning to the topic of good opening lines for meeting men, you're a comedian, you must have a few?

The best way I met other gay men, is <u>not</u> to have a line. I will quote an old theatrical saying: "Cause a line will always smell like a line." For me, it's a very strange tightrope. I try to act as if anybody I'm interested in is not immediately available. If there is somebody who's interested in me, or, if I'm interested in them, I get very nervous. I start "playing all these tapes that echo in my head."

Instead, I put all the sexual innuendo and longings aside for a while and I just talk to them as another human being. It's easier for me to meet people when I'm with other people that I'm already comfortable with. Then, I'm more myself, and that's always the best way to meet new people, when you're really being yourself.

Yes. I remember you being at my last party; you seemed comfortable there?

Yeah. I was at the home of a good friend. I was there with another good friend. I just talked with other people in an open and friendly manner. I didn't start "coming on" to anyone. I think people really appreciate being seen as a whole human being and not, just as a potential sex object.

What physical attributes do you find attractive in another gay man? Or, what non-physical attributes do you find attractive and what attitudes do you find unattractive?

A relaxed smile and someone who is comfortable in "his own skin," I find very appealing. Somebody who I know I can laugh in bed with or, can have a discussion over breakfast with; that, is an enormous "turn-on" to me.

You simply want someone with whom you can comfortably talk to following a night of sleeping together?

Yes. Someone whom I can laugh in bed with following a night together and can have an intimate discussion over breakfast. As far as negatives, I personally can't stand smoking! Kissing a smoker is like kissing an ashtray. Other big "turn-ons," are a positive outlook and a worthy goal in life. They don't have to be successful, but they have to be happily pursuing their dreams.

What if they're having some difficulties achieving their goals at the time?

That's fine, as long as they're working on it. I used to run the biggest "lost puppy agency in town." I've closed my doors for that type of rescue work years ago. I get "stuck in my stuff" too, but I keep working at it.

What types of behaviors or attitudes do you find unattractive?

I do not care for people who are "emotionally shut-down." Don't get me near anyone who is "emotionally shut down!"

How would you classify "emotionally shut-down?"

Those are people in my estimation who can't emotionally express themselves. Every word they speak is very measured. You never know what they're thinking or feeling. It's hard to trust anyone like that?

What do you envision for yourself as your potential goal that you hope to accomplish in your lifetime? And, how did your acceptance of your gay identity help you toward achieving those goals?

Career goals are my present goals of course! I want continued success with my acting and writing. I can't imagine how someone can be an artist of any sort, and not be "fully in touch" with the many facets of themselves. I just read a great quote from Marc Chagall, "I'm grateful for my art, because it is through my art, that I have learned to become a man."

Your theater work and your gayness are intertwined?

Yes, of course. Not, that I necessarily play gay characters all the time. I usually play "straight" characters, but, if I'm not "comfortable in my own skin," then I'll never feel comfortable playing those roles.

Then, your acceptance of your gay identity did help you to feel satisfied in your theatrical work, that it is all a part of the whole? That you can't play Othello, Iago, Stanley Kowalski, or any theatrical character unless you're comfortable with whom you are?

Yes, to be any kind of artist you have to be in touch with all the many parts of yourself, and be comfortable with those parts as well.

Or, working toward that level of comfort?

Yes, it's all a process. It's progress not perfection. My personal goal opposed to career goal, is to meet "Mr. Right" and have a nice, Jewish wedding.

Would you have a rabbi officiate?

Oh, yes.

Who would break the glass?

I once officiated in a gay wedding, and we had the two grooms break two glasses!

With regards to the focus of this book, do believe there is a problem in gay communication?

Yes, but I say that there's just problems with human communication in general, especially in America.

Why do you say that?

Because between television and social media, people don't communicate anymore! We turn on all these "garbage" television shows like *Jerry Springer* or *Murray Povich*, to see people talk "at" one another. The reason people need to watch talk shows, is because, nobody is really talking to one another.

Thank you so much for your clear insights and wonderful stories.

You are most welcome Dr. Vince.

End of interview

In retrospect, it is surprising how my friend here, aspires for a loving partner and has so many wonderful insights on his gay identity and our culture and yet, ironically, fears of being identified in this book? It's almost saddens me that someone who loves being gay and wants so deeply to find love, has to be concerned over whether a religious institution or government agency in today's more progressive climate, can still hold so much power in his life. But, despite his trepidation, his clear self-analysis and detailed stories, have provided important information not only for myself, but for all of you as well.

Wayne at his 60th Birthday Party

Wayne is my best friend and manager and I am very grateful for his time and honesty here.

"WHO AM I ANYWAY; GAY, JEWISH, ITALIAN, WASP, INVISIBLE?"

Wayne Scherzer - New York City, August 9, 1997 in Wayne's apartment on West 85th Street following a light lunch. Wayne is sitting comfortable on his couch in the living room. I have also incorporated data collected from Wayne up till present day as well.

A BRIEF HISTORY

Can you give me some background about yourself, specifically, your childhood experiences of being gay or, simply different from the other children around you?

Can I simply start out with what I do now?

Yes, of course.

I've been a professional actor for more than thirty three years. I work in a theatrical community which is very accepting of gay people. Certainly, at this point in 2006, it's much more accepting then they were years ago.

In terms of my childhood experiences, I didn't even know what the term, "gay" meant. I don't think it was a term used when I was a growing up. I was not conscious of anything homosexual until I was in the eighth or ninth grade. I remember having experiences with my cousin. I was fascinated by him. We used to play sex games with each other. In retrospect, I believe it was my first homosexual experience and they continued until my first year in college! This all started when I was eleven. He rejected me when I approached him during my freshman year in college. After that, I never approached him again. We never even talk about it anymore!

What did these sex games entail?

It was exhibition. It was fondling. There was no anal or oral sex! There was no real sex. There was ejaculation through manipulation or "jerking off." I believe that the penis became a substitute for breasts! We went to boy's school together and there were no girls.

How long were you in a boys' school?

I attended a boys' school from eighth grade through college. We were in the same prep school, but not in the same class.

Was it one of those Ivy League type schools that catered to a more WASP clientele?

No, that was another school that I attended. The second school where my cousin and I went to had a lot of Jewish kids. A lot of "upwardly mobile" middle-class children of Italian and Jewish descent. Those were the primarily nationalities, but as time progressed, that too became more "Waspy." Originally though, it was more mixed.

The school that I had attended prior to this one, was a co-ed, private school that was almost exclusively "Waspy," where I was the "outsider."

How did it feel to be an "outsider?"

I have always felt like an outsider! My background is Italian and Jewish. So, I've never felt like an "insider" until I entered the theatrical business, which is more open and accepting of "outsiders." Being an "outsider" in my religious and ethnic background and, an "outsider" with my sexual orientation, it was nice to be part of a community of peers.

Is there any other information you'd care to share about your background, especially, your childhood experiences of feeling different from those around you?

My parents provided us with a loving household, but a household that infused me with some of the expectations that were part of the Fifties. We lived a fantasy version of what family life is; a "whitewashed" version. When I discovered these feelings that we not a part of the norm, or what was being considered the norm, there was a lot of shame and guilt that went along with being different.

So, it has been a learning process to try to identify that shame and guilt in my life and try to work through it. I'm presently working through accepting my gayness in my therapy, and have been for some time now.

The focus of this book, which may be of help to you, is the search toward acceptance of one's gayness, and how shame and guilt play a large role in our difficulties with intimacy and our communication with other gay men.

So, then, did your feelings of being an outsider, affect your relationship with your parents while you were growing up?

I think there has been an expectation of me as a child and have always sensed a disappointment in them regarding my "difference." But, I was really a practicing heterosexual until after college. In college, I began to experiment with both men as women, but honestly, I "got farther" heterosexually, than, homosexually. I didn't really "come out" till after college, when I came to New York and got involved in the theater.

In terms of my parents, there seems to been a disappointment in me, because they had concerns over my not having a "normal," heterosexual life.

They envisioned a life, where I would have a girlfriend, get married, and have children. I do feel that there is a disappointment in regards to that. There was a revelation in college, where I had fallen in love with this friend of mine, which was unrequited. I remember that he was the first person with whom I fell in love with, and it was pretty agonizing for me.
I went to my parents and told them about it. I remember distinctly my father saying, "I don't think that there is anything worse that you could of told me unless, you told me that you murdered somebody." Which is a pretty "damming" statement? His suggestion was to go to a psychiatrist; which I willingly agreed to do.

At the time, there were things being done in the psychiatric profession to "cure" homosexuality, such as, electroshock therapy to reduce one's desires for the same sex. I went there with the thought of doing this. Most fortunately, my psychiatrist responded, "If you are going into the theatrical business, I wouldn't suggest electroshock. Being that you went to an all-boys school, it's not uncommon to have had these experiences. Why don't you just go to a bar and pick up a girl." That was his suggestion at the time, which I considered to be a very stupid one! I never went back to therapy with him.

It is astonishing how trained professionals would prescribe such inane advice to someone who goes to him or her for help in dealing with one of the most frightening times of their lives and the sadness as the result of a cruel and ignorant father?

The initial revelation to my parents was pretty devastating to me. My sexuality is something to this day, that they still have difficulty handling but, are able to deal with it better today. It is still an uncomfortable subject to talk about with them, which does sadden me, but they do profess to want a close relationship with me. And yet, the close relationship that they seem to want, is one that they seem to have imagined differently, and I simply can't deal with that.

Wayne is one of many gay men who have struggled with their relationships with their family as a result of being gay, and feelings of dissatisfaction with his present situation despite, possibilities of having the relationship becoming repaired over time.

MY THEATRE LIFE

Do you feel that moving to New York City and the theatrical community helped motivate you toward "coming out?"

There are really two issues here. One is the career issue, with the background that I have given to you with the parents and their expectations. Fortunately, I was given singing and dancing lessons as a child. I began with the dance lessons, but I didn't like them, because I was the only boy taking the ballet class. I felt it was too "sissy," and I did not enjoy it. But somehow, at the same school, there was a singing class, and they found out that I had a big voice, and that was it!

Finally, there was encouragement for something that I did, which felt great! I remember as a child of being so violently nervous, that whenever I performed, I would throw up before each performance, and then, sing and get reinforcement. The positive feedback always felt terrific and that would motivate me to continue. My parents nurtured all these extra-curricular activities, particularly in the arts.

I had every lesson you could possibly think of with dancing, singing, acting, ice-skating and tennis. I think it was their attempt for me to be well-rounded, rather than thinking, I would choose any of these as a profession. When I went into the eighth grade, I was cast with many other kids, in a production of an opera on the Jersey shore.

Suddenly, I discovered opera and loved it! I wasn't cast for my talent, my cousins were tone deaf, and they were also cast in the production. I was just a fortuitous thing to happen to me, and I discovered a whole world that I loved and felt comfortable. It was my intent to become an opera singer now. But somewhere along the line in high school, I was convinced that I should have a career to fall back upon, and that career was medicine. So, I entered college with the thought of becoming a doctor.

I was going to be biology major, but within the first week of attending school, I accidentally met the head of the music department and decided to visit his office. I recall saying to him, "I'm going to be Pre Med, and I'll probably never see you, but I just wanted to see what was here." He gave me a pamphlet and told me I could be a Pre Med/Music major, which was the perfect solution! But in my sophomore year, I failed Organic Chemistry which was a Pre-Med prerequisite and I had to make a decision. I decided to become an actor/singer instead and surprisingly, my parents were supportive!

The sexual issue continued, but now, I was in New York in the early seventies. Being gay was not as open as it is now, so living the gay life was not easy. Despite Stonewall, it was very difficult for me to "come out of the closet." I still felt a need to be "normal."

I saw that the theatrical community was populated by many gay people. But, still, I felt that it was completely "under wraps," and no one in "normal society" at the time, talked about gay people. Fortunately, there was a sense of belonging in terms of the actors and actresses in that community. There was also a sense within the theatrical world of having to be careful in revealing that you were gay for fear of losing jobs.

Similar to my previous interviewee's experience, Wayne also benefited by feeling a sense of belonging and acceptance within the theater community, where his creativity and uniqueness was encouraged. Unfortunately, Wayne had to keep his gayness "on the down-low" for fear of not getting jobs if his true sexuality was known. But, in playing another role, Wayne and other gay actors I interviewed, have reported to enjoying the opportunity to "live in another man's skin," and take the focus off themselves and onto the characters they got the chance to portray.

At times, I had considered myself to be bisexual. I was not really "out" in full force. It wasn't until I did my first professional production, where eighty percent of the performers were gay, that I took an action. I had never before been in an environment like that, and it was "eye-opening!" That people could be free about this! There were bars with lots of "hot" gay men in them! There was an entire community that I was totally unaware of! I now had a new support system too!

I recall first meeting you in tap class? Was it 1974 or 1975?

1975. I believe I had just "came out of the closet" in 1975. I recall, that it was also in those years when I met Tony. That was right after the show when I was began to acknowledge my being gay.

Did you meet Tony before, or, after finishing the show?

I had met him prior to the show. It was at the show, where I met Sal and George, my oldest gay friends. The show was The Student Prince, and there were some twenty six gay men in the cast! During the entire tour, I never had sex with any of them, nor, did I acknowledge to them that I was gay. After the tour, I did pursue relations with some of the cast.

When did you make a more conscious "coming out?"

Well, the first formal "coming out," was to my parents, when I confessed my love for the man I met and befriended in college. The period of doing the show, was more of a beginning of my involvement in the gay community but, I do recall a more quiet gay community at my college.

In college, I had a best friend there who was gay and we discussed my feelings for that unrequited love. After college, we remained good friends, despite his living in San Francisco. With him, I could discuss my feelings for other men and soon, there were other gay men in my fraternity with whom I discussed my feelings, and listened to theirs as well.

That time was a very confusing period for me. I don't know how to describe it? There was this special feeling toward other men, but somehow, we were able to emotionally distance ourselves from the "label." In other words, your perception was basically, that of a "straight" man who has strong feelings for other men. Where you could engage in relations with men, but could say, "I'm basically straight." That was the mentality of the time.

That period after high school when gay men enter college or, find themselves in the working world is clearly a time for introspection and experimentation with one's sexuality. I recall my experiences in college and those times were not easy for me, especially, with one "hot" dorm-mate who loved to rub his "washboard abs" while watching television with me alone in the student lounge. I was a fool for not taking the opportunity to pounce on him when I had the chance, only to stop myself due to my fear of being rejected by him and possibly shamed.

It wasn't until I was exposed to the "gay world" playing in The Student Prince, that my thinking began to change. It was during that time, when I began to view myself as a gay person. I recall being exposed to all these gay bars in various cities on the tour and that, changed my perceptions of gay men. So, that was how I "came out of the closet."

When you were in _Student Prince_, you made a conscious choice not to pursue anyone in the cast?

I remember being attracted to guys in the cast and wanting to experiment with them, but I was very young and didn't pursue it.

How old were you at the time?

I was twenty two going on twenty three at the time but they were reluctant to engage me as well.

Did you have sex with anyone you met in the bars on the tour circuit?

No, never! But, I'd love to tell you about my first experiences in those gay bars on the tour. I remember vividly the first time I went out with my buddies from the cast. There was a discussion at the time of the two different "camps" in the company. Of course, the "straight camp" was accepting of us, but, they were very much in the minority! I recall finding myself drifting more and more into the "gay camp" during the course of the tour.

FEAR OF ATTACK

On one special night, I recall going into my first gay bar in Washington D.C. I had never been in Washington. I was so frightened! The images that were perpetuated about gay people at the time were they were "predators!"

Somehow, they were; and I speak of "they" because I viewed them as "they;" because "they" were the ones that "converted" you! "They" were the ones who "induced" you into gay sex! "They" were the ones who were "dangerous" and could have "control" over you! These were my fears. I don't exactly know where "they" came from? I'm assuming "they" came from the perceptions of the time, and the material that I read. I believe the parental shame that was imbued in me at the time had a strong effect on my thought process.

Wayne's comments are very sad to hear but, only confirm the ridiculous statements made by politicians, church groups, and the media at the time, based on rumor and innuendo.

Unfortunately, many young gay men have fallen victim to this racist propaganda, due to very little gay literature or credible information available for gay men to read at the time. I personally remember looking up homosexuality in the encyclopedia and hearing information similar to Wayne's experience, with regards to homosexuality being an abnormal condition.
I remember "shaking like a leaf!" Feeling so uncomfortable and out of control! But, with all those fears inside of me, I still felt the need to go there! I recall planting myself in one place in the bar and being surrounded by all my friends using them as a buffer!

Sadly, I also recall feeling very much the "victim!" for some reason? I don't remember meeting many people in those bars, unless they became close to one of my cast mates first.

Feeling victimized for being gay, as well as, being fearful of being gay, are common emotions and thoughts experienced by gay men in those days. A time when there was cause to be fearful due to society's view of gays at the time as being "freaks" or abnormal, and should be punished or feared.

It was a very scary time for me! Literally, there was physical shame when I would go to those places! I felt so guilty about going there. What were people going to think about me? These feelings of shame and guilt were so strong within me, but I had to be there!

When you met these men in the bars, did you realize that your earlier perceptions of gay men were incorrect?

I really don't remember meeting anybody! I was always surrounded by cast members, and would only meet anybody unless they were accepted by the group! I don't remember dating anybody new! The image I have of what occurred there, was "cattle!"

Why cattle? That sounds like the theatrical term for a "cattle call."

It was the image of cattle protecting their young from danger by surrounding them from the potential predators!

The same holds true for all animals including, humans. Were your friends aware of the roles you had given them of protectors?

I think so, yes! In fact, my friend Sal was my chief mentor. He was very protective of me. A lot of the guys were. They viewed me as being fragile. I have remained friends with most of them, and they all agree that they played those roles with me.

Do you feel that their perceptions of you were accurate?

Yes. Yes! Because, I was ill-equipped to handle my sexuality at the time, and I'm still dealing with those issues!

Then for today, how do you feel about being gay?

I feel better now about being gay. I feel part of the community. I still have concerns about revealing my sexuality to everybody! I continue to feel that there is a prejudice toward us in many situations. Although, with the media being more vocal and portraying gay people in film and the theater as being more normal, the prejudice has only lessened somewhat. The general population appears to be more aware and savvy of us, but there still appears to be a pejorative connotation to the word "gay." As such, there is wariness on my part, to reveal it to everyone. I have an immediate circle of friends and family with who, I do confide in.

The only thing that I can endeavor to do to make myself happy, is to be "out" and more upfront with people, because it's freeing. Adopting an attitude of, "This is who I am, you can either like me or not! It doesn't really matter to me. If you don't like me, then I don't have to deal with you. But this is who I am!" I'm getting to be more militant about that attitude. Militant with myself for living the way I chose to live, and militant toward others who are intolerant of gay people? I am intolerant toward them for attempting to stop me from living my life!

Wayne's anger not only suggests his unwillingness to allow others to control his life or his choices with regards to his lifestyle but, that he is motivated toward defending his choices and will be an effective advocate for other gay men who have been abused or devalued.

I think there are people who classify themselves as "professionally, gay people, but I don't believe I am one of those. To me, being gay is just like having blue or brown eyes. I don't believe the majority of society accepts the recent statistics of a genetic predisposition for gayness, as there is, for having blue or brown eyes. I don't know whether they'll ever attain that vision of what being gay is, but that's the goal.

I had a dream last night of being accepted and supported at my last job for being who I am. I viewed myself as being militant in asserting myself for what I believed to be true.

Yes. With the situation I was in with my relationship, I realize now of how much I lost myself. How much of my essence was being compromised. That realization of what I did, and the results of it, both in terms of the outcome of the relationship and the outcome of my self-worth, made me realize that never again, will I allow myself to be compromised.

I will endeavor to be truthful to myself for the rest of my life. That's the process or, "thrust" of how I am determined to live my life. Never again, to be emotionally dominated or shamed for simply being who I am! It won't be easy, but I'll give it my best effort.

Yes. I recall at the time I couldn't sleep, and simply hugged my boyfriend at the time. Hugging my lover helped to deal with the "demons of the past." Looking around, and seeing how we decorated our home, the meal I prepared earlier, and how we enjoy one another, helped me to acknowledge the beauty my life.

Yes, that acknowledgment of those simple things, definitely helps to deal with the more painful aspects.

LOVING MY GAY SELF

What is being gay like for you today? Is it simply an aspect of who you are and not of whom you define yourself to be?

Yes. It's just as aspect of who I am. It's a facet of who I am. It's not a definition of who I am! I'm also an actor, a manager, a singer, and a good person. Being gay is a significant part of me, but it's not "the" major part of me.

Are you still struggling with your gay identity or, do you feel more positive about it?

I'm very positive about it! I feel "at home" with it. I feel accepted. In the theatrical community, I feel accepted by both straight and gay alike. In terms of the job I have, the top management are all gay. There is not prejudice for being gay there, but there is a prejudice toward being gay in casting! If casting directors know you are gay, there is shame and guilt in that! They have their own shame and guilt, which results in a "reverse prejudice!" Despite actors like Neil Patrick Harris and a few others, they still have difficulty casting openly gay men in heterosexual roles.

New York is more accepting than Los Angeles! In L.A., many actors who are gay keep their sexuality private for fear of never getting work. They endeavor to be "careful." That "carefulness" may also be true in New York, but in Los Angeles, it's a necessity!

In movies and television, you have to deal with big, corporate money. It's a liability to have an actor reveal he is gay, and still play a "sex symbol." If the masses find out about it, a pejorative context is placed on the actor. The fear continues to be perpetuated in Hollywood. Producers need to protect their investment, so no gay actor will be hired who may prove to be more of a liability than an asset. So, there is less openness in Hollywood.

Harvey Firestein, Sean Hayes, and Nathan Lane, still appears to be getting all the "stereotypical, gay" roles but John Travolta is right in there.

Yes. The roles continue to be overly flamboyant. I rarely see exceptions to that rule. I don't ever recall ever seeing a gay actor play a heterosexual, romantic role until Neil Patrick Harris got the role of a heterosexual lover in popular television show: *How I Met Your Mother.* Until then, I didn't think that would ever happen. Charles Nelson Riley did it on the stage, but he's never played a romantic lead in the movies. But, this topic is more relevant to Vito Russo's *Celluloid Closet* than for this book.

Yes, but it is relevant that so many actors are gay and have to continue to "stay in the closet."

Yes, that's true. The film industry is mostly "closeted" and shameful.

That's very interesting because I often seen theater actors say on the <u>Tony Awards</u>, "I'd like to thank my lover," but you rarely see that happen on <u>The Academy Awards</u> unless, it's a gay-themed documentary with gay producers.

And you probably never will!

But, you discovered a "breakthrough" toward your acceptance of your being gay during your time performing in the <u>Student Prince</u>, but are there other experiences which promoted your positive or negative feelings regarding your sexual identity? But for today, do you still feel shame and guilt associated with being gay?

As I have evolved in my life as a gay man, I met Tony, with whom I had a very long-term relationship. That relationship helped expedite my acceptance of my gay identity. But, I would say that after my involvement in The Student Prince, I was on my way toward accepting my gayness. So, there was not necessarily an event that promoted my acceptance, but an evolution.

Would say that being in <u>Student Prince</u> and your relationship with Tony were the chief experiences that helped to move you toward your acceptance of being gay?

I wouldn't want to say Tony. Crediting him with this acknowledgment really bothers me, because we had an "open" relationship for a long time, mostly on his part. He obviously, was an important part of my life but, I never felt like an object of desire with him.

Would you care to talk about your relationship with Tony and why you have difficulty giving him credit?

(*Pause*) Our relationship ended badly when he confessed to loving another man; someone with whom his told me was only a friend and after that revelation, he said he didn't love me anymore.

Wow, that is very callous and self-serving but the two of you did love one another and I know being his friend too, that he still cares about you. But on a lighter note, how did you two meet in the first place?

We met at Radio City Music Hall. He was a ballet dancer and I was a singer. I had worked there before he came into the show. We met at a rehearsal and I thought he was very cute. He was being a "wise ass" and I was quick to retort. We both enjoyed the game we were playing. He quickly became a part of the group of veterans at Radio City, like me. He would always go to lunch with all of us, and our friendship slowly evolved toward becoming more of a sexual relationship.

How long were you and Tony together?

We were "together" from late 1974 to 1996. When we moved to California and formed what I thought was a committed relationship in 1981 that lasted until 1994. We remained housemates until 1996, at which time I decided to move back to New York City to perform in <u>Les Miserables</u>. It was when I was living in New York City when he told me of his other relationship and admitted to all his lies.

Wayne and Tony are both good friends of mine and it was very painful to hear of Tony's deception and the emotional toll it had on Wayne. But, since Wayne was temporarily living with me in my apartment at the time, I knew that I had to be more supportive of him and would talk with Tony on my next visit to Los Angeles to get his side in the breakup.

Following my trip to Los Angeles and my time with Tony, it became clear that neither person was completely satisfied with their relationship but, Tony felt unable to be honest with Wayne for fear of hurting his feelings. Wayne was aware there were problems but, did not want to deal with them. In hindsight, their relationship was very similar to many failed relationships where honest communication was not occurring and resulted in the breakdown to their long-term relationship.

It is pretty obvious that your relationship with Tony was not your most satisfying gay experience? 'What would be considered a satisfying gay experience for you today?

The most satisfying gay experience is when you're with somebody with whom you are having sex and everything is "out in the open." Meaning, you can "look into their soul" and they can "look into your soul," and there are no lies. That is the defining experience!

I just can't imagine that happening with a woman for me, but that has happened with a man. It validates my belief that being with a man is where I should be. It is the ultimate experience, or at least, what I envision that ultimate experience to be.

Are there any other satisfying experiences that you recall?

Being gay is satisfying!

How is being gay satisfying to you?

Because, it is who I am! I'm comfortable living in a gay-friendly environment. Being gay, allows me to express who I am. If I'm allowed to be who I am, I am happy!

When do you feel guilt and shame with regards to your gay identity? Can you identify when those feelings have affected your behavior?

I expressed earlier of the shame in going to a gay bar for the first time. As for today, there is the shame in reconciling myself to the unhappiness which I seem to bring to my parents. I continue to have a lot of difficulty in trying to maintain my identity as a gay man when I am around them.

I love my parents. They have been incredible parents in many, many ways. Materially, they have given me everything that I want. They have always been supportive. But, "deep down," there isn't an acceptance of this gay part of me! But, my relationship with them seems like something at times, that I can't do anything about! I can't do anything about being who I am. And, I can't seem to make them feel better about who I really am. It disturbs me that I may be inflicting any sort of pain on them.

I know that my being gay or, if I express my gayness in a very open way around them, it pains them. So, there needs to be some modification as to who I really am when I am around them, even though they are aware of my gayness.

You feel guilty if your actions around them are perceived as appearing too gay?

There's guilt about not being able to be who they expect me to be. Not being able to "deliver." And yet, there is a sense of determination despite all this, to be who I am. So, there will always be something between us that appears to be in conflict.

Will this conflict ever be resolved or lessened?

It has been lessened! But, it's hard to for me to imagine there being full acceptance on their part. And yet, full acceptance is what would make me the happiest.

How would that image of full acceptance look like? How differently would they be treating you? How would they behavior toward you change?

They would be more involved in my life. They would ask me more questions about my life. I would have no compulsions about telling them anything! I wouldn't be so worried about editing the information in our conversations so, not to hurt them. It would be much freer and comfortable for me to be with them.

What it actually would be like, is what my mother seems to want, a closer relationship with me. And yet, every time I give her the opportunity by revealing a truth about me, or, problems I am having, she's incapable of hearing it. The result being, the frustration continues to continue.

Wayne's mother's reaction to his being gay is quite common within the gay community since he is the only son and the namesake of the family. Also, his mother had clear expectations of what she wanted for Wayne though her determined efforts in sending him to prestigious private schools. Plus, her promotion of a career for him either in the medical, law, or financial professions, certainly, not in the theater; despite her own love of the theater.

As a result, Wayne has had to experience both a lack of support from either parent for both his career choice and, his sexual identity; which his parents are among many, who choose to view being gay as a choice, and not an integral part of who we are.

Then you feel the origins of these feelings of shame and guilt first occurred in your relationship with your parents?

I believe we covered that, although, it's not only my parents, it's social! It is the society we live in which dictates this! It is though those dictates or, beliefs, that my parents become slaves to! The dictates of what is expected of both society and the world that they live in. In the case of my parents, it's not coming from any religious perspective. But instead, it is coming from a perspective of right and wrong as dictated by social norms and peer groups.

Do you believe your mother feels your being gay draws negative attention toward her?

Yes! I think that is definitely an issue. That it somehow shames her. That she is more worried about what other people perceive about me! She often says to me, "People don't think that's nice!" I view that statement as an inducement on her part that I change! As if, I have a choice in the matter.

But, it was a choice that I don't follow my heart and to follow the precepts of being true to my essence of whom I am! Both those choices are unacceptable! Those are unacceptable options!

Does she want to place a heterosexual microchip in your head to stop you from being gay?

You're absolutely right! But, they don't perceive that! Their perception is that it is a choice.

But, what I am concerned about with you, is how this shame and guilt has adversely affected your relations with other gay men? For example, you must have observed the obvious class system based on physical attractiveness within the gay community? Do you perceive something shameful being the "root cause" for the attitudes of superiority and indifference which is pervasive in the gay community?

I don't have a clear answer to that. I don't know how shame and guilt has affected my relationships with other gay men? I can only tell you my experiences of relating with other gay men in gyms and other social arenas.

The Age of Calculated Indifference

There is a fear of engagement with other men that seems to be pervasive in the gay community. There is this accepted axiom, that if you engage with another gay man in conversation, it is an opening to pursue them sexually. So, if you meet somebody whom you do not know and have not been previously introduced to, then there is a sexual connotation apparent in the meeting. If the response back is friendly, then you know the possibility for having sex is clear.

But as a result of this accepted axiom, there is a fear of engaging with anyone unless you can entertain the possibility of it going further. Therefore, you have a lot of people who put up "fronts" of disinterest, or, just plain unfriendliness!

They don't want to have themselves exposed to the pressure of this conversation becoming a sort of "mating ritual!" Eventually, you have a lot of people who are either ignoring one another or simply being unpleasant. The resultant affect, becomes an environment of isolation and hostility.

That is the type of environment being created by what I term as, "calculated indifference!"

Wow! That's good! That makes a lot of sense. Fear of sexual overtures or mating rituals!

Wayne's term "calculated indifference" is another term for selective communication that not only occurs between gay men but, with men or women alike, especially toward others with whom they feel no attraction. Therefore, there has to be an obvious reason when first meeting these men and women to desire increased interaction, whenever they feel no clear benefit in befriending or pursuing a more intimate relationship.

This type of behavior is common for all people with regards to interpersonal communication identified as the Social Exchange Theory where people weigh the costs and benefits of pursuing a relationship with another. For example, what benefits will occur if I engage this person for increased interaction; such as, a good friend, a sex partner, a career opportunity, or, more?

Yes. Very often these conversations are exactly that, sexual overtures! Which many people are reluctant to engage in because they don't want to be put in the place of rejecting others? I don't know if that's true or not? I do know personally, that I'm guilty of this! If there is an older, unattractive guy with whom I have no interest in, it's difficult for them to engage me.

I just don't want to be pursued! I think it comes from those old feeling of losing control and seeing a gay man as a "predator." There is this sense of being objectified, even if it is a friendly encounter. I, personally, would not want to be objectified as a "sex object." As a result, there is a protective "shield" that prevents perceived predators from engaging me, and exposing myself from being "preyed upon!" Which is actually an unrealistic fear, because you have the control?

I believe that this dislike for having to reject others has become the "norm" within the gay community. In other words, most New Yorkers have put up this "shield" to protect themselves from unwanted intrusions, and from persona harm. It is not until one has been introduced to someone, then their defensive "walls" mostly come down. Similarly, most gay men put up these "shields" to protect themselves from unwanted sexual advances!

But a smile can often result in another smile.

Yes, but that smile can also produce danger! If the wrong person smiles back at you, then, you could find yourself embroiled in troublesome situation. It's a fear thing!

Do you still perceive yourself as being vulnerable to the predators?

Yes!

Have you been attacked?

No.

But, you have fears of being attacked?

Yes, at times. In the street, I fear it all the time!

I recall a time when you were bumped on the street in Chelsea. Some "low life" bumped into you and he dropped his liquor bottle. He blamed you and screamed for payment for his broken bottle. You immediately gave him ten dollars! I was upset with you for paying him. I was ready to confront him and call for the police if needed.

So, why did you pay him? Was it part of that fear of being attacked?

Yes, I didn't feel I was in physical danger, because you were there. I was fearful though of being screamed at, and have undesired attention drawn toward myself. I felt that by paying him, I was avoiding an ugly confrontation.

Wayne being a close friend of mine has frequently confessed of being invisible to most attractive gay men since he is sixty years old and not feeling as attractive as he was in his past. His fear of being attacked by predators even today, is curious to me still, since, he has admitted to being victimized by both by Tony and with men in his past.

This feeling of victimization appears to originate from his past relationship with his parents and their unwillingness to come to terms with Wayne's sexuality and chosen career, therefore, he feels a need to overcompensate for their affection by always playing the role of caretaker with a defensive posture or behavior.

FEAR OF FAMILY REJECTION

You are fearful of confrontations with predators, or, hostility, but, can you tell me about your interactions and relations with heterosexual friends and family today? For instance, do you feel shame and guilt when interacting with them or, do you hold back information about your sexuality from them? I recall your prior statements of bonding within the theatrical community, but is it different with your family members?

Yes. I have heterosexual cousins with whom I feel could not "handle" my sexuality. I am not "out" to them. They never ask if I'm dating anyone. There's this non-confrontational dynamic that goes on between us. I don't bring women to family functions in order to "mask" my gayness. But, there's definitely a reluctance to open myself up to people who would not be accepting of gays or, me, since I am gay.

When we interact, you appear very comfortable being gay. But, are you saying that when you are with these family members, you don't relax and let yourself be who you really are?

Yes, but there are several other factors that "come into play" when I am with my family. Even, so far as being an actor. I don't perceive them as accepting that lifestyle either. They're just not accepting people in any area!

But, you're a successful theatrical manager and have appeared in several successful Broadway shows and television programs! Isn't that acceptable enough for them?

There's economic prejudice, as well as, sexual prejudice! So, there is this shame that enters into my interactions with them on both those fronts.

What careers are the acceptable careers to them; a doctor or lawyer?

Yes! They are ALL doctors. Their lives are based upon money and status! I have a cousin whose husband was severely injured and became a paraplegic. She has found her family to be dismissive of him, because of his handicap. They've been financially helpful toward her, but tend to "keep their distance" with regards to their relationships with either of them. As a result, I am fearful of being perceived as an "outsider," as I believe he is!

Yes. I perceive similar dynamics between my family and my brother's "developmentally challenged" daughter. There appears to be a sense of shame and guilt that prevails when a family member has a physically or mentally handicapped child.

What makes me angry as well, is that I often feel there is a parallel dynamic between my being gay and my niece's handicap! That both these "circumstances" are something deemed either shameful or, unacceptable, to certain family members. I have spoken loudly of the vast difference between the two, but I do feel a certain bond with my niece as a result of all this!

Yes, that's why I choose to keep quiet. I don't want that confrontation, and yet, I know by not confronting them, the secrets continue to exist.

Ironically, I know this shameful gay man who lives a gay lifestyle but, refuses to promote being gay as a positive choice. He is negative toward gay rights. He believes that we have certain "human rights" stated with the Constitution and that should suffice.

He also seems to enjoy debating his skewed beliefs often during dinner parties. These debates usually end with the disagreeing parties leaving the party in a furor, or, simply choosing to walk away and not to continue the discussion.

Are you going to interview him?

No. He refused to be interview.

That is too bad, for he would be a perfect example of the "other side" of gay men; those who continue to deny or accept their lifestyle as a source of pride.

But in a sense, that's what you're doing by not "coming out" to your cousins. By not speaking out, the stereotypes continue to exist and thrive.

Yes. I guess, I simply choose to "keep my own distance" from them, because I don't really like them and what they stand for.

Did you feel your deliberate choice to "come out" to your family and friends, signified your desire to feel emotionally closer to them?

Yes, and for that reason, I chose to tell my parents when I was in college! "Coming out" to me was a means by which I could begin to "define myself." That for some, "coming out" is an early process of self-affirmation.

For others like your friend, it never happens! It continues to be perceived by them as something shameful. That although they have lived a gay life, they choose not to involve their family in their lives! That if they choose <u>not</u> to accept your lifestyle, and they, then, refuse to be an active part of your life.

So if they learn to accept our lifestyle, they can be more involved in our lives? But if they don't accept it, they can't be?

Right, then they can't be a part of your life! Or at least, my life! How could they be? What are you supposed to do? Bring women to social events?

I refuse to be having to function on both levels with my own family! Despite having "come out" to them and told them some very personal experiences, there still, isn't a lot of in-depth discussion that I can have with them, because they are unwilling to deal with it.

Didn't you have a lover for many years with whom they were close with?

Yes. I brought Tony there many times, but there was never any discussion with regards to our relationship. It was simply never discussed! There was never a discussion to say that we weren't lovers. I don't know if my mother would have insisted that we sleep in separate rooms if she knew we were lovers?

My sister had to sleep in a separate room than her boyfriend, because they weren't married. They had been "living together" for several years, but she insisted that they sleep in separate rooms!

Did you and Tony sleep in separate rooms?

No, because when we visited, we slept in the same room in separate, twin beds. But, I don't think that it would have been an issue for them if we slept in the same bed! The subject of two men being lovers is so foreign to them, that it never crossed their minds to question our sleeping arrangement. They wouldn't know how to process the information!

What do you mean?

To think about putting us in separate rooms! They would think to put my sister and her fiancé in separate rooms, but not us! They wouldn't put my lover and I in separate rooms because they viewed as only as friends and nothing more!

So they were simply denying the simple truth of your relationship?

Yes! Their denial is very strong and immobile. There was no precedent for this situation. If there's no marriage, why have separate rooms? I can even visualize them saying, "Separate rooms? What's that about?"

This game of family denial is a common game being played by families and their gay children who cannot be honest with their sexuality, due to fear of losing that family support and comfort. Therefore, Wayne had to sacrifice who he truly is due to his need to be a caretaker for his family and continue playing the role of the "good son; "a self-defeating role to be sure.

For example, in playing the game of the "good son," one loses a part of himself. Not only does the son have to always act in an acceptable manner to others but, has to be ever-vigilant of his or, her, communication for fear that the truth may escape and expose the "dirty secret." Sadly, this game takes a great deal of energy and attention to keep playing and only serves toward prolonging the shame of the "secret."

"COMING OUT" PROCESS

With regards to your "coming out" process, your family were obviously not your role models but, was there a special person who helped motivate you toward "coming out?"

You continue to view my "coming out" as an event and not a process. It never was an event! Meeting Tony and having a relationship was a major force! Yes, but, my friends David, Greg, and my friends in college with who I had many in-depth discussions, were all very important toward the over-all "coming out "process. Perhaps, even more important than Tony with regards to my "coming out."

With them, I discussed my feelings of being gay for the first time! The excitement of discovering that I was not alone in having these feelings and that others had them too! That even though a lot of us did not perceive of ourselves at the time as being homosexual, we all knew that we had sexual feelings for men. Now, that was truly exciting!

Were these friends in college were even more important toward your "coming out" process than your friends in _The Student Prince_?

The entire *Student Prince* experience provided me with an entry into the whole world that existed at the time. But, in college, there was this "subterranean" gay community that existed. I wasn't involved in that group in college. With the *Student Prince,* I was introduced into the many gay subcultures of the major cities we toured.

It sounds as if your experiences in both _The Student Prince_ and, in college, were very positive.

Yes, absolutely! They were both instrumental toward my "coming out" process. It was very comforting to find somebody else who was gay, with whom, I could share my feelings with.

I recall the many discussions with my friends in college of why it was considered wrong to be gay? Intellectually, it made perfect sense as to why so many people were gay. But morally, it felt wrong to be gay! Inwardly, it was very difficult to accept being gay, because of the thought of being labeled "homosexual." That was a term that was still very upsetting or demeaning. **Demeaning?**

Yes, it was a demeaning term! It meant you were inferior, dirty; not acceptable!

REGARDING GAY COMMUNICATION

What advice would you give to the gay men of today with regards as to the ways in which they interact and relate to each other?

My only hope is that they can learn to be civil with each other and to not be so fearful of one another. We would be a better community if we try to be more civil and less fearful. After all, we all have the power to disengage from a situation if it progresses farther than we want it to.

In many of us, there is a fear of being sexually pursued that causes a "wall" to go up! A wall that is ages old, probably since birth, that is there to protect us from harm. A wall that prevents us from being engaged in a situation that may become uncomfortable and compromising! An "emotional wall" that allows us to not have to deal with anybody!

I say this, because there is always this perception that somebody is "putting the moves on you!" And with those "moves," there is this perception of oneself as a "potential victim." It is that fear that often separates us from others. After all, don't you put up your "walls" when being approached in a club by men you're not attracted to?

Yes, I do, but, that's in a club or bar! As I continue to write this book, I find myself becoming kinder and more open with all types of gay men. I'm smiling more and becoming less resistant to saying "hello" to a familiar face at the gym without having a "sexual agenda" behind my actions. Every so often, I have also observed gay men at my gym appearing perplexed as to whether or not they should say "hello" to either me or, to one another! Is that true for you?

Yes, but there is this fear of being "hit upon," that prevents us from saying "hello." As a result, the walls go up!

For myself, I would like to see gay men take the responsibility of dealing with a sexual advance appropriately. So, if you're being approached and you don't like it, then stop it from going any further! What's the big deal? Why is this issue? Why can't you just say, "I'm not interested?"

Making that type of statement could really hurt the other person's feelings so, we avoid it!

But is it? Do you? After all, how much can you hurt somebody's feelings if you've never met them prior to that first encounter? How much true damage can be done if somebody comes up to you who you don't even know, and you reject them? Will it cripple them for the rest of their lives because you won't go to "bed" with them? So all I am saying is, that I too am guilty of this, as I've already admitted! But the guilt is totally unrealistic!

Wayne's comments are clearly indicative of both frustration and anger at gay men who avoid or, ignore him as a perceived suitor or sex partner. As I recall, his frequent comments with regards to poor communication between gay men, is that he often feels "invisible," to them; meaning, that as far as some gay men are concerned, he does not exist for them, because, they are not physically attracted to him. Ironically, in Wayne's role as a successful theatrical manager, he is very visible to everyone he associates with, men and women, gay or straight. And in this role he is both powerful and direct.

I personally choose not to pursue anyone sexually unless I get some positive eye contact or clear body language first! Otherwise, I am setting myself up for rejection! With all my lovers, there were very clear signals prior to our introductions to one another.

That does make a good deal of sense, thank you.

But before ending this interview and on a lighter note, is there one really good "pick-up line" that you could share with us?

I don't know? Perhaps that's the chapter in your book that I would love to read: "Great Pick-Up Lines From Successful Cruisers!"

Why so?

Because, I don't really feel that "pick-up lines" really work, unless you're physically attracted to the other party! In addition, I don't think the "venue of a bar" is an appropriate place for me to meet another lover. I do feel there are many men, gay or straight, who enjoy the "hunt!" These are the men who clearly enjoy the thrill of "bagging" a date for the evening and of "putting another notch on their wall of conquests" are simply, "not my cup of tea!" But, I'm simply not one of them, and I really hate the idea of it!

But what I am truly hoping to achieve by being gay, is to find another human being with whom I can relate to and be totally comfortable and trusting of him. I have yet to have experienced that feeling but, I know that I want to feel closer with someone I love.

The "hunt," is only one small part of achieving that end, and yet, it is a very necessary one to accomplish. It is simply the one part of the process that I don't enjoy, because within our community, it is all based upon "a look!" If you don't happen to fall into those narrowly defined parameters, it becomes a difficult process. And, someone who is facile with clever lines, is someone with whom I would not be interested in listening to.

It's more about how we as a community, have limited ourselves to the pursuit of the fantasy; the "ideal" mate. Besides, how can one hold a good conversation in a loud and noisy bar? Bars are meant for meeting someone and leaving as quickly as possible! The loud music does not allow for in-depth conversations!

The most success I've had, is through meeting people and becoming friends with them, and then we date. Meeting though other friends helps. Discussions of common interests are a major factor toward moving toward a relationship. But getting through the initial "ice-breaking," is something I hope to learn from your book.

Thank you. But, you are basically saying that the best way toward meeting someone new, is through mutual friends?

Yes. For me, that is the most comfortable and successful means toward meeting a potential partner.

But in speaking about looks, what do you find physically attractive in another man?

I am as guilty as everyone else! I like well-defined bodies. I like beautiful eyes. I like dancer bodies! I'm not attracted to large, big-muscled bodies, because they intimidate me and I feel overpowered by them. So, I gravitate toward smaller, well-defined bodies with a sweet smile.

What non-physical attributes do you find most attractive?

One of the most important qualities for a relationship is someone who can make me laugh. I love someone who has a great sense of humor.

What aspects of gay men do you find most unattractive?

I guess the "coolness," the "bitchiness," the competitiveness, all are unattractive aspects of the gay man of today. Men who are extremely effeminate are unattractive, but as I get older, that quality doesn't bother me as it did before. But, I don't think I could have a lover who is a "drag queen!" I feel if I wanted a woman, I'd choose to be with a woman.

Lastly, the most unattractive gay men to me are the guys who just want to "score" for a "one night hookup."

You're list of unattractive qualities that gay men display: "coolness, bitchiness, competitiveness, effeminate," are all qualities that are classified with most women. Do you feel that gay men are trying to emulate women in some way? Although, the first three qualities are mostly negative, they are synonymous to many women, especially, fashion models, whose careers are based upon young, beautiful looks? Do you agree or disagree?

I think that being gay, meaning, attraction to the same sex, can be very confusing today. There is this "push/pull" or "male/female" dynamic of seeking a mate (masculine) and being someone's mate (feminine), that are the heterosexual dynamics we all were raised with. These dynamics stem from the heterosexual role models we had of a mother and father of opposite sexes.

When we are involved in a gay relationship, we are forced through those heterosexual terms, to play both the male and female parts. Those roles are the "norms" we are forced to use for our relationships, because those are all we have to go by! They are the "benchmarks" of our relationships!

Gay men, by virtue of being gay, are exercising their feminine side. It becomes confusing in terms of mannerisms and dealing with other people, especially, with other men! We are all raised to be "bread-winners" and "hunters!" There is this "machismo" in being the "hunters" but, what does that mean when two "hunters" are making a "home" together? There is a feminine aspect that we are expressing by being in a relationship with another man.

Yes! For instance, who cleans the animal after it is killed? Who cooks it?

Yes. It tends to be difficult to "come to grips" with what form in takes within us to express ourselves in a relationship?

The terms of "coolness and bitchiness" appear to be the manifestations of "coming to terms" with our feminine sides, as they exist in the gay world. Perhaps they are exaggerated in some way because they simply don't feel comfortable "in our skins?" So when they are exaggerated by others and I perceive it, it becomes unattractive to me.

I am interested in a man, not someone who is more interested in being more of a "woman!"

Wayne's closing comments are indicative of the complex interactions between gay men with regards to social identity and personal life satisfaction. The question of who plays the female role or, even defining what the female role is, has been a constant dilemma for many gay men.

For example, some gay men view the man who plays the "bottom" role sexually, as being more feminine or submissive when in truth, many gay men enjoy that role as well as, the "top" role. Also, in the equation is, who cooks and who cleans; do both work, or, does one go to work while the other stays home to take care of the home and either the kids or pets?

All these questions and dynamics are all important to understanding gay male lifestyles and are good subjects for another book but, the focus here, is on how to talk and interact with one another, and how to do that with more respect and consideration.

Thank you Wayne, talking with you was a lot of fun and eye-opening as well.

I had fun too. It was very thought provoking for me as well.

END OF INTERVIEW WITH WAYNE SCHERZER

CHAPTER VII- DAVID PEVSNER
"A GAY FOR ALL SEASONS"

This interview was conducted some thirteen years ago but I want to demonstrate here if there is any significant difference between the David of thirteen years ago and today. A second follow-up interview that occurred as of more recently will also be included in this chapter.

Interview with David Pevsner in his Chelsea, N.Y. apartment on July 3, 1997 and a follow-up interview ten years later– *Similar to Bob Dobson and Tim Rogers, David also exudes a clear confidence and air of sexuality and masculinity, His eye contact is direct and clear. His sits in his chair ready for the interview as if this is not the first time he has been interviewed but not about his gay identity but for his extensive theater and film work*

Please tell me something about yourself?
Do you want to know about me physically or, personally?

Whatever comes to you first; if physical is more important, than describe yourself physically.

That's really tough! Physically, I'd say above-average build, dark hair, a little-bit-better-than average looking. Personally, I'd first say that I am lazy; I'm very lazy. Although, I'm pretty driven when it comes to my career! I'm very disciplined about going to the gym. And, I would say that I'm one of the most loyal people I know, especially with friends and people who have been good to me. I hold grudges pretty badly. I have a "way-above" average intelligence! I'd like to think I have a good sense of humor and, a good conversationalist!

I like people! I don't mean to sound like Miss America but, I really do like people if there is something about them that's "open." I love having great late-night conversations with people. I love staying up late at night, talking. But I only want to talk about things that are really important to one another and not just "small talk.

So, I guess in general, I'm a typical Capricorn; which means I'm smart, stubborn and ambitious!

It's interesting how you started to describe yourself physically, and then went immediately into describing your other qualities.

Well, I think I'm in a phase now, where I'm putting less emphasis on the physical. I sort of fell into the "Chelsea-Boy-Gym-Thing" for a while, where I used to work way too long at the gym! I spent much, too much, time there! I mean, it did good things for me such as, building up my self-esteem and physique. But, when I realized that I was constantly judging others based on their own physicality, I got myself into trouble.

I was involved in a relationship which made me very aware of my judgmental attitude. I essentially, threw away a really wonderful person because of their physicality! It was an "eye-opener" for me, because, it was a lousy thing to do!

BODY OVER MIND

How did you throw this person away?

I told him, "I am not attracted to your body as much as I thought I would be." It really hurt him, because at the time, we were being really honest with each other. Everything was about honesty with us. After I told him that, the relationship took a downturn from there! I hurt him, and I think that was one of the "shittiest" things that I've ever said to anybody!

The question in my mind was the same. What would motivate someone to say something so cruel to someone he seemed to care about? A quick analytical response would be, that his comment came from his own feelings of inadequacy and low self-esteem, where one needs a partner who is similarly attractive to themselves or even more attractive. In that case, they would look "hot" when walking together in public or, with other gays.

Now, when I think back on it and ask myself, "What exactly I was thinking? What was holding importance to me at the time?" He was a great person and was very attractive to me!

But for now, I'd like to think that I've changed. In the last year, I've done a lot of thinking about it; a lot of reading about it. I'm involved with somebody now who doesn't go regularly to the gym. He's really attractive to me and I think he's really sexy; without being one of those "big, gym-built guys!" I simply love who he is, and he seems to love me for who I am! Plus, I don't feel that I have to "put any airs on" with him.

So far, this has been the longest relationship I've ever had! I hope that when this book is published, we may still be together?

How long have you been together?

Seven months! But, that's the longest relationship I've ever had!

Are you monogamous?

Yes!

Are you monogamous because you chose to, or, can it be more of a result of what's going on in the world today with regards to AIDS?

No, we chose to be monogamous. I think we both agree that it's for the best, especially, coming from the world I come from; having been only into great bodies. It's now a matter of trust! I want to prove to someone that they can trust me. If they want to be monogamous, then you really have to make the attempt to follow suit. It's all individual!

I think everybody has to set their own rules. But, whatever the rules are between the two of you, then, those have to be the rules you stand by! So, if you want to prove yourself trustworthy to someone, you simply have to abide by those rules! You just got to do it!

Sounds wonderful. Good luck to you both. But at this point, I would love to talk about your theater work since it is so connected to the gay community.

Yes. I've been performing in *When Pigs Fly* for almost a year now. I've been involved with a couple "out there" gay theater. pieces. I did *The Party* first, for almost a year, and now I'm in *When Pigs Fly*. They are both, very entertaining shows! I feel I've done, and am presently doing, really good work in both of them. I'm very proud of that! I'm also proud that they were gay pieces that also provided wonderful entertainment for all audiences. I know that neither one of them were Shakespeare! But, they provided a lot of entertainment for a lot of people, and I am proud to have entertained audiences for a couple of years straight in both these shows.

I saw __The Party__ in Chicago during a business trip, but you were only in the New York show?

Yes, I was only in the New York cast. I know *Party* was not a great play, but we had a lot of laughs!

Were you okay with being nude in the end of the play?

Yeah, it was okay. I had no problems with it.

David clearly is proud of his physique and it clearly holds a great deal of significance for him with regards to his attractiveness to other gay men and the power it affords him. The problem here, has more to do with how he chooses to interact with other gay men who may not be as well defined or, as "hot" as he, with regards to his interactions with them in both a romantic and social level.

You appear to have been doing a considerable amount of "soul searching" and making changes in your behavior within the past few years?

Yes! I have made a lot of changes in the last year or so.

You admit to be carrying some shame with regards to the ex-boyfriend whom you insulted. Have you given it some thought as to why physical attractiveness holds such a high priority for so many gay men?

People with great bodies and who go to the gym a lot, are perceived by many gays of only going out with their own kind! It's true! You see it every day! When I go to brunch in Chelsea, I frequently see a table of six beautiful gay men sitting together! I often ask myself, "How did these guys meet and "get together?" My first thought is that they're probably friends from some "circuit party" or the gym, who continued to stay together after meeting.

I believe a lot of people think that if you have a great body, then that's the type of people you "hang out with!"

A lot of times, that's just the way it is!

Yes, I know that it's just the way it is! But, that's no saying that it's a quality relationship! Some of them are I'm sure, and some of them are not!
As for myself, I felt that I had a really great body for a couple of years there, and I too, fell into the trap of only going out with other great bodies! I was only attracted to other good bodies and they were attracted to me! I was becoming a part of the group that Michelangelo Signorelli called the "Cult of Masculinity!" So, I simply fell into it!

But, I never did the drugs or, the steroids! I rarely went to the "circuit parties." In fact, I went to the "circuit parties" before they were called "circuit parties!" I just hated all that stuff! So, I was never a "circuit queen!" But, I did become friendly with plenty of "circuit queens," as did a lot of other people!

Having gone through some pain in past relationships, and always wanting more than just a beautiful body, I still took the beautiful body when it was offered to me!

David is clearly presenting the "clique mentality" which I mentioned earlier in this book, as being one of the basic problems which result in the "Gay Communication Game" at its worst. Where the communication between others can be at its most demeaning and ostracizing for those who are seen as not fit or, beautiful enough to belong within their clique or group.

For now, David is claiming to be feeling a sense of guilt over his actions, where he indeed, hurt others in his past who wished to become romantically intimate with him.

I can hear some guilt with regards to your past actions, which affirms the major premise of this book: that many gay men because of the environment we grew up in, even if you were popular, such as the "Prom King" or "Star Quarterback," you were living a double life!

Right! I believe that too!

Many still do even those who live within predominantly gay-friendly communities.

Yes! For the most part, we lived a "retarded adolescence" because we couldn't be our true selves when we were young. We focused our lives on acting in a certain way to please others.

Exactly! That's an excellent term! Although, I believe that many gay men would take exception to that term.

Well, there are exceptions to everything! I know that my adolescence was not a normal adolescence for me, because if I had a normal adolescence, I would have dated the boys that I was attracted to! Since I could not, I had to stop those feelings, otherwise, I would have been called a "fag" when I was six years old! *(laughs)*

My own adolescence was as a time when I had to wear a "mask" in order to hide being gay.

CHILDHOOD EXPERIENCES THAT LEAD TO THE GAY "CASTE SYSTEM"

*Within this book, I want to make special mention of the obvious "caste system," as it presents itself within the gay community. As my previous interviewee described it to be: "We separate the gay community into two groups: one, being the group of men we're sexually attracted to, and the other, being the men we aren't!"

This "caste system" I suspect, is a direct result of years of shame and guilt for being gay and not fitting in with the heterosexual world. Therefore, we experience the need to feel and act superior to others, which is based on those years of feeling less than perfect from those family and friends who fit into what our society deems "normal."

In addition, there is this focus on physical beauty and status, which appears to parallel the physically beautiful, heterosexual female in our society. In doing so, we often feel this need to separate those who are less physically beautiful from those who are not. There is also this impetus to pursue physical beauty at the sake of emotional and spiritual stability.

The fact that many film icons with the gay male community are "bitchy" and powerful women such as: Joan Collins, Bette Davis, Madonna, Joan Crawford, and so many others, that appear to arise from this place of competitiveness with the "straight, white male."

What it can be with the female film icons, is an attraction to strength; which could be either male or female. I, myself, am very attracted to strength, and I don't mean physical strength. I love people who are very passionate about what they do. I love people who are very verbal and vocal about what they do. Those are the people, both men and women, whom I am attracted to.

I've never been attracted to someone who can't make up their mind or, who's "wishy-washy." When I'm that way, I feel unclean or "yucky!" I just want to hide my head in a bag and not walk out of the door! I believe, a large part as to why I feel that way, is the result of spending a good deal of my childhood acting like that! I felt like I was always being "wishy-washy."

Why did you feel like that?

It comes out of fear! Fear of being beaten up! You just can't say what you definitely want, or, at least, I couldn't say what I definitely wanted. I was being geared in school to be a doctor or a lawyer, but deep inside, I felt I was an artist! There simply was not a lot of positive outlook as an artist in my home! So, I found myself attacking something that I really wasn't interested in. As a result, I began to feel "wishy-washy," because I wasn't doing something that I felt passionate about. Now, I feel I overcompensate for feeling weak or insecure by building up my physique. In terms of relationships, whenever I started feeling sexual, I couldn't go after what I really wanted, which were boys instead of girls!

Were you aware of all those feelings back then?

I don't think I really knew it.

But, you sensed it?

I sensed it! I don't think I really understood it when kids would call me "fag" as a little boy. I always thought they called me that name because I liked to read, and didn't like to play sports! Little did I know, was that they were absolutely right!

How old were you when they started to call you "fag?"

120

Oh, God! I think it was around the fourth or fifth grade. It really got intense in the fifth grade! That was when I was really scared of some of the other kids. I would stay away or avoid eye contact with these guys! If I made eye contact with any of them, they would look at me with such hatred! They had power over me! I let them have power over me!

Why do you think you did that?

Because, I felt deep down inside, even if I couldn't put my finger on it, I knew I wasn't, in quotes; "as good as them! I just knew that I didn't conform as to what was considered "normal!" Besides, being one of the smartest kids in class, nobody likes a smart kid, except the teacher! And if you were liked by the teacher, the rest of the kids despised you!

In terms of the other boys, it was the fact that you couldn't throw a football! It was a real hateful thing not to be able to throw a football! I hated gym class because I was afraid of their scorn! Gee, it's not as if I'm alone in feeling that way, but just the same (*pausing for the moment*).

David is providing clear information of how his feelings of inadequacy, as well as, the fear of being exposed, which resulted not only his need to get that perfect body but, his desire to demonstrate to others that he was better than most of those who abused or demeaned him in those painful school years.

Were you afraid to be caught looking at the other guys changing in the locker room?

No, I didn't even want to look at the other guys in the locker room. I didn't want to be naked with the guys in the locker room! I didn't look at the guys. I just looked down! I was afraid to be naked with the other guys, because I was just afraid to be naked in general! But, to be naked with guys that I may have been attracted to, didn't come into my consciousness until much later. I didn't even become aware of my attraction toward men until my mid to late teens! But early on, I just knew that I was different somehow, and I was scared of that, because I simply knew it wasn't "normal."

On that note, I just read this interesting interview with Will Smith in *Us Magazine*. I find him to be an incredible jerk! Did you know that he refused to kiss his male co-star in the film *Six Degrees of Separation*? He initially signed a contract saying that he would do it, and then backed out on the agreement at the last minute.

But in this interview, he was asked how he would feel if his son was gay? His answer was, "Well, I hope that my son would conform to nature!" The interviewer responded," What exactly do you mean by that?" He simply went on about the "need for the male to procreate" and so on. It is now down in print for all these little kids who think he's so great! It is just so disturbing to read about him "going off" on how being gay is not "natural!" Well, "Fuck you Will Smith!"

Will Smith's comments of years back, come to mind Tracey Morgan's more recent comic rant during a show where he was attacked for his anti- gay rhetoric; which happily, resulted in serious damage to his career and professional image? But how was Will Smith able to "dodge the bullet when Tracey Morgan did not? Perhaps Morgan paid the price for his hateful rant, due to the efforts of the GLBT community and its leaders, where there is now more respect and dignity for us among today's more accepting culture, thanks to President Obama and his constituents. A similar situation occurred when Isaiah used a homophobic slur against his gay co-star T.R. Knight and was subsequently fired from the television show, Grey's Anatomy.

What is also of significance here, are that all three actors accused of homophobia are African American. Ironically, a race which suffered their own centuries of slavery and persecution who would clearly know of hatred and prejudice but now with these notable examples, have found a group to verbally attack and demean which in the long past, they never would be able to do.

As a little kid, all I knew about the words "fags" or "faggots," and how it was "unnatural," and that's what I was called! All I knew was that I was unnatural, and because of that, I was less than them!

Can you specify with who you mean as, "being less than?"

Less than those bullies who were name-calling me, as if, it was their way of saying," You're not as good as me!" Therefore, when you have no way of fighting back, because you're a little, skinny kid, and if you don't want to get into a fight; you retreat.

What was it like with your parents?

They were fine. I guess you could say that our relationship followed a bit of the stereotype. My mother was a very opinionated woman; very smart and "on the ball." My father was a quieter sort of guy. He went to work and came home at night.

My family was not the most demonstratively loving family. I felt loved and wanted but, not all the time! There were times when I used to watch a lot of television. On the television shows, the families used to always hug and kiss in the end. Well, that wasn't us! My parents showed their love for us, in the ways that they learned how to do it. I guess looking back, I sort of think that "It wasn't great, but it wasn't bad."

What were your favorite television shows?

On Friday nights I wouldn't go out! I would sit and watch *The Brady Bunch*, *The Partridge Family*, and *Love, American Style*. Whatever that Friday night line-up was, I would stay home to make sure I never missed an episode; I used to just "die" for that! The guys were always so cute, and I was just this little "teeny-bopper!" They were just such great families, not like mine. They were just great!

Again we see children who grow up to be gay, finding solace in the fictionalized versions of families where the home is a place of safety, comfort, and support. A place where these children could easily retreat to that safe place where there was abundant love and acceptance. Where everyone was happy and every crisis was resolved by the end of the show.

How old are you?

I'm thirty-eight.

My favorite television shows were __The Donna Reed Show__ and __Leave it to Beaver__.

They were around when I was a kid too, but my prime time for watching television was around the late sixties and early seventies. But, I watched television always! I used to watch re-runs of *Father Knows Best* and *Leave it to Beaver*. I loved all those family shows! I guess it was something that was ingrained in us, because I used to watch a lot of television.

Why did you watch all those shows? What was it about those shows that attracted you? Was it because they didn't look like your family?

No, it was because I wanted to be an actor! I wanted to be an actor, and these shows had a lot of actors in them who were my age or younger. I pretended that I was those people! So, that's really what attracted me to those shows more than anything. But, I did put myself into those situations that were shown each week. So, even though I was looking at them as a kid wanting to be an actor, I was still Mrs. Partridge's son for a while or, a Brady kid for a moment.
That's very believable. I recall having similar feelings, and all this information ties into your childhood experiences of feeling different or separate from the other children around you.

Did you ever want to "fit in" more at the time with the other kids? What was your general feeling about yourself as a kid?

Well, the overall feeling was that, I should have been something else, but, I not sure what? I do come from a pretty sheltered upbringing. I lived in the suburbs and the problems that we had we not terrible. We didn't have any terrible diseases or craziness in the family until I was old enough to deal with it.

As a kid, I wasn't faced with a lot of difficulty. My parents had enough money and we lived in a nice house, and we had a lot of friends. But, with all that normality, I felt that: (a) I didn't want to be a "breadwinner." (b) I knew there was something different about me, in terms of the object of my attractions.

So, because I come from such a normal, sheltered background, I felt really guilty and "pained" about who I was, and what I wanted for my life.

You felt pain about what?

I knew there was going to be a struggle. I felt I was "setting myself up" for this huge, gigantic struggle, which is why I always got good grades. I knew that I needed good grades in order to be a doctor, even though, I wanted to be an actor. I always had girlfriends because I really wanted to fit in with everyone around me.

Did you have sex with these girlfriends?

Only fondling! I was very innocent, because I was scared of sex with women. I was scared of sex in general!

Have you ever had sex with women?

Yes, but later in my life.

When was your first sexual experience with a man?

It was late in my grammar school; sixth or seventh grade. My friend and I did some experimenting under the covers once. We used to play the game "Feely-Meely."

Is "Feely-Mealy" something like playing "Doctor"?

Yes. But, it wasn't really sexual. We never got erections or anything else. It was mostly, "Oh, look at that!"

Just with that one boy?
Yes. It wasn't really sexual, even though, we were touching one another's genitals. But, it wasn't arousing. Come to think of it, there was another time in the sixth or seventh grade with someone who taught me how to masturbate!

Did you continue to masturbate with him after that?

No, I only would masturbate on my own.

I had a friend too who showed me how to masturbate.

Yeah. It's a shame that we couldn't figure it out for ourselves back then.

I kinda liked being shown, and we ended up having a very sexual relationship for years.

Yeah. But at the time, I acted really bored. (Acting bored) "Come on. Come on." But worst of all, I told people about this friend who taught me how to masturbate!

Oh, no! Another victim of your actions?

Yes. Now, how horrible was that?

Gay shame was clearly at work here where David must have felt either shameful for his feelings toward other boys or, feeling intense guilt over masturbating with his friend. As a result of his shame and feelings of intense guilt, David exposed his friend as being the perpetrator and not himself as the willing participant.

This type of shameful behavior was the beginning of placing the blame or, negative focus on others, rather than on himself; all over his fear of being viewed negatively as a homosexual.

So, what happened?

Nothing happened as far as I know, because this kid was very popular and it didn't hurt his reputation at all. As for me, everyone looked at me thinking, "I can't believe you told people!"

Why do you believe caused you to tell on him?

I think it was because I wanted so much to be part of a popular group back then.
Was it a matter of prestige for you to have that popular boy masturbate you?

Yeah. But, I still wonder why I did what I did? I really don't know. I think it was just a stupid thing to say!

Your rationale for doing it must have come from someplace?

I'm sure, but I really don't know.

Well, the desire to be popular runs deep in a lot of us.

I'm sure. But, I think it came more from a place of "putting someone down" in order to "bring myself up!" Maybe that thought was running through my mind at the time. All I know now, is that I still feel pretty "shitty" about what I did!

We've all done pretty "shitty" things at one time in order to make ourselves feel or look better to others. Finding a common ground with others by criticizing or taking notice of someone else's behavior is very human. It's good that you can acknowledge your behavior now and try to rationalize your motives.

(*Feeling a little pensive*) Yes. But, it's funny to think about all that now.

As a therapist, I considered going further with David's reporting of a second incident of shaming or insulting another gay man as a means of either protecting himself or, emotionally distancing himself from them. Both incidents are clear indicators of displacing his negative self-worth on others as a way of avoiding intimacy or his attempt to fit in with the "cool kids." Either way, his choices don't exactly come from a good place but a shameful one.

Going back to previous statements of "not fitting in" or "knowing it was going to be a struggle;" of "having to get good grades or girlfriends," and such. When did these feeling begin to lessen in intensity?

That is the main problem that I still need to deal with in my life. That is the main problem that I have as a human being. For, in order to gain happiness, I still look for approval way too much from other people!

What if they don't give it to you?

Well, I used to get mortified! Now, I'm learning to take it for what it is. It also depends on how much sleep I got the night before, on whether it bothers me or not. It's getting better! I've really worked on this issue over the years! But, when you're struggling in a career where you have to put yourself above so many other people, I still feel very vulnerable to people's opinions. I try not to read reviews! Although, I enjoyed my reviews for this last show, I try to stay away from reading reviews about my work.

I feel that I've learned to enjoy myself as I'm working. As of late, I been satisfied with the good work I've done.

THE THEATER IS MY LIFE

In the theatrical world there is amazing competition. What is it about you that will attract directors and producers to hire you? Do you believe that your success in the show business stems from that need for approval from others?

Yes! I want them to really like me.

What do you feel works for you in getting roles?

Nothing special, I used to do a lot of smiling. I do a lot of "reaching out" to the audience to get them to listen to me. Then, I decided to go back to studying acting again, and realized that acting is NOT "result-orientated."

If you come from a place of: "You must love me," then you will fall into a trap. What I've learned to do, is to do the work and not to be lazy about it, and to know my character's motivations as to why he behaves as he does? A good actor needs to look at the relationships within the script; and, do all the work that actors need to do technically to make his performance work for the play.

Then, you put your special "stamp" on the work. Find what makes you laugh? Discover what lines make you laugh or cry. Create moments that relate to special times you've had in your own life. That, is what creates a whole performance! If you do that work, the result is, that it works!

It's making the work yours which is most important. Put your "personal stamp" on it and don't go looking for approval from the auditioners. Get the "bad angst" out of it! It's when you care about what they think and go looking for their approval that, the nervousness comes in and screws you up! You end up trying too hard and "pushing for results!" A lot of actors do that! I've sat on the opposite side of the table and watched many auditions.

What have you seen?

You can always tell if someone is going to be considered from the minute they walk into the door!

How so?

Because, there is a desperation that some people take on the minute they walk into the door that is really unattractive. It's really hard to watch!

What do they do?

They come on too strong or, they appear as if they're putting on a "false self" or mask on top of who they really are! It's the ones who come in simply saying, "Hi, how are you?" that get the jobs!

Even if the people you are auditioning for have a reputation of being real "hard-asses," you have to walk in being yourself. You also need to be well prepared and have done your homework to keep from being "thrown off your lines."

Also, don't push too hard or not enough! In other words, you have to know where the "special moments" can take you. Have enough calm to recognize the moments when they arise and use them instinctively. You'll go farther if you show them who you are. Don't be one of those singers who sing Mandy Patinkin's or Sam Harris's versions of "Over the Rainbow!" Give your audition piece your own personalized signature and you'll go much farther.

After all, why should they hire you over everybody else? If they want Sam Harris, they'll try to get Sam Harris, not a copy of Sam Harris!

So, you really learned to find clarity in your acting techniques? You've also found some emotional balance with regards to your acting career.

I'm much more experienced now. I've learned a lot of life's lessons and they've taught me well. I know I have plenty more to learn since I'm not as successful as I'd like to be. That comes with more learning and more "letting go."

"Letting go" is an important step?

Yes! "Letting go is very important. It's huge! "Letting go" of all your ideas of how you believe you should act.

Yes. "Letting go" of your need for validation; fearing as if you're not talented enough to get the job. It's especially important during the audition to "let go" of that fear that you're good enough to get the job.

Yes! You can see that too in people's faces as they are auditioning!

That makes a great deal of sense, since many actors go into show business looking for validation and approval. As a drama therapist, I've seen the importance of validation as a means to satisfy our intense need for self-approval.

That's why when a lot of actors decide to give up on show business, they become therapists! They understand the human need for approval and learn where it stems from; a desire to be loved! Therapists such as you, learn to understand the "inner workings" of a person through their educational background. But as actors, you have been through the difficulties of pursuing an acting career.

Sometimes when I feel frustrated with my life and my career, I think to myself, "I live in New York City, I'm gay, and I want to be an actor." I then realize that I've set myself up with some very difficult situations, and I've done pretty well for myself so far.

So, I know that somebody like me, who hasn't "hit in big" already, who's not twenty-three anymore, who isn't beautiful or "hip," it's going to take time to make it in showbiz. It's going to take a lot of learning and a lot of "letting go." The "letting go" part is most essential. You got to stop caring about what other people think about you because it will make your work go much easier.

Thank you. Your advice is not only important for actors to hear, but everyone.

I follow my own advice as much as I can, but sometimes, I still care too much. But, I'm getting better.

It's a one day at a time process.

Yes, it's totally a one day at a time process! It also helps when you audition for somebody who's a great auditioner! Who will say after you finish your piece, "That was good, now why don't you do it this way," instead of, "Thank you!" Because, when they say, "Thank you!" It makes you feel like the biggest piece of shit in the world!

It would be nice if someone just stood up and complained when they treat you like that!

Some people are just not like that. They just imply "You're not what we want! Now get out!" It would be nice if they just said, "You may not be what we thought of so could you try to read the script more like this?" Then you try it again, following their direction, and all goes better.

SHAMEFUL EXPERIENCES HAVE THEIR CONSEQUENCES

Going back to the first question, is there anything else you'd like to share about growing up feeling different from the other kids around you?

Just that I hated being seen shirtless! I was very ashamed of my body.

Did someone make fun of your body?

My two older sisters would always make comments about my body in a bathing suit. They thought I was too skinny. Whenever I wore a bathing suit, they would go "Woo-woo!" It was embarrassing.
I was on the other side, chubby!

Yeah. I think a lot of times, fat people and skinny people have gone through the same thing.

Be they gay or straight?

Yes.

So, when did you "come out?" Where and how?

For me, it was when I was in college during my freshman year at the University of Michigan. It was after meeting somebody and who eventually told me he was attracted to me, and I did the same. It was September 1, 1978. Nothing happened that night. We just talked about it and went for a walk. Down the line, it became sexual. We were boyfriends for a couple of months.

Before that, I went to a therapist over the summer in Chicago. He was a jerk, but he was the first person that I "came out" to! The only good advice he gave me, was "to meet somebody who had the same feelings that I did." I think that gave me the strength to eventually say to this guy, that I liked him.

Were you shaking with anxiety at the time?

Oh, God! He had to get me drunk!

Do you think he purposefully tried to get you drunk?

Uh, yeah! I had never really had that much to drink before.

Was he older than you or, the same age?

No, he was definitely the same age. We were somewhere between nineteen and twenty years old.

How did that "coming out" experience feel?

It felt good. It actually felt great to be so free with somebody, but it was always tinged with shame. Like, there was no way that we were going to hold hands while walking on a public street. We didn't want our friends to know about it. We wouldn't touch each other until we were either his dorm room or mine. For some reason, it took quite a while for us, myself especially, to get comfortable enough to touch. So, our relationship was really tinged with shame.

Was it guilt or shame that you were experiencing? Were you feeling guilty or wrong over the acts that you had doing or, shame in feeling wrong for who you were. Guilty means our actions were wrong, while shame, is the person.

Then, it was more shameful!

Do you recall what thoughts went through your mind when you were with him?

Mainly, that I didn't want anybody to know about it!

What would happen if they did?

Well, eventually some of my friends did find out about it! They ended up feeling more hurt that I didn't tell them. But, I didn't feel comfortable telling them about it! So, eventually we were able to talk about it and be more open with each other. But, I still felt very "closeted" in certain ways.

What was the fear that kept you "in the closet?"

I guess I was afraid that people weren't going to like me if they found out! Until, I eventually found out that half of my class was gay! You just think that people were going to judge you. And for someone who's afraid of being judged, it was going to be rough hearing: "You're not normal! You're not regular!" It's just one more thing about you that was not as good!

This fear of being judged negatively appeared to happen first with your sisters, correct?

No. It was with me, from when I was a little kid. Not just with family!

Then, when did it start?

I don't know? All I know, was they expected me to be the best in school and I so I had to be the best in school!

I guess I could blame it on my family, but I guess they were just doing the best they could.

No brothers?

No, it was just me and my two older sisters but, I did feel pretty "picked on" by them.

Were they jealous of you because you were the son and the namesake?

You'd have to ask them, I don't know? I think it was simply the "family "pecking order!" Mother "picks on" the oldest, the oldest picks on the next in line, she in turns takes it out on me, and I have nowhere else to go! I didn't have a pet to take it out on. So, I can't go kick the dog! Not that I would if I did!

Glad to hear it! With regards to your "coming out" process, was it a more positive or negative experience? Are you still struggling with being "out?"

It took me a few years to get comfortable with being gay. I didn't do anything sexually for a couple of years following that initial experience. I believe I began to feel guilty again, because it didn't work out as it was supposed to. I wanted this "big, romantic thing" but he wanted to go onto other things. He was "feeling his oats" as much as he could.

So, he was "feeling his oats" and you didn't want to?

No! I was in love.

You were feeling hurt.

Yes, I was hurt. Yeah. So, for a couple of years I didn't do anything.

When were you most sexual with a woman?

Eventually, I had one situation with a woman who had to get me drunk! And, I had a perfectly great time, but it felt dishonest. From a sexual standpoint, it didn't feel dishonest. From an emotional standpoint, it felt totally dishonest. And that was the one and only time.

So, it was a one shot deal?

Yeah, that was it! I wasn't really that attracted to her, but I hadn't had sex in a very long time. At the time, I was in this summer program. I was interested in this one guy, and she was after me and so, eventually, I "gave in" to her. Don't get me wrong. She was young and beautiful, but I was more attracted to this guy. Although she was sweet and wonderful, it didn't feel right to have sex with her, because there was no chance for a relationship happening.

I recall feeling very guilty about sleeping with her afterward, because I ran away from her. I did end up sleeping with the guy I was after, and we became boyfriends for the summer. One day, she eventually got tired of my avoiding her and ended up coming up to me and saying, "Look, I know what it was, so just relax!" But, I did feel very bad about how I acted with her.

Sounds like you had a large case of the "guilts?"

Yeah, you could say that!

It also sounds as if you've had several bouts with guilt during your "coming out" process?

Yeah, that all comes about with one's upbringing and being raised by America's standards of being incredibly "normal," and then, finding out that you're not! That awareness tended to make me feel shameful and guilty about a lot of things!

You appear to have been struggling toward accepting your own gayness amidst the teachings of your family and society? Asking yourself questions such as, "Where am I" and "how do I fit in?"

I must say, that after that summer program, I really had no problem being "out!" From that point on, I became more willing to connect with people on a sexual level.

Did you want to connect with men on a regular basis?

Actually, I used to make a list of the names of men I had sex with. Before I came to New York City, the list was very small; very small. Then, after I had been in New York City for a few years well, you can forget the list! They just don't make books big enough!

How many men?

Well, not as many as a lot of men, and more than quite a few.

Did you find that your sexual experiences with these men felt so right that they affirmed who you were as a gay man?

Not early on in my gay life but, I think a lot of times, even if I was really "into it," once I had my orgasm; I just wanted to ran away! Unless, it was somebody I really liked. But, just to pick somebody up to have sex with, once it was over, I just wanted to get the Hell out of there!

Why was that?

I think a lot of it was that basically, I'm somebody who has always wanted to fall in love. So, when I realized that the person I just had sex with, was not the "somebody" that I could possibly fall in love with; that the attraction was purely sexual, I end up feeling really bad about it, because I feel as if I just used them.

Yes, but they used you too!

Yes, but everybody feels different about that kind of thing. I think I tend to get mad at myself. I end up getting moody and sort of, run away. But, not all the time with some of the people! It sometimes depends on the day I'm having, or, whether I've had enough sleep or, protein in my system.

One issue that continually arises with all my interviewees is the fine line between meeting for love or sex. In fact, it appears at time that the Gay Communication Game has more to do with sex than it has to do with taking the time to really know the person you're having an intimate relations with. In fact, I question at times, whether gay men can get beyond the sexual innuendo and are able to view one another as just guys "hanging out" without it having to get sexual with men we are physically attracted to.

What has been your most satisfying gay experience?

Right now, I would say the fact that my boyfriend and I being really honest with each other. We've talked though a lot of issues that we both have. And, instead of running away, as I normally do, I've stuck it out! As I said earlier, it's only been seven months! But, it's longer than I've ever been with somebody and I'm really proud of that fact.

I'm really holding onto all the great qualities that he has about himself as my reason to stay in the relationship. And, it is my hope that I won't be running away for some stupid reason.

What do you believe is the reason for having such as history of short-term relationships?

I get bored over their inability to fulfill every item of my checklist. I carried that checklist along with me for many years. Always believing that there is someone better just waiting for me right around the corner! Or, what I thought, was better for me right around the corner.

By better, do you mean a better body or more attractive?

Sometimes, I'd think, "What if I meet someone who is cuter?" or "What if I meet someone who has a better body?" What if I meet somebody who I have more in common with?" For example, if I meet somebody who's a computer programmer? If he loves his work, and, if he is passionate about it, that's great! If they're not; if I meet somebody who's dull and lacks goals or initiative, forget about it!

I want to meet guys who are passionate about what they do in their lives! They win out over the cute guys any day!

When was the last time you felt shame with regards to your gay identity? What do you feel is shameful about being gay?

I'll tell ya. A couple of years ago, I was in the Gay Pride Parade. I was on the <u>Party</u> float. Behind us was a float protesting the government monitoring the sex clubs and on that float, there were these guys wearing jock straps simulating sex acts on the street!

So, during the entire parade these guys were doing their own thing in order to try to shock everyone. I kept thinking, "This is the Gay Pride Parade, why don't you guys go take your protest somewhere else! There are kids watching the parade! These kids had two watch these guys wearing practically nothing, "dry-humping" each other, simulating fellatio! This is not Gay Pride! That has nothing to do with Gay Pride!

There are many who would disagree with you. But, I heard similar sentiments about the Gay Pride Parade in Boston.

Well, that made me really ashamed that day to be in the Gay Pride Parade! I'm getting to the point now, that being gay doesn't mean throwing away all the rules that society has given you! I'm proud to be gay, but that really turned me off to the parade!

Yes! The government does tend to stick it's nose in where it doesn't belong, but that doesn't have anything to do with being gay right now! It's about Gay Pride! Are those guys helping to increase understanding and acceptance for gays during a time of an AIDS crisis? Are they helping to increase funding by acting like that? What impression does it instill in the heterosexual community, many of whom already view us as acting like that?

I never had a problem with ACT UP. I think they've done some great things in the eighties. But to simulate sex acts on the street for kids to see, that just crosses the line! I can just hear the little kid saying to his mother," Why are those two men doing what they're doing Mommy?" What can she say to her child?

Because they're angry, but also, because they're not being entirely compassionate to their audience or their fellow marchers.

I wouldn't have minded a float saying, "Stay out of our bedrooms!" But to have to show the whole world that image! I was just really appalled by it all! I felt it was a real misuse of the entire Gay Pride Parade! A lot of times, I find that many gay people are "heterophobic!" They look at the family unit as being almost hateful.

Are you referring to the term "breeders?"

This is a very devaluing term used by some gays in reference to heterosexuals who have children. I have always equated the term to be similar in distaste to "faggots!" Both terms are used by bitter and angry people within both groups, against those they fear or dislike, often, based on assumptions that the opposing groups will view the other group negatively. Thereby, by making these insulting terms on both sides, it makes the offender feel better about themselves; which we all know, the opposite is true.

In my opinion, both terms should be banished from the English language entirely and never used..

Yes, exactly! I've used that term before as well. But, it is really a terrible thing! It's not as if we should hate them. It's that they shouldn't learn to hate us! We should all try to appreciate what everyone else wants in their lives. WE are not the members of hateful political parties such as the Nazis or the Klu Klux Klan! But for the most part, I shouldn't hate you simply because you are married and have two kids! Then please, don't hate me because I'm not!

Maybe, I don't want to have kids and instead, want to have a boyfriend, a lover, or, a husband. That's all I ask of them is to accept my decisions and not be so quick to "shut me down. "

But, as far as the ACT UP float, that was probably my least favorite moment as a gay person, to walk in front of a float like that!

It's good that we're talking about the shame visible within the gay community, but what about the origins of your shame and guilt with regards to your gayness? I recall your mentioning specific abuse as a child; could you perhaps expand upon them more?

Well, I don't know. I used to do volunteer work for The Henrik-Martin Institute where we would talk about what it was like growing up gay.

The Henrik-Martin Institute is a school for gay and lesbian youth. They used to have an education program where I would volunteer where I would go into schools and corporations with someone from the institute, and conduct workshops on homosexuality.

We would talk about what people think about gay people and why they thought gay people were gay? Eventually, we would "come out" to them and talk about our own personal experiences. One of the things I felt was most important, was how teachers didn't want us to talk about their homosexuality!

I recall them not wanting us to go into grammar schools, because they felt the children were too young for this program. And yet, the kids weren't too young to say the word "fag" to each other on the playground! You'd hear five-year old boys calling each other "faggots!" Well, if they're allowed to use that word in a derogatory way, then they're old enough to know what a "faggot" is, and how "shitty" it is to use that word. They needed to know that some of the people in their lives could be "faggots" too!

The negative aspect of homosexuality it what always has been focused upon! You hear that negative aspect all your life, until some "cool" teacher or a family friend tells you different. But for all those years, all you heard was the negative! So, if all you ever get is that negative thrown at you, then deep down inside, you just know that something must be very wrong with you!

Like for me, I was not attracted to "that girl," I was attracted to "that man, since I was five years old! But, don't tell anybody that you're attracted to "that man!" So, you don't tell anybody anything , and, you keep your secret to yourself! A secret that as your grow older, if someone does find out your secret, you're going to die! You're just going to die!

Was there a fear that someone was going to kill you?

Either someone will want to kill you or for myself, I did get beaten up!

Why?

Well, I "hung out" with the girls mostly. I wasn't athletic. I was very smart. So, guys would come by and call me "faggot!" Every so often, it got physical
.

How often would they get physical?

They'd push me around a little bit.

Were you looking at them?

No. I was on the other side of the playground!

Do you think that if you openly confronted them, things would have been different?

I don't know.

With those upsetting images in mind, what if you could put yourself as you are now, into the body of that little boy, what would have been different?

My favorite joke was always if they called me "faggot," if I knew as I know now, I would look at them and say, "It is Mr. Faggot to you!" But to your question, I really have no clear response to that. I can't even imagine it being any different! There were just too many of them and I was very much in the minority.

Also, that question smacks of, "What would you have done if?" I just can't possibly imagine it going any differently than how it did.

It's obvious that some of those boys were having difficulty dealing with their own "homophobia," or, were gay themselves.

I'm sure they were. They acted it out in one way but, I chose to run away! I think it's all about having a secret that you can't tell anybody. It's not like a happy secret. It's the type of secret that gets buried in a painful place in your being and just sits there.
Do you see that painful secret turning into an ulcer or a tumor?

Absolutely! I remember this one kid in high school who wasn't very popular. I, on the other hand, had my secret but, was still very popular. I was in all the shows there and had good grades.

Sure, there were people I stayed away from, but I didn't have any real problems with getting picked on in high school. But, there was this one kid, who was definitely gay, and, he was a nervous wreck! I remember he wanted to dance and he did perform in the shows, but he was sort of ashamed that people knew about it. When I think of this kid, I recall him being all "twitchy" and nervous. It was very sad to watch, because he was a really nice kid.

Years later, somebody just mentioned him to me, and I asked how he was? The reply I received was, "Oh, he's great! He looks incredible. He's this big, strong, handsome guy."

Well, obviously what happened was, he continued to be a dancer. He got away from high school. He escaped from the "cocoon of hatred," as I would call it, and "came out of his closet." He probably took the dance classes he wanted to take, and got to do what he always wanted to do without anyone telling him "no!"

I remember him. He used to stutter when he talked. It's amazing to hear about his transformation!

Hearing David's painful stories evoke my own painful middle and high school experiences of being viewed as a sissy or weak; the prey for bullies and their followers. But, it was powerful to hear the success made by both David and his classmate, at surviving and escaping their persecutors, just as did I. Not only to escape and survive, but to thrive, especially, the boy who stuttered and twitched. Obviously, the tormented boy found a world which comforted and supported him and provided a safe place to promote himself and his skills.

He flourished once he was out of that hostile environment.

Yes. But, I had my share of nervousness. Grades made me crazy! I had to get good grades!
That makes sense. You had to get approval from somewhere.

Yes, but, I also had girlfriends in high school.

Did you have good male friends as well?

Yes. Two of my friends were guys.

What were they like?

My friends were just "regular" guys. Actually, one of them turned out to be gay and the other turned out to be straight. There was never anything sexual between us. I never even dealt with sex in high school! In fact, I was so amazed years later when I found out that some of my male friends in high school were having sex too!

And you didn't know about it?

No, I didn't know about it! I thought everybody's dates were like the dates that I went out on. You go to dinner, you "hang out" at the girl's parent's house for a while, and you go home. At least, that was what I thought they were doing?

Well, I think you've made up for what you've missed.

I think so too.

THE GAY COMMUNICATION GAME AT PLAY

But as for those feelings of shame and guilt, do you those feelings had an adverse effect on how you interact with other gay men today?

Yes, definitely!

How?

It's funny. I saw that question on your questionnaire and I'm actually better at dealing with other gay men than I used to be. For the longest time, I couldn't make eye contact with people at all! I couldn't say, "hi" to somebody, because I thought that they were going to think I was "coming on" to them. As a result, I had a tendency to cut myself off too often from other gay men, for fear of having my intentions misunderstood.

Did you feel that your sentiments would be equally shared by other gay men?

Most definitely! For example, when I'm cruising somebody and they're cruising me, I can tell if they're attracted to me from the "sneer" they give me. They don't smile, they don't say "hi," they just go like this. (*David pantomimes a sneer on his face*). Then, I know that they are fully "into me."

Why do they sneer? Do they think its sexy?

I think gay men are afraid to make themselves vulnerable to somebody else for whatever reason. I also think that a lot of gay men don't make themselves readily available by smiling first, because they're afraid you might get the wrong idea! The smile is interpreted as "I want to sleep with you," instead of meaning, "Hi, how are you?"

For example, when you walk into the steam room at my gym, you are in a sense, "slicing through" this sexual tension. I tend to want to stretch and even talk to a friend, but that's less of the norm. What occurs instead, is nobody talking to you or even looking at you, unless they know you. It's funny, you can almost see a "wall" between people, unless somebody makes some kind of "overture" that causes the other to smile. But if you smile at somebody, there has to be a reason behind it. It's as if, everybody has this "secret agenda" all the time!

In the gym, especially, as you are working out, the people there can be downright nasty! I mean, there are people in my gym with which I've seen working out for some seven or eight years, and if I say "hi" to them, they will <u>not</u> say "hello" to me!

Do you think it's because they think you have sexual intentions toward them?

I can't see any other reason why? I do it just to be friendly, but I think most gay men tend to spend inordinate amounts of time categorizing! For example: "Attracted to that one, I should say "Hi! "Not attracted to that one; I'm going to ignore him!" "Who is that person? I've never seen him before. Let me see if he says "hi" to me." I think people do that!

For the longest time, you couldn't tell if someone was gay or not. Therefore, one tended to be afraid to say "hi" or smile, for you never knew what reaction you were going to get? But a lot of times, you just knew someone was gay, and, they would look at you and I would make this face. (David pantomimes a sneer)

You gave that response because you thought they had a sexual agenda?

Right! They were going to think something of me.

What were they going think of you?

That maybe I was communicating that I was attracted to you and wanted to sleep with you. That you found out that I was attracted to you too!

Then what would happen?

It makes you vulnerable! It's all a game! It's ONE BIG, FAT GAME! It's hard to explain the game because its works differently with different people. But in general, people don't want to be the one who initiates the game, because it puts them in a vulnerable spot! To go up to somebody and say, "I'm really attracted to you" is frightening!. The power then, automatically goes to that other person! They could say, "Yes" but ,they could also say," NO!" You've already given away your power!

But, I tend to look at the situation as being honest. I even have more admiration for the person who says "Hello," instead of the one who goes like this: (*pantomimes turning his face away in disgust*).

That's an excellent point with regards to "giving away your power!" But don't you think that some guys like to play the game?

Absolutely!

Even love the game?

Absolutely, yes!

Even devote their lives to it?

Absolutely, it is true.

They don't even want a relationship!

Yes! The really beautiful ones that you see strutting down the street, they know that everyone is looking at them. So if you look at them and smile, they're also the ones who sometimes just turn away and won't give you the time of day.

And that attitude is what I find totally unattractive.

Yes, but people do it! And I know it's horrible. It's a horrible thing.

It's as if they're dismissing you before you have the opportunity to dismiss them?

Yes, exactly. I think that's EXACTLY what's going on. When you think about when two people connect, you think of two people looking into each other's eyes and saying, "hello." That's a natural thing. Then, think about another two people who connect, but one person suddenly breaks off the connection! How many times a day do people do that?

In New York City it happens all the time!

Yes! In New York City it happens all the time! But, think about how it must build up inside of you? That instead of going by your natural impulse, which for many people, is to say, "hello," you choose to continually break off the connection and thereby shut down the energy! When I realize how many times in my life I would do that, it makes me sad.

Then why did you do that?

Because, I WAS AFRAID! IT'S ALL FEAR! Fear, that I'm going to smile at somebody ,and they are going to ignore me!

Which is exactly what happened, therefore your fear is based on reality.

Yes!

David is clearly describing how the "Gay Communication Game" operates and how the game simply does not work! The clear root of the game is FEAR OF BEING REJECTED! This fear is what keeps David and all others from taking the risk of approaching someone they are attracted to and then, let the "sparks fly, "or, on another, make a new friend.

This desire to approach and engage in conversation is called the Social Exchange Theory where two communication partners weigh the costs and benefits of getting to know more about someone they are attracted to either physically, sexually, or personality-wise. Unfortunately, gay men are more sensitive to being rejected, as a result of living in a world that for the majority, simply rejects them for being gay, even as a child. Therefore, they are less willing to take the risk to approach someone who may continue the rejection cycle and as a result, the game begins.

Returning to your former classmate who was a "nervous wreck," it is amazing how he flourished once he was outside of that hostile environment.

I was told he did. I never saw him.

I don't see any reason why the person who told you would exaggerate his description to you?

But for the sake of argument, say he did flourish within a gay-friendly environment; do you see him becoming one of those "body boys with attitude" or, do you envision him treating other gay men with respect and equality, unlike the way he was treated as a child?
He was always a nice guy in school despite, all the abuse.

Do you think he stayed a nice guy? Or, was he a nice guy because he had to play that role within a clearly hostile environment? Do you think he had no choice but, to be a nice guy?

No, I think he was always a nice guy, and he'll continue to be a nice guy.

But, do you think he might have changed to be more like those aggressive types who bullied him? Or, maybe he freed himself from playing the role of the "nice guy" and is now the aggressor?

I am illustrating for David how some gay men, similar to any abused child, could take on the negative character traits of their abuser, as a defense mechanism to avoid further hurt by harming or, abusing others he perceives as being more vulnerable or weaker than himself.

He probably won't allow himself to treat people in a similar way to the way he was treated. At least, that's how I feel about myself!.

Okay, then what is it about you that relates to the boy?

That, I won't treat people the same way as I feel I was treated. I can get really angry, especially now! For example, when I say "hi" to guys in my gym and they ignore me, I get angry! I mean, I'm not making any sexual overtures! I'm just being friendly! (*David begins speaking in a loud voice*) When you see somebody every day for seven years, and you finally make eye contact and they ignore you! Fuck you!!!

That's what I'd like to say to them when that happens to me at the gym or a bar.

I do! I don't say it to them, but when they walk by, I murmur "fuck you."

What if they hear you?

I don't care if they hear me!

*It is for that exact reason, and for other similar situations, that I chose to write this book! *(I recount to David my Hampton's story of being ignored by my supposed gym friend) I still feel conflicted on whether I should greet this guy in the gym when I see him?*

I generally don't give people more than one chance. And then, I know there are times when I feel real "bitchy" too. When people address me and I murmur "hi" and walk on. Its times like that, when I think I should give people more than one chance.

I am considering giving him another chance to redeem himself.

You never know what's at work inside a person! I'll try to give people lots of chances if in the past, they were more social with me. I don't expect everybody to say "hi" to me when I walk by them. But if you make eye contact with somebody and you start to smile at them, and then they pull away, it's upsetting! I find that behavior to be a very unhealthy thing to do too much! For yourself, not even for them! If somebody is not friendly to you, you're simply denied a basic human connection with them.

With regards to my experience, if the person who was uncommunicative to you on one day was more friendly and communicative the next day, would you still talk to them? Say for instance, in the gym?

I probably would, but I wouldn't be as happy to see him!

Would you have asked him why he didn't respond to you the other day?
Yes, somewhere down the line I would have. Especially in the gym, since I'm there to work out. I'm not there to make close friends.

Well, with this particular guy, I shared a lot with him and vice versa.

Well, then, that's different. I would have said something because I think it gets to be really unhealthy to say nothing.

It's rejecting.

To me, it's not even about rejection. It's not about that. It's about the communication being cut off, which feels very unfulfilled.

What do you feel unfulfilled about? Is it about the relationship or, the connection with the other person?

Well, it plays upon the question: "Why did they cut the connection off?" It's usually about their not wanting to be vulnerable. Their discomfort about whether you're "coming on" to them? It's for all the wrong reasons!

I actually did this experiment at a party with someone famous with whom I had been friendly with; in fact, we I slept together! I saw him a year later and he was very cold to me when I came up to him! Later that night, I saw him at a party. Again, he was acting the same way to me! So, I went up to him and said, "Listen, I just wanted you to know that when I came up to you earlier today, I had no agenda, whatsoever, other than to say "hi," and I walked away. Later on, he came over to me and said, "Oh, hi. How are you doing?"

David's experiment clearly indicates how fearful we tend to be when approaching someone we wish to know but, stop ourselves from taking the opportunity to meet them when we get the chance. It all sounds very much like teenagers who play games and secret tests with one another in order to try to get the upper hand with one another.

Sometimes, I just believe that people feel you have a special agenda with them that keeps them from being open with you. I mean, he must have thought that I had some sexual agenda with him or, I wanted to take advantage of his celebrity status? That was NOT the case! I simply said "hi," because we shared something special before. I didn't hate him! He didn't hate me, I didn't think it was that much to say, "hi, how are you?" Is that asking too much?

For some people, I guess it IS TOO MUCH to expect, that everybody needs to connect with each other? But sometimes, there's no reason NOT to! As I said, I don't expect everybody to walk up to me and say, "Hi David, Hi David, Hi David!" I don't expect that! But, there are times when there's no reason NOT to! If you've made eye contact and your choice is to turn away, or, to either say "hi;" to smile, and acknowledge the other person, that's your choice! But, I think we do too much turning away in general.

But, it also takes a lot of emotional energy to keep turning away from people.

Yes! It takes a lot of energy!

So then, how much energy does it take simply to respond with a greeting? It's offensive not to respond within our gay culture, but in other countries, it's a grievous insult!

But this issue fits right into the attitudes of superiority and indifference that many gay men demonstrate to one another. Do you feel these attitudes stem from their own shame and guilt about being gay?

(Indifferent) Well, I'm sure. But, I just think that behavior is inherent in a lot of people.

Do you mean the behavior of the general gay population?

Yes. I remember going to this bar one night, and there was this cute guy from the neighborhood. He was just standing around with his shirt off, and obviously on some drug. There were a bunch of guys "hanging around" him and he was just oblivious to all of them! It was as if there was no one there who met with his approval! It wasn't as if he couldn't turn and smile to somebody?

Instead, he would look totally past people! It was all about: "What do I want? What do I see? What do I like?" His choice to ignore people was based on: "You're not beautiful enough for me. Why isn't his shirt off; what's he hiding? You're not dancing with me until I see what you've got!"

I just continued to stand there and watch him perform his act, and I said to myself, "Yech!"

(I have a difficult time containing my laughter).

David's comments of this egotistical and rude gay man reverberate with what the primary focus of what this book is all about. That as a means of validating his own superiority over others, this man is choosing to demean and dismiss others he deems as inferior or unacceptable to be potential suitors. That is anyone was fortunate enough to be acknowledged by him, it would be an affirmation of one's "hotness! "similar to that of a movie star.

Unfortunately for this man and others like him, they more often cause others to feel bad about themselves, and become increasing hesitant of taking potential opportunities to approach other attractive men for fear of rejection.

I did see him occasionally give some eye contact to some people. It was this kind of eye contact! *(At this point, David begins to pantomime this egotistical man's attitude. His posture has this pompous, muscle-bound caricature of a snob to it. When he glances in someone's direction, the glance is full of disdain and disapproval).*

So I ask you, why couldn't he give anyone polite eye contact and then look away? For instance, if you say "hi" to somebody and they want to talk further, but you're not in the mood, then find some excuse to politely move away. But, don't act in the same gross manner as that guy did!

I remember seeing men act in an identical manner as him, when I went to the old Roxy or other NYC dance clubs. I often had the strongest impression that I was being judged and failing dreadfully!

Yeah, it's gross. It's really gross.

Do you feel that the whole "meat market" mentality of: "I'll talk to you if you're Mr. Perfect!" needs to change?

Yes! I am tired of men in general "acting out" in bars, where unless you're interested in someone sexually, for the most part, you have no reason to talk to people! That's how it works out to be.

Understand it, because there are a lot of people who think that way!

Also, there are a lot of people in those clubs who by avoiding you, they leave themselves available for the "right one" when he comes along.
It's a "sexual arena!" Asking someone to dance is usually a prelude to "let's fuck!"

You are very right! But sometimes, there are some pretty interesting people out there; some pretty nice people to dance or socialize with as well. Yet, how many times have you stood next to someone in these clubs and you see this? (*David demonstrates a person with a rigid neck that appears determined to only look straight in front*). I mean, you see these people making sure they can't possibly turn their heads in your direction, and if they do, their head will break off!

They can't look at you because they're not interested in you OR, "I'm really interested in you so, I can't look at you!"

Why can't they look at you if they're really interested in you?

Because, they don't want you to know that they're really attracted to you!

Why?
Because by looking at you, the message is being sent that he is interested in meeting you and that puts them in the vulnerable spot of being rejected.

Then they end up going home alone or, with someone they don't really want!

Because most people are afraid of rejection so, going home with a "second choice" or alone, is the result of their fear of saying, "hi," As a result, if this person really doesn't want you, they will go away and you will be rejected.

And you will feel like what?

You will feel like a reject! That's why we're ALL afraid of rejection, not just gay men!

What can you do to prevent that "angst" from happening night after night? What's your advice to that person who goes through that silent torture?

For myself, I finally learned how to make the first move!

Say, I wanted to meet somebody for whatever reason? Whether they were attracted to me or, whether their tits were nice! Whether they were talking to a friend of mine or, they just looked like they were having a good time and I wanted to meet them. I force myself to smile at them or in the least, say hello to them!

Guaranteed, it put me in some pretty uncomfortable situations because I'm not really good at doing that! But, I've met some of the people that I would normally have been afraid to approach. In fact, I eventually met the guy that I wanted to meet, because I forced myself to say hello.

How did you do it?

I'm a pretty good conversationalist. Once I get past saying hello, I'm pretty good about talking. It's hard! But, it's all about going after what you want! Like I said before, as kids, we didn't go after what we wanted because we were afraid to. As adults, in the theatrical world as well, the more you know about what you want, the greater the chance that you'll eventually go out and get it! But, you have to after it and not cut the communication off!

Your advice to my gay readers is to do what?

Is to try!

(Dramatically-crying) **"But, I'm going to be rejected!"**

So what? You're going to be rejected? It's going to happen. We're all going to be rejected! Even the most beautiful man in the entire world whom you think is your ideal, is going to be rejected by somebody!

Yes, because somebody is going to think he's either going to be arrogant or would be too self-focused.

Yes, and that's going to make him go more "into his shell!"

Or, put on his mask!

What I mean by "mask" is similar to what David is referring to as "his shell." It is simply the place we retreat to when we are fearful of the reaction we may receive from the outside world or, fearful of appearing vulnerable or weak; simply put, the operative word is "fear."

Yes, and what I'm saying is, "Get out of your shell!" Force yourself to say hello to somebody. Force yourself not to break eye contact and continue that connection! Once I said to myself, "I do that too often! I cut myself off!" It made it so much easier for me to meet someone that I wanted to meet instead of running away from it!

I know that many of heterosexual men could easily identify with your statements having experienced rejection themselves. But for the gay man, rejection has so much more emotional impact than it appears it has for "straight men on the prowl."

For example, I've observed "straight guys" pursuing women in the bars and dance clubs, and have been shocked by the vicious responses that some of these women give them. I have even asked my female college students as to why they respond to these men in such a hostile manner, and their response was, "they want more than to meet or dance with me, they want sex! And no matter what men think, we're not always looking for sex!"

I think a lot of it has to do with nobody being honest! But a lot of these guys approach these women saying, "Hey!" Or, they're checking out their tits while they're talking. I don't know? I'm not a woman, but as a man, I think these guys need to work on their approach!

Yes, but these guys also seem unfazed by the rejection. They just shrug it off and move onto the next woman they see.

In general, "straight guys" have gotten a good deal of support for their egos over many years, while we gay men have not!

That is very interesting; why do you say that?

Because in high school, where many of our gay tendencies were formed, we were not allowed to go after who we wanted to go after. We couldn't get together in groups and say, "Hey, I think that guy is really, really cute! So, I think I'm going to go and try to get some sex off him in the car!" Straight guys can say that about getting women but can we?

I agree.

Well, we were NOT able to do that! Not only that, a lot of times, you don't know who's straight and who's gay? Maybe New York is a little easier. You could be at work and say something, thinking that guy is gay, and end up in an embarrassing situation!

Don't you have working "Gay-dar?" (A gay man's ability to recognize another gay man)

Say what? Yeah, my "Gay-dar" is good! But, living in Chelsea and being in the theater, it's easy! How hard could it possibly be in the gay ghetto?

Yeah, it's pretty evident around here who's gay and who's not! But, in your interactions with others who are not just gay men, do you feel the issues of shame and guilt with regards to your gayness has had a positive, or, negative effect on your interactions with the heterosexual community? Being involved in the theater, did relationships form more easily for you?

Well, for the most part, I am really "out!" Not for the most part, I am really out! I "make no bones about it." I don't walk around with a sign saying, "I'm gay!" But, in natural conversations with anybody, I will mention my boyfriend as casually as they would mention their partner. I live my life as a fully gay man however, there are situations when I'm in the minority.
If I'm in one of my married friends' houses, and I can sense when there are people around who have not had a lot of experience being around gay people, I'll pull back! I'll monitor myself for them. Not really **for them**, but for me!

There are times when I get the feeling, "I'm not as good as you because you are married. Society loves you! Society doesn't love me!" All those old tapes come up in a situation like that! Or, if I'm auditioning for a group of "Good, ole boy," casting agents and directors, who say when I enter a room, "Oh, here comes another fag!" I can still feel a little sensitive about that. I usually "wear my homosexuality as such a flag!" But sometimes, people pick up on it in the wrong way.

In Hollywood, there is a good deal of "homophobia." Do you feel it's that mentality that works against you and other gay men in pursuing more romantic leading roles?

Yeah, but I'm not giving up on pursuing those roles. There are a lot of gay men in Hollywood playing romantic leads and getting away with it! They're just not "out" yet.

Yes, it's said to be "professional suicide" for most gay men to "come out of the closet" in Hollywood. But some actors have decided to "come out" and their careers continue to survive. Yes, some gay actors have made good career for themselves in Hollywood playing gay roles. All it takes is a good filmmaker to make a gay role become a more positive image. It's going to take some strides from among some of the talented writers and directors who "don't give a shit," to bring about some positive change. If you leave it up to the "Hollywood, money men" forget it! But if you leave it to the more positive-thinking directors, they won't care what your sexuality is if you're right for the part.

Yet, there are actors like your "friend" Will Smith, who will refuse to "go the limit" in playing a gay role. What we often see, is Harvey Firestein panicking in <u>Independence Day</u>.

I love Harvey Firestein. But, it was scary for me to see him play that role in <u>Independence Day</u>.

Why was it scary?

Anytime I see the stereotype being played, it bothers me. But, I love Harvey Firestein. I think he has done a lot of good for us and I have a lot of admiration for him.

So, what are your impressions of how heterosexual men and women relate to us now? Do you feel that there still is a barrier that comes between us in our communication with one another? For example, "Society may accept you but, it still doesn't fully accept us!"

It depends on the situation. There have been many times when I've been with heterosexual men and women, where it's not about sexuality. It's not about being heterosexual or homosexual.; it's all about being a person! In those situations, it's very easy just to talk as a person.

I'm uncomfortable, when the subject turns to be about my being a homosexual and they're being heterosexual. I've been in situations, where I've had to defend the behavior of my community in a political discussion. For the most part, the situation does not have to be about who's straight and who's gay. Everything doesn't have to be about being gay! It's more about "Hi, How are you?"

What advice would you give to our readers about how to communicate with their families and friends on the subject of shame and the acceptance of their gay lifestyle?

First, it has to do with your accepting that you are a gay person! I'll put it in actor's terms; you ask yourself, "Why did you get the role instead of someone else?" It's all because you put your own "stamp" on the work! You personalize the work, meaning you put your own little idiosyncrasies into it. You also put your sense of humor and your keen sensibilities into it. That's how you play the role. You own it and make it yours!

Well, it's the same thing in dealing with people. When you are talking with somebody, you want them to get to know something of who you are. You don't just want to shout out to them, "Hey, I'm a gay man!" That's only a part of who you are, but as a gay man, there's so much involved in being gay. I've really learned that with dealing with my family, as with others, it's all about who you are!

If you're funny, and if you like to make people laugh, don't try to make people laugh because you're afraid of them! In other words, don't lose who you are because you're afraid of somebody or, because you're afraid they won't accept you! You have to fully be who you are in any situation, otherwise, you let FEAR win and fear has no place! Fear has no place in my life!

That's easier said than done.

Yes, but we have to all find out what makes us afraid and face it! Otherwise, we just don't get what we want, and we don't connect with one another!

Did you feel that "coming out" to your family and friends was an important step toward dealing with your fear of their possible rejection? Was it an important thing for you to do?

Yes, it was something that I had to do! I knew it was inevitable. But again, I can relate this question to my theatrical work. Somebody can say to me, "I thought you were really great in the show!" If I don't think I did a good job, it doesn't matter what they say, good or bad! I really need it to come from ME in order for me to feel comfortable with myself. It helped that I had the support from those around me but, I still needed to feel comfortable with myself.

What was it like "coming out" to your parents?

They were great. We were sitting in their home watching *Star Search*. I was home, coming from performing in an out-of-town engagement before returning to Chicago. I said to my mom that I wanted to talk to them something important later in the evening. My mom replied, "Why don't you just tell us now?" I agreed. So, my father came into the room and I told them. My father seemed okay with it. My mother played more of the devil's advocate, "It doesn't sound as if it's something you really want. It sounds like its perhaps something you're no exactly sure?

"I said, "Mom, I'm gay today, down the line anything can happen I guess, but today, I'm gay and

I probably will be gay for the rest of my life!" I had been gay for some time already when I finally told her, "Mom, if you're trying to find an "out" here, it's probably not going to happen."

Did she cry?

No, they were good about it.

Do you think that they already knew?

They sort of did. They had been really good about it. Originally, they came from a position of: "Don't tell anybody," to actually telling all my relatives! They did all that, because they wanted me to feel comfortable around them. Since then, my mother has done a lot of reading and she's become really sensitive about things. She comes to my shows! She knows how important being "out" is. I've trained them all!

You're funny. Are you the only son?

Yep! The name stops with me!

That statement screams of gay shame and is constantly being uttered by gay men because with that statement comes a strong sense of guilt. Guilt mainly because we know that with that statement we are acknowledging that we are disappointing our parents with little to no possibility of ever having children (boys especially) and carrying on the family name.

Did you feel a certain amount of shame about that?

For a while, when I realized that the name stops with me, I did. But then I thought, "That's just one more pressure in my life that I won't have to deal with!" That I don't have to get married and raise children, so the name doesn't stop with me! I was finally able to put my happiness first! That my own happiness was more important than having the name continue.

Do your sisters have children?

Yes.

So, your parents still have grandchildren to love? That helps to relieve some pressure?

One of my sisters has three children. The other one isn't married, but she wants to be married and have children.

When did you "come out" to your sisters?

I decided to come out to my sisters before my parents, in the early eighties.

What was their response?

There was no real response. Everything was fine.

Do you feel it changed the dynamics of your relationship with them?

No, it didn't change how they reacted to me. They were great to me sometimes and "bitchy" to me at other times. There was no difference, which is good!
Yeah, it's great! Nothing changed with regards to the playfulness you had with your sisters.

I got lucky. I know that a lot of families are not like that.

What advice would you give our readers on how they can treat one another better and not carry on the shame.

Force yourself to say "hello" and not to cut off the communication! If someone smiles at you or looks at you, at least acknowledge it and move on.

What was your best technique for meeting men in social places such as bars, clubs, and parties? What line worked for you? Your technique need not to be verbal, it can also be nonverbal.

(David makes a big smile) It used to be a tight t-shirt, a shy smile, and a friendly "Hello."

And it worked.

Pretty much; when I got up the nerve to do it!

Better work out at that gym then?

Some of my self-esteem is still in my body, but it's getting to be less and less important.
As long as it's not totally who I am! I don't want to be with somebody who's only interested in my body!

I know when you want to meet somebody you want to put all your best assets forward! But the way that I met the man I'm with now, was through friends. It was winter, and we were both wearing heavy sweaters. It had nothing to do with our bodies. For me, it was his smile and his intelligence that really got to me! I think it was the same for him. Just like with the acting, just "show up and be who you are!"

That sounds perfect but in focusing on the physical, what physical attributes do you find unattractive in a man and what non-physical attributes do you find unattractive in a man?

When I see men who look uncomfortable in their bodies, I get unnerved. They could have the most beautiful bodies in the entire world, but if they look uncomfortable in it, then it's a big turn-off!

How do they look uncomfortable?

Being stiff or, showing it off all the time! Also, if I can tell that they're taking steroids to pump up their overdeveloped bodies, then that's also a big turn-off!

Non-physically, I find it really unattractive when I smile at someone and they sneer back at me! Or, they refuse to acknowledge my smile! That really pisses me off!

You said earlier that you knew that, "a man was attracted to you if they smiled at you." But, you actually found that sneer to be an unattractive behavior?

No, I don't like it! They think they're being sexy, but for me, it means "Fuck you!" It is really unattractive when people sneer like that!

I think it's really unattractive when you see this big, "butch" guy walk into the room and he turns out to be this big, huge, gigantic girl! I mean, it's okay to be this "big girl," but what are you trying to put on with the "butch act?" Then again, it's just the "shell" covering over the fear, which is the truer self!

What non-physical attributes do you find attractive?
Intelligence is number one! If you're smart, that's A-number-One for me! I don't think I could be with someone if he couldn't "get" my sense of humor. He also has to make me smile at least once a day.

I don't want him to be less successful than me! I don't want him to be struggling like I have been struggling! I know how painful it is to be struggling in my career. This sounds really shallow, but I know how depressed I get when my career is not going the way I want for it to go. Therefore, I really want to be with someone who's happy in his career, so that, only one of us is miserable!

I know how difficult it can be when your lover is struggling with his career while you're struggling with your own. Even if your career is successful, it's difficult when his is not going as well. The competition between two men in a relationship has to always be addressed and not ignored. (See: The Male Couple's Guide by Eric Marcus)

I'm also saying, "Don't negate people who are less successful than you are!" I'm just saying that it's really hard when your whole relationship focuses on having to "buoy" him up all the time! I think one of the biggest reasons why I've never had a long-term relationship, is because my career is just too important for me! I've always given my career the highest priority! I was not ready to hear my lover constantly say, "David, it's going to be okay. You'll get that next job" or, "Don't worry you'll make more money next year." I didn't want that either! I didn't want them to constantly feel the need to tell me, that I would be okay.

So, what would you tell the reader who's lover tends to do that or, vice versa?

There's nothing wrong with telling your lover, "Honey, shut up!" Your lover doesn't need to have you constantly reassure him. He should know that everything is going to be okay! Or at least, inside, he should know that everything is going to be okay. You have to be careful not to be pitying him a little bit too much.

Is there anything else you'd care to add about those unattractive non-physical attributes you find in others, including, gay men?

I just don't like "bitchiness!" I don't mind a little gossiping, but I hate it when the gossip gets to be really mean. I don't like mean people! Especially, a mean gay man!

"Here, here" to that comment being that there is nothing worse than a mean gay man and the nasty comments that comes out of their mouths when they spew that bitchiness. I for one, have a friend who when in drag becomes one bitchy queen who when out of drag, is less bitchy and mean. As far as that friend is concerned, I see him as sad and lonely who has never had a mutually loving intimate relationship with another man. Instead, his closest relationship is with his elderly mother who has embraced his gayness and enjoys his large grouping of friends.

As far as his "bitchiness," I believe he uses it as a source of humor and not to be completely mean- spirited. But, his comments have often provoked angry responses from others including his mother that has gotten him some unexpected backlash including being sued by a former friend.

Sometimes I hear people being critical, but they're very funny about it. I can accept that, because there's at least something sort of constructive about it. But, if a person is just being mean, and there's nothing else but meanness in what he says, I really hate that! Being mean and judgmental is a very unattractive combination.

I tend to believe that those mean people come from a place of poor self-esteem. They truly feel less than those with whom they tend to criticize.

It's easier to criticize others than face your own failings or deficiencies.

This one gay man I once associated with was constantly critical of others and the opinions of others. He once responded to me when I mentioned the upcoming Gay Pride Parade, "What's to be proud about? Being gay is shameful!"

Yuck! I'll pass on meeting him!

Yes, I quickly admonished him and separated myself from getting to know him any further but on the other side, what about arrogance in a gay man?

153

Sometimes, I think a little arrogance can be very sexy but only sometimes. It all depends on the person. Sometimes, it's a little misplaced. But arrogance, can also suggest confidence, and I think confidence is very sexy. It's a great attribute to have! That's always been a problem of mine so, I very attracted to people who are very confident.

That makes good sense but what do you envision as your future with regards to your gay life and what goals do you hope to accomplish in your lifetime?

Right now, I'm hoping that this guy that I'm seeing and I will have many years together. I don't know. This is the first person that I've ever really felt this way with. That a long-term relationship can be a definite possibility!

What is it about him that separates him from the others?

He wants me for more than my body! He also doesn't only tell me what I want to hear. He's very honest with me. I like his politics! We have similar careers. That's about all I want to share about him at this time but there is a definite possibility that he may move in with me.

Is it a possibility soon?

Yeah. We did talk about it. Let's just say that, he's the first person with whom the possibility of his moving in doesn't sound like a crazy scheme.

Would you plan to live in either your place or his?

I don't know. I like my apartment.

That all sounds good but other than love, what goals do you hope to accomplish in the near future? Specifically, has the acceptance of your gayness aided you toward being more assertive in stating your needs and desires to others?

Well, I don't want to play gay roles all my life! I would like to take some of my experiences and put them to work artistically. Either theatrically, in a screenplay, or, whatever. I have a lot of stories to tell and I think they are stories that many people would find interesting. So, I'd like to bring those situations forward in an artistic way, somehow? Not just to say other people's words!

You mean writing about them?

Yes! I do write! What the writing is going to be, I just don't know yet? That's one thing I would like to do.

I would always like to be a spokesman for the gay community. I view myself as somebody who can be "totally out" and can still have a thriving television and film acting career. I just want to be somebody who doesn't give in to the homophobia that appears to dominate the Hollywood community. I believe that I can have a full career and be a happy and "out" gay man!

Yes. I know from my own experience, that once I started to "let go" of that shame and guilt associated with being gay, it allowed me to become an active participant in shaping my own destiny. I began to feel "freer" about who I am. "So, you can support me by allowing me to be who I am, but it's not essential. I'd love the support but, I'll still be okay."

Do you feel that by taking a stand on asserting who you are as a gay man have allowed you to shape clearer goals in your life?

Well, you certainly find out who your friends are! And, I feel that I've been a good instructor for people just by being who I am. I know that my niece and nephews know that their Uncle David is gay, and through me, they should not have any problem with people who are gay as they grow up. Maybe when they hear one of their friends say, "He's a fag" in a derogatory way, then, they'll turn around and say, "Hey, my Uncle David's gay and he's a great guy so, you shouldn't put them down!"

I think that's a great opportunity to do a little instructing about what it's like to be gay. I know that I have instructed people about being gay in my theatrical work! For instance, when I was in a production of *Jeffrey* down in Florida, the majority of the audience was over sixty-five, and many of them didn't know what being HIV was!

With that specific show they were able to see a very positive portrayals of gay people, specifically, HIV-positive people! They were able to see two men, one HIV-positive and the other, HIV-negative, fall in love and have it be all about the love that bonds them!

Theater, film and the arts can be so instructive for people. You can use them creatively in a really wonderful means toward expressing your beliefs! I always wanted to do that! That's why I'm an artist!

And, you are an artist!

I'd like to think so.

Being gay is only one role that you play in life.

Yes.

It's a large role, because it has a lot to do with who you are.

Totally, but we're not just gay people, we're people! I know it sounds so, "Pollyannaish." But, when people begin to realize its only one aspect of the person to whom we are is when they begin truly understand us! It's like what I told these kids when I went into their schools and talked about being gay. I would say, "We are more alike than we are different! And, if all you do

155

is concentrate on our differences, and you don't understand them, then you will continue to be afraid of us! But, if you start to concentrate on what we have in common, then our differences will not seem so different to you! You'll begin to say, "Oh, that's just sort of, who you are."

That reminds me of a time when my lover of years ago and I, were attacked by a group of young men at Santa Monica Beach. I recall that after they kicked him, I started beating up on them and then everything stopped, as if they were in shock!

At that point, we began to talk about our similarities rather than our differences. I remember one boy who said, "You had girlfriends?" It was an amazing experience! He struck me at the time as being very gay-looking and wanting desperately to come to terms with his sexuality. But then all of a sudden, one of the angriest boys started fighting again, and we were back in the fray until more gay men arrived to help us and the boys ran away.

Sometimes, I just want to throw my hands up in the air and give up on all this violence. Why can't people just talk to each other? Why do people do what they do?

I believe that maybe these sad boys "gay bash" because they're latent homosexuals? Sometimes, they just believe that they hate you. Sometimes they believe that, "Well, if they're gay, then they must be weaker than me." You never know why right away. The fact is, nobody should do it! I don't care what your reasons are, you just shouldn't do it! Nobody is going to listen to me, right?

I'm listening and my readers will listen.

Thank you.

And thank you so much for your time and your wonderful stories and insights.

Thank you. I had fun.

END OF FIRST INTERVIEW

**July 27, 2011 - Updated Phone Interview with David now living in Los Angeles*

David, what has changed from 1998 when we had our last interview?

Living in Los Angles is very different from New York City. Out here one feels more isolated. I don't get to see gay people all the time. New York is one big "melting pot" but, in Studio City there are less gay men around unless I go to my gay gym or go to West Hollywood but I don't even see that many gay guys in West Hollywood unless you go to the bars.

What about at the bars and clubs?

I'm just not into cruising like I used to be. Mostly, it's just a waste of time and bars that cater to men more my age are not as plentiful as the bars for younger gays. And anyways, older gay men tend to talk more all about their homes and their possessions and that bores me.

Sounds as if you're not in love with living in Los Angles?

No, I don't love Los Angeles because my life has been a bit frustrating as of late and I am trying to figure out where I want to be in the next five years.

Work has always been very important and the work I choose is acting. I have always measured my self-worth with my acting and right now I am in this terrific show.

How are your relationships with men going?

With men, I know what I have to offer. But as of late, they all tend to have boyfriends and want just to play on the side; that is not what I am looking for.

What are you looking for? Are you attracted to younger or older men?

As I have gotten older, I find that the young ones are more attracted to me and are the ones who will approach me but, I tend to prefer men closer to my age.

That's makes sense to me as well but with regards to a relationship, what is your primary concern with regards to finding love?

I just don't want to be the guy who becomes the "cat lady!"

Wow, that's an interesting image! Are you saying you're afraid of becoming an unmarried spinster? What can you do to prevent that from ever happening?

I have to get myself out there and meet more guys in a more social setting; not just the bars or clubs! Also, I have to try to keep from getting too "jaded," and make up my mind that this is what I want to do and not hold myself back from going up and introducing myself to a man I am attracted to.

Then what excites you now?

I am very excited by the challenges before me and in my work I am challenged! I also want to be more spontaneous! For example, "Let's go to Vegas!" I want to be able to just be spontaneous and do something like that!

How has gay communication changed in the years since our first interview in 1998?

It's all about the Internet and one's I-phone! I have even seen a group of gay guys sitting together and everyone is texting other people and never even looking at one another, unbelievable! I see this type of communication occurring everywhere and it is very frustrating to say the least!

With regards to texting or the internet, what problems exist in that type of communication?

Don't text me if we are talking about something emotionally charged. Call me on the phone if you want to know what's going on in my life! Don't text or email anything emotional and don't text me with highly emotional feelings!

I know exactly what you mean and I tell my students not to text when they have something emotional to say to someone!
Yes, communication has definitely changed especially with the younger generation. And I have to tell you that all of these websites get pretty old real quick! Especially with all these online chat rooms or "hookup" sites such as Manhunt!

Yes, what do you think of these online sites such as Manhunt where there is a clearly a lack of tact when interacting with gay men online for a quick "hookup!" Such as people contact you, you start chatting and no response?

If you have good photos on Manhunt you can get laid! AS far as poor communication, that's the chance you take when you chat online. For instance, I know when a guy is not interested in me online – they just stop typing! There's less face-to-face interaction unless you meet up and play, otherwise, you're just a non-entity! You don't really exist for them so they can say or do almost anything they want with no consequences!

I guess your suggestion is to hire a professional photographer to get those great shots if you can't do it yourself?

Well, I'm not spending $500 on a professional photographer! I know I still have a good body at fifty but I am still gay and single!

Why are you still single then?

I don't know because I have never been more ready to meet someone wonderful for my boyfriend but I know it's not all about the body but the personal connection!

So, what do you think is wrong with you that could prevent that connection from happening?

I also know that I am a recovering narcissist and I refuse to ever get fat!
Is that a good or bad thing to be?

Well, by being a narcissist you have to watch what you eat constantly which does promote good health! But as to who I am today, I know I am more politically interested in what happens in the gay community that I used to be and my life is more emotionally and spiritually balanced.

When I was living in NYC in the nineties when we last met, there was less room in my life for a boyfriend and I wasn't that interested in finding one since my primary focus was on my acting career. But if I was to return to NYC now, I know it would be easier to find a husband as that in NYC, I would be that new face in town which sparks interest!

Yes, I recall going to a party in Laguna California while visiting a friend where I met three prospective boyfriends in the first ten minutes! I couldn't believe it!
That's one of the advantages of being the "new face in town" but, they also knew you were on vacation and you were with another man, which makes the challenge of having sex with you more challenging and exciting!

Do you feel that going to friends' parties is a good place to meet prospective boyfriends?

Yes, I like to go to more parties and meet guys one on one.

What upsets you at present with regards to gay behavior today?

What "gets me" is how many guys don't care about "bare-backing" and have unprotected sex! In fact, I once met a sweet boy who once asked me to have unprotected sex with him but I refused to do that. Then I heard he did have unprotected sex with someone who told him weeks later that he was now HIV Positive and that he should get tested.

After my friend got himself tested and found out that he was negative, I really "laid into him," for his stupid behavior and his reckless choices. I held back initially from getting angry at him prior to his getting tested but afterwards, I decided to not hold back and screamed at him!

Have you ever heard about "Bug chasers?" Men who want to be HIV for a variety of reasons, one being the decision to just be free to continue having unprotected sex!"

Yes, and I think it's ridiculous but I also believe it's a pressure thing through their foolish peers and that they think that all they have to do is take a pill and no problem! To them, treating HIV is just like treating asthma and IT'S NOT JUST LIKE TREATING ASTHMA!

David sounded very angry with this type of behavior as if he had experienced more than his share of foolish behavior by gay men and knew that this type of thinking reflects poorly on the gay male community. Also, that this young man may have been someone he contemplated having a relationship with but could not accept his poor decision-making and immaturity.

What do you think our community needs to do in order to stop this foolish thinking and reckless behavior?

Here in Los Angles, there are billboards and advertisements that show men who have HIV with distended bellies as the result of medications to treat HIV. Those advertisements have definitely had some effect with some gay men but not totally.

All I know is that I will never allow a man to put himself inside me with putting a rubber on his penis first!

When did you first experience bare-backing? Was it with that guy who wanted you to fuck him without a rubber?

No, it was at a sex party where everyone was having anal sex with one another without condoms! I must admit that I did enjoy watching them having sex but I did not have a good time. I was just too shocked seeing all this bare-back sex going on!

Yes, I have a friend who enjoyed bare back sex and later found out that he had AIDS but, happily continues to be a long-term survivor. Unfortunately, he has both swollen jowls and a distended belly which has seriously affected his self-esteem since he too is an admitted narcissist! I know too he is very sad due to his appearance and puts on a brave face!

That is exactly what I am afraid of being that I too am an admitted narcissist. But instead of having anonymous sex, I am trying to enjoy my life more. I would like to see men who are like your friend who walk through their life with a positive spirit and try to be happy!

There are so many men who are miserable in their life because they have no money and no boyfriend!

I am getting the impression that David is referring to himself and that he refuses to be miserable and feel defeated in any way.

That's why I am so impressed with people who have cancer because they truly appreciate their lives and won't allow themselves to feel defeated! They always seem to live by the line, "I'm alive!"

Then what are your plans for the future?

I have decided to not waste my time living here in Los Angles anymore. I have to work on spending more time by myself being it even feeling at times that I am living in loneliness and poverty. But in NYC, I know that I would be running around all over town!

What is life in Los Angeles like today?

Well for one, you're in your car a lot so you feel pretty isolated and spending a good deal of time by yourself. In New York City you're in the subway and surrounded by people!

You would really like traveling on the crowded NYC subways?

That's why I love my Kindle. I would be reading on it whenever I am not being busy people watching.

What about buying a pet while living in LA?

I want a pet but financially and time-wise, I am not in the best shape!

It sounds as if David is going through what many of us are experiencing in these financially taxing times in our lives and believes that NYC will offer more beneficial and exciting new opportunities that LA doesn't appear to be offering.

I noticed on your website that you are in a new show and have a new business.

Yes, the show is called, *It Must Be Him* and it's a ton of work! But fortunately, the show is just now beginning to gel!

What else are you doing?

I have a business which helps people organize themselves but it is not doing as well as I had hoped. I have also been getting work in television, film and print.

What did you do last?

I played an attorney on *Law and Order: LA.*

Then there are some advantages to living in Los Angeles?

Of course there are but I am looking for new opportunities that I believe moving to NYC would afford me.

So, what is your present plan for your future?

I am looking forward to what's next! I want to feel more hopeful and positive in general and I am looking forward to the next chapter in my life.

I also want to get more work in film and theater and having a long-term relationship.

Then what is the difference in you now when compared to you in the nineties?

I show up more now! I am not "into my head" all the time and I know that if I want a good relationship, I have to be there for him and not all about "what about me?"

I also want to be more present and not about the past! Plus, I want to be working in NYC again; I miss the city.

What advice would you give my readers with regards to planning a positive future?

I live every day to learn something new about myself instead of bemoaning my present situation.

Meaning you will never become the "Cat Lady?"

You got it! No, to Cat Lady!

David at present, is still single and living in Los Angeles continuing his theatrical career. But as far as his political activism, he constantly posts articles and videos that depict injustices in the LGBT community. Also, many of the theatrical productions he is involved with appear to frequently focus on important subject matter that affects our community as well. His anger and frustration with the slow political process to promote changes to benefit our community is clearly expressed in his frequent posts, and he expressed his frustration recently on my radio show Talk it OUT. The theme of the show was: "Growing Older Being Gay," of which David had many humorous and thought-provoking comments on our ever-increasing lack of community within our culture and stressed the importance of safe sex practices.

CHAPTER VIII

"TOO FUNNY FOR MY OWN SKIN"

INTERVIEW WITH AN ANONYMOUS GAY WOMAN on October 7, 2007 – This is a dear friend of mine who identifies herself as an "out" gay woman known in her past as a successful comedienne and songwriter. Coincidentally, with regards to David's parting statement, my friend is very much, a "Cat Lady."

HERSTORY

As with my other Jewish interviewee: "I'm Just a Nice Jewish Boy," my friend also asked not to be identified due to her concern with regards to her workplace becoming aware of her lifestyle. But, as you will see in the following interview, there are other issues being raised here which may have also prompted this fear of being "outed." in this book.

Please begin this interview with telling us a little something about yourself. For example, tell us who you are and what information you could provide our readers on communication between gay men?

As a <u>gay woman</u>, I will answer that question. But first, I would like to refer to myself as a "gay woman" and not a lesbian, because a lesbian is an "a" and gay refers to a "we!" People say, "I am gay, not, "I am an (fill in the blank)."

I think we should have gotten a new word for gay women in order to distinguish that difference. "Gay" should stand for everybody, but we do need to distinguish between gay men and women! What is the appropriate term? It would be more appropriate to refer to us as "gay women" or, as a dear friend of mine would often say, "Lesbi-anns and Lesbi-andys!"

I do think "lesbian" is a nice word. The denotation of the word is lovely, but the connotation of it is negative! That's why I feel as a community, and as a civil and political rights statement, we chose that word! The movement wanted to have a new word to make their own. Homosexual men chose "gay" meaning "happy," and homosexual women chose "lesbian." Once, I remember a gay man saying to me, "We're kids!"

Most of the gay men that I know tend to be happy and vibrant. Their attitudes reflect the denotation of the word, "gay!" Yet again, they are mostly drawn to the arts! They pursue interests that enrich their lives! Therefore, I prefer the word, "gay women," to describe lesbians, or the term, "Gays and Feys," or, "Lesbi-anns and Lesbi-andys!"

Semantics or true word meanings can be extremely important when one is seeking to define themselves as unique and individual in our world at large. Gay men and women have been struggling to define who they are for centuries, and now, that it is more acceptable in our society, it is even more important to distinguish who we really are. This woman is clearly seeking to do that, and is not afraid to speak her mind with regards to her opinions, despite her concerns over identifying herself for this book.

Was there a personal experience in your childhood which helped you to become more aware of your true sexuality?

Yes, I do! When I was in sixth grade, I recall talking to this girl. I know that I wasn't particularly attracted to her, but, I recall her saying, "Stop talking to me! Please get away from me!" I didn't think I was standing that close to her? I was just leaning toward her and telling her something I felt was important! She was in my class, but, I also recall that she used to "hang around" the theater group, which I now find to be very interesting. But she did say to me, "Ooh, get away from me! What are you, a lesbian?"

I recall at the time, that I had no idea what a lesbian was; but I knew it was bad! I remember asking my mother later that day when she was in the bathroom. I recall her being at the sink. Don't ask me why, but I remember that specific scene a lot!

There were not a lot of conversations with my mother that I distinctly remember, but, I do remember asking her "what a lesbian was?" She immediately questioned me with, "Why am I asking her about such a thing!" It was also during that conversation, where I mentioned a best friend of mine who was gay.

"Mommy, what is a lesbian?" That's how I recall asking that question in the bathroom. She then began to explain that a lesbian was a woman who liked other women. She did indicate to me then, that perhaps I should be a little cautious about "hanging out" with this very effeminate boy who lived down the street. She must have feared that he might try to infect me toward becoming a lesbian! I knew right then, that the way she said, "Lesbian" that it must be bad!

I knew that she was shaming me by saying something negative to me! So, that's a personal reason for why I don't like the term, lesbian!

It all makes sense to me now! So, let's get some new words here! To me, I equate "lesbian" to the insulting word, "faggot!" Both of those words have a strong negative connotation!

My friend's opinion are clearly not shared by many in the lesbian community otherwise, GLBT, standing for Gay, Lesbian, Bisexual, and Transgender, would not be used to designate that specific grouping within the GLBT community. But, it appears as if the word "lesbian," does have a significant connotation with regards to her own personal history with the word and her relationship with her mother. After all, our parents hold considerable power and influence for us when we are children, hence as to why she remembers her mother's reaction to the question so many years later.

So, tell us more about your growing up and how you've learned to be so outspoken?

First of all, I am a daughter of a pension planner and an actress. My mother was known to be quite the renegade when she was younger. She exposed my family and my father to music and the theater from the beginning. My mother sings Jazz and the Blues and had an extensive repertoire of folk songs that she used to perform in concerts.

I have a brother who is three years older than me who is "straight" and divorced. I look up to him a lot! Through the years we've had good communication as brothers and sisters should.

As for myself, I did a lot of acting. I've acted in many television commercials. I also do impressions, as my mother also used to do impressions. In fact as a kid, I would "hang out" with two fellas all the time! One of the boys was the effeminate boy who lived down the street from me. Despite my mother's protestations, we became best friends, because he was the one guy on the block, other than my mother, who liked theater!

Soon after, he met with this other guy during a high school production of *Guys and Dolls*. We used to call ourselves "The Three Musketeers." I remember going on a bus with them to all the shows in New York City! We also used to do theater in my backyard. The three of us would eventually work backstage in this theater where all the big stars would come in and do these shows! It was a lot of fun! Betty Grable and June Havoc were only a few of the stars who would perform there. Scott, my effeminate friend, would wait till the theater closed at night and try on all the stars' dresses!

How long did you and Scott remain friends?

Scott and I had a bunch of years together, from eleven to sixteen! But, the three of us were always together! My other friend Billy was a lot of fun. He was a wonderful artist and a good actor. Both guys knew a great deal about movies. I even remember doing Tennessee William's plays in my backyard! Can you believe it? Here we're doing Tennessee Williams at twelve or thirteen years old! We did the play, *This Property is Condemned,* and another of his plays about this demented guy who lives with his mother and ends up burning his house down. I played the boy's mother, being the character actress that I am.

In terms of my "coming out," I didn't "come out of the closet" till years later. My formative years were with these two male friends. I do remember seeing a good deal of theater since my mother was very involved in the community theater in town. But, it was with these two guys, where I found myself going to all the Broadway shows, especially, the musicals! Scott was the big theater enthusiast. He simply loved the theater!

THE GAY COMMUNICATION GAME/ A GAY WOMAN'S PERSPECTIVE

You know, I remember Scott being quite nasty a good deal of the time. You could even say that he was sadistic. I usually find that type of personality tends to be more present with boys who are especially effeminate. They tend to have this nastiness about them.

That statement is beginning to sound like a popular stereotype. From where did you come to that opinion?

There's some sense of hatefulness that comes with the "drag queen persona." What makes people nasty? Part of it comes from insecurity, and part of it comes from being hurt; nastiness and hatefulness because of this natural feminine tendency. There is this innate desire to become women, and they're angry because they're <u>not women</u>!

Again, my friend has a very interesting perspective with regards to "bitchiness" in gay men and the desire to become women. This point reflects to my earlier mention of a gay friend who loves to dress in "drag" and when he does, he becomes an even "bitchier queen," than what he is when not in drag. It's as if they a playing a role in the play where they can be someone other than themselves.

But to take a more analytical perspective here,, I see this "bitchiness" as a means for acting in a dramatic fashion and conveying a superior attitude as a defense mechanism to not expressing one's true self. As if one's true self is being viewed by them as being less attractive and less empowered than when they are in their drag persona or acting-out in an effeminate manner.

Scott's very comfortable now with who he is, this is being a man. It took him a long time to get to that place of acceptance; just as it takes everyone a long time to get to that place of comfort. We all take that journey toward maturity, which includes a desire to settle down and become comfortable with ourselves.

But, I think part of that nastiness comes from being angry at the world, and anger at women, for not getting to be born women! I really don't know why effeminate men have that nastiness? I think it comes from watching all those movies from the forties and fifties, where women were always being "catty" with one another.

Yes, I too, am a big fan of the movies of the thirties and forties with such stars as Joan Crawford, Bette Davis, and Olivia De Havilland, all, who played "larger-than-life" characters to which handsome suitors revolved around their world hoping for their love. If some gay men choose to embody those roles either in drag or acting in a similar manner to these archetypes, perhaps they are doing so in hopes of obtaining that same sense of entitlement and superiority over others as these women did in their films. I realize to some reading my friend's comments and my analysis, that there may be a difference of opinion here and I look forward to hearing from both drag performers and transvestites to hear their perspectives on this matter.

 I just read this cover story from *New York Magazine* about drag queens! Men who do "drag," partly do it for of artistic expression. The other reason they do "drag," is to fulfill themselves in being women. But the women they play often exemplify qualities in women that are not particularly attractive for other women to see! It's as if they're expressing their anger at not being women through playing the nasty, unattractive aspects of some women!

Are you equating the "drag queens" as being the angry ones? Or, are we talking about gay men who are effeminate-acting and make "bitchy" remarks to everyone?

I'm talking specifically, about the effeminate-acting, gay men, not the drag queens! Especially, the young, nasty ones! They haven't attained that maturity and acceptance of who they are yet.

They can't really be women! They may want to <u>be</u> women according to their perception of what women should be. But since they are men, the two sides seem to always be always in conflict! The result being, a third sex! A whole other kind of person: the effeminate male! It's not a female and it has this unacceptability of being a male!

All this gender confusion! These guys are caught in this "in-between" place! Everyone should have their own sense of gender, but when you're different, something else comes up! You have a "little bit of this" and a "little bit of that!" Part of it is anger at not being born a woman. Part of it is what they think of women. To me, I see it as a mockery of women!

But, when I relay this feeling to one of these men, the quick response I get is, "Oh, No! We love women! We love women!" So, I respond and say," Well, why do you portray them as such hateful creatures?" I personally don't know, you'd have to interview these effeminate men who love to dress up in "drag" and get the answer from them. Do they dress up as women for "art's sake" or, is there a sexual need being satisfied with all this cross-dressing behavior?

Men that have operations and become women, aren't they really gay? No! They respond and say, "I'm really a lesbian!" That I don't get! It's like a "straight" person questioning whether we choose to be gay! But to me, it's not a question of choice! It's who I am! It's all about attraction to the same sex! But if these guys get changed to become a woman and are attracted to women, why don't they just stay being men?

That sounds like a great topic for another study, and I may consider interviewing a professional drag queen or, transsexual male, and get their opinions on that subject. But, let us return to the subject of gay men and what differences you see between them?
Well, you see there are the "butch, Butch" and the "fem, Fem!" There's the "soft, Butch" or the "fem, Butch" and the "butch, Fem!" I'm not able to follow all of it! It's kind of interesting. I try to understand it.

I mean, wouldn't the effeminate gay man be viewed as being submissive to a more masculine man? What you do in the bedroom has an effect on how one behaves outside of the bedroom. It carries over in terms of how gay people role-play both sexually and with intimate relationships, especially in terms of drama!

Again there is the reference toward semantics and the need to define who we are and equate that word or term to how we choose to live our lives as gay men and women or, gender identified. Indeed an excellent study for another day but important to be mentioned here, with regards to how we view one another and how that view affects our communication.

I see a lot of drama between gay men. Drama associated with an overindulgence of alcohol and drugs. Gay people have a lot of drama without alcohol too! Gay people tend to be happy, artistic and creative. They tend to be drawn to the vibrancy of life, which often includes theatricality, and the drama that is contained within the theatricality.

The "transgender community" may be a fascinating area to study with regards to how other people communicate with them within the gay community.

But, for the purpose of this study, I want to investigate the supposed "class system" within the gay community. This choice of: "People I want to talk to vs. people I don't want to talk to." If the transgender or transsexual community or, the "drag queens" feel they are on the "in-group" or "out-group of this "class system, then I want to know why?

Another important issue to discuss is how do we classify "normal" and "not normal" according to other gay men? Just where do those of that specific community fit in within the unwritten, but clearly imposed "class system?"

Yes! It's almost as if you're forced to touch upon this issue, because there are gay men who are effeminate and gay men who aren't effeminate! Do we talk about sexual preference within the gay community, for instance, do you like being a "top" or a "bottom?" Sometimes, that is clearly indicative if a man is acting in an effeminate manner, and sometimes it doesn't!

I agree. I personally have enjoyed dressing in "drag" on special occasions, such as, Halloween and various parties. My dressing in "drag" is not indicative of my sexual preference. I tend to view it as play and a desire to let my "feminine self out of the closet!"

I agree. It's both theatrical and exciting!

Yes. I also enjoyed the fact that men found me attractive dressed as a woman! But for the case of this study, I primarily want to know from you information about how gay women identify and relate to gay men?

Specifically, how they feel gay men interact and relate with each other? And finally, how do you as a gay woman see similarities between how gay men interact to how gay women interact and relate with each other?

What's the common thread is the sense of fun that many gay men have, while many gay women do not! Sometimes I hear, "Lesbians don't have a sense of humor!"

Most of my gay and "straight" women that I know do have a wonderful sense of humor but, other lesbians tend to have a different kind of humor. From my own personal experience, the types of men and women I associate with have a great deal of humor. I need to be around people who laugh at my jokes and aren't so quickly offended by my type of humor. I'm a professional comedienne for goodness sake!

But, I do want to return to the subject of the "nasty men!" I'm very interested in knowing how these guys operate in such a manner because I view them both as sad, and hateful!

How are they nasty, can you go into a little more detail?

They say cruel things to each other. They gossip in ways that are unhealthy. And yet, I know that gossip like that goes on in other groups throughout our society. Everyone talks about things they feel are important; a lot of time they talk about nothing!   So concerned with externals! The death of their "inner being" is unimportant. Sometimes, there's drugs and alcohol involved. It's all about everything except having feelings; of having a "heart-to-heart" with a close friend.

Even their definition of a friend, is someone with whom the "cruise" with; do drugs and alcohol with! Just running around and doing "things" together. The focus is all about having fun! They're serious enough to go out and earn a living, but to me, it seems like an empty life!

The fun is great! It's a very important part of being gay. But, I find it very sad to think that there are a lot of gay men who are not happy.

Why?

They're unusual! (*Said with a great deal of humor*) They're not regular gay people!

What do you mean?

(*Still laughing*) Something went wrong for them!
Are we just talking about gay men, or do you include gay women as well?

Gay men and gay women; more so, gay men! There are more gay men, and they are more visible than gay women. Gay men tend to have more money and they congregate more in masses having more fun!

Don't gay women have fun?

I think that they do. You just don't see them out and often as you see gay men! Women are more emotional and enjoy more intimate settings. They tend to do more things with a select group of friends. They're simply not as visible spending money and having fun as the men are! Gay women go out for more political causes and dances. Especially, with the younger generation of gay girls! They're even into doing what the gay men do; having anonymous sex with multiple partners! These girls even have sex bars like the men!

I find the whole scene quite unique. Women tend to be more emotional. I'd hate to see the young gay women becoming more like the gay men in terms of the emotionality.

Wow! That's a strong statement to make about gay men! Are you saying that gay men tend to run away from their emotions?

I'd say that men in general are not as emotional as women. Remember the book, *Men are from Mars and Women are from Venus*?

You would include gay men in that classification? What about the belief that gay men are more in touch with their femininity?

I think, men in general are less emotional, and gay men also tend to less emotional, because they don't have to worry about getting someone pregnant! They don't usually have somebody making them wait a long time for sex. I mean, if they're mutually attracted to one another, they tend to have sex right away! They simply have the freedom to have more sex, even with the AIDS epidemic in the eighties and nineties when they would just have "safe sex" right away!

I don't really know how often they have sex, but I have quite a few friends who are quite promiscuous! I also have some gay friends, who tend to go on more dates than I do! I make it a point not to have sex with somebody right away! Once and a while, it just winds up being that way. I'd rather date someone for a while, before having sex with them. At present, I'm dating someone, but on the night we met, we had sex!
I think that gay men, with some exceptions, think: "So many men, so little time."

Truer words were never spoken.

Well, because a man's penis tends to tap him on the shoulder all the time and says, "Come on. Let's get laid! Let's get laid!"

This woman's perspective on gay men and their tendency to let sexual gratification somewhat numb their emotional state is most fascinating and her views are supported by textbooks I use for my communication classes, which state than women are more relationally focused while men are more task focused. Meaning women enjoy the emotional complexity within relationships while men are more focused on a task; such as sexual conquests or completing a job well done.

Men period! When women were on the same wavelength, straight men were always saying, "Wow! I'm getting sex all the time! It's so great!" It's just like gay men! They quickly meet one other and go have anonymous sex with no commitments! That type of mentality tends to be very frustrating for people who want to get more emotional or even want a second date!

I don't know if men just don't want to get attached, or they're too excited about having more and more, and different partners? They wouldn't want to stop with one, or their partner didn't want to stop with one. After all, we all hear about the problems gay relationships have with monogamy.

Where did you learn to be so intuitive about people? Did your theatrical background have a direct effect or, was it from your childhood experiences?

Well, my mother did expose my brother and I to theater and art. But, being around gay men is very stimulating! I started doing impressions very early for my family and their friends. I remember doing George Burns and Gracie Allen, and characters from the 60's television show, *Hogan's Heroes* for their enjoyment.

But, I learned to perfect my Bette Midler and Joan River's impersonations specifically, from my gay friends! So, they were a big influence on my life! I would find out about things from them that I was too lazy to read about.

My friends would always talk about these stories with great interest. They could look at a magazine and know just what to focus on. With me, it was simply too much information to take in. But, they got me excited about what was new and trendy. I would listen to them and follow along with them. I remember going to see Julie Wilson at the Continental Baths! I was disappointed that I missed Bette Midler when she performed there.

It would appear that you've experienced a good deal in your life? Can you tell us more of your childhood?

Yes! I've had "depth" since I was twelve years old. I don't know why? I was a little bit nerdy. I had this curly hair that they didn't know how to cut it then! I hated it! I remember setting it with curlers and having to sleep on those curlers! I would try to straighten my hair and wear a headband. I had glasses and braces and I was involved in the theater. So, how popular was I? Fortunately, there were four or five of us. The art department was also included along with us, so there was strength in numbers!

I remember the audio-visual guys always hanging around with us. I used to call them the "A-V-babies!"

What are the "A-V- Babies?"

They were the audio-visual guys in the art department and I liked one of the guys! He used to sit in front of me. I felt at a certain age, that I had to pick a guy that I liked, and he was the one. I was already having feelings for girls by then.

There was also this really pretty girl in my study hall. Noticing her, I knew something "was up" with my feelings for women so, I felt that I better start liking guys! I also tried acting more feminine, because, before that time, I knew that I was acting more like a "tomboy."

I started wearing mascara and eye shadow and when I went to the theater, I would be an usher and learned how to be more feminine in public.

Martin was the name of this boy who sat in front of me. He was nice looking, but I never became romantic with him. Years later, I went to my high school reunion and I met him and his wife. She came up to me and said, "I understand that you had a 'crush' on my husband?"

I replied, "Yes, I did!"(*Makes another loud laugh*) It was funny to admit to it, because part of it was true, but another part of it was untrue. It amazing, he knew I liked him, but never mentioned anything to me about it. I recall that there was some "chemistry" between us, but nothing happened!

I did have a boyfriend years later when I was nineteen. I lost my virginity to him. As it turns out, he was bisexual!

You've had some wild experiences but I would like to return to your intuitiveness and where you learned to be so perceptive with regards to others?

It terms of my being intuitive? I don't know? All sorts of influences I guess? The theater, being gay, and, all the amazing gay people I tend to associate with most definitely helped.
Perhaps, it has something to do with my hair! I have this "thing" about my hair. For one, nobody seemed to know how to cut it! As a result, the "tough girls" in school used to corner me in the bathroom and poke fun at my hair. I was sensitive as a kid, so their teasing always hurt my feelings. I knew that I wasn't this great beauty like my mother! Well, not at that time! I hadn't found myself and my femininity.

Having known this woman for such a long time, I have seen her hair change in several ways but as of recent, has been softer and more relaxed. Consequently, the change in her hair has somehow resulted in her personality becoming softer and more relaxed as well. As if her hair is no longer an issue or concern as it once was, along with the painful history associated with it.

Okay, so I wasn't Miss Popular; it's not that I really wanted that role. I guess I felt "less than" and inferior to others for "no damn good reason!" I mean, just because those kids were more popular, it didn't mean that they were any greater or any better than I was! But, I felt that if I had long, straight hair as did those kids who were popular, then, I would have been more accepted by them. Instead, I was being poked fun at because I didn't fit into their image of what a popular kid should look like.

Years later, when stylists finally knew how to cut my hair, the situation changed. Now, I get compliments from women on my hair instead of being teased. "Oh, I love your hair. I wish that I had hair like yours!" Instead of being grateful, I want to say "Get away from me! You remind me of all those "trendy-minded" kids who used to say, "Ouch, icky, your hair!"

In retrospect, I should thank those kids for their nastiness, because all their nastiness helped to give me character. What a screwy world we live in but, it did give me material for my act.

I won't disagree with you there but I in concluding this interview, I would like to know how your experiences as a gay woman or lesbian, differ to those of the gay men that you know or have observed?

That's a tough question to answer. We <u>do</u> have different experiences! Gay men seem to have a more sexual life and have more sexual experiences. You go to more places where gay men congregate and as a result, have more sexual episodes. They tend to have more money which allows them to see more theater and travel more. You guys can do a lot of things that I can't afford to do, and do them more often! (*Loud laughter*) That's a big difference.

So, you feel we have more sex and more money than gay women?

"Ab so-fuckin-lutely" I so envy them!

Thank you so much for your time and wonderful insights about gay culture.

CHAPTER IX – AARON & ERIC

The following gay men I interviewed more recently and their perspectives on their gay lives, although similar to the previous interviewees, there is a significant difference in how they view their gayness and their opinions of themselves and others.

I interviewed Eric with his friend Aaron in a coffee house in Chelsea and in Aaron's apartment. The two young and handsome men were in a brief romantic and very sexual relationship that ended all too briefly. When I first entered Aaron's small apartment in Chelsea I did excuse myself to use the bathroom.

Once I entered the bathroom, I could not fail to notice the extensive amount of sexual paraphernalia present including at least eight to ten dildos.

I immediately felt as if I had unwittingly interrupted a very passionate sexual encounter despite the fact that I had an appointment with Aaron for this interview. Being a gay man, I felt as if I was expected to join in on the sex even though they were now fully clothed. If not meant to join in, for some reason Aaron and Eric wanted me to be aware of their sexual behavior and tendencies. As this interview continued, some of my questions are answered by both Aaron and Eric's comments with regards to their goals and life choices.

AARON   ERIC

ERIC – 2009

"ERIC - LITTLE BOY LOST"

Eric is a handsome "twenty-something" who is visiting Aaron and in town to have fun and party. I am very glad he volunteered to be interviewed and I am excited to hear his outlook on his life and choices he has made. I know he and Aaron were having sex prior to this interview and I can only assume they used protection since Aaron is an advocate for "safe sex."

Tell me something about yourself Eric and what goals you want to accomplish in your lifetime*?*

Eric: I want to leave my mark on this planet since I really feel as though I am an activist and I very outspoken. I believe that I have "swum against the stream" my entire "coming out" process. I know that at some day I will be somebody.

I do want a partner, and want something more for my life than just "bar-hopping" or "clubbing," and using that as validation for who I am.

I cannot tell what I see for my future, I can only tell you that it's going to be appropriate and safe. I hope to be sober and as long as I live and follow sane sexual appropriateness as I continue to have sex with men because I intend to stay HIV negative.

But, honestly, I really do want to become somebody, I do not know yet what that somebody is going to be, but I do have high ambitions for myself and I have yet been able to figure out what that is? In terms of long term boyfriends, sure I would want the idyllic life where, (*acting dramatically*) "Oh, I am so in love with you. I crave no other man. I am so in love with you that I will stare into your eyes forever… Of course I want that to happen, who doesn't?

But since I am not close-minded to open relationships, I do not think by accepting an open relationship, I am in turn, accepting a "way out." I am only accepting things as they are in reality. I have had so many nonsense, forgettable, unnecessary "blow-jobs" in my life that, if my partner that I've been with for five years; who I know loves me and I love in return, if he were to get a blow-job on some business trip from some nameless dude, is that really going to affect the love that we shared for the last five years? Because in my view, that it is only a wet form of masturbation!

How are you going to find out about his having had sex with someone else?

Well, when I do find that partner, I want to be completely and inexplicably communicative. I want to talk everything out because, I want to try to understand him to the best of my ability without judgment. I don't want one of these relationships in which I see so many gay men falling into; which is falling in love with the idea of having a relationship!
(*Spoken very fast with some anxiety*) I want to meet a guy where it goes really well, where we

will meet for drinks on Tuesday, and we'll see each other on Sunday.

I want to know that this guy that I'm with I will want to see again. That I already had sex with him and I am still "turned on" by him where I know that the next day, I will see my cell phone and I immediately want to call him and make plans with him. I want to be around this person because, I want to share my life with him. I want to make it work for the sake of having a relationship because I know, that for every successful relationship, there are some twenty lonely people without one.

That sounds very sad.

(*Emphatically*) It isn't sad ;it's a matter of fact! There is someone there for everyone and it's only a matter of making it work. (*Stumbling over his words here as if unsure of what he wants to say*).

I do want monogamy. I don't believe it's easy to do but, I think that monogamy is great and I do believe that true love really exists, I really, really do!

As I was listening to Eric for the past twenty minutes rambling on about love, I began to feel sad for him, since it appeared as if he was trying to convince himself that true love existed for him and others. Also, I know that he and Aaron were having an intense, drug fueled, sexual relationship that clearly Aaron was not committed to, which appears to have had some bearing on Eric's insecurity about love and finding a meaningful relationship in his life.

I, personally, have several good examples of couples that I know of who are so much in love with each other who are content with being monogamous. But, I think that they are maybe only a few couples out of hundreds that I met, that can do that!

(*Struggling to convince himself*) I just think that, and I don't want to sound that I am forfeiting coming up with an easy answer but, I don't think it's realistic to put monogamy upon the human condition. It is simply asking way too much of our biological human need. To declare monogamy for the rest of their lives is going against biological nature! You can't work like that!

Again, you can see how Eric is attempting to understand the complexities of obtaining and sustaining a long-term gay relationship given his past experiences in the gay community. But his opinions do not come out of nowhere, since recent statistics confirm that many gay relationships are unable to sustain a monogamous relationship. Especially, given the climate of the gay community toward seeking multiple sex partners in order to validate one's own sexuality and sense of personal validation.

In addition, we live in a culture where there are frequent gatherings of attractive gay men who love to flirt with one another similar to a beautiful woman flirting with men other than her husband in order to validate themselves as being both attractive and desired. But what is true for both gay and straight men, as well as, the beautiful woman, there is a deeper insecurity that needs to be satiated in order to feel validated. And it is that compulsive behavior that is what needs to be addressed in order to stop or lessen the potentially destructive cycle.

It sounds as if they are giving up on that person before the relationship even got started. That even the idea of being monogamous with the same person for the rest of their lives is so overwhelming to them, that they don't give the relationship a chance to work.

Exactly, exactly, I agree with you.

They're too busy looking for who's next?

Or, they are looking at the relationship with the idea that they cannot be monogamous. I just think it's just a matter of communication, and with being okay with the idea that monogamy may not be a biological reality.

What would happen if someday your boyfriend confesses to you that he just met some guy on the street, and went to his apartment or hotel room to have sex with him, what would you say to him?

(*A brief loss for words here*) I would really plan on establishing the ground rules. If I were to go into an open relationship, my open relationship would be one with clear parameters of everything being okay except, for anal intercourse. I put intercourse in a completely different pedestal. If you want to "jerk off" with him that's fine but, …

(Interrupting Eric and role-playing the cheating boyfriend) "But, I used condoms, we played safe."

(*Spontaneously responding in character*) "I still think that intercourse is what we have and that is not to be shared with anyone but with me!"

So then he cannot cross that line once that line is established?

That's right.

Despite Eric's validation of the inability for most gay men to sustain a monogamous relationship, he still has clear parameters with regards to how far one's partner can go with regards to following the rules and sustaining their relationship. Perhaps he is a little unsure of what he wants with regards to being in love or in a relationship?

Ok, then let's move on to the next question with regards to social communication between gay men and whether it is based primarily on physical attractiveness?

Uh, what do you mean? (*Eric is at a loss for words here, not really sure of what I am referring to in the question so, I further clarify the question for him.*

It means that good looking men only want to "hang out" with other good looking men.

Yes, without a doubt! That is very prophetic! I mean, there are incredibly attractive men, (*changing what he planned to say*), I know incredibly attractive men who have friends who are not that attractive but, there are cliques that are usually comprised of men who look similar. Such as, there are hairy, beefy guys who "hang out" with the hairy, beefy guys.

Even in Los Angles there is a something called the "Bear Patch" where all the "Bears hang out!" It's not just the comfort level; it's also a matter of fitting in. It's "now that I look this way, now I want to be with guys who look like me." It is adult high school! It's always comes back to that. It really is a sense of prolonged adolescence. I don't know why it is or for what reasons but, I often fall into that trap myself!

Eric is pointing out a clear example of one of my major points with regards to gay communication based on age-old shame. That due to not being comfortable in our skin as teenagers because of having to keep our gayness a secret- when one finally "comes out of the closet" they are experiencing that delayed adolescence because now they have given themselves the permission to play with the other boys in their special group/

It almost feels as if I have had to "come out" twice! Not only have I "come out" to the "straight" community as a gay man, but I have also had to "come out" to my gay brothers with the fact that I like older men, and that I am also attracted to men who you may not view as aesthetically attractive. For example, I like men that may be a little chubby, hairy, older, and I get judged as being a little weird.

(Interrupting him- playacting one of friends judgmental friends) "But Eric, you are so young, you have this great build and look, what are you doing talking to him? Sorry, but I don't find him the least bit attractive!"

(*Not responding in role play but talking to me as the interviewer not as the friend*) I would get that all comment all the time, and it would take me a long time to get over that! But in that case, I would just tell my friends to "get over it!" I just can't be concerned with what people would be thinking of me or, would say about me.

Now, I can express who I am with a sense of pride because this is who I am, and I am not going to be making any apologies about it. I like the men I like, and I am not going to settle for something less, because you are going to be "chit-chatting away with whoever else about who Eric is picking up or talking to. I like the men I like and I'm not going to apologize about it!

I find it most puzzling with regards to what Eric is saying about liking older, hairy, and chubby men when he is presently dating Aaron, a sexy, former porn star and very popular party promoter within the gay community. Perhaps Eric was trying to convince me that he is not just someone who only follows what his friends tell him is attractive or, not attractive, and that he has his own mind. But, I am still unsure of who Eric really is and what he honestly feels? I hope that the more he shares about himself, the stronger the impression he will make with regard to who he is and what he truly wants in a relationship and in life.

It sounds as if your group of friends are acting a little bit like a "clique; "similar to a group of teenage girls.

No, it's not that, there is just a sense of bewilderment among them because I am good looking!

So you should be with good looking men!

That's right. Yes!

Or, one that they would view as good-looking!

Or, I am good-looking so I should be with good-looking men! Or, I am good looking therefore everyone should know that I can get good looking men!

I don't really understand why Eric feels so defensive about his choice of men being different from those of his friends, when he is clearly dating a very attractive man at the moment with whom his friends would clearly envy? Perhaps, he is promoting his position so that he will be viewed by me as being a nice guy who isn't so quick to reject men that others may not view as attractive. and is open to all types of men.

I expect to will learn more about Eric's choices as the interview progresses. At present, I have some indecisiveness with regards as to how honest Eric is being here, even to himself.

One of the requirements that I have for my future boyfriend or long-term partner is that he be exceedingly handsome in my eyes. One of my ex-boyfriends Ron, who I still consider to be one of the handsomest men that I ever laid eyes upon, was completely unattractive to other men. In fact, people used to ask me all the time, "Whatever do you see in him?"

My response to that was, "he is so hot, why don't you see him as attractive?" It's all about status and, it's all about who's seen with whom? It's really gross to me; the entire situation!
Everything you are saying has clear bearing on the subject of this book which examines gay male communication and basing it all on a game; similar to a chess game, where it is all about the moves that we make to reach our goal to win.

Do you see that game being played with your friends, and the gay community, where these games are being played to win; but, at what? Do you think the goal is to win the "hot" man that fits my specific criteria for what I see that hot man to be or, what my friends consider a "hot" man would be?

Yes, definitely. The majority of moves made by the gay man are in direct correlation with the way they want to be perceived by others, and they want their lives to be perceived by themselves.

Where there is more going with what public opinion would approve of, as opposed to, what one's "gut" feeling tells him to do.

Eric is making a very insightful comment here with regards to "peer pressure" within the gay social culture, that causes us to act in ways that may be contrary to our true desires. Thereby, questioning our own instincts and following what others believe would be better choices for us to make. But, are those choices going to serve us in the long run if we are not following our true desires and instead, allowing others to model our behavior?

That's an excellent point you are making here; is there anything else you want to say about that?

I can honestly say, that I know all the right moves to methodically make my way in this community, because, I know the right things to say. I know which hands to shake and, who to meet. But, I will always view myself as an individual. I'm not concerned with who I'm "pissing off!" If the gay community wants to "dump" me that's fine! I've got my straight friends to fall back on and they're never going to go away!

(*Working himself up into an emotional fervor*) And the gay community is never going to "dump" me anyway; I'm too much of a nice guy. I'm too much myself. I'm way too confident. I'm not concerned with being unpopular at all! And, I am so incredibly grateful, and I'm so incredibly fortunate, to have glided through this community as someone who has stood out from the crowd! As someone who has been attributed both respect and success based solely on my looks as opposed to what I have to say. In fact, I believe I have gained something and even given them something in return.

In terms of the gay community; in terms of those who "give a shit," about what one another says to one another, I could just give my middle finger to the whole thing. I look forward to "going against the grain." I look forward to "pissing people off!" I look forward to challenging gay men where they stand!

Eric is being extremely vocal here with regards to challenging those who attempt to change or influence his beliefs when they feel contrary to how he chooses to conduct his life. In fact, there is a clear arrogance with regards to how he views himself and his role in the gay community based on his physical attractiveness, that sets him apart from others.

This sense of superiority based on the power of one's looks is clearly indicative of not only the gay community but on society as a whole. Where beauty holds high criteria for those who possess it or desire it, and is illustrated further by the billions of dollars spent annually by Americans in gyms, tanning salons, cosmetic surgeries, diets, and all the trappings that go with that pursuit of beauty and the power it possesses in our society.

How would you rate your communication skills with family, friends, and other gay men today?

(Appearing somewhat overconfident) I feel as though I have a tremendously; highly appreciated reputation. Other than "oh, I met him twenty times and he doesn't remember my name." Or, "I met him ten or twenty times and he is still rather standoffish." I can't think of one thing that someone would say that would be bad about me. I really strive to be the best person that I can be and be the most caring.

(Briefly interrupting) Do you ever forget people's names?

Of course, there are only so many Jim, Bobs, Johns, Pauls, Sams, Toms, and Oscars that you can possibly remember!

I do too.

I've lived in Los Angeles, New York, Northern New Jersey, Tucson, Arizona *(At present, Eric is somewhat homeless living only temporarily with Aaron until he finds other accommodations. I also questioned whether Eric had any money or access to money)?*

All these men that you see again on the dance floor, out and about in bars, and all these faces just begin to merge together where it's impossible to remember them. So, if I don't remember these guy's names, that's fine. I don't take offense if someone doesn't remember my name.

I can't tell you how many times I have been on the dance floor on drugs, nonetheless, and someone comes up to me and says, "We've met some twenty times and you don't remember me? Are you on drugs?"

I appreciate Eric's honesty in admitting his drug taking but, he clearly seems to be in a bit of trouble with both his drug use and sexual compulsion. Also, there appears to be an attitude of superiority based on his narcissism, where he is not feeling accountable to his actions.

Despite my past drug usage, I do speak out adamantly against Crystal Meth and GHB usage! But, I do go on the dance floor and use Ecstasy. I snort Coke (cocaine); I have snorted Special K in the past. I do all these drugs! I've never in my life done GHB or Crystal Meth! And, I believe there has to be a line drawn between these dangerous drugs and just having fun!

We see people on the dance floor passing out on GHB one after another, people getting infected with HIV while on Crystal Meth, and that is when recreational drug use goes past the line of just being recreational to being just plain dangerous! And,

I am not going to just stand here and say that I have not done Ecstasy. I "party" and I plan to still use these drugs in the future. I pose myself as no saint! But I still feel that I have every right to protest against such drugs as GHB and Crystal Meth!

Eric's feelings about such drugs as GHB and Crystal Meth are clear but there seems to be a denial of his own drug problems and sexual compulsion. Although I agree that those two specific

drugs are indeed dangerous and have cost the lives of many gay men, the other drugs Eric mentioned taking also contribute to drug addiction and sexual addiction.

Thank you for expressing your honest feelings with regards to these dangerous drugs and I hope that gay men will begin to lessen their drug usage and sexual behavior for their own sake, but in closing, do you feel your communication with gay men has changed over the years and how so?

I believe that I'm just a little wiser as to what I want. I've never understood the distinction between just being friendly and lingering too long. Nowadays, I try to be more direct and to the point. I no longer try to be everyone's best friend.

Any closing thoughts you would like to say about the gay community or gay culture?

I would tell them to stop "bare-backing," and, no matter whether your just "coming out of the closet" or, have been "out the of the closet" for twenty years; just be yourself first and foremost! Don't compromise any thought of your own or ideas of your own for the sake of someone else. Be a man, whether you're the biggest sissy on the planet or, whether you're the mostly overtly masculine dude on the planet! Learn to stand up for yourself and what you believe in.

Always wear a condom, care about others, and be a brother or mentor to another gay man. Get your "head out of the fucking sand!" Stand up for yourself and be proud of who you are. You're worth it; each and every one of us is worth it!

We are some of the most creative and imaginative people on the planet so, don't doubt who you are for a minute! Fight against HIV. Be somebody, and be in control of your own life!

Eric's last words were definitely supportive and inspirational but some of his action and comments prior to these last words were indeed concerning and sounded a little too permissive of his behavior which could cause him potential harm. I simply hope that his advice for his gay brothers would be words he would use for himself and his refusal to compromise will not be in effect with his future drug usage. Now, it is Aaron's turn to speak.

"PORN STAR, DIVA, BAD BOY"

To be clear, I first met with Aaron and Eric in a Chelsea coffeehouse and then, privately, with only Aaron in his Chelsea apartment. Aaron volunteered to let Eric go first but, appeared clearly bored and mostly disinterested with Eric's share and was on his cell phone or, chatting with friends in the coffeehouse while waiting for his turn to tell his story. Despite his behavior during Eric's interview, Aaron still appeared excited to tell his story once it was his time to speak, and was more respectful and listened patiently whenever Eric interjected at various points in the following interview.

"*Give Me French Fries Not Potato Chips!*"

Aaron please tell us a little something about yourself and your role in the GLBT community?

My background, well, I am from Orange, Kentucky, by way of Cincinnati. I went to college in Atlanta and felt like I was the only gay person on campus. I joined a fraternity, got drunk with dudes but, had sex with women.

When did you first have sex with women?

My freshman year in college when my frat brother saw someone he really liked so, I had to "nail her" to prove to him and myself that I could. Sorry if I am being graphic here.

That's perfectly okay. Did you feel you had to perform for women to assure your frat brothers you were "cool?" Did you like it?

Not really, I just felt I had to fit in with the crowd but I knew I wasn't being honest with who I really was. That's when knew I had to stop and accept who I was, and that is also why I had to go to a bigger city. So, I graduated with a degree in Marketing and Finance and a successful investment company hired me "right off the bat" and I immediately became a stockbroker in Cincinnati. I climbed my way up the channels to Proactive Sales, getting people to bring all their money to the company.

Shortly thereafter, I was in a major car accident when a drunk driver hit me in my Jeep where I was out of work for six months, getting reconstructive surgery to get so much prettier.
That gave me the decision that life was too short and I decided I wanted to move somewhere else. I never thought I would ever move to New York since it was never in my registry! New York was just too scary for me!

I looked at other cities but the only opportunity that came up with my company was New York. So, I flew up here, interviewed, and they took me right from the limo to the interview and right back to the airport to fly home and pack up to move to New York City.

I got the job and began working in January of 2000 for Fidelity Investments for Private Access, which meant that all my clients made five million dollars or more. Regis Philbin was a client of mine and people like him. But these people were mean; they were typical of clients who make a lot of money. They were rude. They were never satisfied; meaning that I could never do enough to satisfy them even though I was considered one of Fidelity's best brokers.

I knew I was going to be stuck in that position for five years and really wanted to do something else with my marketing degree. So, I quit after only one year and lived off of my savings. Lived in Fire Island for the summer and I had an internship lined up at *Genre* magazine and September the 11th happened! (*Pause – takes a moment*)

In the meantime, I kept getting calls from a certain porn person named Chi Chi LaRue saying that she wanted me to do porn and the funds started to dry out and, the rest is history! (*Aaron laughs in a somewhat embarrassed manner*).

I wasn't planning to do it; it was horrible! I cried. It was a bad experience.

How many porn films did you do?

I did thirty seven in all! But I cried after the first one.

You did thirty seven films? That's pretty impressive.

Yes, I did thirty seven films but, after my bad first experience, when I got the call a few months later to come to New York, I demanded more money and a certain amount of respect; co-star approval. So, it got a little easier. And I kept doing the films, working my way through them.

I remember one day on my last film when the director yelled, "Cut," I remember saying, "I want French fries with my meal, not potato chips!" I knew that I had this thing covered, that I was done with this!

What did you feel was the significance of demanding French fries instead of potato chips?

That I was no longer "in the moment;" I was just "doing the actions" where it was just, here's the line: "fuck me, yeah!" Everything was robotic and just a job. Although, I was doing the best that I could and I was having fun, there was just no reason for me to keep doing it anymore. There was nothing more that I could gain from it, other than to be having hot sex with hot men!

That doesn't sound so bad? But, weren't you an Eric having hot sex together before I arrived at your apartment for the interview?

(*Pause*) Yeah, we started to. (*Both laugh*)

Well, then, if you still love having hot sex with hot men, why don't you keep getting paid for it?

Why, would you have wanted to join us if we asked you to?

Maybe so, but I just wanted to know if you love hot sex, why not stay in the business?

(*Seeming a bit uncomfortable with my line of questioning becoming a bit defensive*) I just wanted you to know about my porn history since I know you knew about it.

Yes, of course I want to know about it. So then, let me ask you how the two of you met?

We met through a mutual friend. Plus, I knew that Eric wanted to meet me and I was interested in meeting him too! *(Eric nods in agreement).*

So, when did you guys first meet?

We just met this morning.

Wow, you guys just met! So, basically you are just "tricking" with one another?

Eric is also interested in doing porn.

So, are you going to be helpful in getting Eric some work in porn?

*At this moment in Aaron's interview, Eric rejoined the discussion when Aaron mentioned his desire to do pornographic films so, I continued to interview Eric with Aaron listening in and interjecting his comments.

Also, at this point in the interview, I was very curious as to the casualness of Aaron's statements about his horrific car accident and his resultant porn career. It was as if the change in his appearance promoted Aaron to seek the approval of other gay men, as well as, become an object of desire for many gay men through his popularity as a porn star.
So Eric, why do you want to become a porn star after hearing Aaron's negative feelings about his pornographic history?

Eric rejoins the interview but not before Aaron interjects:

Aaron: (*jokingly to Eric*) You better watch what you say about me here.

Eric- I want to do it because as I stated earlier, I want to make a name for myself, I want my life to become my own and that's one of the things I just want to do. And, after I do it for a while, it will be one more thing that I could check off from my list of things I wanted to do in my lifetime.

But why do you want to do porn?

Because after having so many years of being ridiculed as not being like my peers, I didn't care anymore. I want to do what I want to do and not have any regrets about it! I just don't want to wake up one morning and have regrets about not taking risks and "following my heart."

I am very interested in the ridiculing comment since that is the basis of my book being that early gay shame has caused people to act as they do. That we had to survive through our adolescence by wearing a mask of what we felt people wanted us to wear but, that mask was not honest. And once we "came out" in the gay community, we still don't know how to act?

But, what I don't understand with you being so tall and handsome, how specifically did you get ridiculed?

When I was eighteen and at my present height, I was only 156 pounds! Here I was trying hard to "fit in" with everyone else in Middle America. Where everybody drove a truck and drank beer!

But why do you want to turn to porn?

Aaron: (*Jumps into the discussion and answers this question first*). People turn to porn to get affirmation; to be valued! They want to get the validation that they didn't get in childhood.

Do you wish to be admired now for what you didn't get when you were young? Now, you can be admired onscreen; larger than life?

Yeah, just like when I was growing into my new look after the surgery. Getting used to this new person with this new lease on life I wanted to feel better about myself. I honestly knew that I look better now than I used to look, and wanted others to validate my new look as well.

I wanted to try new things; take calculated risks that I knew would make me feel better about myself in the long run.

As we are talking, I am feeling that what you are saying would make for good television or radio with this new transformation of yours. Hearing your story and the changes you have made in your life, shows me that everyone has a story to tell; especially, gay men. Perhaps the two of you can come on my radio or television show and Aaron, you can tell your story of how pornography became a means of validation for you after a horrific car accident; it certainly helped boost your self-esteem within the gay community.

Yes, I wanted to feel better about myself doing porn but I never watched any of my films!

You never watched yourself in your porn movies? Why? I thought you liked the attention you received from doing porn movies?

I remember going to social or charity events with my fellow porn actors and there would be groups of guys who would say "oh, look at the porn stars," acting as if they're better than I am because I do porn and yet, I know that they watch my movies and "get themselves off" in the process! A bunch of hypocrites! It is so sad but no surprise to me.

It's interesting on how you Eric are just beginning in your porn career and you Aaron are leaving it!

Aaron: Well, I'm in it to build up my savings, which are pretty low at present with the exception of my retirement account.

Eric: Well. I just want to have fun and show up all of those kids who made fun of me when I was young. Now, they can jerk off to my movies?

Speaking of your youth, what were things like for you as a child Aaron?

Aaron: I knew I was gay at an early age of fifteen. My parents were very young when they had me; my mom was only sixteen. We lived in a trailer and it fit every stereotype that is associated with that image! And as sad as it may seem, my dad and I at present are like best friends.

My mother went crazy but back in the day when they just didn't know what they were doing and did everything she could in order to keep her husband's love; he came first and the children came second. Unfortunately, I would take all the abuse from the both of them, because I wouldn't let them touch my sister!

Aaron is telling the story of his childhood in a very "matter-of-fact" way, as if, he is emotionally distancing himself from the trauma. But that "false persona" is merely hiding his emotional pain. Also, his porn career with the drug abuse and sexual addiction associated with that lifestyle, is his way of running away from his true feelings. Telling his story today could be very therapeutic for him just by being honest about his true feelings, because his presentation of the details doesn't seem to fit the images being depicted.. I hope Aaron is able to find someplace of safety to talk honestly about his life and the struggles he endured just to survive.

Were you being the best little boy in order to avoid the punishment?

Yes, I was.

What about you Eric?

Eric: Yes, I was too.

I have heard many similar examples of gay men as children, who would try to be the "best little boys in the world" in order to hide their shame and guilt for being gay. Also, of feeling different from other children around them, often believing that their physical attraction to their own sex was very wrong and they deserved the abuse they often received.

Eric: Nothing is perfect in life. My mom and dad are still married. There was always food on the table and the house was always warm. I may have resented some of the things they did but, I realize now, that they did the best that they could, and I am still close to them.

Aaron: My relationship with my mom may have had its difficulties but, my relationship with my father was amazing!

I would like to change the direction of this interview and ask what about being gay scares or worries you?

I purposefully chose to change the direction of the interview because I felt both men were making excuses for their upbringing. Also, Eric and Aaron were talking over and interrupting one another as if in competition with one another, and I wanted to illicit more intimate information from both of them but specifically, Aaron.

Aaron: I am afraid that they will never find a cure for AIDS. Living in a generation where AIDS now has a "cocktail" coming out that is saving lives. At the time when I became HIV positive, I was a successful stockbroker living the good life and I began to think that everything was going to be okay for me.

Now, I wonder if there is ever going to be a cure. I did become positive only after a couple of months of living in New York. I was invited to a party where I was given something that I didn't really know what it was; a drug. I remember being videotaped and I just "played it off," not really knowing how to "play it off?" I walked out the door. A year later, the guy who raped me committed suicide; long story short.

That's terrible Aaron! I am so sorry for you. Was the man gay?

I asked Aaron that specific question, because I wanted to know if the man who clearly had "inner demons" identified himself as gay or, was simply acting out his gay shame while living "in the closet." Tragically, there have been many documented examples of gay men infecting other gay men with full knowledge of the HIV status, simply to achieve their own sexual gratification without taking responsibility for their destructive actions. Take for example, the flight attendant "Patient Zero" who knowingly infected other men even after he was diagnosed as having AIDS.

Aaron: He was a model so, I assumed he was gay.

Can you both see that this type of behavior where someone rapes and infects another of his peers, is a callous, self-destructive act that only serves to perpetuates the gay hatred. Would you both agree that someone would do such a thing to another human being is self-hating?

Aaron: There were eight people involved in this sex party.

That further supports my position that not just one person but, eight people played a part in

infecting you with the AIDS virus! Eight people playing a part in infecting an innocent human being? What do you have to say about that?

Aaron: I never really figured out how I felt about that, because part of me says, "I got what I deserved." I don't know if I feel what they did was right? I mean, I definitely feel that what I did was wrong , and I feel horrible about that. After all, people always tell you to be careful because you're living in a big city, and, I was an idiot.

That particular experience perpetuated a lot of other things in my life. Trying to find myself, and, what do I want from my life? Such as, why I decided to do porn? Does that answer your question? (*Aaron appears somewhat unsure of where to go at this point in the interview, looking a bit confused and unsure of his answers but, he was the one exposing all the painful details).*
Yes, it does for now but ,what about you Eric, what scares you about being gay?

Eric: Almost the same thing Aaron said verbatim happened to me. When I found out my HIV status, I went through total rage that someone could do that to me! It happened to me in California.

Did someone slip you a drug, rape and videotape you?

Eric: Not exactly videotape me but I remember being in a similar situation.

Is that when you felt you became positive?
Eric: Yes. I remember being afraid to be tested but, I do remember feeling right then and there that I was most likely positive as a result of that incident with another man. I recall playing out a fantasy where I was a straight boy and he was raping me so, we definitely were not playing safe.

Aaron: I went to a party where everyone was on drugs and sex was "bareback."

Having heard of these sex parties where one or more individuals were known to be HIV positive and the other participants willingly engaged in high-risk sexual activity is well known in the gay community, I was not surprised by Aaron's and Eric's stories. In fact, I believe the term for those who willingly risks being infected with the AIDS virus are called "Bug Chasers." Those gay men who choose to be infected with the HIV virus believing they would get the virus eventually and they wanted to have sex without protection.

But these fantasies being played out and these sex parties where there were no limits can be as dangerous and the consequences as horrible as a man raping a child!

Eric: (*speaking in a casual manner*) I was a child! I was as naive and innocent as anyone coming into the big city from the Midwest.

Now, Eric views himself as the victim or, the innocent in this scenario. When he states that he was a child or as naive and innocent as one, does that make him less responsible for his actions?

Also, what does that truly say about his self-worth or esteem to take such irresponsible risks with his life for the sake of his own and others' sexual gratification? In addition, the sense of competition between the two is clearly evident with the dramatic elements of their stories.

My overall feeling after hearing from you gentlemen is that there still is a considerable amount of self-hatred being perpetuated within the gay community with gay men raping, drugging, and infecting other gay men in order to achieve a higher level of sexual gratification? Hearing these stories is comparable to raping children and women but instead, you two appeared to have willingly chosen to place yourself in dangerous situations?
Both: Yes!

Aaron: That's why we have so many gay men having sex parties with drugs.

Yes, I believe on such sex sites as Manhunt it is called: PNP (Party and Play), right?

Aaron: Exactly. That's what we've got now!

There was a brief lull in the conversation as all three of us mulled the most recent confession of both men divulging their HIV status and the causes of their infections with the AIDS virus. It was as if we had to ponder as to why we as gay men allowed such behaviors to perpetuate within our community for the sake of sexual gratification, as if that alone, was sufficient reasoning which resulted in such self-destructive and self-hating behaviors.

(Changing the tone of the interview to another direction) **Okay then, let's change the direction of this interview and tell me what do you both find beautiful about the gay community?**

Aaron: The good work I have done for the Department of Health and at gay expos for "Safe Sex and Condom Usage." For example, I am responsible for condom distribution in NYC, where it is my job to make sure that gay clubs and events provide large jars filled with free condoms and lubricant in order to encourage increased safe sex practices.

Ironically, safe sex behaviors that neither man follows in their own sexual practices but that Aaron promotes in his more public persona. What exactly is this man playing out in his life?

Aaron: The people I work with and those I help have become my family; we care about one another. It's sad that many people view gay people as being all about drinking and partying and not about caring and loving one another. It really makes me sad.

This new family that you created of friends and loved ones, they inspire you?

Aaron: Their love for me makes me cry. I'm proud of the community that I am in.

That's really good to hear. But what specifically to you see to be esteem-able acts within the gay community?

Aaron: That's easy, charitable acts! And, my God, I don't want to sound like a broken record but, condom distribution. I will go to the former Saint's Black Parties and similar events where there are sex rooms and will distribute condoms and lube; helping to prevent others from getting what I got!

I am also a big advocate for marriage equality. My boyfriend and I even marched for Marriage Equality at the last Gay Pride Parade. I chose to do that, because I remember the time when we tried to apply for a marriage license, and it was freaking impossible for us to get one!

I can appreciate the desire to have marriage equality but, do you think that those advocating gay marriage may not fully understand the possible repercussions to the marriage contract when in case of divorce, you could lose half your assets to your now ex-husband?

Aaron: I do hope to have someone take care of me too and if we break up, I would expect to receive a fair share of his assets and vice versa. At the end of the day, I don't care how much he has or how much I have. But, if he has it; then yes, I expect a part of what he has, yes! If I have it, then he has a right to get part of my assets; that's just how it works!

It is similar to when we go to dinner either he picks up the check or I do; it's as simple as that.

*As a point of information, the last time I met with Aaron several years after this interview, was during his engagement party to a successful doctor and apparently they have moved to another part of the country to "set up house." I wish them both well.

Got it. On another point, what are your feelings about the term "gay mob psychology" meaning that everybody is doing the same thing, or, following the leader? How do you believe that plays out in the gay community here in New York City?

Aaron: Well, it's different dependent on where you are. What goes in Cincinnati is different than what goes on right here. I specifically remember reading an article in the *Advocate Men* when I was living in Cincinnati, which made reference to the term, "Chelsea boy." I never heard that term before and was intrigued by it. So, knowing that I could get corporate housing due to my job I asked to be moved to NYC and wanted to live in Chelsea and become a "Chelsea Boy!"

If it was Aaron's intention to become a "Chelsea Boy," he achieved his objective, being that he sexy, well-built, clean-cut, stylish and ambitious; all clear attributes of the quintessential "Chelsea boy" type that he desired to become.

Then again, I wonder whether Aaron is truly happy being a "Chelsea boy' and whether his life is truly less satisfying to him as he presents himself to be? My main question with regards to Aaron, is whether he is at "peace with himself?" In my professional estimation, I would answer no, he is not, but trying to give the impression to everyone that he is.

Aaron (*continues*) That "mob psychology" desire to be a "Chelsea Boy," like so many others here, I believed was just not going to happen for me. When I arrived here, unpacked my luggage and looked around and saw what a "Chelsea Boy" looked like, I said to myself, "I could never be a Chelsea Boy; they were all way too 'hot' for me, I would never fit in."
This last comment I view as an attempt on Aaron's part to be viewed as modest, because he clearly embodies the Chelsea Boy" image. His statement is more indicative of someone who simply does not honestly believe in himself and questions his life choices.

But you became one!

(*Taken aback by my statement but, not refuting it*) Okay, if you say so. But I don't see that as a "bad thing." But, as a party promoter I see from nine hundred to twelve hundred people a night and everybody knows my name and I love it!

I'm sure there is that "A List Chelsea" type, whatever. Different crowds; different gyms where there are muscle boys at the gyms; the "Bridge & Tunnel," types that go to Splash (*a now closed gay bar in Chelsea which was very popular*). I also see how they don't tend to interact with one another and I know that we tend to talk to some and ignore others.

So you see this happening, how these guys don't communicate with one another? That's what this book is about.

Aaron: I see it happening but I never really recognized it.

Eric: You were simply not conscious about doing it to others?

Aaron: I didn't recognize it because it's not my job to introduce them to one another so, I just tend to walk away and that gets me out of it, especially, if they are "coming onto me."

You know that you exude a strong sexuality about you?

Aaron: I always did. I know I do.

Do guys ever get "pissed off" if you "come onto them" and then walk away?
Aaron (*getting defensive*) I "come on to them?"

You do flirt with them.

Aaron: Yes, I do flirt; I was voted the Class Flirt in high school. I flirted with everyone; even girls.

Did it ever get you in trouble?

Aaron: Yes! It already got me in trouble.

I decided to pursue this potentially dangerous aspect of Aaron's personality which may have resulted in his being raped by others or, other painful incidents in his past.

How? What happened?

I remember a teacher saying, "Is that your girlfriend? Are you passing notes to your girlfriend?

What was your motivation for flirting both back then and now?

(Pausing to think) I guess back then, though I never thought about this. I guess, it was for the attention that I wasn't getting from flirting, since my own home life sucked!

Aaron's comments here further support my initial perception of Aaron as a little boy still looking for positive attention for others in order to make up for the lack of attention he was getting at home from his "crazy mother?"
But beyond that, flirting has always been a part of me. Also, another thing that has always been a part of me ever since I was a kid, was whenever I was at a party, I would go up to a girl I saw standing alone in a corner and talk to her, even when nobody else would.

If you look at me now, I would always go up to a guy standing alone at one of my club events and talk to them.

Yes. I remember you going up to a friend of mine at an event and talking to him. He really appreciated you doing that. You even gave him a little shoulder massage.

Thank you. That type of interplay comes easy to me and that's why I chose to be a party promoter.

Listening to Aaron talking about his more caring self, where he would befriend others he viewed as being ignored, relates directly to Aaron's charitable work for the NYC Department of Health. As a member of the Board of Health's Safe Sex Awareness campaign where I volunteered as a part of his team toward increasing safe sex awareness for gay men, I got to know more of that caring part of Aaron, in contrast to the "party boy/porn star" image.

(To Eric who was waiting patiently for his turn): **What about you Eric? What do you think about "gay mob psychology?" I saw you make a face when I asked the same question to Aaron. Where do you see it happening in your life?**

Eric: *(referring to Aaron)* Well, it can happen right here in Starbucks! But as far as my experience with it, our backgrounds are basically the same. I met my first relationship in a nightclub where I modeled. I saw that "mob psychology" happening every day when sexy gay men congregate and act the same. It happens everywhere all the boys go to "see and be seen!" I heard about it happening at the Pines Party in Fire Island. I just hope I live long enough to be there, and if I do, I better wear sunscreen; I burn easily.

I mentioned earlier in this interview with regards to how we learn to play the game toward getting our needs met through strategic moves to get what we want from others. What strategic moves do you use with other gay men to get your needs met? For example, what specifically are you looking to win at in life?

Aaron: That's a great question. I didn't know what I wanted to win? I wanted a boyfriend, a picket fence and a house. Just as many in the "straight community" say that they want as well. I am really no different! We all want the same thing and, we as gay men are no different! We simply choose partners of the same sex rather than someone from the opposite sex!

Eric: *(affirming Eric's statement):* Yes, they are no better than me!

Who are you referring to Eric?

Eric: The "straight community!" We all go to the bathroom. We all want to be happy and want our lives to mean something. We are no different!

Thank you guys for your time and I want you both to know that it is my plan to create a talk show at my university for the purpose of having gay men like yourselves tell their stories on the air for all to hear; similar to my goal for this book.

At present, Talk it OUT with Dr. Vince is both a show on Hofstra Radio- WRHU and a featured column of the same name on www.edgeonthenet.com, both with the primary purpose of providing a forum for members of the GLBT community to tell their personal stories.

Aaron: I would love to come on your show when it happens.

Yes, maybe you could come on and talk about your life as a porn star and on the gay community's fascination with gay porn?

Eric: I'll be one of your first guests.

Aaron: Yeah, on that subject. I love it when guys recognize me in the streets or at events and say, "Oh, there goes one of those fucking porn stars," and then they'll go home and "jerk off" to one of my videos!

That is exactly what I am talking about with regards to the "gay communication" and how we can't be honest and supportive with one another. How we are so quick to criticize someone and then lie to ourselves, as if "putting others down" makes us feel better about ourselves but then, those who criticize are not being honest with who we really are.

Aaron: You got it! Sounds like a great show in the making, and I would love to be on it and tell things as I see it from my perspective. I feel strongly that someone needs to increase awareness within the gay community of all the bullshit!

You got it and thank you both for your time and I wish you all the things you hope for to happen.

Aaron and Eric: Thank you, we had fun too!

END OF INTERVIEW

FOLLOW-UP INTERVIEW WITH AARON *(Held in his Chelsea apartment one week later)*

I appreciate you meeting with me again to talk about your life and your work with the NYC Dept. of Health. So, what exactly is the nature of your our work with the Dept. of Health?

Aaron: Basically, I am a gay liaison. When they have a campaign or project to do with the gay community, they call on me for help. I was involved with a project to help with a survey for HIV drug users, another on safe sex education on HIV prevention for gay men under twenty-one. I helped organize focus groups of gay men on sexual activity and as a party promoter, organizing social events with a focus on the Dept. of Health's "Safe Sex Awareness" campaign for the past three years including, my condom campaign.

Yes, you are very involved with distributing condoms in clubs but, what specifically motivated your activism?

The club owners with whom I worked with as a party promoter, agreed to have me be in charge of distributing condoms and lube to some forty bars and clubs in the metro area. They picked me, because I am a "hotshot" and attract large crowds. They knew I would have no problem greeting guys with my line; "Hey, we are doing a condom campaign here and you're going to sign up for this aren't you? And the response I got was always, "okay."

Clearly Aaron was using his sexuality and charisma to his best advantage and to the advantage of whatever charitable cause he was advocating. In a sense, Aaron was bringing his "winning game" to a really good cause.

The next question I have is, do gay men really use condoms?

Well, a lot of guys who are already HIV Positive tend to like to "bareback" and not use condoms. Bareback parties are very popular whenever someone opens up his apartment to these parties where no one uses condoms because many guys feel it decreases sexual pleasure.

(Quickly changing the subject) But what I do for the Department of Health is to make sure all the clubs and bars have condoms for everyone to use free of charge, to promote safe sex behavior.

From an earlier interview with Aaron and Eric, it was made clear that during their sex sessions, there were no condoms used therefore confirming that Aaron clearly didn't practice what he preached or, advocated for others. This paradox is very curious to me; one on hand he is helping others and on the other side, he is taking very serious risks to his health, as are many of his fellow "bare-backers!"

By my doing this condom campaign, I felt as though I was in a sense giving back to the gay community and giving people options.

In interviews with other gay men who were positive, they reported that men who were HIV Positive tended to be more sexual than men who are HIV Negative because they had a more "devil take care" attitude. What are your thoughts about this?

It's hard for me to answer that, because most porn stars have to be extremely sexual and many porn stars are HIV Positive. Also, porn stars have to keep their erections going so, they give us Viagra and have guys giving us oral sex to keep our erections going when having to wear condoms in the anal sex scenes.

Wow, that's very interesting but the main point of my book and my new radio show: "Talk it OUT I deal directly with issues about gay shame and gay guilt. On both subjects, there is a tendency for many of gays to having lived "shadow" lives as we were growing up, and how after "coming out" many young gays simply do not know how to be gay? They get into cliques" and act foolishly, and leave themselves susceptible to being taken advantage of

(Aaron cuts in). Yeah, and acting as if they are in high school all over again.

Exactly!

I love seeing all the "carrying on" between the guys in clubs. I also love watching gay men in relationships being depicted on television in such shows as *Brothers and Sisters* and *Modern Family.*

Yes, I love those shows especially, the gay couples!

Yes, I think they are great role models for young gay men to see.

What role models are better choices for the young guys "coming out" to see? Do you advocate any particular groups such as: the drag queens, the leather community? It seems as if neither group want anything to do with the other because one group advocates "hyper masculinity" while the other promotes femininity. What do you think?

I don't think it's true that neither group want anything to do with the other. I personally know a drag queen called Trailer Trash who is always seen in clubs and bars that cater to the leather community. She's won awards at many leather community events.

It seems as if the heterosexual community is more fascinated with the drag queen persona while the gay community is more "jaded."

That's true. But I would check that with members of the heterosexual community.

What do you want to say about yourself as a gay man today? Also, what is something you want the gay community to recognize about itself? Where should we go; what is our future? (Aaron is taking a deliberately long pause) Okay, then, let me ask you what is YOUR future? Such as, what are your strong qualities that work for you or not?

Let me tell you. I was raised Southern Baptist. My church and community "turned its back" on me. I had to find my own way, which wasn't easy. I had to become my own role model but learned from men who I got involved with either as friends or boyfriends. I learned some from the media about how gay men act....

Who were your media role models?

(*Giggling*) Believe it or not, but, I would say Elton John. It was men we viewed in the media who modeled for us how to act, since we weren't learning anything at home.

Your generation certainly had a good deal more role models in the media than my generation did for sure.

Yes, you are right about that.

So to conclude this follow-up interview, what do you foresee your future to be?

I take it as it comes. I "go with the flow." Right now I am working parties at Splash this Saturday and Fire Island this summer. I don't know? For a long time I debated if I was going to be successful if I worked hard every day. Now, my "heart is just not into it." For the most part, I have a loving family but, I don't want to predict the future. I want to be in a relationship but I'm just not sure. I enjoy promoting parties and I'm good at it but I know I can't do it forever!

Then what do you foresee for the gay community? After all, we are still in our adolescence being only a community since the early seventies and we're still trying to find our way. What do you see for the gay community's future? How do we define ourselves?

I don't know, I think it depends who we elect for our next president?

Just when in your adolescence do you remember your first gay experience?

I remember playing in the dirt with my cousin when I was really young and getting excited. I remember finding magazines that my dad owned and only looking at the men in the magazines and not the women.

When I was a teenager, I remember watching a television show where the gay character was crying about being gay and I felt sorry for him. Then, when I was in college, I dated women and had sex with them but, wanted to have sex with my male friends instead. But, being raised Southern Baptist, I also knew it to be a "major sin" against God.

Well, you certainly moved away from that viewpoint of it being a "major sin" when you were a porn star.

(*Laughing*) I guess you could say I did it and never looked back.

I want to thank you for taking the time to meet with me again and I look forward to working with you in your Safe Sex Campaign for the Department of Health.

So am I, and I too am looking forward to it.

In the next months following this interview, Aaron and I worked together interviewing gay men on video talking in a similar fashion as the interviews in this book with a focus on issues important to the Department of Health such as Mental Health, Community Activism, Substance Abuse, Aging, and HIV Awareness. With Aaron, I interviewed other porn stars, transsexuals, gay men of various ages, and celebrities such as Robin Byrd and Peppermint. After the campaign was completed, Aaron met an anesthesiologist and they moved to another part of the country with plans of getting married and creating a home for themselves.

Presently, I have been unable to contact Aaron or Eric and wish them both good health and happiness and pray their questionable choices haven't led to any serious consequences.

END OF INTERVIEW WITH AARON TANNER

CHAPTER ELEVEN

ROB ORDONEZ – "ONE SEXY SPANISH FLY"

Rob Ordonez and I met in his apartment in Queens and began this interview after a light dinner in the summer of 2007. Rob, like Aaron, Eric, Bob and Tim exudes a playful sexuality and a "come on let's get in on" attitude that made him very popular with a large group of gays such as porn stars Aaron Tanner and Michael Lucas. He initially identified himself as a "budding artist" who planned to become famous in any way possible; being a porn star was one of those possible career choices.

So Rob, tell me something about you such as what was your growing up gay like for you?

Rob: I remember that I tried to grow up acting "macho" like my brothers but, I had a problem in school with "fitting in." I had friends at the time but, it was still not easy for me. I dated girls to keep up the image of being "macho," but, I couldn't wait to drop off my girlfriend to be with guys!

What was your first gay experience? What was it like?

(Giggling) I "blew" a taxi driver because I didn't have enough money for the fare. He was very cute. So, he parked in a dark alley and I "blew" him. I know I took a risk but, I enjoyed it!
I'm sure he did as well. When did you have your first real relationship?

I was nineteen and met him when I lived in Cancun. We were friends first, and he was a lot of fun. He was a psychologist but, he was also a little "coo-coo."

He was a little coo-coo?

He was a nice guy but very possessive. We are still friends but, long-distance friends.

So, did you ever feel any shame about being gay?

No, not shame, but I sometimes wish I wasn't gay, because I would see all my brothers and sisters being happy with their kids and sometimes in the mornings I would feel I had nothing to look forward to in life. Being gay isn't easy for me because I don't like to be lonely.

I can identify with that, but what was your "coming out" experience like for you?

When I was twenty-one, I would go to the gay clubs every weekend, mainly, for the dancing. I didn't tell anyone in my family until I was twenty-five. That was the age when I finally told my family I was gay and leaving Mexico for New York.

Knowing Rob to being a very sexual guy, I knew that this "coming out" statement was not only for his sexual freedom but, for his freedom to be himself without having to "check-in" with his family all the time and seek their approval.

Okay, so you were planning to leave for New York anyway but, you wanted to tell your family first. What would have happened if they rejected you? Did you plan to leave Mexico anyway for your new life as a back-up plan. What happened when you told them?

Well, my dad said he was glad that I was leaving because my brothers were ashamed of me. They told all of their friends that I was leaving for New York to be with my girlfriend. None of their friends knew that I was gay, because my family were all ashamed of me.

How do feel about that now?

I get along well with them okay but, they are so "macho" that they don't want to talk about my being gay. Even when I went home to my sister's wedding five years ago and saw that two of her bridesmaids were my ex-girlfriends! Nobody mentioned anything about my being gay.

What did they ask you?

They asked me about my girlfriend and whether we were still together? But instead of playing the lie, I told them that I didn't have a girlfriend but had a boyfriend which shocked them! My sister ended up getting mad at me for telling them and disrupting her wedding.

As Rob was telling his story, I felt a wave of sadness come over me, not just him but, for the countless other gay people who have felt forced by their families and friends to keep up the lie that they're heterosexual, when they clearly are not! This mask of shame that many gay men such as Rob are forced to wear only leads to a propensity for depression, compulsive behavior, and even at its most severe, suicide. Rob clearly experienced the shame that others felt toward him but refused to allow them to make him feel shameful; good for him.

(*Changing subject*) So, Rob, how is it that you know so many gay celebrities such as Aaron Tanner and Michael Lucas? (*Aaron being my prior interview, was introduced to me by Rob*)

I walk their dogs. I also worked as a waiter in a popular restaurant in the Village and meet people there. I, also, "give good service." (*Smiled mischievously*)

Of course I immediately picked up upon the sexual innuendo in Rob's last statement, and knew he was being playful and flirtatious with me. He knew that I would know the subtext to the "good service" comment; being of a sexual nature.

Got it, so, if though it seems pretty obvious, what exactly do you like about being gay?

Being gay is just like being a kid again! Being like a kid, in that we get to sometimes dress up young; trying to look like a boy. Just like boys, we break up quickly like we did when we were teenagers, and then, we date someone else!

We like to go dancing, go to the beach, always trying to look good. My friends and I are always concerned about how we look and, I think we all look good.

What is something you don't like about being gay?

I would like to have kids.

Are you feeling that way because of the pressure you received from your family?

Maybe, I don't know. But I would like to have kids and feel I need a boyfriend to do that.

You can always adopt kids.

I have the feeling that Rob's comments come from a feeling of loneliness and isolation for his family and country, and may not even be aware of his sadness by "masking" it with sexual compulsion. Also, Rob has begun involving himself in his efforts toward becoming famous as a performance artist in the leather/bondage communities. All to which, I perceive as a way of showing his family and himself, that he has become a success without having them in his life.

Okay then, so what else do you dislike about being gay?

We are all gay but, we are all very different! We get jealous of one another and we separate ourselves from different groups of gay guys, such as the Latin-Americans stay together, Blacks stay with one another, the Asians stay together. The lesbians have their own place. And, no one interacts with one another! We are all so separate.

Then, we have those gay men like, those in South Beach, Florida who have all this major "attitude" because they think they're so beautiful and better than everyone else.

We stay separate; we don't connect.

Yes. I can blend in pretty easily, but that is not true for everyone else.

This is very true with regards to Rob, since he is very familiar with many different types of gay men from the porn, leather, and bondage communities, as well as, celebrities in the LGBT community who are good friends of his as well. It does seem as if Rob has achieved at least one important step with the gay community ,as being both sexually and socially desired by many.

Where do you think you blend in best?

I blend in with the leather/bondage groups, even with the "Chelsea Queens," who have accepted me into their world; which is nice. But still, there are some who don't want me around them. It's just a matter of knowing with what group you blend in best.

Rob's comments remind me of Freud's "latency stage" where adolescents find the right clique or, gang of friends to associate with where he/she feels the most accepted and supported.

Do you sometimes believe that some gay men like to "put other gay men down" for their personal enjoyment and if your do then, why do you believe they do that?

Yes, they do that so that they can feel superior to everyone else, gay or straight!.

Why do they need to feel superior? (Trying to get an emotional response from Rob)

Because just like all human beings, we like to compete with one another; we love the competition!

Good point, so, what are you hoping for in your future for yourself as a gay man?
My dreams are to become a famous artist and find a good husband. I want to have a couple kids, get a couple dogs and travel everywhere with my family.

Travel where?

I would like to travel to Europe, South America, everywhere, with my boyfriend.

Interestingly, Rob did not mention his home country of Mexico to show off his success and his new found family to his original family of origin, who dismissed and pushed him away from them because of their shame and disappointment in him?.

What don't you like about being gay? It sounds as if you really don't want to be alone.

Yes, I don't want to continue being alone, I hate being alone. (*His tone becomes sad and reflective of his life*). I am tired of being alone; going to a movie or out to eat alone. I do a lot of alone things. I have traveled many, many times alone and even though I always meet new people. But, I am tired of it. It's scary…

I hear Rob's sadness and loneliness but I personally know that Rob is sexually active and men who tend to be sexually active tend to have very short-term relationships comprised primarily of "one night stands," which rarely go from that one night of passion. Perhaps Rob is setting himself up for disappointment without really being aware of his self-defeating actions?

Do you sometimes think of the words of others, such as my own mother, who say that if you are gay, you are most likely going through life alone?

Yes, of course. Those were exactly the same words my father told me when I told him I was gay!

This exchange brings to mind a potential Self-fulfilling Prophecy, where what we are afraid others say will happen to us, comes to be true, for the basic reason that we believe the prophecy, and unconsciously perform actions that cause that prophecy to occur.

I, personally, believe that many of us create the prophecy to become a reality for ourselves, which then, results in many gay men living alone. All, because we have accepted the belief that being alone is what they deserve, primarily due, to gay shame.

Fortunately, we could just as easily turn that curse into a lie and celebrate our gayness and tear down those walls that others tell us we deserve. After all, in order to honestly love another, we must first love ourselves first. Therefore, I question whether Rob and others like him truly love themselves, especially if they feel rejected by their primary caretakers; that, being their parents.

What did your father say?
He said that I should try going out with girls so I wouldn't be alone. That a girl is less likely to leave you because they want children.

Do you think your father and family believe your gayness is a choice?

My parents think I am confused.

Denial is an easy rationalization that many families of gay men and women go to whenever they refuse to believe or accept their loved ones decision to "come out of the closet" to them. Also, if the parent stays in the place of denial, they can convince themselves to believe their child will change and follow the correct and more acceptable path in life, which would give them comfort.

How long have you been "out" to them?

Nine years.

And they still think you are confused?

My dad and my brothers think I am confused. They say that all I need is a "hot girl" to love; that all men are "pigs" who just want to "get laid."

Surprisingly, Rob makes no mention of his mother and I am wondering what role she plays in all of this or, does the mother let the father do all the talking and decision-making. As for his father and brothers, I don't think Rob is ever going to change the way they think, and the "pig" comment is more of a reflection of themselves.

So, you said earlier that you love being gay! What do you love about being gay?

I am part of the artistic community here in New York but, there are many gay artists. I am trying to make a lot more connections. I love men and I like looking like a kid!

You sort of still look like a kid in that you are slim, boyish, and playful.
Yes. I do like still looking and feeling young.
What has been your most memorable gay experience?

Well, watching guys in bars standing alone all looking like they are right off the cover
MetroSource Magazine. I remember asking this handsome guy if he was gay and he said,
"the only "straight" thing about me is my smile. I loved that! We ended up going home
together! *(Another big smile- a conquest)!*

That's a great line! So, what is your most upsetting or negative gay experience?

That I became HIV Positive from a guy who I dated, who ended up dying of AIDS?

I am so sorry for you. How do you feel about what he did to you and having to live with AIDS?

I'm healthy; I have never been sick. The pills are working, and my viral load is very, very low.

Excellent, I am so happy for you. But. what about the popularity of "bare-backing?" Guys sleeping with other men whom they know are HIV Positive, do you do it?

Yes, but I never let a guy "cum" inside of me; never! Also, I don't swallow "cum."

If a guy chooses to use a condom, will you let him "cum" inside of you?

Sure I would, that would be fine*!*

Rob's sexual behavior, even though he is taking some precautions, is still potentially dangerous and he is playing "Russian Roulette." And with "bare-backing," one has to look at why someone would take such risks with their health, especially is they know of others who died from the disease? Again, gay shame and a lack of self-worth, both, due to Rob's family and cultural heritage where it was inferred through their communication to him that he is not special, causes a "ripple effect" where Rob's decision-making may be fueled by rebellion and an intention to prove them all wrong about him,.

A belief that one is not special as a human being due to what is believed as their chosen abnormal lifestyle which often leads the shamed party to seek comfort and support from others. It is my belief that Rob through his actions, has chosen the art, leather, bondage, and "bare-backing" communities/cultures in order to gain the comfort and support that was denied to him by his family and country of origin.

On the subject of this book, gay male communication, what do you think about the way that gay men communicate with each other?

I think we are basically insecure and fearful of rejection?

Why do you believe that so many gay men are insecure?

Because it's all about our looks, the house in Fire Island, who has the sexiest boyfriend, who has the best clothes; who travels more? It's all about competition and seeking approval.

Who are your more positive role models? I remember you mentioned earlier that you love Madonna, right?
Yes, she is my number one role model! She is both strong and rich.

Yes, but, she's a woman not, a gay man!

But she was bisexual for a while and is a big supporter of the gay community!

That's very true. What other role models do you like?

I love gay artists who pursue their art and sexual identity. I just love that!

There is also this wonderful gay couple I know; Brad Carpenter and his lover Chris who are wonderful role models for me. Everyone wants to be like them and I love being a part of their life.

Thanks to Rob, both Brad and Chris agreed to be interviewed and will appear later in this book.

Was there anyone in your family or country of origin that were role models for you? Specifically, was there anyone who you looked up to and helped you to feel good about yourself? Or, were there just people who made you feel bad about yourself?

In school, I was always picked on by the other boys because they thought I was gay?

Why did they think you were gay?

I was in a school for only boys, and I was very shy and small. Also, I had a friend who was very effeminate and they thought we were boyfriends. Also, I was being abused by my family.

How were you abused by your family?

I was always getting beaten up. I was verbally and physically abused.
What did they say to you?

That I was ugly, that they were ashamed of me; that I was dumb?

Did you believe what they were saying was true?

At the time I did, yes.

What about now?

No, I don't.

What changed you?

I felt many times that I was like a butterfly. Like before you are born, you are small and shrived up like in a cocoon, and when you come out of your mother's womb, you become a butterfly. People tell you that you're beautiful and everyone loves you.

Rob's image of being a butterfly is perfect analogy for almost all of us growing up and trying to find who we truly are. But, the desire to fly and be beautiful sounds as if Rob was longing to escape his abuse and be recognized for his beauty, both, inside and out.

Also, the feeling of being in a cocoon, although a safe place, can also represent a sense of hiding in fear of the world and those who abuse and devalue us in this self-destructive process of keeping us in fear and shame based on the abusers anger and disappointment in the child..

But then, you tell stories of how your family abused and rejected you. Do you feel that coming to New York and now living within the gay community, that you were given the opportunity to fly? That by rejecting you, they gave you a gift in finding another family to love and support you?

Yes, I do. Here in New York. I can be myself with my gay friends and in my work. People support me and I feel wanted. Similar to when girls who wanted me when I was a teenager because I was so wild and crazy, but, also, unattainable!

The focus of this book is that many gay men said they didn't come alive until they came out into the gay community. Does that hold true for you?

Yes! That is what I'm talking about.

As an artist, how would you paint yourself prior to "coming out of the closet?"

Well, I had girlfriends. Girls liked me because I was wild and had money. I even used to get all the prettiest girls because I was wild and had money. So, I would paint myself as a star!

Maybe that is why your brothers were jealous of you?

Yes, they were. I was the youngest-acting of them too! I used to "show them up" too, by getting the best looking girls! They would look at me and say, "What is this some kind of act?" They just couldn't believe I got all these girls and, I loved 'showing them up!'

Rob is providing clear example of normal competition between siblings and especially men who have a natural tendency to compete with one another with the objective of winning the game as referred to in Sarah Trenholm's Pragmatic Model in Chapter One. (see: p. 11)
How many brothers do you have?

Seven brothers but, I am the second oldest? Also, I have two sisters.

Nine! So statistically speaking, one of you was bound to be gay.

I also think that my youngest brother may be gay! In fact, my parents once asked me if I thought he was gay, because he was so effeminate. They even wanted to change him and make him see a "shrink." But, they didn't bother wanting to change me because I was leaving Mexico.

So, if Rob was out of sight by moving to another country, he was also going to be out of mind as well, as it no longer necessary for his parents to try to change him. How sad the lengths to which some families go in order to change their children, even if the potential damage they may cause is ten times worse than allowing their children to become who they truly are meant to be.

So what happened once you began living in New York City?

I started going to discos where all the good-looking gay guys went and I could get hot sex and drugs. I went wild but, I was also scared, because I was all alone in a strange country. And, I knew that I wanted to "party," do drugs and play "rock and roll." I got some tattoos and didn't communicate with my family back home; they thought I died or, was in the hospital.

Again, Rob's self-destructive behavior continues to suggest his lack of self-esteem and worth by following a very dangerous path. In his own words, "went wild, do drug." Clearly, rebelling against his family and their abusive and devaluing actions toward him for being gay but, his actions could also have led to his eventual destruction due to his lifestyle; as they predicted,

Would you say you were being self-destructive?

Yes, very!

Why were you doing that? Were you trying to kill yourself?

I was scared, depressed, and lonely. Plus, I was very young at twenty-five. I said to myself, "Fuck everything! Do everything that I never tried before. I even "blacked out" due to taking drugs!

Rob's words are a sad affirmation of my earlier conclusion that he was clearly "acting out" against the world, and that once he had his independence from his dismissive family, he clearly tried to act out their belief that he was wild, immature, and following the wrong path in life by being gay. And if his actions led to his potential demise, his death would have only served by proving his family correct, and the gay community would have lost another young, sweet soul to gay shame.
Continuing) Somehow, I met the right people who helped me find the right path; they saved me!

I know that you know all these influential gay people in the community and today, you feel more important and part of that group. Thankfully, instead of becoming another casualty to gay shame, you "came out" and despite being scared, self-destructive, and almost suicidal, you survived thanks to this people!

Yes! I always wanted to be part of the "in group." But, I was still afraid and unsure what to do?

What were you scared of? Dying of AIDS? Being alone?

Yes, I was scared not only of all those things but, I thought one day, I would pick up the wrong man who turned out to be a "psycho" who could kill me. I felt I was terminal because I was HIV…so …why not?

Rob, are you saying that you were willing to take risks with your life because you don't care or, do you want to be loved, respected, and part of the popular group of gays? Which is it?

Because the first question very likely could lead to your death!

Rob's fear of being killed, sounds as if he saw the movie <u>CRUSING</u> with Al Pacino, where a serial killer chose gay men to kill during sexual intercourse. That movie scared more than a few gay men and caused many of us to be extra cautious of whom we chose to bring back to our homes.

But, what concerned me most upon hearing Rob's statement, was his 'devil-make-care" attitude with regards to his own self-preservation; as if he didn't care if he picked up a potential killer now that he has been diagnosed with HIV; clearly another example of "gay shame" and low self-worth despite his desire to be famous and admired for his work.

I noticed that sex for me was a way to feel accepted and wanted. So even now, I am getting very sexual. I feel that sex cheers me up and boosts my ego. I always feel better after sex.

Some gay men say that after sex they feel emotionally "empty" after anonymous sex but, not you?

No! I always look for the next sexual experience; the next thing?

Rob's statements are indicative of someone who is sexually compulsive or has a sexual addiction, similar to drug or alcohol abuse, where he is looking for his next "feel good" experience. Although he admits to feeling better during and after sex, he denies that his behavior may be compulsive. After all, denial is acknowledged as a basic behavioral tendency for someone who cannot come to terms with his addiction or compulsive behavior.

How would you classify your life to be like now?

It's the best! I love my life right now. Because even though I have been living alone for the past three years, I am working on my book, my own website, and I just finished filming a documentary on my life; all my goals are being met. My dreams are coming true.

That's maybe why I haven't found a boyfriend right now, because I am focusing on my career and if I had a boyfriend, I wouldn't be getting all my goals met because my focus would be on him. When I am ready for a relationship I hope it will be someone who is "into" the same life I am involved in? Maybe he'll be a famous artist? Maybe we'll be famous together? Maybe our career paths will cause us to come together and then, I will get all I want?

Maybe, maybe, maybe? Rob's comments are indicative of a dreamer but his dreams also keep him energized and focused on the prize. But the prize here is not only on getting a boyfriend and finding love but finding fame and acknowledgment for his artistic talent.

What do you believe energizes or motivates your dreams? Do you think the rejection and ridicule you received from your family had something to do with your desire to become famous?

Yes, I think I had a very tough life but, that toughness only made me stronger. Having my life not go as easy as I might have liked, makes you appreciate the little things and doing things for me.

Do you get any financial support from your family?

Yes, I do.

Do you feel any guilt for taking the money and not making it yourself?
No, I don't, because it was really my grandmother who died and left me the money in order to live here in New York. But, my dad still helps me when I ask for it because he worries about me.

What about your mother? You haven't said anything about her, only your father?

They are divorced. My dad is rich but my mother is poor? My dad remarried and he has the money.

Does she know you're gay?

Yes, she likes all my friends and boyfriends. We get along great!

Anything else you want to say about your family right now?

No, other than we get along great and love each other. It was the best thing I ever did to move up here, because now, they all miss me and wish me well.

Do you have anything else to say about gay communication and how we treat one another?

I think we're a little "jaded" because we don't want the party to end. But some of my friends have mellowed and are more "into" relationships.

In closing, what are your last words about the gay community? Specifically, what do you think gay men need to do in order to make their lives work better for themselves? Do we need to work more on how to talk, interact, or "be" with one another? How is your communication with other gay men for example?

Well, I only have two or three good friends who I can count on, where there is no competition between us. One of them is an artist like me. Another enjoys sex like me. Another one likes to go to shows. So, I don't want to really open myself up to anyone else, because I am not "into" too much "partying" and drugs!

But you do want a boyfriend?

Yes!

Finding a healthy and loving relationship for some, takes a long time to find.

Yes, especially in New York! It was until I started working out all the time to look good that I began to attract the "right" people.

So, then, your focus is really about finding that "hot" boyfriend and by working out all the time, you will find him, and in the process, will help you toward feeling better about yourself?

Yes, if I have both a career and a sexy boyfriend, I know I will be happy.

As I listen to Rob, I wonder if he will still feel content even if he finds that "hot boyfriend" and success in his chosen profession, since rejection from family and home for being gay is not easy thing to recover from. Despite receiving financial support from his father, money does not replace love.

At this point in the interview, I wanted to get Rob to respond a little more fully by touching of his emotions.

What makes you cry?

(*Pause*) Sad stories or sad movies will make me cry.

What specific movies do you remember crying at and why?

(*Another long pause*) The last scene in the HBO series *Six Feet Under,* where in the end, it showed how everyone in the cast died made me cry. I felt badly seeing them die.

What makes you happy; what makes you smile?

(*Smiling*) My friends, and going to the beach in the summer; feeling sexy. I smile all the time. I love to smile.

What do you believe would make the gay community happy?

Like me, I think they all need to settle down. I love to see couples together holding hands and they look so happy, as if, they're not only lovers but, they are best friends too. It's just a great feeling to be with someone you love.

You sound like a real romantic. But you are also very sexual; are both hot sex and love for you related?

Yes, I am a romantic and I love hot sex. With my sexual partners, I love to be dominated and I am a very submissive bottom. I like it rough!

With someone I am dating, I want romance and kissing for a long time.

What do you consider to be a romantic date?

Going to a Broadway show and have dinner after. I love the beach. I would love to get away to a romantic place for a weekend, such as going to a lake or hiking in a forest.

I hope you get what you want and I appreciate you taking this time to talk to me and share your intimate feelings and desires.

You're welcome. I had fun.

As I ended the interview, I felt a little sorry for Rob in his pursuit for love and acceptance for who he is, and his need to have artistic talents recognized. But in many ways, Rob sounded like a little boy who just wanted all of his dreams fulfilled. But then, who doesn't want their dreams fulfilled?

My only concern for Rob is whether even if those two goals are achieved, will those goals be enough to replace the gay shame perpetrated by his family and whether some of his potentially self-destructive actions, despite all their fun and excitement, may end badly for him, I hope not.

.

Follow- up Interview with Rob Ordonez – July 2012

Rob is presently single and working as a photographer hosting monthly sex parties at a club in New York City and has self-published the art book, Lustrous. Rob is also involved in charitable work within the LGBTQ community.

*At a recent dinner with Rob and his friend Monica, Rob confided that his father still gives him money from his successful businesses with his eight other sons, who live near him and work with him.

Me: How is your relationship with your family today?

Rob: They still make fun of the way I talk when I go down to Mexico to visit them, and my youngest brother told me he was gay but ,our father refuses to believe it, and blames me for poorly influencing him due to my own gayness.

Me: Maybe they'll send him to New York as they did you?

Rob *(laughs)*: Yes, maybe he might just do that, but, I think he's going to try to convince him he's straight and keep him away from me.

Monica:(*emphatically*) Rob, I wouldn't have anything to do with people who don't love and respect me. I am sorry they still don't accept you; you're a wonderful man.

Listening to Rob and Monica I felt very sad for Rob and his on-going dysfunctional relationship with his family and their continued disrespect and cruelty of his lifestyle and mannerisms. It is also clear that Rob wants dearly to have his family's love and respect, and tries to prove himself as a photographer and artist but, his sexual compulsive behavior continues to work against him. It is a paradoxical situation where Rob wants his family's admiration and yet, his sexual promiscuity, although it gets him attention within the leather community, keeps him within a lifestyle that would never get him the respect from the family he loves.

END OF INTERVIEW WITH ROB

I met with Brian at a well-known bar in Chelsea and was very pleased to see that this well-known recording artist was a sweet young man with a big smile and lots of charisma. Having

seen him shirtless and sexy dancing in his music video, I was surprised to see him looking as if he just walked out of his college philosophy class looking casual and "laid-back."

Thank you very much Brian for taking the time to meet with me.

My pleasure, I am looking forward to it.

I would like to start off by asking some questions about your personal background, specifically, with regards to you childhood experiences of how you felt different from other children around you?

I grew up in Los Angeles; a big city that was very progressive. Even though I remember being "closeted" at a young age, I still "came out" very young and found a group of friends like me. I remember going out to clubs; doing "my thing" at thirteen, fourteen- years-old with my friends.

My father was a single parent and he really didn't know what was going on with me. So, I continued going to the club scene and met this gay kid when I was fifteen who took me to this gay underage club and I would "hang out" there. So, I created an environment that I felt comfortable in, because I was always there, especially, on the weekends "hanging out" with my friends.

So, on some level, that all helped, because I didn't feel so isolated with having so many gay friends at such a young age. My father was a military pilot so, being gay was not okay at all. So, it was tough on one side having to hide that side of my life as we all did, but, I felt fortunate that I had so many friends like me while growing up.

I moved out of the house when I was seventeen, almost eighteen, to go to college so, I started living my gay life on my own at a very young age. From there, I was able to "do my own thing" because I wasn't living at home. But, I still had to hide that lifestyle from my family. I finally "came out" to my mother when I was twenty-one and she was as supportive as she could be.

I have been very lucky that my parents ended up being very supportive of my being gay and eventually they told me that they knew I was gay for years, and even knew that my boyfriends were my boyfriends, and not just friends. They just couldn't come to terms that I was gay and ask me if I was gay until, I announced it.

I just couldn't bring it up with my father being in the military; even having gone to military schools.

How is it you lived with your father and not your mother?

I lived with my mother for most of my life but, when I became a competitive ice skater as I reached my teen years, I had to move away from my mother and my brothers to live with my father who lives closer to ice rinks. So, when I was thirteen I went to live with him to pursue that career. In hindsight. I enjoyed living away from my brothers and kind of "doing my own thing."

How many brothers?

I have three brothers including a step brother but, I had two brothers when I moved away from my mother's home.

Do you know if you're the only gay one?

Yes, I am the only gay one.

Do you feel that you being the only gay one in the family takes away some of the pressure with your father, being that you have two other brothers to sire offspring, reducing any shame you may have felt for being gay?

(Spoken very quickly) I don't think that was the case, because my parents were proud of me and the things I have accomplished in life; the one who "had his shit together," so to speak. Not to say my brothers don't, but I was the one who stayed out of trouble, and always did the right thing!

You were the "best little boy."

Yes, I was very goal orientated and I worked hard.

Why did you work so hard Brian?

Although I didn't always attribute wonderful qualities to him, as I got older I learned that specific quality to my dad. I was always a hard worker growing up. I started my first job when I was thirteen years old, working at an ice cream store across the street.

Do you think there was a bit of the "best boy" dynamic in there?

Absolutely, yes!

Brian, I believe there is this desire within many gay men to be the "best little boy in the world" in order to counteract the shame of being gay and a sense of inadequacy. With this sense of inadequacy we tend to form a type of survival instinct where we want to show others we can take care of ourselves without their assistance.

Specifically, that in order to survive in our young gay world, this "best little boy" behavior took over so we could keep any negative attention away from us. Do you agree or disagree?

For me, it was always about being a survivor. I lost my stepfather who acted just like my real father who, tragically died in an airplane crash, so, when that happened, I had to "step up to the plate." My mother was an "emotional mess" and my brothers were too young; it was definitely a survival instinct; knowing I could make it on my own, and that I didn't have to rely on other people. I think it was definitely that instinct at play there.

Brian is being very open and honest with me, providing many intimate details, but, what I find most striking with his sharing, is the speed in which he is delivering that information. The pace of his storytelling suggests a need to disclose but, there was some anxiousness as well being conveyed in his fast pace delivery, and I questioned where that anxiety stemmed from? That fast pace was most in evidence when sharing of the death of his stepfather, which suggests a defense mechanism to avoid becoming emotional.

How and when did you "come out of the closet," and how would you define "coming out of the closet?"

To me, there was no one official day when I decided to "come out." I felt that I was "out" around fifteen or sixteen to my friends, and then, I "came out" to others along the way. As for my family, my mom was my first, and my dad was much later. But by the time I got around to it, he already knew, and was so okay with it, that it wasn't even an issue

Evidence says that most parents already know.

Oh, yes, he knew, and had already met my partner. It was never actually said, but, he never said anything otherwise to make me feel uncomfortable for being gay.

Brian is coming across here as one of the lucky ones who received the love and acceptance from parents that many of us were denied. His clear work ethic and ability to deal with adversity through considerable charm and intelligence has worked well for him. Happily, he appears to have obtained many of the goals in life that many of us aspire to achieve in our lifetimes.

Did your family ever make any negative comment with regards to your being gay that hurt your feelings or caused you to feel shameful for being a gay man?

(Stumbling a bit here-trying to find words) At that point, I didn't. I'm glad that I'm gay! I have the opportunity to experience so much more as a gay man, having success as a recording artist and a loving relationship with both my family and close friends.

Did being gay ever cause you to feel challenged; with gay men, as well as, the "straight" community?

Yes, to some degree. I came here with all the masses, and just did what I had to do to become a success. Sure, I had certain challenges in life, such as the death of my stepfather but, those challenges often come with life. I learned so much in life and the challenges that come with it, and being gay has helped me so much in dealing with those challenges.

So you affirm that being gay has helped you to be who you are today?

Yes, absolutely, and I am proud of that and own it! I own those experiences. There are some things about the gay community that challenge me but, have not stopped me in any way. It took me a while as an artist to get there.

Do you feel that your comfort in being a gay man has helped you in your career as a recording artist, as well as, a human being?

Yes, on one hand, and no, on another. A lot of people want to "pigeon-hole" you into one category or cross you over to another market, because you are gay. I think we are changing things slowly but not right away. That is why I didn't "come out" right away as a gay man in the music business, because I wanted to develop myself as an artist.

Being a professional actor, I fully understand what Brian is sharing regarding the categorizing gay men into one category or, into one fan base, because of our sexuality. Fortunately, artists such as Neil Patrick Harris have proved that stereotyping is incorrect, since he plays a "straight woman chaser" on his television show: How I Met Your Mother. And although Brian has earned a high level of respect and acknowledgment in his chosen field, his music does primarily play for a mostly gay market of fans.

Going back to your childhood, how did you feel yourself to be as a child? Were you talkative, outgoing, isolated, creative, scared…?

I was talkative, outgoing, and the first kid to run out onto the dance floor and dance.

At what age?

(Smiling) My dad told me the story about the town having a big dance, that when the music started, my dad asked where I was to my mom? Immediately, she started to panic until they saw me up on stage where no one was, dancing. They ended up cracking up with laughter while I danced all around the stage.

How old were you?

I think I was five.

Wow, do you think that event had some influence on who you are today?

Yes, I do. I think for a lot of us, it's just inbred. It's in your makeup!

Speaking of being in our makeup, do you think being gay had something to do with your decision to become a recording artist/singer? I assume you felt that you had the ability?

I have always been a performer but it wasn't until I accepted the fact that I was going to be an "out" and open" artist, is when my music started to evolve. As an artist, if you can't really be in touch with yourself and accept yourself, then it's really hard to then go out and try to represent that creativity, and establish a connection with your audience. I don't feel its right to be hiding your sexuality, for then you're wearing a mask, where you're holding yourself back.

I am very pleased to hear Brian talking about wearing a mask, which is a very common behavior for gay men who feel the need to hide their sexuality from those who could abuse or reject them. Brian's purposeful intention in not wearing a mask to hide his sexuality, will show others that he is both healthy and confident about who he is and, a fine representative for change and acceptance for the GLBT community. His choice to just be himself, is another affirmation of the strength of his character and an excellent role model for other gay men to follow.

For me, to just go out there and do whatever I do in life without worrying whether people will think I am gay or not, has totally opened me up, and I wouldn't have it any other way!

If that is the case, what are your goals with regards to your music?

I am a firm believer in the universe, and it is my job to simply be creative. Where it goes and where it's going to take me, can go many different ways. I am just so happy to be making music.

My album is coming out and I am performing; getting out there and meeting people who connect with me and my music.

What is the name of your album?

I'm Not Crazy!

That's a very interesting title. When I saw your video, I saw some similarities to George Michael. I assume that was something you purposefully wanted people to see because of his being a gay role model? Isn't he "out" as well?

It depends on the day; some days he is, and other days he's not. For myself, I think role models need to contribute to my community, and therefore, I tend to open myself up to many types of audiences as a gay performer. The main focus in my life is performing, so, the more places we are accepted, the more places I can perform!

How well do you communicate with other gay men?   Do you see the way we communicate with one another is different from the way we communicate with the rest of the world?

For me, I am very much a communicator. You never have to wonder what I think, because I will tell you immediately how I feel if something bothers me. If someone offends me, I will let you know that as well. I think I communicate very well but, I have had years of psychotherapy at a very young age so, I think that helped me as well in telling people how I feel.

Why did you start therapy at such a young age?

My parents divorced when I was three. Between my stepfather's death and both my parents being married four times, it was not easy for a kid. On top of that, with all stuff of my being gay, it was just not easy for me to deal with it all. A very "LA Story," but, I came out alright despite of it.

Where are your parents today? Are they still married to other people?

No, my parents now are both single again.

With Brian's latest information of the poor relationship history of both his parents in their inability to maintain long term relationships, I question his ability to recognize his mask and the emotional blocks which may arise for him, when he finds himself in a long-term relationship. In fact, I recently saw Brian is a well-known leather cruise bar being playful and flirty with a variety of men having a very good time. Of course he could be there simply to talk about his latest album or, be allowed to be there with his partner's knowledge and acceptance. Then again, Brian could be single again and like most everyone else there, looking for a fun time.

In a follow-up interview with Brian, I will be interested in his own relationship patterns and whether there are any similarities to his parents' histories and patterns.

What is your relationship life like?

My relationship life is very different from most gay men. I'm very "into" monogamy, and trying to make it work with just one person. I think our biggest challenge is trying to get to know just one human being; I think that's what relationships are all about! Too many of us just run away when things start to get rough! As a result, relationships are not really evolving. We stay stuck in our old patterns, and are a little fearful of change.

Brian is very correct here with the tendency of many Americans who have decided to leave a relationship or marriage when things become difficult. According to recent statistics (2012) "17% of divorces are due to adultery with either one or both partners. In the book, Sex in America: A Definitive Survey "100% of all couples surveyed experienced infidelity in their relationships within the first five years." (July 24, 2012).

So, my relationship history has been really evolving. Sure I have some good relationships and they have gotten better as I've grown up over the years. But, I am not in a relationship now.

How long have you been single?

I just got out of a relationship.

What are you looking for in a man now?

I am looking for a lot of things. The "bottom line" for me, is someone who communicates and is honest. I'm not "into" the drug scene or, the sex party scene and, all that comes with that!

Are you a romantic?

I am very romantic. I love it! Just like what everybody says they're looking for, I also want someone who is "real" and honest. Someone who "gets it" and really has that sense of humor about themselves and a strong sense of self-worth; self-love, as well as, a love of the world they live in and, live their life to the fullest!

What Brian is sharing, is something many of us say we are looking for in a partner but, in order to be available to a man like that, we first have to work on ourselves, and lessen those negative behaviors that tend to keep a man, such as the one Brian described, away from us!

As for me, a sense of humor about my own self is something that has always challenged me, as with many gay men and women who have been the focus of ridicule and scorn for our differences and sensitivity.

I want to make it perfectly clear, that I am not saying that heterosexual children have not faced similar scorn and ridicule for their appearance or behavior but, many gay men and women have. As a result, for many of us, we often choose to live our adult lives mostly with our own kind, while the heterosexual man or woman does not necessarily have to, unless they choose to do so.

Do you think that gay men don't have a sense of humor about themselves?

I think a lot of gay men take themselves way too seriously because they are trying so hard to overcome whatever issue they have for being who they are. They just tend to overdo it and they "get" real serious. (*Brian is having difficulty finding words here*) I think it's really hard to find somebody who has a good sense of himself, because we all have our faults and our difficulties while growing up.

I think for many gay men over their formative years, were told over and over again that they weren't okay; that they weren't good. So, they would overcompensate in order to get that approval. They would look a certain way; be built a certain way and follow a behavior that complements that look so that they could be okay and, be accepted.

So these men would mold themselves into a certain way in order to gain the approval they were denied earlier in their lives?

I think that all of us have to follow our own path; go on our own journey in their own time.

Sounds as if they are following this path based on a fear of not being accepted for who they are unless they look a certain way or, act in a specific manner?

I just think it's difficult to find a gay man who can laugh at themselves and not care what other people think.

Brian has touched on the main dynamic of gay shame with molding oneself to either blend in with everyone else or stand out as a model of beauty, success, and confidence to be admired. Many of us secretly want to be envied in order to avoid any further rejection by a culture that seeks to shame us for what they believe to be our "chosen" lifestyle.

When is the rest of the world going to get it into their heads that we did not "choose" out lifestyle but, were born into it, and we need to love ourselves more than those who say they love us, but, secretly want us to change.

That's something I personally struggled with Brian because I grew up with an older brother who enjoyed making me feel bad about who I was, not just for being gay, but in many other ways.

In fact, when I finally "came out" to him and other family members, he said, "I feel responsible for you being gay." I replied, "Dennis you are wrong about you making me gay but, you did take away my sense of humor about myself, because I always felt the need to defend myself with you."

As a result of that abuse, I am seeking a life partner who is confident, happy, and has a good sense of humor about himself, and doesn't take himself all that seriously. What about you?

I am looking for the same things. I think it's very important that we don't take life so seriously, because at the end of the day, we need to acknowledge that everyday life is a gift. If I died tomorrow, I don't want to say, "Why didn't I do that?" "Why did I get so upset about that?" "Why, do I take things so to heart?" I mean, you've got to laugh at life's events sometimes!

In a previous interview one of my guests talked about gay men in bars and gyms that are always scowling and acting all serious even in a bar? What do you have to say about that?
That's exactly my point! We just have to be gay and laugh and say, "hey, sweetie." Stop being so serious, severe, and scowling, it doesn't serve any purpose.

On a similar subject, how do you believe your own self-image affects your communication with other gay men?

I look at myself, in that, I can be so many different things depending on the occasion. For instance, did you know that I was once Mr. Eagle? And, as Mr. Eagle, I would go out on many different social gay venues and circuit parties and meet so many different gay communities and they would say to me for instance: "You are the only Mr. Eagle who is a leather guy and has a "Chelsea nose" and it's weird, because you cross all these different lines?"

A "Chelsea nose," what the heck does that mean?

It means that I am sort of the "Mayor of Chelsea." They just couldn't picture me as Mr. Eagle and that is what I am talking about; people couldn't see me outside of the type! That I could actually cross so many different lines and be so many different things!

Brian is clearly presenting here how our community does tend to congregate in groups of similar types such as: Chelsea boys, leather men, bears, drag queens, and body builder;, just to name a few.

*If someone like Brian does choose to cross over into a different category, there may be some sense of discomfort or confusion from others within that community when someone who exhibits that prettier "Chelsea boy" image, could also be viewed as being representative of their leather community. A culture which clearly advocates "machismo" or, a scruffier, more "hyper masculine" image. *(This is assessment is based more on an empirical view of these various cultures based on my more subjective observation).*

It appears as if you are indeed very comfortable in any role you take because you are clearly "comfortable in your own skin." But, how are you able to discern when to disclose more personal information to another person? When do you know you can trust to disclose?

I try to be very upfront and honest with everybody but, as to how much information I reveal to somebody? Of course I have a meter, especially, when you are in the public eye as a performer, you have to be cautious as to how much you can reveal about yourself.

Where do you hesitate in revealing about yourself?

Anything that is extremely, extremely personal. But, I am not afraid to go there with somebody I'm involved with or dating, where I would want to be open and honest. But. I will definitely hesitate with someone I don't really know! In a normal, everyday, conversation, I'm there! But, I'm not going to tell them about my childhood for example.

With what type of person would you hold back in sharing about yourself?

With me, I would hold back with someone I found to be superficial or, only wanted to talk about superficial matters. Someone who was just not that interested in what I have to say.

I would also be hesitant to share personal matters with someone I would consider to be "shady" and not to be trusted. I think it's all about the type of energy you get from them.

Do you feel that there is "shadiness" or a good deal of superficiality within the gay community?

I don't think they mean to be "shady." I just think that many gay men have their "guard up" and so, they are very defensive about what they have to say; almost being "bitchy" or "catty" at times. Of course, Lord knows, I could be as well, but, it comes from a different place..

Where does it come from?

For me, it comes from a place which is never serious, but, I think for a lot of people, that "bitchiness" or "cattiness" comes from a place of insecurity. So, they keep their "guard up" and when something is said that they are uncomfortable with, they will "throw it back on you" to make themselves feel better. They will go so far as "put you down" to make themselves feel better.

Yes, such is the case with my older brother, who would often poke fun or "put me down" at times to make himself feel better, and, try to make me feel worse than I already did. I also realize knowing him, that there may have been no conscious intention of making me feel bad.

Yes, that's exactly what I am talking about but, I am mainly referring to gay men. Of course it can certainly pertain to family members, most especially, siblings!.

With one to one communication, do you find yourself to be a leader or follower?
I am a leader when I have to be, and, a follower when I need to be.

Clearly you were a leader when you were Mr. Eagle.

Yes, it was a fun experience. I enjoyed myself in playing the role.

As a public figure, do you believe there is a gay "mob psychology or mentality" where one tends to always go along with the crowd?

I don't know. I think sexually, it's almost a "calling card" that you have a profile listed somewhere. It may be true in the "straight world" but, it is more of a necessity in the gay world.

I for one, am an energy person, and not someone who is always on the internet. I don't believe in it. I like to get out, go to bars, and meet people face to face. I like that kind of energy much better.

A point of fact: Face to face communication is a richer form of communication especially, when expressing emotion, unlike the internet, which is more emotionally detached and where communication can be more easily misinterpreted.

I think a lot of us are doing what we are supposed to do, just like everyone else but in different ways. For one, we have to go to the gym to keep looking good. We often feel the need to go out and "party" and be with our friends instead of "shutting ourselves up" in our room in front of the computer.

I, especially, need to get out there and be in the public eye since I am a performer and I don't want people to forget about me.

I do see a real problem within the gay community of an excess in using drugs. For instance, I will see the same people a hundred times and yet, they will never say anything unless they're "high." And I will say to them, "why can't you say hello to me when I see you? Why do you only say hello to me when you're "high" or drunk?'

Good for you Brian. You don't hold back! I don't see fear in you or, in anything you've said thus far today.

I think we're afraid because we don't want to continue what we've heard our entire lives; that we were wrong for being gay. Then, to be told by members of our own community that we are wrong or not acceptable within a specific group; it's just horrible!

So many people try to just fit in within their own community and it's that fear of not fitting into their own social circle that many of us work so hard to avoid.

I recall when growing up of trying to fit in with my family, school, and other social settings, and how so many of us are fearful of being rejected by something we hold in such high esteem; the pressure can be incredible!
Right, it sure can be!

In fact, in one of my main points of this book, even the most successful athlete or beauty queen can still face a world of rejection if they "come out" as gay or lesbian. Therefore, we tend to live "shadow lives" and act a certain way in order to keep our sexuality a secret. Then when we decide to "come out of the closet," we don't know how to act, because we had no role models to follow.

Now, the media has many more role models for gay men and women to follow but, that certainly was not the case for older generations like my own.

Exactly! But now, I think that many of my generation tend to "go with the flow" even, when that flow is a "downward spiral." For example, some guys see everyone taking steroids and doing drugs, and then they we think that is what we are supposed to do in order to fit in, which I think is very sad.

You feel that the gay community can be sad? Why?

I think deep, deep down, a lot of us are very unhappy. If you ask anybody what they want, they always say they want to find love. They want a relationship and all these things, and yet, they don't know how to go out there and get it! Because when they do go out there to get what they want, they're not going about it in the right way.

Which way are you talking about? Maybe it has to do with the culture?

Perhaps so, I do not know.

As I have studied in historical documents, in ancient Greek and Roman times and even American Indian culture, gay men were considered acceptable in society as long as they played the dominant sexual role or "penetration" position. Although there was a stigma to homosexual relationships, there was more universal acceptance especially in the military.

But in today's world, we still have that stigma, even though many rules and laws have changed both, in our government and military, and still, many gay men are simply too cautious in allowing their sexuality be exposed to those they don't trust. But to be honest, I believe we as human beings are all connected, and yet, we deny or dismiss that connection and live in our fear. That's why I always feel better when I walk around with a smile rather than a frown or scowl

But I always see you with a smile. Did you ever face ridicule or scorn for being gay when you were younger?

Yes, as a kid I often felt like the "odd man out:" being called gay, faggot…

Why? Did you show a certain behavior?

No, I don't think so. Maybe it had to be because I loved performing onstage and was a little more flamboyant being a show person.

Were you in musicals in high school?

Yes, of course!

I hate to play up the stereotypes here but, being a little flamboyant, a dancer, and singing in high school musicals does sort of give it away to others that one might be gay. Thank God for the television show Glee in helping making the musical gay boy more popular in today's culture.

I do think being musical and loving to dance, created a good deal of problems for me and contributed to the teasing.

How did it make you feel?

Oh, it was horrible.

Was there anybody there to comfort you?

No, not really. It wasn't all about that, it was simply something I had to learn to deal with; develop that survival instinct. You had to learn how to defend yourself as a kid; protect yourself.

Yes, I used to make fun of the teasing and would often join in on the humor and laugh at myself, even though, I hated the bullies and those who loved to taunt me.

Memories came flooding back to me as Brian talked of developing a "survival instinct" with the constant teasing he faced in school. As continued on, I recalled my many attempts to make fun of the teasing as if I was joining "in" on the joke, even though, I, was the subject of the teasing. I hated it all, and hated the teasers most, but couldn't shout out against them; feeling powerless at the time. But, not anymore!

I recalled going on the bus to my new high school which was predominantly attended by African-American students, who I would "hang out" with since I loved to sing "disco" songs with the girls. So, when I got on the bus, I would get picked out by the Caucasian kids not just for my singing, but for being a "nigger lover!" There was just no winning, no winning!

It seems at times, as if there will never be any peace between racial groups despite all the strides we have made in recent years. Gay boys and girls will still be the brunt of jokes for every bully or angry child one seems to need their "scapegoats." in order to feel better about themselves; some things never change. Just like the song with the lyric: "You've got to be carefully taught."

Do you feel that with the adversities you faced when younger had some effect on who you are today and what you have become?

Absolutely! Because, I felt what I went through was a gift that despite everything I went through. I just continued to carry on and make the best of it; their cruelty made me more open minded.

So, you're saying here, that you never became someone who chose to pick on someone else to make yourself feel better for being teased yourself? For example, you don't comment negatively on other gay men for being too effeminate or, people who are too overweight?

We all can be stereotypes! I just choose not to be.

What category or stereotype do you think that people might want to place you in?

People may want to put me into a certain category but, I just don't see myself in any specific category. I know I was mostly popular in school, and I feel I have maintained that popularity today as a performer and an artist but, I don't see myself as being "better" than anyone else.

Don't you feel that in the LGBT community, attractiveness gets more attention and more popularity as a result?

I think that holds true everywhere, not just in the gay community. I have no problems telling people how I feel but, I don't feel it's necessary to say something negative such as, "I don't find you attractive." I also would never shy away from talking to somebody, even if I didn't find them attractive.

One of the behaviors I have focused on in this book, is in regards to the dismissive communication within the gay community. Where I see gays in groups demeaning other gays even when they are attracted to them; similar to teenage girls in their little cliques. Do you see behaviors like that in gay social settings, and what is your comment about such behavior?

I think there are two things: it is very similar to heterosexual men who are afraid to be around a gay man, because they feel they are going to be "hit on." Or, they are so afraid of not being accepted, that they won't cross that line and talk to the guy they like, so, they don't have to face possible rejection. Basically, I think it's all about insecurity. That's just my opinion.

Brian touched on a very important point regarding ignorance being the primary reason why stereotypes continue to exist and how fear and insecurity keeps many of us to become "stuck in our ruts!" As a result, we don't move forward toward making more positive changes based on our fear. We are so in fear of rejection that we hesitate to take risks that could move us forward.

I agree with you in that if one needs the comfort and support of the group when they are not secure about themselves. But in switching gears, what I am most concerned about with our gay community is gay shame. So, let me ask you, when did you feel shame with regards to your gay identity? Or, was there a time in your life where you felt guilty about being gay?

(*Pausing to think*) I think for me, it was some four years ago when I felt I was a little bit out of control with "partying" in Fire Island. I was doing drugs and I was going out too much until I said to myself, "you have to stop!"

So, I reached out to a friend in a Twelve-Step program and he helped me "get myself together." I didn't feel I had a problem with alcohol or substances but ,that I lost focus on where I was going in my life. So, I "got myself together" and identified myself as an "out "gay artist. Now, I am much more comfortable about whom I am today, and I don't hold myself from being honest about myself and others in the gay community.

Sounds very positive so, what exactly do you find attractive about the gay community today?

You're asking attractiveness within the community but to be honest, I find a lot of gay men to be very unattractive. (*Laughs*) Only kidding. But, we do tend to overwork our bodies at the gym and try to be more health conscious; which is a good thing. But, I think our community as a whole is very pretty. We have a Gay Pride Parade and there are a lot of hot bodies who love to "strut their stuff" and the audience clearly loves it; I love it!

It may feel that way at the parade but sometimes, I get the feeling at times, that they don't love us! For instance, do you ever desire a woman? And if you don't, as many of us do not, then, how do you think that truth would affect the way they truly feel about us?

I find some women to be very beautiful and, I find them very attractive but, I don't want to go to bed with them. Frankly, I have never had a problem with "straight women." That animosity may be there but, it has never been my problem! *(Laughs)* In fact, I don't really interact that often with that many "straight woman" at my shows or in life, so, that has never been an issue for me.

I hear you. But, was there someone significant to you as a role model for "coming out of the closet?" Someone who helped you or, influenced you to want to "come out?"

Not really. I didn't make any big announcement at a wedding or at a family event. It was more of a slow process of "coming out." I guess, that whenever I felt the need to let them know who I am, I simply would.

OK, so what is your best technique for meeting men? Do you charm them with your smile?

I hope that when I meet someone at a social event or a bar that, I will smile at them. I used to love living in LA but, the bar "cruising scene" always confused me. For example, I would walk into a bar there and I would see men scowl at me, and I didn't know whether they liked me or, wanted to kill me! After a while, I realized in time, that if they scowled at you in LA, they liked you, but if they didn't, they ignored you! *(Laughs)*

What I love in New York, is that the men who find you attractive will look at you and let you know that they were interested.

Obviously, there are many who live in both cities who would question Brian's statement and say that the reverse is true, but, for myself, I have seen both behaviors, both positive and negative, in each city. And, to be perfectly honest, I enjoyed the challenge of meeting men in LA who are known to scowl (see: David Pevsner interview, p. 146), as do men in New York. But a smile is always a good nonverbal expression that works for most, unless they are truly not interested in meeting you.

As for my best technique for meeting men. it is, that, I like to smile at them and let them know I'm interested. I have no problem going up to someone and introducing myself to them. I'll say, "Hey, I'm Brian, what's your name?"

What physical attributes to do you find attractive in a man?

I've been attracted to all different types of men. I like someone who takes care of himself; no smoking. I like cute and boyish but, never set limits. Don't like them real, real young, because I've been there already. *(At that very moment, a young fan comes by us and tells Brian, "I love you. I love you" and Brian responds),* "I love you too!"

(Addressing me again about the boy after he happily walks away) He was at the bar last night and saw me perform.

That was fantastic, and just like that boy, what personality traits do you find attractive?

I like a guy with a good sense of humor for sure; someone who is fun and witty. Love "catty" but, it has to be a fun type of "catty:" not, "bitchy!"

What personality traits do you find unattractive?

Snotty people are simply people who I won't put up with. People who think they are better than everyone else.

Do you find snootiness to be something more prevalent in the gay community or in society in general, and what do you believe causes people to act that way?

I think that is a true generalization of the gay community. I remember when I first came to New York, everybody was more open and honest but, I do see an attitude present with some guys who feel the need to set themselves apart from everyone else. I just don't "play" into it.

What do you envision your future with regards to your gay life?

I feel being gay is part of my life but, my career has to be my primary focus. I enjoy my life but don't let it run me. The gay community has been terrific to me as fans, and they show me their support all the time. *(The young man who came over earlier makes it a point to say goodbye)*.

What do you feel the gay community needs to improve itself?

I think we need to be honest about ourselves. If we have a problem, talk about it. Do something about it; don't get drunk, take drugs, and "sleep around" as a way of life. If you have problems get help! Go to therapy or a Twelve Step group.

People who went through 9/11 refuse to acknowledge the trauma and act as if nothing happened but, I see a lot more anger out there as of late! Like the other day, I was walking home and some asshole yelled "Hey faggot" from their car. What cowards! I basically laughed at them.

There is a lot of ignorance in society and those assholes are still around. I have had the same experience several times, one time, they threw a beer bottle which landed close to my feet. But, unlike yourself, I find it hard to laugh at these criminals, having once been physically assaulted by a gang of punks and had to be saved by my boyfriend.

I think all those who attack us are all cowards and ignorant. They don't know who we are. They think we're going to jump them or try to molest them; which is something far from the truth!

 I only want to be with a man who wants me as much as I want him. Basically, I believe the guys who attack us have issues about their own sexuality. If you weren't so afraid of yourself, then you wouldn't be afraid of me.
I agree, it's those "closet cases" who are the dangerous ones.

That is why gay men work so hard on their externals.

Why is that?

Because we have so much to work on with our "insides," and it's easier to focus on the outside by bodybuilding or looking "hot."
But, do you think gay guys have difficulty communicating with one another?

(*Laughing*) I think we have a problem with our pronouns! Such as, we use the word "gurl" instead of "man," when we talk to one another, which often confuses the "straight" community. Also, we say "she" instead of "he."

Otherwise, I don't think we have a real problem communicating with one another.

So, we just have a problem with our pronouns otherwise we are no different from one another. But, do you feel your communication with people has changed over the years, especially with other gay men? Are you more honest now?

I have my limits. I try to be honest and not "play games" with people. I try to avoid difficult situations with difficult people. I enjoy myself and feel comfortable with who I am.

I can see that and thank you very much for your time today.

You're welcome. I enjoyed myself.

End of Interview

Leaving that interview with Brian, I had the impression that among everyone that I had interviewed thus far for this book, Brian was the most successful in his communication and interactions with others within the LGBTQ community. His openness and honesty was prevalent throughout the interview, and I never had the impression that he had to hide or felt ashamed of whom he was also a child or, as an adult.

His adult presentation appeared similar to the five year old child dancing on the stage with reckless abandon. His smile and positive demeanor generated good feelings for both me and even the young man who approached him at our meeting place; to tell him how much he loved him. I see nothing but positive things for Brian's music career and himself in general, and he is a role model for others with his upfront and genuine communication. At present, Brian is still performing his music in clubs and music festivals throughout the country in mostly gay venues.

CHAPTER THIRTEEN

IRA SMITH

I interviewed Ira Smith, a talented artist of male erotica in his beautifully decorated East Village apartment in June of 2007 with his two pet cats. Ira did not refrain in the least with talking about his life and art.

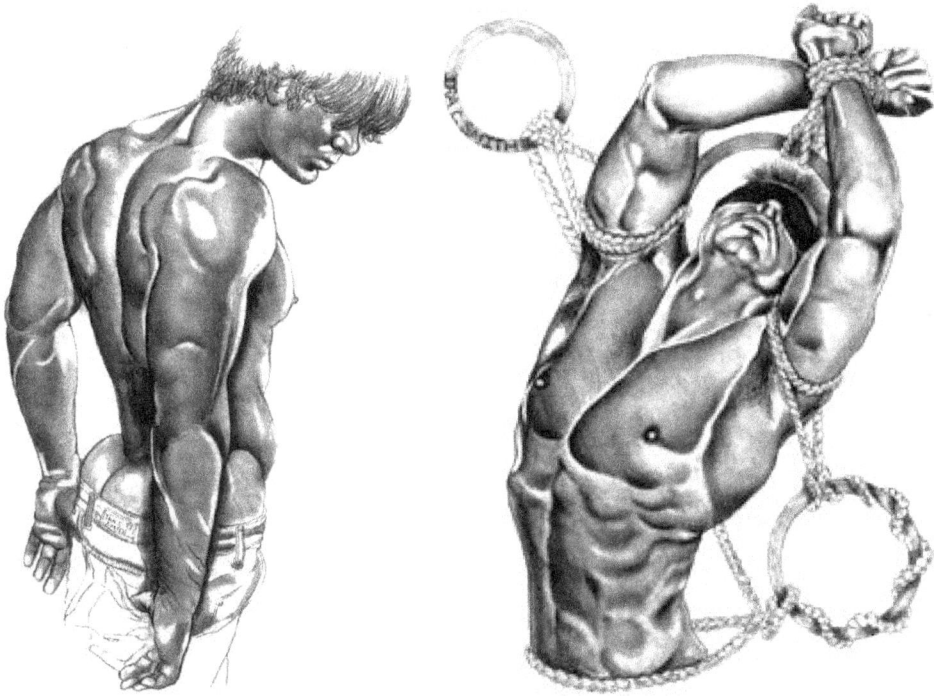

Growing Up Gay and Artistic

I am from an Orthodox, Jewish family. My parents divorced when I was five years old. I grew up in Stuyvesant Town around 20th Street in New York City. I went to school in the neighborhood. Being in the city, I knew there was prejudice everywhere else but, I did not find it here!

I went to an art design high school where everybody was gay! So, I really didn't really have to deal with a lot of the abuse others had to deal with growing up gay and facing abuse.

The only thing that happened to me that was a painful experience, was when I went up to this guy at my junior high school to whom I had a "crush" on, and asked him a month before graduation, "did you ever wonder what it was like to go to bed with a guy?" His response was an unequivocal, "No."

The next day, everybody in the school knew and they were all pointing, laughing, and stuff. I was pretty humiliated. But, moving on to graduation from high school, that night of the graduation, I ended up at the Plaza Hotel with him! And now, of course, he is an "out" gay man.

Wow, what does that say to you about what you experienced with him and the others who pointed and laughed at you? How were you able to rise above it?

I think it all says, that I was a little bit more open. My parents were divorced and I lived with my

233

mom, so, I didn't have to deal with my father that often. I would visit with my father every Sunday. He was very loving; he never hit me or anything like that. He was known to be quite the disciplinarian but, I never did anything to annoy him so, it was always a pleasure to be with him.

It sounds as if the "good little boy" analogy could be at play here in your relationship with your father?

Well, we never argued but, the question of my being gay never came up! At the end of his life, he opened up about his past and the struggles he went through. He had a rough life in comparison: I was really lucky.

Did he ever find out that you were gay?

Yes, but we never he never said the word. I had a lover for twenty-seven years. My father could never understand why I lived upstate, and wondered who this person was that I was living with, and why he had such a hold on me? But, I never could say that this person was my lover!

Why?

I don't know.

The answer is gay shame. Ira simply feared telling his father of his true sexuality and about the role his lover honestly played in his life. As a result, the father and son continued to live a life of denial where the word "gay" would never be uttered and the denial was kept alive by deceit. Sadly, I sense that Ira and his father were never able to experience the potential joys and honesty that a relationship fueled by lies could enjoy.

Perhaps Ira felt his father suffered enough in his life and that if he chose to tell him, it would only make things worse. Unfortunately, Ira would never know that relationship since his father in now gone, and there is no going back to change things to see if their relationship could have been more fulfilling and joyful. It is obvious they loved and cared for one another but, living a life based on lies simply denies any potential for growth and truthfulness.

Did you ever think that if you told him the truth of your relationship, everything would have been "over and done" with?

No. No.

Why not? Do you think he would have looked at your differently?
(*A loss for words*) Perhaps, I don't know. I denied everything from him. (*With renewed enthusiasm*) Never with my mom! I could talk to her about everything and anything, even about sex! She would give me advice. Ironically, she's been married six times!

Wow, I guess she would know about sex and relationships having been married so frequently.

Her marriage to my father was her first. She would marry five more times, and my father did remarry as well, but, only one more time. I, also, have a brother, so a lot of pressure was relieved for me, since he was "straight" and had a family. Of course, he is now divorced like my parents but, he had a boy, so a lot of the pressure of having kids was taken away from me.

That pressure does permeate within the gay culture toward having children, specifically, boys, in order to keep the line going for our families.

With Jewish culture, that's for sure. I was benefited living with my mom in the city. I had the option. I could have lived with my dad but, preferred living in Manhattan, so I would be able to go to the shows and museums. I just didn't want the hour and a half to two hour commute back and forth from Queens.

Getting Even with a Traitor

Got it but, in returning back to the boy at school who "outed" you to everyone. Did you ever realize that by asking him that provocative question, it was opening yourself up for possible trouble; which it obviously did?

I did it because I knew he was gay.

How did you feel about what he did to you in school with the other kids?

I was embarrassed but, not angry.

Why not? I would be. I know that a lot of gay men are known to have suppressed their rage to those who abused them for fear of retribution; was that true for you? For example, if someone "outed" you now at work, what would you do?

I would sue! But at that time, the only option would have been getting beaten up, and that didn't happen! I was not threatened that way, I was just embarrassed. But, I was just being me. I didn't play sports, even though I love to swim, but we didn't have a pool. To be honest, I didn't really care what happened, I just did it!

You say you didn't really care but then you had sex with him at the Plaza right? How did that feel?

I felt vindicated.

I heard from Rob Ordonez (previous interviewee) that you are a "top" guy, and are well endowed so, you must have "topped" the boy. Did you have a good time?

Oh, yes! I "came" three times! (Laughs)

Okay, so what were you feeling when you were dominating this boy who embarrassed you in school by "outing" you? What was running through your mind as you were on top of him?

I remember telling him, "I told you so."

So, you felt some vindication while "topping" him?

No, actually I was more grateful.

Why?

I thought he was gorgeous, and in truth, I still had strong feelings for him.

Still do?

Not anymore. That was some twenty years ago.

Listening to Ira's explanation of his experience "topping" the guy who embarrassed him in high school not only sounds to be a form of retribution but also, an affirmation of his assertiveness in approaching the boy all those years ago. Ira knew the boy was gay. but also, wanted him and went after what he wanted, which suggests determinism and a "devil may care" attitude.

I still question Ira's tendency to deny his feelings and in giving others emotional power over him; such as his father and his "crush." For example, he never was honest to his father about his gayness and never reproached the boy for his betrayal. Therefore, by keeping his identity secret, he never fully enjoyed a completely honest relationship with his dad or, the boy.

But, with the boy, he allowed his sexual aggressiveness to prevail over the need to reproach. Although, I perceive that his "fucking" this guy three times, definitely demonstrates clear emotional satisfaction. But, in addition, there has to be some vindication for Ira in being proven correct, as well as, dominating the "crush" sexually and thereby, achieving a long desired goal.

What exactly was your motivation for going up to your "crush" and saying what you said to him? Was it for sex?

Oh, yeah!

Even back then, were you horny for him?

My First Sex

Oh, yeah! But, my first sexual experience was pretty stupid with another man. I was shopping in Bloomingdales and saw this guy walking around whom I briefly met before.

How old were you?

I think it was just before my thirteenth birthday. And, I remember just grabbing something from the rack and heading for the dressing rooms shaking, because I wasn't sure what was going to happen. Before I knew it, the guy opened the curtain, came in, closed the curtain, "blew" me, and walked out. That was it! And, that is NOT what I wanted to happen!

Talk about a shameful individual to give oral sex to a minor in a public area. I am sure some might consider it hot and sexy but, it "speaks volumes" for someone to have sex with a minor and leave without saying a word. As for the teenager, I am sure it was "hot" as well but, for the man, I am saddened by the chances the man took in having sex with a minor; with a high potentiality of being caught by security! I could only guess this was before security cameras were placed in dressing rooms but, it "screams" of a need for help for the adult perpetrator, to have sex with a minor.

Why did you not want it to happen?

My great sexual urge at that time was simply to be kissed by another man.

So, he didn't kiss you?

No! But it felt good.

When did you finally get that kiss?

Probably not long after my first sexual encounter, but I don't remember that! It's funny. I don't remember my first kiss but, I can remember my first "blow-job!"

That's not surprising for a man to say. Remembering one's first kiss sounds more like a romantic comedy for the ladies, rather than for the boys but, boys would definitely remember their first orgasm from their first sex partner.

More significantly, what strikes me more with Ira's story, is the feeling that he didn't feel victimized or taken advantage of in some way; which in my estimation, is exactly what occurred, being that it was an older man taking his virginity, rather than the boy (his first "crush"); which he truly wanted.

Finding Love

What is your present relationship status?

(*Very seriously*) I have been with the same lover for the past twenty-seven years. We met at a dance club on Gay Pride Day those many years ago. He was in a spotlight surrounded by his friends, when he looked over his shoulder and saw me standing there watching them. He looked directly at me and I nodded. We ended up spending the night together at "The Trucks."

The "Trucks" was the term for a very popular sexual acting out place where several tractor trailer trucks were parked in a secluded lot, and gay men would have mostly unprotected sex in this public area. The "Trucks" were one of several sex areas back in the seventies and eighties as well as in Central Park, the Piers, and sex/dance clubs such as the Mineshaft, and Anvil bars.

You spent an entire night at "the Trucks" with just one another?

"The Trucks" were rarely known as a place where a couple could be sexual or intimate without others nearby to watch or want to participate.

Yes, just me and him, with no one else, because we kept in the dark part of the truck away from others. I wanted him to myself! He was only in town for the weekend, staying with friends since he had his home in Upstate New York.

He didn't stay with you afterward?

No, I had a female roommate at the time, so, staying in my place was impossible!

But you've had twenty seven years since that first meeting!

(Again, very seriously) Yes, twenty-seven years but, here's the best part. He went back to his home upstate and gave me his phone number to call him. So, I called him to ask when he's coming back to town and guess who answers the phone? His wife!

(I am truly shocked) **Wow!**

He told her all about me, and she was gracious and wonderful.

What type of marriage did they have?

(Acting surprisingly naive) How do you mean?

I mean, what type of marriage arrangement did they have? You have to say, that her reaction was most unusual. I remember the wife's reaction in the movie Brokeback Mountain, where she sure didn't open her arms to her husband's lover and wasn't all that happy finding out that her husband was gay!

(Very calmly) No, I don't think it had anything to do with her; as much as it had all to do with him! He was the type of guy who liked to "do his own thing."

Did he "go both ways? Did he have multiple lovers?"

Yes, he had multiple lovers. But, he did, I didn't! He loved to come into New York and play. His wife's name was Karen.

Is she still married to him and are you still with him too?

Sadly, he passed away recently.

You said earlier that you "have" a lover of some twenty-seven years.

I had a lover of twenty-seven years.

Okay then, so you're a widower?

No, I am presently dating somebody else. My deceased lover passed away on October 25,[h] two years ago.

Was he still married when he died?

Yes! In fact, I was watching television with her in her room while he took a nap, and one of his family members who lived there with them, heard a gasp. He went into his room and quickly came back to her room, telling us to quickly come into his room. He had died after suffering a major heart attack.

Didn't you mention earlier, that your lover has cancer?

Yes, but it the lover I have now, not the one that died. My present lover lives in Ft. Lauderdale, and I go down there to be with him. I wasn't always a fan of going down to Florida but, some of my fans asked me to come down to show people my artwork and, I did just that.

It was during one of my visits to show my work that I met Eric. He asked me to come back to visit him, and I did; whereupon, he eventually became my agent. We ended up having six art shows in six different clubs, and have been together ever since.

<u>My Artwork</u>

That's great. So then, tell me about your art. I can see it all over the room.

Ira's apartment was well decorated and comfortable but his artwork of mostly male nudes, was in display throughout the rooms. The artwork focused significantly on very masculine and muscular men in detail. The sketches projected a sexual aura about them, perfect for displays in leather gay male bars such as the Eagle in NYC and the Ramrod in Ft. Lauderdale.

Well, none of the art hanging in here, is my art! I purchase art from other artists in shows I attended, and whenever I can, I try to publicize their work to get them published.

That's a very kind thing for you to do. I can see that kindness within you; in that, you care so deeply for your lovers, and are so involved in their care, plus, your generosity with other artists. I can even see that kindness with your cat , who clearly loves you and doesn't want to leave your lap!

I get that from Frank's family; my first lover. I still keep close ties to his wife and children, and they with me. I even go to the house in the summer while they're away to watch it and take care of it. We still get together every once in a while when I go up to Maine.

Tell me about your work and how it represents you? It "oozes" sexuality, looking very much like a cross between Tom of Finland and Michelangelo.

I actually got a letter from Tom of Finland. His work definitely made an impression on me and he was aware of my work, and complimented me on it. Especially, with the fact that I was having art shows in gay bars! He was very flattered on how his work helped inspire me.

How did you get started with your sketches?

I actually got ideas from photographs I saw in magazines. I would use men in those photographs as my models.

But, what inspired me to draw what I draw, was strongly influenced by a club I used to go to, called The Cell Block at the Triangle Building on Fourteenth Street.

I made an appointment to show my work at the bar and since I never been there, I was very unsure what this place exactly was? I remember going to the Cell Block during a terrible snowstorm and meeting this girl named Janet who worked the front window. Inside, there was a big bar and a little alcove.

Janet told me that the Cellblock was actually a "straight" hangout that turns gay on certain nights with very strict rules. You could only "jerk somebody off" but you couldn't "blow them" or "fuck them." She told me I had to wait for Lenny who would have to approve of my work.

Within moments, Lenny walks into the bar and he's this big teddy bear of a man! I loved him! He takes my work and we walk over to the alcove area where there is this naked woman in a sling with a gag in her mouth under a spotlight!

He places my sketchbook on her stomach holding her breasts up while I flip the pages! When I get to the end, he says, "you got the job!"

That was the first time I showed my work to the public, so I said, "thank you." The woman thinking I was referring to her, said in a muffled voice because she had a gag in her mouth, "you're welcome." That was also my first experience with a club like that, with the naked people and the "bondage scene. "And so, my first art show, was at the Cell Block!

Of all the stories I have heard from my interviewees, this story was the best! Just the image of showing one's artwork on a naked woman's body while someone holds her breasts up is something I have never heard before. Ira surely has the best stories with his revenge on the "tattle-tale" and the lover with the gracious and accepting wife. I still feel somewhat sad that he never "came out" to his father for fear of being rejected; something I do not believe would ever happen, since the father must have suspected something (most parents do, but, do not reveal it).

The art itself was not for sale, it was more for creating a mood; an atmosphere for the bar.

It sounds like the same atmosphere that I see at Rawhide Bar where they have sketches of graphically sexual situations between men on the walls.

Yes, more or less. Boots and Saddle Bar on Christopher Street used to hang my artwork on the perimeter of the bar for years before their renovation. I had shows at the Hanger Bar, also, on Christopher Street and many other places.

During one of my shows, David Wambaugh from GMSMA asked me if I would like to show my work for his organization, the Gay Men's S&M Association, and, I said I had not. He gave me the information and I joined. They produce the Leather Pride Night, and all these events and street fairs including, the Folsom Street Fair. He even asked me if I wanted to have a table to present my work to the public at these events at the Gay and Lesbian Community Center. The showcase of my work became known as "Leather Art."

It just proves the point, being in the right place at the right time. I was very lucky.

But earlier in my career, I would like to tell a similar story. I did not know what is right and what is wrong because I was very naive.

There was this gallery down on Broome Street that was having a show on Tom's work *(Tom of Finland)* before he died. I show up and mind you, everybody was in full leather. There were Harleys parked all over the street. Here am I, coming into the gallery with my portfolio and ask to speak to the head of the foundation to show him my portfolio. *(Laughs)* You know what he did? He looked at it and said I had talent; a month later, he called me and asked me if I would like to become a member of the foundation, for which I quickly responded, "yes!"

How were you dressed? Were you in full leather too?

No, I was dressed similar to how I am dressed now; in jeans and a pressed shirt. I don't think I even had that much leather at the time. Certainly not enough to make an outfit, let's put it that way! I even sent a sample of my work to Tom a month before he died, and he wrote a letter and addressed it to me saying that he was grateful that there was "somebody who can follow in my footsteps." He also said, that I knew the male anatomy well and wished me the best; soon after, he passed away.

When I went out to California, his friends put me up in Tom's room and they opened up his vault and let me hold much of his work. I became very prolific after that experience; inspired by Tom.

Ira seems to want to impress me as being naive and somewhat innocent, but similar to his actions with his "crush," it appears as if he set a goal for himself and achieved it; not shy at all.

So, what do you feel your work says about the gay community? When people view your work, what strikes them?

I have been told that they find my work hot and sexy. They say, that they would love to do what the models in my art are doing, such as: bondage, group sex scenes, and wrestling naked.

Now, sex and bondage is brought up as something that inspires Ira in his work but, I believe that the situations are similar to the sexual gratification of Ira with his "crush." In that incident, he reported that he felt intense pleasure in not only having sex with his "crush" but, that he did it several times and clearly dominated the man. A similar scene as depicted in much of his work.

Which is what you primarily depict in your paintings.

Yes, right. Just to let you know, I don't get involved with my models. I don't pose my models. I tell them just to sit and get comfortable; hold onto a pipe or whatever. I don't draw background. It doesn't matter where I take the pictures, as long as they're clear. When I see the photo afterward, I will be inspired as to whether I want to put wings on them or have them holding rope, chains, or, in full leather. I would never tie anybody up. I don't know how to do it!

I notice that many of your models are muscular men.

Not always; anybody that would like to be photographed could be my model but, most people decline to be photographed saying, "I don't look like the men that you draw. "My reply often is, "it's only a drawing." I could photograph anybody, even you!

Thank you, I may like that. But, your work appears very sexual when I look at it. Do you feel that the gay culture is pretty much obsessed with sex and sexual domination?

Yes, absolutely. I see it not just with the gay community but everywhere! We had Women's Liberation before Gay Liberation; and sexual freedom is a large part of it. I think it's good. I see us a very repressive society and sexual freedom is one of the ways of liberating ourselves.

Are you talking about the world, or, primarily the gay community?

No, I am mainly referring to the United States.

What about the Arabic cultures?

I am mainly concerned about America. Many of us take our freedoms for granted living in New York but, things are very different in other parts of the country.

Can you give me some specifics?

Well, I have a friend who lives in Oklahoma. I had the opportunity to show my work there. He runs a gay leather organization there. We had a private event there but, they still had to put Post-its on all of my artwork and seal my catalogs closed. Ironically, it was against the law to display even drawings that depict a gay man in a sexual act.

Why the Post-its?

To cover up the penises of the men in the drawings! Even at a private event!

Ira's story reminds me of Victorian times, when people were ashamed of their own sexuality and it was not uncommon for husbands to never see their wife's genitalia; where the married couples were often separated by a sheet with a hole in it to perform sexual intercourse. "The ideal Victorian woman was pure, chaste, refined, and modest." (Wikipedia, October, 2011) "Men were allowed several lovers."
Living in New York City and its "ilk," we are definitely more fortunate when compared to other less accepting and permissive cultures in our own country and, the world in general.

At this art event, was it predominantly a gay crowd?

It was a totally gay crowd.

Who insisted the genitalia should be covered?

The organization running the event, and, even the contributors had the work covered up, because it's against the law and they were afraid of being raided by the police. I thought it was completely ridiculous that something like that could happen in today's day!

What do you feel it's says about today's society?

I find this repressiveness to be very similar to the Orthodox Jewish culture, as well as, all the proselytizing from within the Catholic Church as well.

That would be quite hypocritical of them with all the pedophilia scandals within the Catholic Church of parish children and altar boys. In fact, I rarely see altar boys at Catholic masses unless it is a High Mass or special events. Nowadays, I see altar girls and adults serving that role which is very sad to see.

Yes, I completely agree.

But to change this subject to a more positive one, what would be your most pleasurable gay experience you can recall? Would it be being sexual with your first "crush?"

I love having sex with men. I find men very attractive; I find women attractive too but, I don't want to be sexual with them.

Have you been monogamous with your lover?

Yes, and with my first lover who died as well.

Did you ever feel tempted by other men you meet at your art exhibits who "come on" to you.

Yes, but I never act on it. I am completely satisfied with my lover. But going back to the earlier question of what I loved best within the gay community is marching in the Gay Pride Parade in full leather. I loved marching in full leather despite sweating in the hot weather but I love it!

Ira, as I said earlier, is well endowed and loves showing it off in tight jeans. There is definitely an exhibitionist attitude that he seems to enjoy, as do others.

Another high point of my gay life was when I was exhibiting my artwork and was being filmed by this camera crew. I exhibited my artwork at Robin Byrd's home in Fire Island and received a lot of positive response.

But, the worse part of the gay community, is how the leather community is prejudiced toward drag queens.

How so? Tell me more about that.

I can only tell you what I know from several years ago in Oklahoma, in that, it is very similar to the way we used to treat Black people who were entertainers in the 20s and 30s. They could entertain onstage but afterward, they would have to leave by the back door; they couldn't stay and interact with the audience.

With drag queens, they would come in and perform, then, give the money they would earn to the charity they were performing for, but, they couldn't stay around and mingle with the guests!

Why not?

Because it was just not done! Certainly not in the leather community!

So, the leather community won't let the drag queens interact with them? What is that about?

I have no idea.

Do you think it's because they don't like the way they look and act; that by interacting with men dressed as women, it says something about their own masculinity?

Maybe so, but, I think it says more about their stereotypical view of what gay men should look and act like from the days of being "limp wrist-ed" and "fey." The leather community wants the general public to see this big leather guy who is full of muscles and "ripped" instead.

Even if the "drag" is so well that you can't even tell that he is a man, as soon as someone realizes that it is a man dressed as a woman, they are out of there! And, I sometimes would wonder how the "drag queen" felt about being treated differently as a man, than, when he dressed up as woman, by members of my community?

Ira is clearly questioning why the "hyper masculinity" within the gay leather community is threatened by having another man dressed up in the opposite gender. That somehow by even interacting with this cross dressing male, it makes the other visibly uncomfortable; as if talking with this effeminate looking man will somehow communicate something negative about his own masculinity? Basically, the "leather man" fears that the other gay man's effeminate behavior will somehow "rub off" on him.

This type of fear-based mindset is clearly another example of "gay shame" within the gay community dating back to the days of Quentin Crisp of the early 1900s. In those days, the more "straight-acting" gay men tended to dress very formally in tuxes and suits when they met in private clubs, as clearly depicted in the film Victor, Victoria (1982). Men such as Mr. Crisp were often ostracized by the other gay group since they were too effeminate to be around; behavior which was portrayed in the film, The Naked Civil Servant (1975) starring John Hurt.

Freud often referred to the Latency Stage in child development where children would develop a tendency to identify themselves with the groups or "cliques" they interacted with most. According to Wikipedia (July, 2011), "The latency stage originates during the phallic stage when the child's "Oedipal complex" begins to dissolve. The child realizes that his/her wishes and longing for the parent of the opposite sex cannot be fulfilled and turns away from those he originally desired. He/she then begins to identify with the parent of the same sex. The "libido" is transferred from parents to friends of the same sex, clubs, and hero/role-model figures."

As a result, we see the gay community's tendency to segregate themselves into clearly identifiable groups such as the leather community with "Bears" and their varied categories/ based on physical build. Also, "Chelsea Boys, "Drag Queens," The Stonewall era/Baby Boomers gays(50s, 60s, and above)/ transvestites, transsexuals, etc.

*(Please excuse me if I fail to mention your group or named it incorrectly but there are so many it's even confusing for this aging queen). And yes, I acknowledge that many of us gays find ourselves in several of these groups depending on the occasion.

You made reference earlier to your friendship with Kevin Aviance who is a well-known drag performer who was savagely beaten by homophobic thugs outside of a gay club for his effeminate appearance. What are your thoughts about what happened to him and others?

Yes, you should ask him about his view of how he has been treated in and out of "drag." From knowing him, I recall him being upset at the way he is treated differently when he is dressed as a woman, as compared to, when he is dressed as a man. Also, when the group he has been performing in front of is "straight" or gay; there is a definite difference in how he is viewed.

The "straight" people will treat him great as an entertainer but, not true with the gay community.

Yes, I can see that happening in the gay community.

Have you ever attended the "Night of a Thousand Gowns?" *(*This is an evening where men dress up in opulent "drag" with escorts of both genders but the women are also dressed in "drag" as a man. I have personally attended this event as a male escort of a friend dressed in "drag" and playing homage to the King and Queen of the event).*

Yes, I did, and I had an interesting time. I was a friend's date, but, I have to honestly say, I didn't really enjoy myself. Even though I had dressed up in drag several times for Halloween, and I felt that I was able to "pull it off" well. (I even had a taxi driver try to "pick me up" while dressed as a woman). I did feel quite uncomfortable at the event.

I do acknowledge on those specific occasions, that it brought out a certain aspect of my personality when I put on the high heels, makeup, and hair. I had a friend who was a very talented beautician who did an amazing job with my appearance, and stayed with me as I walked the streets of Greenwich Village.

Also, I recall, it felt pretty grand at the time. I even remember this time where I was standing in front of the Rivera Café when I was fixing my hair and didn't realize people could see me through the glass. The next thing I knew, people were standing and applauding for me; I was so embarrassed but secretly thrilled as well. (Okay, I get the attraction to dressing in drag)

But for me, I am honestly more comfortable at the Eagle where there is a predominantly leather crowd, since I am physically more attracted to more muscular, masculine-acting men. Drag queens just don't do it for me until they get out of the "drag." I am not attracted to the woman but, the man. If I wanted a woman, I know I could get one, and I am still attracted to certain aspects of a woman that a man simply cannot imitate, such as, the nape of a beautiful woman's neck, their smooth skin, or, the line of their buttocks.

Yes, I feel the same. I also find certain aspects of the physical beauty that woman have that men dressed in drag, simply can't "pull it off"!

As I am listening to both myself and Ira, I am surprised at my own reaction to "cross-dressing" and gender identity debate, and wonder how men dressed as women creates a level of gay shame within myself and others. But the truth is, I like a man acting like a man and despite being gay, find myself strongly attracted to certain aspects of a woman's beauty that a man dressed as a woman can not completely duplicate. *(I know that some of you may disagree to my honesty, but that is how I personally feel, and yet, I know my view is not shared by everyone in the gay male community).

But, I can also acknowledge my own sense of self-satisfaction when I was dressed as a woman and received such positive reactions in people of both genders and sexual orientations. It is no wonder why so many male celebrities and other males, gay or straight, are so willing to dress up as the opposite sex; not just for fun during festive occasions but, as a chosen lifestyle.

This discussion on gender is very interesting and something for another occasion but, the predominant focus of this book is on gay male communication.

So then, what have you observed about gay male communication not just between the leather and the drag communities but, by gay men in general? Specifically, how do gay men tend to interact with one another in social situations. For example, do you feel there is a strong sexual dynamic in how we interact with each other or, is it dependent of the context?

I would say that it is depending on the context or, the situation. But in general, I do not know. I can only talk about what I have seen and personally experienced.

Okay, tell me something about that.

People who are HIV Positive have tons of sex!

That is interesting. Why exactly do you feel that dynamic to be true?

They are just so much more sexual. It's as if they are trying to prove or fulfill something before their imagined end. Which I think is great!

Then why are so many HIV positive men practicing bare-backing (sex without condoms) with all the risks inherent in such behavior?

Because they are living under the assumption that "I've already got, so what does it matter if I get the virus again from someone else? It's one less thing that I have to worry about."

This was something brought up in my earlier interview with Aaron Tanner and his partner on having "bareback sex" with one another since they are already HIV Positive.

I don't want to comment on Aaron's behavior because I had a negative experience working with him but, I do know that such sexual behavior is rampant with HIV Positive men who feel they have nothing to lose.

But don't these men realize that they are opening themselves up to another man's virus load or, strain, with all the bare-backing. It's all so mystifying?

In a recent article from the web post, <u>The Body: The Complete HIV/AIDS Resource</u> (February 17, 2010) a HIV Positive couple asked a HIV Specialist Robert J. Frascino if they could continue having unprotected sex since they both have the virus even though one identified himself as a top, "Poz on poz couplings are at risk for "Superinfect ion" (acquiring a different strain) and for other STDs that could make your HIV disease flare out of control!"
It is clearly indicative of a shameful culture to have so many gay men practice unsafe sex despite the inherent risks as if tempting fate? I know that sex is more satisfying without the use of condoms that often desensitize the sexual experience but, the consequences of unsafe sex raise the question of the risk taker's self-worth. Specifically, what is the impulse that would cause someone to engage in such self-destructive behavior.

Reckless behavior is further exemplified by the following statement: "If I am already considered shameful by many in our world, then why should I bother swaying others from that negative opinion of gay men?"

Is getting HIV something that you ever worry about?

Not me, I am a "top! Also, I have no intention of ever letting anybody into my anus! *(Laughs)* I personally wish that things would go back to where they were back in the seventies before AIDS.

Who wouldn't? But, AIDS is still here and we have to learn to live with it.

I am still HIV Negative and am monogamous with my partner. But, I don't give oral sex to my partner although he does with me.

In a sense, you are what we would call "trade." Meaning, you mostly lay back and have your partner sexually gratify you without reciprocating.

Yes, and my partner and I are perfectly okay with that.

I wouldn't be. But, in going back to the topic of AIDS and "bare backing," where HIV Positive men are having sex with men who don't know their status?

If they are looking for it, let them find it!

It just sounds so suicidal or, in the least, self-destructive!

Sex is an urge, and if guys are having sex with one another without asking their HIV status then that's their problem. You're just not going to change the behavior. Sex is just like going to the bathroom; you can't stop the urge to go.

Gay men, positive or otherwise, are still going to want sex with desired sex partners and nothing going to change it. I wish something could be done to stop risky behavior but, you're not going to change it until they want to change it.

This risky behavior clearly supports the premise of this book about gay shame and how it effects our actions. It is as if our lives are not important enough that a quick sexual encounter could endanger our lives? Are the risks worth the potential consequences?
Do you find the gay culture to be shameful in that we're still playing out the "victim" act?

In what way are we victims?

In that we are allowing ourselves to get fucked figuratively and literally. As if the world owes us something? That by engaging ourselves in such risky behavior, we are denying ourselves opportunities for growth!

I view it as an individual thing. The guy who allows himself to be the "bottom" for another guy without taking precautions will have to take responsibility for his actions. He has the control in the matter, whether he tells his partner to cover it.

I am not going to pass judgment on him. I think that point says a lot about one's pride in oneself.

Also, we're not just talking about unsafe sex but, the excesses of drug usage within the gay community, especially, Crystal Meth!

I happen to enjoy Crystal Meth myself when I am working. When I use it, I know I will be up and working for the next eighteen hours without sleep. I take a capsule and within five minutes, I get that cold "rush" and know I will be creative and engaged.

Do you get horny?

No, I work. I don't even have company around when I'm on it.

So you use it to enhance your creativity?

Yes, I do. One time I did it for one week and worked the entire time.

That sounds a little like Michelangelo when he worked on the Sistine Chapel for weeks with little to no disruption.

But I wouldn't ever do that again! I ended up hurting myself without getting sleep for all that time, since I tend to hunch over when I draw, resulting in being in a good deal of back pain. A pain which has resulted in my having to use a cane to walk and being unable to carry an object more than twenty pounds.

Hope it was all worth it?

I thought it was, but all my medical bills cost me more than seven thousand dollars! Now, I am much more careful never to do that again to myself!

Listening to Ira, I was clearly shocked at his choice in taking Crystal Meth in order to be more creative and engaged while clearly risking his physical health in the process? Consequently, he will have chronic back pain as a result of his intensive artistic pursuits, reckless actions, and drug usage. All of which prompts me to question Ira's choices and their self-destructive potentiality, and why he is making such risky choices. Perhaps they are a result of gay shame as with many gays; created by feelings of low self-worth stemming from childhood.

Ira, let's return to what it was like growing up gay. We touched on that earlier and I would like to hear more about how those experiences had an effect on who you are today as an artist, and, as a gay man? You do appear as someone who feels "comfortable in their own skin."

I think my mother had a lot to do with that.

As being someone who is also "comfortable in their own skin?"

My mother was someone who taught me how to be self-sufficient, because she was a hard worker who held a couple jobs and a new relationship, so, she really didn't have the time to raise me. But, she did teach me how to cook, sew, and basically take care of myself.

I never resented my mom; I was grateful. I even remember her saying to me, "you see, if I was around, you wouldn't know how to do all of these things!" And, she was absolutely right! My brother cannot do the things that I could. He didn't even know how to change a light bulb and called me on how to do it!

So, thanks to my mom I learned how to do all these things.

So you never held any resentment toward her for not being there for you?

No, no, but we didn't speak for years for several other reasons.

What? You didn't speak to her for years for what reason?

(In a very calm tone of voice) For one, I didn't even see my mother for years! She had an accident and was placed in a nursing home where she became very demanding and mean.

She always depended on me and I had to do everything for her. She always called me and never called my brother, even though, I was living in Upstate New York and he lived near her.

The worst experience was, when I was I got this phone call from this man who identified himself as the husband of the woman who was my mother's roommate at a hospital in which my mother was being treated for Diverticulitis. He berated me on the phone saying," Are you aware that your mother is here in the hospital with no money, no phone, and no television? What kind of a son are you? Why haven't you made any arrangements for her?"

I responded to this stranger with: "Sir, I didn't even know my mother was in the hospital and I do not live in the city. If I did, I most certainly would have made all the arrangements for my mother. But I live in Upstate New York and there is a blizzard going on. Did she bother to tell you that she has another son who lives in the city who you could have called instead of me?
He responded with a timid, "no."

Everything always fell on my shoulders and not on his, and I was tired of her constant dependency on me and not on my brother.

So then, do you feel the relationship you had with your mother had an effect on who you are today, other than forcing you to become more self-reliant?

Self-reliant, yes, but she also gave me the freedom to be more creative. I could do anything I wanted.

Your creative freedom is clearly present in your work and I truly appreciated the opportunity to get to know you and have you in my book. Thank you.

It was a pleasure Vince, I really enjoyed talking about my life and work with you.

In concluding my interview with Ira, it was clear that despite some dysfunctional dynamics within his relationship with both f his parents, that Ira's artwork and the dedication to his work, has been a creative outlet for expressing himself and giving his life more value. But, I would be doing Ira and other gays a disservice not to mention my concern over his drug usage, even if he said that he used it for creative purposes.

It is my hope that Ira will continue doing his excellent work and be cautious over any excesses that will eventually lead to serious consequences if not lessened or eliminated. Good luck Ira.

END OF INTERVIEW WITH IRA SMITH

CHAPTER FOURTEEN

<u>BRAD CARPENTER & CHRIS ARUDA</u>

I met this charming and partnered couple in their apartment with their adorable puppy dog and interviewed them after Brad prepared a delicious dinner for the three of us. Both men were excited to tell their stories and talk about their impressions of the gay male community.

BRAD: I was born and raised in Des Moines, Iowa in the nineteen sixties. I am forty-six years old; forty seven in September. I didn't really "come out of the closet" in my Des Moines years; there were inklings of it, especially in the summer following my high school graduation but it was all pretty unclear to me until I decided to move out to California to attend Stanford University. I did "come out" when I was in Stanford University (*chuckles to himself at the thought of it*) in 1978 which you know is near San Francisco.

So, you can just imagine "coming out" in San Francisco in 1978! The first thing I did when I got to campus was to walk around and check things out. Of course, I soon found the Gay and Lesbian Student Union, which happened to be this little red firehouse! I remember thinking to myself, "Aha, I found it!" I think I was just waiting for a time when I would be away from everybody, specifically, my family.

So, how did you feel once you found that little red firehouse?

Oh, I was totally relieved! I remember thinking that I finally found a place I could go to and be myself! So, I went to the first meeting of the semester there; I must have found a public notice advertising the group somewhere? Now, you can just go online and find the information listed easily but, of course, there was nothing like that then!

Once I was there, I quickly met two people to whom I became really close to. One was another freshman who was from Seattle, Washington named Cam, who had been "out" since age sixteen, and his parents were totally accepting. I remember really looking up to him because he had the kind of growing up experience that I wished I had had, because he was in touch with his sexuality and his parents were so supportive; they were even active in PFLAG. He had all of that, and I didn't! (*Brad paused to take a moment to reflect on that memory*)

My other friend was Lonnie, who was a graduate student in Psychology so, he was already in his early twenties. He was from Arkansas and looked like he just stepped out of a gay magazine; he was blonde and muscular and really well spoken. He was really comfortable with himself! We started dating like, immediately! I had not been going out on dates other than a couple sort of "botched" dates back in Des Moines; while I was confusingly trying to figure myself out!

But when I met Lonnie, he was ready to jump into this whole relationship, and I still had no clue as to what I wanted! I was just barely nineteen and not that sure of myself but, really looked up to him because he was such a good role model.
Lonnie was just so comfortable with his sexuality that I soon became comfortable just being around him! It was also such a relief when I finally figured out that I was gay. I suddenly knew who I was and remember thinking, "That's what all that means!"

As I am listening to Brad tell his "coming out" story at length, including his meeting with his first boyfriend Lonnie, I was a little concerned about his lover Chris's reaction was going to be?

It seemed pretty clear that Brad had a very "hot" sexual experience with the guy, and when Chris was listening, he appeared somewhat uncomfortable and impatient for his turn to tell his own story.

It was evident that Chris was somewhat fidgety while Brad continued, and I wondered if he was uncomfortable with Brad's clear appreciation of his first boyfriend Lonnie or, simply wanted him to stop talking and give him his turn to go which suggests a sense of competition between the two of them.

So, I continued going to meetings there and remember one year when they had the Bridge Initiative, where they were going to fire teachers suspected of being gay!

Did this have anything to do with Anita Bryant and her evil campaign to have gay teachers fired back in the seventies?

No, this was the Bridge Initiative, which had nothing to do with Anita Bryant since, this had occurred in California. Bridge was the name of the outspoken senator who initiated the initiative.

One of my mentors was this professor of mine who was the head of the Alternate Studies Program at my school and was partnered with another man named Michael. They had been together for a real long time and to me, they were the epitome of this healthy gay couple who were older and wiser. I recall going there often to visit with them to cry out my woes and share my worries with them. They would always listen patiently to all my little "broken heart" stories.

You suffered from a "broken heart?"

Well, I sure thought I did. But, I still felt like an adolescent! I didn't really date at all in high school. My sexuality was really repressed! I had "crushes" on guys but didn't really know that they were "crushes!" I didn't put two and two together until college! Then suddenly, you have all the freedoms of being an adult to explore with no emotional development to go along with that freedom!

I would go out with a guy and immediately think I was in love! I would be experiencing one week of bliss, followed about a week of uncertainty, followed by, another week of not knowing what was going on, and then it was over! I was having all these three week relationships! At the same time, I was "out" in a big way! I was involved with all these political awareness groups, speaking in dorms to educate people about the Briggs Initiative and somebody would always ask, "Are you gay? And I would be like, "Well, yes, I am!"

How did that feel to admit you are gay?

It felt great actually! In fact, there was a documentary about me when I was a freshman by Ann Makepeace, who was a well-respected filmmaker in the graduate film program. I was thrown out of my dorm as a result of it! I mistakenly "came out" to my roommate, who was concerned about having a gay roommate so, he went to our RA, who was a practicing Mormon.

With my family, I had yet to "come out" but, when my brother came to my school to visit me, I decided to tell him, because I felt he was the one most likely to be an ally. Although it was difficult for him to accept it at first, he was really good about it.

But, the next night, I decided to take him to this gay leather party where I ended up getting "stoned," because, I really needed to relax! Lonnie my boyfriend was great to my brother trying to make him comfortable. But, at the party, I remember there were friends of mine trying to "hit on him," where I finally had to say, "Stop it, he's straight!" Other than that, it was great to have him there, since it was the first time I had family around to support me.

How old were you?

I was nineteen at the time and in time, I tried to integrate my gay life with my old life. Now, that I understood this part of my life, I felt relived, even great, and wanted my family to be part of it! I wanted to share my life with them. I didn't want to go backwards and hide some part of myself. Once I discovered myself as a gay man, I didn't want to remain private at all. That didn't feel right to hide. I was in this environment when it was gay revolution everywhere in San Francisco.

What year are we talking about?

1978. And with my brother at the time we talked about my "coming out" to my parents who lived in Des Moines, Iowa knowing it was a going to be a lot for them to accept.

But at my first visit at Christmas break, my brother had already spoken to my Grandma Jenny who was really "cool" and agreed that we should talk about it. But instead of having that talk around the kitchen table, we went to a restaurant because my mom was renovating the kitchen. So, instead of an intimate dinner around the kitchen table, we ended up talking after dinner at a restaurant.
After the dinner, my grandma told me to just tell them so I decided to just do it, which was not the easiest thing for them to accept, because when I called a family meeting, they were half expecting me to tell them I had a new girlfriend.
So, they were sitting there with big smiles on their faces when I said, "I have discovered in these last months, that I'm gay!" There was a long pause for a moment, and when they responded, it was with a quiet, "Oh, I see," which I translated in my mind to: "No, you are not."

I remember my dad having his head down the entire time with watery eyes, and my mom was real quiet. My brother sat there the whole time trying to be helpful. In the end, it went okay but for my father, there was a delayed reaction where he said, "it took a lot of courage to tell us about this and I feel really bad, because you are going to have a really tough road ahead of you."

So, I went upstairs to my room and called my Grandma Jenny and she immediately said, "well, I'm waiting." I quickly told her that it went okay, and that they cried. I told her that it was difficult for all but, I think everything went alright," and the two of us laughed with relief.

For the rest of my two week vacation home, we didn't talk at all about it and we carried on as if we hadn't talked at all; living in denial. But on the last days, I realized that they had been talking about me together and started making suggestions to me about my life and ways to change it.

Listening to Brad continue his story while not giving Chris the opportunity to talk, seems clear that Brad needs to tell his story of "coming out" and the inner conflicts he experienced. Conflicts that many gay men and women have gone through but, with the same relief and honesty that comes with sharing intimate details of our lives. And with that honesty, many of us get to experience the relief that comes with the opening of those gates of denial. Gates that keep us stuck in the same place; forced to live shameful lives in order to protect those we love.

I had given my mom a book called *Loving Someone Gay* by Don Clark which was pretty famous at the time. My mom and dad thought that I had been taken over by some cult like the "Moonies" who brainwashed me while I was living in San Francisco. They pretty much figured that someone had changed me because when I left for school, they thought I was normal and now, three months later, I wasn't!

So of course they wanted me to go right into therapy and wanted to fix it! Of course, I said that if you want me to go into therapy to help me with being gay I am all for it but, of course, that is not what they wanted. But I to be honest, I was afraid that they weren't going to allow me to go back to Stamford, which they did not do!

It took them a number of years to finally come to terms with my sexuality and that was mainly due to the wonderful men that I were in my life; one of which, was a man who was a minor celebrity in my town who dealt with troubled kids and met with Nancy Reagan during her "Just Say No!" campaign and was on the front page of the *Des Moines Register Tribune,* which my mom had just happened to see. Even my father was real impressed with him!

It took time, but, eventually, they got it! It took about eight or nine years. In hindsight, they just wanted me to be happy and in time, became very supportive.

How are they today?

Well, they are both gone.

I'm so sorry to hear that.

Thanks, but my mother got to know Chris; my father had already passed away. But my mother really loved Chris and thought he was *(very affectionately)* Great! And all my nieces and nephews began calling him Uncle Chris.

Now how long have the two of you been together?

Chris finally chimes in and answers my question.

Chris: (*very causally*) It will be ten years in September.

It was really nice to finally hear Chris come into the conversation waiting for Brad to finish telling his story and patiently waiting for his turn. I had a strong feeling that Chris's story was going to either equate or even surpass Brad's "coming out" experiences, perceiving some sense of competitiveness from the these two men; similar to male siblings.

Hearing Brad and now hearing from you Chris, I would like to know what your thoughts were while listening to his story? Do you always let him go first?

Chris: Oh, so that is what we're talking about? I just gave him room to go first. Brad wanted to go first, and I let him. I have heard this story before and always hear something new.

I have a good story too and will be happy to tell it. His story is not that different from mine. We are some six years apart but, those six years to me are a big difference since he came out in the mid-seventies and I came out in the early eighties.

Coming from a Catholic Portuguese family in Massachusetts, I always knew I was gay from an early age. I have a story that I love to tell people about when I was around seven or eight and would go through my dad's collection of *Playboy* magazines. I knew where he kept them, and would sneak into his room and go through the magazines looking for that one photograph of a half-naked man to get myself excited.

It is funny how I went through all these pictures of naked women in order to get to that one picture of the half-naked man! I was too young to masturbate then, but I recall being excited by the pictures of half-naked men.

Listening to Chris's story of his exploration of his sexuality at an early age reminded me of similar investigations and explorations into my own sexual identity. But, I am sure if Chris's dad ever happened to come upon his son going through his Playboy magazines, he would have been amused, thinking his son was exhibiting a healthy and more "normal" sexual attraction toward women, not being aware of his son's secret desire for his own sex.

I did have a girlfriend in high school named Amy whom I just saw this weekend, being that she is like a sister to me and such a good friend. Surprisingly, I am very close with the people I went through my adolescence with still. In fact, I was just with them all this past weekend! They all know Brad.

I am very proud of those friendships and the fact that they have lasted over the years! As I look at those friendships, I also recall, that many people thought I was "straight" when I was in high school, because I was always with Amy. It was always Amy and Chris from my Sophomore years in high school till graduation.

Of course, I had those "school-day crushes," and my first "crush" was with my good friend Chris Lately. Chris and I am still good friends. In fact, we just saw him this past month. I remember that he played Jesus in *Godspell* and I was completely infatuated with him. I was a Freshman and only fifteen, and he was about to graduate so he was a bit older; but, he was my first sexual experience! We only "made out," and then we gave one another oral sex, but, that was about it!

Funny, but, I recall thinking that I was only fifteen years old and I am an adult so, I can do this!

Then of course, I now have nieces who are fifteen, and the idea that they might be having sex absolutely horrifies me!

You have a problem with a fifteen-year-old boy being sexual?

Yes, I would have a problem with a fifteen-year old boy or girl being sexual, because it just feels too young to me.

But, you didn't feel that way about yourself?

No, no, of course not. But if I was a parent, I may feel differently, I don't know. It's just that I feel somewhat protective of others' children, while I was not as concerned about my own wellbeing as a child, since I explored my sexuality at an early age. I simply felt I could do anything I wanted to do when I was that age.

When Chris and his family moved away, I didn't really have any other relationships in high school and that was fine, but I knew; even before Amy and I got together, I knew I was gay.

Did you ever tell Amy that you were gay?

Not until I went away to college, and I remember her becoming very emotional and wept. *(abrupt change in tone)*

But Amy was very special to me, I felt that maybe we could make this work anyway!

What did she say when you told her that you were gay?

When I told her, I told her about Chris, because she knew Chris, and we both cried. She wasn't shocked but, she was upset; we were both upset.

Do you believe that she had expectations?

Yes, absolutely.

To be married to you?

Probably yes.

But, she didn't perceive that you might have been gay; that thought never came into her mind?

I think when I told her she wasn't completely shocked. I think she already knew but didn't want to admit it. After all, we hadn't had sex in over five years. So, she probably already knew something was up! *(laughter)*.

Of course, you're a good-looking guy and of course something must be going on for you sexually, somewhere?

Of course, yeah! But with Amy, I did used to fondle her; mainly feeling under her shirt but, not fondling her breasts, it never went further than that! I don't think the fondling went further just because of me but, on Amy's as well; she was a bit afraid and closed off about sex, which was perfect for me.

It's interesting how gay men always seem to find that type of woman. After all, we're not going to go after that "man-hungry" type of woman but, the one that is a bit inhibited with sex, where our true desire for men would not be so easily exposed.

Yeah, you're probably right. That type of woman would probably terrify me! *(laughter)*
Chris is clearly talking about his own moments of gay shame which inhibited him from being honest with his girlfriend Amy but fortunately, did choose to make his move to "come out" in college, similar to Brad. It also appears as if Amy was honestly hurt when his gayness was finally revealed but, wasn't too surprised by Chris' announcement of his true sexuality.

Similar to his partner Brad and myself, college provided the opportunities to "come out of our proverbial closets" and to that point, we can all be grateful to those women who helped frightened gay men make the move to live a more honest and freeing life and drop the facade..

It's also interesting how so many gay men in my interviews here, and on my radio show, have talked of having relationships with women who were somewhat repressed sexually; which only made it easier to have a more platonic/romantic relationships with them without sex. But, I was also curious as to what Chris's real feelings were about women.

Were you afraid of girls as you were growing up?

Yes! And what's really funny, is that I am <u>still</u> afraid of girls that I think are really attractive to me! There's this little part of me that gets really nervous around pretty girls and I love women! I love having women in my life! But, whenever I find myself around a woman I find attractive, there's still a part of me that becomes afraid and find myself "pulling back" emotionally.

Why?

I suppose it's because..... (*clearly questioning himself*) I don't want to.... I don't understand it fully yet.

Do you feel that you might not be able to live up to their expectations?

Chris is clearly questioning the "age-old" question of what would we gay men do if we were ever placed into the position of being sexual with a woman when we honestly desire men more. The problem is, that many gay men feel a sense of guilt and shame about not being sexually attracted to a beautiful woman and set themselves up for failure.

Having been a similar place as Chris, I too felt tremendous guilt for not desiring sexual relationships with a beautiful girlfriend in my past, and knew that I wasn't not only disappointing her, but, the expectations of my parents as well, especially, my mother.
It's not because I am gay, it's just that there's a little repressed desire. I never had sex with a woman; I never wanted to! I just always, found myself way up on the Kinsey scale of being gay and, so, it never occurred to me to have sex with a woman!

So, that might have something to do with my reaction to a beautiful woman, I find myself thinking, "Wow, if I was 'straight,' I would be all over that woman!" So, then, there is always a bit of anxiety whenever I see a woman I find attractive.

How are you with men? Do you feel anxiety there too?

Such as? (laughter)

Do you hesitate in approaching them or, are you aggressive with men?

I can be.

Do you let them know when you're attracted to them? Are you the pursuer or, like being pursued?

Both! I am very confident sexually with men.

Were you sexual with Jesus from Godspell? I can't help exploring this because it is so rich with drama, especially, with my being a drama therapist!

(*laughter*) It was the same with Jesus. I was sexually aggressive with him but I never had a Jesus fixation. I was a Catholic boy but, there was no Jesus longing.

Who was the pursuer or the pursued?

It was clear he knew what I wanted. He was eighteen and I was fifteen; it was pretty mutual. But,

I was the one who laid the groundwork which led to us finally kissing.

But with regards to my "coming out," my parents only found out about my being gay when I went away to college. In fact, I "came out" to them some four years after having sex with Chris and two other gay men, one of whom I slept with the third night I was in college!

Lucky you. (laughter)

(Agreeing) College to me was the place where I immediately knew I could be gay here. We are talking about 1984 and 1985, when it was not such a big deal to be open about being gay.

Anyway, I wrote this letter to my roommate one day, where I mentioned to him that Chris and I were not going to have sex anymore after four years, and decided that we were only going to just be friends.

But my mother somehow read that letter!

How did she get it?

I was out by the pool in our backyard writing the letter in my college notebook, and I hadn't finished it. So, I closed my spiral notebook and brought it into the house and hid it under my bed. My mother later admitted afterward, that she saw me doing that and was concerned about me. At a later date, she said to me, "I was very concerned Chris, because you came back from college very different and I wanted to find out what was wrong!"

So, when I went away to summer camp where I worked as a camp counselor, I recall planning to either walk or ride my bike home; this being a day camp.

Unexpectedly, my dad came to pick me up at 4:30 when I regularly finish work which surprised me, since I knew he regularly worked till 7:30 or later. So, I immediately asked him why he was there to pick me up when he said, "your mother had read a letter of yours and she was very upset."

I can remember on that very short ride home thinking "I could jump out of the car right now." That the possibility of risking death might be better than the fate I was about to face.

Chris's admission that he actually contemplated harming himself, even for the briefest moments, rather than having to face the potential fate that he feared was in store for him, brings to my mind of all the young gay men who have either committed suicide or, contemplated suicide rather than face possible parental rejection.

Secondly, with that rejection, there is that very real possibility of being thrown out of one's home to a life of uncertainty or losing the love and support of one, or, both parents. A fate that several of my own friends and acquaintances have experienced, including, a respected and caring psychiatrist whom I went to in California to deal with my own "coming out" issues. This amazing man, who was in a committed relationship with another psychiatrist, had parents who rejected him and didn't speak to him for two years when he revealed intimate information about his life; unbelievable!

But instead, there was a lot of crying and a lot of "I love you" endearments. And to my great surprise, my mother admitted to me that, "you may not know this about your father, but your father is an alcoholic and that's a disease. He got help and he was cured. You also have a disease and you too can get help and be cured"

My dad didn't do AA (Alcoholic Anonymous) to get cured but, went to a therapist to help cure his alcoholism. I didn't even know my dad was an alcoholic.

So it was your mother's plan to cure you?
Oh, yeah! They were going to send me to a therapist as well to cure me of my disease.

Knowing that the painful situation Chris faced with his parents was decades ago, long before the general public was more aware that homosexuality is not a disease, I can try to forgive them for their attempts to try to cure him of homosexuality and save him from himself.

What I find more disturbing, is that both parents are choosing to view homosexuality as being parallel to alcoholism; a disease that also cannot be cured through therapy but can be treated effectively to assist the alcoholic in achieving sobriety and keeping it; (alcoholism similar to homosexuality cannot be cured). Fortunately, most therapists know that it is in their client's best interest to moving them forward toward accepting their true sexuality and not, trying to cure it.

Sadly, Chris's parents' desire to try to cure their son will only serve toward increasing their son's gay shame with the knowledge that his sexuality is both shameful and painful towards those he loves. An irony that can only lead toward more pain and suffering until someone takes a stand toward accepting the inevitable and moving on with their lives.

So, they sent me to my father's therapist's husband, being that they were a husband and wife tem and felt it was too conflicting for my father and I to go to the same therapist. Of course, in my mind, I agreed to go to therapy to get help in dealing with my parents rather than seeking a cure.

As far as the cure, on the first day of therapy he tells me, "I can't make you straight; you're gay. It's the same as trying to tell someone who loves music to stop listening to music!"

I love that!

What a wonderful line to use for any young man or woman coming to therapy and being new to the gay scene and, having people who wish to change them to a heterosexual lifestyle. Thank God for good therapists in the world, such as the ones who I had in my own therapy following my "coming out" to my family. Christopher was just as lucky as I in finding the right therapist for himself. Good therapy helps immeasurably in providing gay men and women the comfort and support their own families are either unwilling or unable to do.

So, instead of focusing our therapy in trying to change me, he was more concerned about how I felt about my mother going into my room and reading my letter? He wanted to know more about how I felt about that, and my response was to say, "I don't know."

His response was, "Okay, so let's talk about that!"

Yes, that's the same thought that came to my head as well as a therapist.
Ironically, that wasn't the only thought in my head about mothers reading personal letters of their sons, since my mother did the exact same thing when a letter I wrote to my ex-boyfriend was returned in the mail due to an incorrect address! Except with my mother, she took it upon herself to read letter and confront me on the contents. Of course my first response was to say that I would never act out in being gay again, instead of telling her that she had a "lot of nerve" reading something so personal.

Consequently, her actions only caused the relationship between my mother to widen even farther than it was prior to the letter being read until I wrote everyone letters years later acknowledging my gayness and that I was going to live my life more honestly despite their feelings to the contrary.

I hope Christopher had a similar response in confronting his mother.

To my joy, I had a good therapist and my parents were unwittingly spending a lot of money to help me toward accepting my true sexuality rather than trying to change or cure me of it. But for a while, they tried to ignore the fact that I was gay but, after some time, they learned to deal with it, since I continued to have a boyfriend and was not going to change.

Was that with Chris?

No, Chris and I were never together. We just "hooked up" every once in a while when the opportunity presented itself but, we were never boyfriends.

Did your experiences in college help toward improving your sexual practices with other men?

Oh yes, definitely. I kind of "minored" in Oral Sex 101! *(laughs)*

Wow, that was a strong image to get at the moment, and I thought Brad in the kitchen almost dropped a dish, when he heard Chris share such intimate information. For a moment, there was an awkward moment where I was a little unsure where this interview was going so, I decided to bring Brad back into the interview and hear his response to Chris's straightforward storytelling?

So, Brad, what is your reaction to hearing Christopher's story?

Instead of commenting on Chris's admission of his sexual practices, Brad chose to take the interview in another direction.

Brad: I basically am dealing with the aftermath of that experience with his mother opening his letter, especially when he had hid it. (*to Chris*) I thought she found it in the pocket of your coat?

Chris: No, I had placed the letter in my notebook and put it under my bed. She searched my room until she found it. But, there is a happy story about my mom.

Brad: (*quickly agreeing*) Yes, there is a happy story about his mom and that is what I wanted to say. I have listened to that story many times and I still marvel at it, because his mom is so different now.

Having grown up in Des Moines Iowa, and coming from such a backward place; my parents thought I was taken over by a cult and they made me gay. In fact, my dad thought my Greek professor had converted me.

Chris: (*laughing*) Well, you know about those Greeks!

Brad: (*sharing in on the joke*) Yes, my dad thought my Humanities professor who was Greek had converted me to homosexuality! And I recall responding to his statement with "Oh, dad, you have to be kidding!"

And to think that my parents went from that attitude about my sexuality to becoming the most supportive parents I could ever wish for. Unfortunately, it took a full decade for them to get there, but now, they are great!

Chris: (*interrupting*) Sorry, to interrupt you for a second but just to parallel Brad's parents with my own. In trying to find someone to blame with my situation, my boyfriend Chris was eighteen while I was fifteen when we first met and had sex. So, my parents when they found out about us, wanted to press charges against him because they unequivocally, blamed him for my being gay!

Of course they never did press charges because by then, I was "of age" at nineteen but, they never wanted me to see him ever again or, having anything to do with him ever! He was the bad guy.

As I am listening to this exchange between Chris and Brad, I question how Chris's parents would think if the boy Chris who seduced him was short for Christine and not Christopher!

I am positive that his parents would not have been as upset knowing it was an older girl who was sexual with their son rather than an older boy? And yet, their initial reaction was to press criminal charges against the young man who was most likely simply responding to the younger man's flirtations or, who expressed his clear interest in being sexual with the older boy.

Your parents were in denial and had to blame somebody

Chris: Yes. They had to blame somebody and he was an easy target. I tried to tell them that I had gay feelings before I met Chris, and even tried to convince them that I was the initiator of the sex but, they refused to believe me.

Brad: Yes, they refused to believe he was gay and even denied another boyfriend named Brian, who was with Chris for five years or six years and they didn't accept him at all. The only time that they allowed Brian to come into the family was when Chris's father had cancer and Brian was a medical doctor. In fact, he was an oncologist

Chris: *(agreeing)* Yes, that was the first time my mother agreed to meet with him. Unfortunately, it was too late for my father and he passed away soon after.

Brad: So, when I came into the picture, Brian and Chris had already broken up and I found myself in this very inhospitable environment where his mother was not happy to see me at all!

Chris: *(interrupting)* In fact, I remember showing her this picture of Brad from a television show he was in and she went, "ugh." (laughing)

Brad: Yes, I was in the television show *Hercules* with Kevin Sorbo and the picture was of me having fun with Kevin and goofing around making a funny face. But, she wasn't receptive to me at all, and I remember thinking, "OH God, do I have to go through this bullshit again?"

What do you mean?

I mean that my own parents from Des Moines, Iowa weren't initially accepting of my being gay coming from this more backward place but in time, they became more accepting. But for this woman, time had stood still. She had not moved forward at all! Not one iota!

In fact, there was almost this eerie feeling with her as if there was this third spot at the family plot for Chris; being that he was now the man of the house, and she was fearful of being alone.

In fact, there was this kind of Oedipal energy between them as if I was this invader; feeling very frustrated having to try to "win her over" when I had to work so hard toward getting my own parents to a more accepting place.

Now, I had to try to win her over this woman at my age; being in my mid-thirties and feeling as though I was in high school again!
Brad in his description of the "chilly" reception he was receiving from Chris's mother relates directly to what Kubler Ross described in her book, Death and Dying, (1969) which highlighted the Five Stages of Death & Dying.

The first and second stages of the five are denial and the second, anger. Although the focus of the book was on working through the stages of a terminal illness such as AIDS, it also pertains to an

emotional death of a relationship. As with Chris's mother, we have the envisioned death or desire that Chris will ever wed a woman or, have children. Also, if Chris is the only male heir, the loss of the bloodline continuing; thus, we see her dismissive behavior toward Brad or, any male partner of Chris's.

What do you believe was causing her to attack Brad?

Brad *(answering quickly and clearly)* If she accepted me, then, she would be accepting Chris being gay, and that meant, she would also being giving up hope of his ever being straight! Somehow she believed that her resistance to accepting the truth may somehow change him.

Brad just affirmed my point regarding her irrational belief that by denying her son's true sexuality and refusing to accept his boyfriends, it may miraculously make him heterosexual.

Chris: Yes, if Brad was a girl there never would have been a problem.

Being that Christopher's mother appears to be a possessive woman following the loss of her husband and her fear of being left alone, a woman replacing her would still be viewed as a threat.

What would have happened if your mother found out that instead of you being gay that you were dating an older woman who was unable to have children such as Joan Rivers for instance?

(laughing) Well, Joan Rivers would have been a little old, but then, she had problems initially when I began going out with my friend Amy. Both my parents thought Amy as a little too "pushy;" being that I was a little young when we were dating and they thought I had not "played the field" enough as yet.

Brad: Of course that is way before I came into the picture.

Chris: But to get a truer sense of my mom and what held her back from accepting my gayness, was her devotion to the Catholic church and her choice to consult her pastor for guidance in certain matters, including to ask about what to do about her gay son.

His response was to say, "always love your son but never to accept him."

Wow! What a thing to say! Of all the nerve and hypocrisy. Of all the people to talk when years later, who but the Catholic church and the scandals that arose with all the cases of child molestation by Catholic priests and pastors.

Having had more than a few experiences with Catholic priests myself and all the recent controversy regarding homosexuality in the Catholic church, it saddens me to know all the bad advice given to parents of gay children over the years by priests. Causing me to wonder how many gay men and women suffered as a result of unsympathetic and non-supportive advice given to parents in trying to understand and accept their gay children.

Chris: Thankfully, my mom now is so wonderful. She lives her life on life's terms. She nearly died a few years from an infection from an operation and now embraces life and has welcomed Brad into the family.

I tend to believe she was heavily influenced by the Catholic church and with the death of my father. But in time, she began to realize that the church doesn't have the answers in all things.

Brad: But even when things were rough between her and I, Chris always stood up for me, and whenever his mother asked for him not to bring me for family gatherings and holidays, he would always respond with, "then, we are not coming."

There was even this one time around Thanksgiving when she said, "doesn't Brad have family to spend the holidays with?" and Chris responded with, "yes, and we are more than welcome there but, we want to spend that time with you, and Brad is my family, and he is going to be with me!" I was so proud of him standing up for me but, it was difficult feeling so unwelcome.

Chris: Yeah, the dog was more welcomed than Brad was.

Brad: Yes, and on that point, there was this one time on Xmas morning when we were opening presents, the dog got dog biscuits, and I got nothing from her!

It is so sad the number of families who abuse the holidays by making them times of struggle and stress, instead, of focusing on the true intent of these time honored traditions in bringing families together rather, than tearing them apart.

I remember the Chris's nephew and nieces were curious as to why no one was talking about our relationship when they were "cool" with it. But in time, Chris's mom began to warm up to me a little bit and began to accept us.

The turning point in our relationship was when my mother died and we were all out to dinner before the theater, and no one was talking about it.
Chris: I remember being very anxious during that dinner because Brad was unusually quiet and was pulling away from her dealing with his own grief. So, during intermission of this beautiful production of *Midsummer Night's Dream,* I asked my mother to ask Brad how he was feeling because I knew he felt she didn't seem to care.

So when I asked my mother to talk to Brad about his mom's passing, she said, "I didn't think he wanted to talk about it." I responded, that Brad simply wanted to know that you cared; and so, she quickly agreed to talk to him.
After the play was over and I went to the bathroom, I met them in the lobby and they were in deep conversation.

Brad: *(interjecting)* It was the first real conversation I ever had with her.

How long did it take from meeting Chris to having that conversation with her?

Brad: It took years before we got to that point! This was a number of years! I mean, I was looking after her son all this time, doing so much to help him have a better life and make him happy, as he was doing for me.

But, I kept thinking if she could only understand how much I love her son and what I am doing for him to make him happy? And then, to be shunned all this time, until the time she asked me about my mother. Happily, she really listened to me and I shared some real feelings with her.

Did it feel as if the whole world now was accepting you?

Brad: Yes, it was huge!

What is interesting here, is all the power we choose to give some people in order to get their acceptance of us and a little respect. Brad allowed Chris's mom to speak for the world and getting her attention and consideration, represented more than just one woman but, the world's approval as well.

Brad: That was the turning point in our relationship, because it used to be when she called here and I answered the phone knowing we sound alike, she would always say, "Chris?" I would respond, "no, it's Brad," and there would be this pause followed by, "is Chris there?" Then, I would go and get Chris, because she clearly didn't want to talk to me.

Now, when she gets me, we talk for a while before I give the phone over to him. Or, sometimes, she would be talking to Chris and after a while, ask for me, because there a lot of things I have helped her with such as, her computer. Now, there are a list of things I do for her and she clearly appreciates what I do for her since now she has a Brad list and as well as, a Chris list.

Chris: Yes, she now enjoys having another son.

Brad: Yeah, I cook when I am there so, now, she has a daughter-in-law as well!

Chris, do you have any siblings?
Chris: Yes, I have a brother and a sister.

So, why haven't I heard anything about them?
Chris: They're wonderful people and have beautiful families. I thought I did talk about them.

No, you haven't but, with them having families, doesn't that take the pressure of having kids off of you?

Chris: Well, there's no heir to the family name which my mother has brought up on several occasions because my brother had daughters. So, she has said several times, "well, I guess the family name will die with you."

Which means that Chris is not the only child getting the "guilt trip" from mother. When I hear these comments from gay children of demanding mothers, it simply brings up all the guilt mothers tend to heap onto their children until the child reaches a certain point.

A point to which there is an acceptance of life on its own terms for both parties, or, the point of contention is never reached, and there is a continuation of "guilt tripping" on the children without any resolution, until the day when the parent or child passes on; which is truly tragic.

Chris: Even though she has been wonderful these past years, last weekend we had my high school friends visiting for a memorial. When we all got together at one of my friend's homes after the memorial; my mom was there too, and there we are these kids running around the house. It was simply wonderful but, with my mother, the first thing that came out of her mouth was, "oh, don't you feel bad that you don't have any children." *(Chris makes a dramatic gesture pantomiming his head exploding!)*

Despite all Chris's protestations that his mother is so wonderful, she definitely knows how to "dig in the dagger" of shame and guilt in deeper and deeper. Hence, why "gay shame" is never going to go away anytime soon with parents that don't know when to keep their opinions to themselves.

Chris and Brad, you are my first committed couple that I have had the pleasure of interviewing and you present yourselves as being stable, affluent, intelligent, have self-affirming work and a supportive network of friends, did you ever consider adopting or having a child of your own with a surrogate?

(Brad and Chris discussing this together and Chris answers): We've certainly considered adopting but, we're not going to do it the way some of our friends have done it. We're not going to use a surrogate. I mean we have considered adopting but, as I get older, it becomes less and less important.
Does your mother's voice ever get into your thoughts about this and cause a definite reaction?

Chris: We have considered influencing a young person's life and I know many couples choose to marry so to raise a family; after all, it is a basic human need, and I have certainly thought about it but, I also don't think that I **have** to! But, I am certainly open to it.

Brad: Yes, we may be open to it but, have no plans at present to do anything about it. It is possible but, our careers are also very important to us.

I hear you. But, Brad, in returning to the subject of Chris's mother, how did you feel about her comments? Especially, since you have come so far with your family?

As you know, the focus of this book is on gay shame and guilt perpetrated by comments such as the ones from Christopher's mother of not producing children, but instead of reacting to those comments in the moment, we often displace our anger out on other gay men, by either, not associating with men we don't find attractive or, living lives of shame by leading "double lives" or, in addiction.

Chris: Well, I can tell you that I had many conversations with my therapist about my relationship with my mother and her shame producing comments about my lifestyle.

I can tell you that I had the same experience as you did with my mother finding and reading a letter that I had sent to my ex-boyfriend telling him goodbye. She found it and read it, whereupon, she took it upon herself to call me on the phone and confront me with the new information. She used all the Italian guilt she could think of to make me feel shameful and promise to leave this deviant lifestyle so she could sleep at night. As the dutiful son, I did promise to not be gay but, we all know how that ended up?

Chris: I get the Portuguese guilt.

But you "took the bull by the horns" with your mother Chris and asked her to comfort Brad when he lost his mother. You knew the right thing to do and he needed that from her and here he is so many years later, still visibly upset about it.

Chris: We really do tell each other everything. In fact, I remember feeling a bit guilty about it. I talked to my therapist and our friends about whether I should tell Brad the truth; in that, I asked my mother to comfort him when his mother passed away. He had thought she did it spontaneously.

I know he felt that it was genuine. But in fact, it was genuine! Of course my therapist said, "no!" (laughing) "No reason to be telling Brad right now?" It's just the idea that it was set up by me and Brad believing it was spontaneous.
I am just a little curious as to what the difference is in you telling him that you asked her to do this and whether she did it spontaneously? (to Brad) Did you think she acted spontaneously?

Brad: Yes, at the time I did. I felt that she was reaching out to me spontaneously; which she was! But, by the time Chris told me the truth, it didn't matter, because I loved him so much for doing that for me, and her. I get choked up about it, when I think of it now.

So, you came from a more loving experience of the situation rather than viewing it as being manipulative; that he manipulated the situation?

Brad: He gave her the "edge, and, it provided her the opportunity to get closer to me and ask how I was feeling?

Chris: Also, it was bravery on her part. I told my mother to do something for my lover in his time of need and she did not hesitate for a minute! I was so proud of her.

It is somewhat perplexing on how we act so grateful to acts of kindness by our families and at the same time, are so quick to forgive them for hurtful comments made in the past. It is as if, we are "eating crumbs" for any acts of kindness, as if it will take away the pain of past more hurtful actions or comments, but, does it?

For many of us, it appears as if we are simply denying our true feelings, as if, we are still reacting from that shameful place where we are actually surprised when someone is authentically kind and accepting of us, and willing to "step up" and comfort us in our time of need.

In this part of the interview, Chris is just so grateful for his mother's kindness when in fact, he was the true initiator of the act of kindness. He praises her for her willingness to comfort Brad when in fact, he was the more courageous of the two.

As a result of that action on her part, how did their relationship begin to change?
Chris: That really was the "turning point."

Brad: We began to talk more and slowly got closer. In fact, the times we spent at her house, we found many things in common.

In fact, in the past couple years, I told her how I was enjoying the times we spent together where one Xmas I said, ""You know Mrs. Aruda, I really do enjoy all our Christmases together" to where she said, "please, call me Dolores!"

But not Mom?

Brad: No, not Mom! But, that was really great, because we were able to lose the formality and call her by her first name!

And yet, it still sounds as if you're having to climb this ladder toward acceptance or approval from her. So then, I ask you, what exactly does this woman represent to you? I am hearing this story for the first time, although you know the story well, it sounds very important to you?

Brad: *(interjecting)* What is strange about that is, I have been "out" from a very early age, when I first knew I was gay. I have always been quick to be "out" in the workplace, with neighbors, I don't think about getting other people's acceptance, at least, subconsciously in my world.

The thing is, it's his mother! He cares a lot about his mother, and if we are going to spend a good amount of time with her, it's important to have some sort of relationship with her. The fact that we now have this relationship; it's not just about getting her approval, it's about just having **a** good relationship with her!

Now, I can express all the emotions that I need to express with her. I can express love with her, where I can give her a hug and a kiss. She's now very warm with me.

As Brad is talking about loving Chris's mom, I get a strong sense of him missing his own mother and the lost moments of not getting to experience them with her. It appears as if Dolores is now almost a substitute for the mother he lost and misses deeply.

Does it draw you closer to Chris?

Brad: It also draws him closer to his mother! It helps all the way around. So now, I enjoy our visits to her home where before, I used to brace myself!

And now, with her acting so wonderfully toward me, his siblings are now acting in a similar manner where before, they kept their distance, being more concerned over upsetting his mother. Chris: (sadly) Now that we are mentioning my siblings, unlike Brad's story, my parents were of no help to me when I wanted to "come out" to my family.

I remember my parents for years, saying in no uncertain terms, that I was not to "come out" to my brother or sister for fear of hurting them; that they alone, would "shoulder the burden of my being gay." In fact, when my sister became pregnant, they told me not to tell her, for fear of her losing the baby if she knew I was gay!

The stories get worse and worse. Hearing what a tangled weave of lies, shame and deceit that some parents use in order to make us feel shameful! How ludicrous to think that with our revealing our true selves to loved ones, can be potentially dangerous to others. Thereby, convincing many of us to "mask" or disguise our gay identities and live inauthentic lives. To even consider that by divulging Chris's secret, it could actually kill her newborn infant due to the shock of the news. As if his sister had not already guessed as my younger sister did at fifteen!

(sarcastically) Wow, you're powerful! As if they didn't know you were gay and living with another man?

Chris: No, my brother and sister really didn't know. In fact, my brother and sister were both shocked to find out the truth when I finally wrote them letters telling them about myself. I wrote them the same ten page letter which I wrote out twice in order to get it right!

In fact, when my brother read the letter he cried, because when he read the letter, I said, I was gay on the first page but, after reading nine more pages, he felt convinced that I had AIDS!

When you wrote the letters, were you with Brad?

Chris: No, no. This happened when I just graduated college.

What motivated you to write the letters to them?

Chris: So, I could have a relationship with them! I wanted to talk about my life but I couldn't, because my father and mother asked me not to! But, I felt as if I didn't have a relationship with my brother and sister because I couldn't be honest with them!

So, I went against my parent's wishes and they were not happy about it. But, I remember secretly hoping that they would be my allies. The part of this story that was very sad for me, was that my brother and sis both said they loved me, but, were not going to go against our parent's wishes.

Hearing Chris's story brings up my own painful feelings of loneliness prior to my "coming out" to my family. Feeling isolated from everyone, prior to being honest and truthful about who I really was, until I wrote my letters and received nothing but love and support from them.
Again, I strongly advocate "coming out" to one's entire family as soon as you possibly can. For in the long run, despite any initial hardships due to harsh responses, it will most often result in a better and more honest relationship all around. My family became emotionally closer and more honest with one another after I shared very personal information about myself which allowed others to follow suit and do the same.

So, this all happened soon after the establishment of a closer bond with Brad and your mom?

Brad: Well, it didn't happen overnight! But, they could clearly see that his mother was now more comfortable around me and they acted similarly. Before that, it always appeared a little forced between us, as if, there was an effort to be nice and yet, they always had presents for me under the Christmas tree.
(Chis is laughing at some memory of a past Christmas coming to his mind)

Brad *(noticing Chris's laughter and immediately began laughing himself)* Chris is laughing at the memory of one Christmas where there were no presents for me under the tree and his sister felt so bad that she went out and bought me a Christmas present the very next day.

They just thought because I was not getting along so well with his mom, it would not be correct to buy me a present. So, the only presents for me under the tree were from Chris and no one else, and yet, I always bought gifts for them.

Of course the family is going to follow suit with the parent's behavior or implied wishes, and may continue to either ignore or, deny their true feelings and subsequently, disrespect Chris's partner, as long as the matriarch or patriarch wishes it so.

This behavior is almost synonymous with the Amish ritual punishment of "shunning." A cruel and emotionally painful practice of ignoring a person's presence, where the offensive party is often forced through this continual persecution, to leave the community in exile. A behavior very similar as to how some gay men and women may perceive their treatment by their families.

If this behavior continues, it could lead to a self-imposed exile or, at its most tragic, suicide. This similar situation was dramatized in the sixties film <u>Town Without Pity</u>, where suicide was the result of the two lovers being shamed by their town.

Brad: Now, when we go to his mother's for a visit such as last Mother' Day, it's just so easy. We're all just "hanging out" and having lots of conversations where we are updating one another on what's going on, and I am aware of what's going on with their kids. His niece may even come visit us this summer! We even sent her the latest Fire Island Ferry schedule when she comes. Now, the dynamic between them and I has transformed! But the key was getting past that problem with his mom.

In fact, one of the reasons we held back from getting married officially was because we wanted his mom to be there and be sure that she would come. Now, she is finally at the point where she would want to be there for us.

Have you set a date for your official wedding?

Chris*:* We're planning something a year from September in Provincetown.

Brad: We were going to do it on our tenth anniversary but there's a lot of planning in doing the wedding, right?

Chris: Yes, there is a lot of work planning a wedding, I have a lot of bridal magazines to read.

I would like to transition this interview into another direction now that you are mentioning all the gay vacation enclaves for us Easterners such as, Fire Island and P-town.

The focus of this book being on gay male communication, what insights do you gentlemen have about the LGBT community and, what do you find either uplifting or challenging about how we interact with one another in today's day and age?

(Both Brad and Chris exchange puzzling glances between the two of themselves until Brad responds)

Brad: It has changed in terms of location and time. Back in my thirties when I lived in Los Angeles in the nineties, there was a lot of my trying to get accepted into the group as the "popular guy." It felt like high school again! In fact, I remember one time, when I was at this party where I "hung out" most of the night with this little niche of attractive men, who were all bemoaning the fact that none of them were getting any phone numbers that night.

In retrospect, I realize that the reason they didn't get any numbers, was due to the fact that they huddled around in their own little attractive group, where they were so "off-putting," that they looked too intimidating to anyone who may have wanted to approach any one of them!

I remember the group mentality of the moment, was that if they put on another ten pounds of muscle, they would become more attractive to men and then, would get more phone numbers!

But with all the posing and comparing themselves to the next guy, they ended up with no one that night, when in hindsight, they would have done so much better if they smiled to other gay men or invited them into their group. Instead, they became their own worst enemy and repeated the same behavior over and over again, where they rarely got to meet anyone new and often went home alone.

This need to compare oneself to be either better or worse than the next guy, only leads to never finding something in common. That behavior is what I always find so disheartening; almost like a delayed adolescence where the comfort of being within a "clique mentality" such as in the film Mean Girls, *may provide support but not in finding that loving partner, even for the night!*

The "party circuit" which many of us experienced in our twenties and thirties, leads me back to the times when we never felt included in all the high school festivities that many of our classmates got to enjoy. It is as if we felt denied as gay men in our teen years, and are now getting to "act out" in our later years with the "party scene."

Part of me thinks it's great to be having the fun we were previously denied by partying without responsibility, and go to all these extravagant parties with playful abandon. But, there is a repetitiveness that doesn't go anywhere after a while! At some point, you have to look for more meaning beyond that, and our Fire Island experience has been shifting over the past years.

How so?
Well, for one, we've always had houses with other couples.

Chris *(interrupts)*: Who were more into "partying." Which, when I first came to Fire Island, was a lot of fun. So different from the West Hollywood scene that I was previously used to.

I recall the time when I first met Brad, and I used to go to this gym in West Hollywood where nobody smiled at me. That all changed one day when I met this beautiful man (Brad) who smiled at me in the locker room while fixing his hair. When he smiled at me, I was so surprised that I quickly went up to him and said, "thanks for smiling at me; nobody smiles at me at this gym!"

He quickly responded with, "that's because you are much too beautiful, so no one is going to smile at you."

What does hearing that type of comment mean to you?

Well, here's something else that just happened to me when I was in LA at a bathhouse...

(surprised myself) Oh, okay. . .

Of course, hearing this sudden admission of what I would suspect, was approved sexual behavior outside of their relationship, surprised me and took this interview into an unexpected direction with regards to monogamy and questions of relationship parameters.
Okay, so this interview is now going into another direction.

(Affirming my statement with both men laughing)

Chris: (continuing) Yes, and I hadn't been in one for quite a while. So, there was this very attractive guy and I continued to walk around his room without asking to go in feeling hesitant to invite myself almost as if I was performing some type of dance because I couldn't catch his eye..

As Chris is telling his story of "cruising" other men at a gay bathhouse in West Hollywood with his lover Brad listening in with a smile on his face, I am wondering why the interview has gone in this direction when talking about gay male communication? I am sure Chris had his reasons for wanting to invite me into knowing about their own sexual practices and the need to have sexual relations with men outside of their relationship so I am quite curious to hear more.

Chris: I was just too afraid to go in the room thinking he had a "major attitude" about me. In fact, it felt like we were playing a game until I finally ran into him outside of the room and introduced myself to him which led to us going back to his room and talking and of course, playing too!

As Chris is telling his bathhouse story, I can hear a clear hesitancy in his voice that illustrated to me a bit of nervousness while obviously telling a story about his obvious infidelity which I am assured that Brad has heard several times before. Thinking to myself that these gentlemen definitely give one another permission to play outside of the relationship which according to many research studies, is highly prevalent in many gay male long-term relationship.

Chris (*continuing his story*): After sex, he admitted to also having a boyfriend too, a neurologist, and as he was talking I asked him why didn't he just invite me in instead of having to play this "cat and mouse" game? He responded that he didn't think I was interested in him and I said, "all he had to do was to just smile at me?

Brad (*interrupting Chris to give his own analysis of the situation*): There is this fear of rejection where nobody wants to just "put themselves out there!" They are indeed interested but, this fear of rejection keeps us frozen with inaction. Everyone is keeping at a safe distance while waiting for the first indication of interest and then, they'll make their move. Some guys play that game so completely that they never go for it!

Like those guys from your party in the huddle that no one could penetrate?

Brad: Yes, exactly! And, I have gotten sucked into that too, where all my own insecurities will catch up with me and I'll hear myself saying to myself, "enough!" Like, when Chris and I first met, our first interaction was that honest.

Chris: That's because I went right up to him!

Brad: Yes, he went right up to me, introduced himself and he said, "Hi, I'm Chris," and I said, "Hi, I'm Brad and I'm glad you came up to me because I couldn't fuck with my hair much longer!"

(laughter from both men)

Brad: In our situation, we were both being honest and we indicated right away that we were interested in one another. So, we talked a little bit, exchanged business cards, and arranged to meet for dinner where I cooked for him.

So you had a date. Did you have sex on the first night?

Brad: Of course we had sex but, we had dinner first. In fact, we talked a lot that night during dinner and afterward, before we had sex. But, I was just interested in him and getting to know him. I wasn't interested at the time in having a relationship because I was perfectly fine with staying single

If you're not looking for a relationship, then why did you cook him dinner?

Brad: *(feeling a bit defensive)* Well, that's something that I just like to do. I know it's unusual but, it's just something I like to do when I meet someone I really like.

Maybe it's just an L.A. thing?

Brad: No, I just remember that I was really interested in getting to know him and really didn't know where this was going? We could have gone to a restaurant but, I really enjoyed cooking and, I'm really good at cooking steak.

I really had no hidden agenda or under the expectation of "snaring a husband;" I was just on my own for quite a while and was really looking forward to having someone to cook for. I just wanted to create a really nice environment for us to get to know one another.

As I listen to Brad telling his story of his first date with Chris, I wonder how honest he is allowing himself to be. It appears as if he is trying to convince the both of us that he didn't have a hidden agenda of getting a wonderful boyfriend to end his single life which he appears to be denying, even to himself. Perhaps he is just a born romantic. I certainly would love for a man to cook me dinner and end the night in bed if the chemistry is right.

Of course, this story is ironically coming at the heels of both Chris's and Brad's admission of having extra-curricular affairs outside of the relationship, and still partaking in the "thrill of the hunt" for other men, to reinforce their feelings of personal gratification and sexual prowess.

As Brad continues to speak, I am a bit intrigued as to the casual manner of his stories in desiring and pursuing other men in front of his partner. Clearly the two men have a clear acceptance of the other's sexual activities outside of the relationship and are comfortable with their choices.

Brad: The same as I am doing for us tonight; creating a really nice environment to get to know one another. That's just how I operate with people; which is a quality I have that tends to make me different from other gay men. But as far as getting to know Chris when we first met, our honesty came from our comfort with ourselves from the beginning.

In fact, I remember being told by other gay men in LA, "you're not from around here are you?" Simply because, I would tend to smile and talk to them, and be nice to them. I never got into that mindset of being more "cool" and aloof; which seems more common in West Hollywood.

In New York, I find men to be more open and straight-forward. With regards to Fire Island, that is the one place where if you are genuinely interested in someone, you can smile and be more forward. Maybe it's because it's an island and a vacation destination and removed from the confines of the city. That's why we love going there on vacation practically every summer.

THE PINES "A GAY" SOCIAL SCENE

But to the contrary, some years ago I lived in a house in Fire Island which was a total "A Gay" house, where they had to be at just the right party. A party where one had to get tickets to attend; or, be on a private list in order to get in. Often, there was a VIP list, and you had to be with the right house in order to be invited in the first place.

We would have dinner parties where you invited entire houses of the "right people" and everything was very social, where everyone had to be in all the "right places" at all the right times; which was fun but, exhausting! So, by the end of the summer, I was thinking, "my God, this is more work, than work, just to keep up!"

For those who are unfamiliar with the social scenes prevalent in such gay enclaves as Pines Beach in Fire Island and the Hamptons, Brad is illustrating the exclusive social scene that has enjoyed a long history of parties. Parties that we clearly more elitist than anything I ever came upon, with all the "right people" doing all the "right activities!" A social scene which clearly compares with other "upper class" social scenes where either money or fame is the key to entry.

The prevalent criteria for the parties that Brad is describing in Fire Island (the Pines primarily), is to be a part of the "right house" with the "right people." And being familiar with the criteria for entry to these parties, being wealthy and socially connected were helpful but being, physically attractive especially, if you have a "ripped" physique, would get you entry to any house of your choosing since "hot sex" was always the common denominator with this scene.

Unfortunately for many, getting into those "right houses or parties" was not easily attained unless, you traveled with the "right" group of people. A clear indication of how these gay men would separate themselves from other gay men who do not meet the criteria for entry often based on physical attractiveness and knowing the right people.

The above example is clearly an example of what I call "elitist gays" who are also frequently, members of what Brad named as the "A Gay" houses. Houses who's hosts or owners, would organize the houses and parties with the clear intention of keeping only their friends and their associates on the guest list and excluding others that don't meet up with their criteria for inclusion.

With this type of exclusionary tactics, those gay men who find themselves outside of these elitist groups, often find themselves faced with another form of discrimination but this time, from their own social group; thus, promoting another form of gay shame. A type of shame being created by not being the "right type of gay" and where entry is only allowed if one changes either their physical appearance, friends and acquaintances, and, or, financial success.

Brad *(continues):* I am glad that Chris and I have made the conscious decision to be in "lower key" houses where its more about quiet dinners in the house and relaxing.

But you guys would still go out to the Pavilion (Pines #1 club) and parties?

Chris: (agreeing with Brad): When we go to the beach, it's very rare that we would go out to the clubs such as the Pavilion or Sip and Twirl.

As many are aware, both clubs were seriously damaged due to storms and fires which destroyed both clubs. Sip and Twirl did open its doors in July of 2012 and The Pavilion reopened its doors last year, much to the delight of many.

As far as Chris and Brad's new "quieter" lifestyle at the beach, I question how "quiet" it truly is when both admit to extra-marital affairs but, it does appear as if their previous "party" lifestyle has changed. Especially, with their present desire to keep a more or less, low profile.

Brad (continues): We would go occasionally to "Low Tea" at the Blue Whale for maybe an hour or so of dancing, and then, go to the beach to watch the sunsets together.

Did you fellows go to "High Tea" at the Pavilion afterward?
Brad: I think we did it once or twice last year. It took me almost the entire summer to know that there was even a "high tea" at the Pavilion. When I did, I did enjoy going there a few times that summer and enjoyed it. Otherwise, I hardly went out that much last year, and Fire Island was the one place where I would go out and party.

I mean I love going out dancing but lately, I have not had as much interest in it. I am focusing my energy in other places. I was tired of the repetitive nature of all the parties on the island.

(Suddenly remembered something else to share with excitement) I did go to a birthday party that

Susan Morabito (*one of NYC' and Fire Island's most popular disc jockeys*) played at out in the island a couple weekends ago and that was lovely, because there were only fifty people there with all the pretty music that I loved to dance to.

The people there were not all "fucked up" and I could have good conversations with them. I was completely sober the entire night and it felt GREAT! I remembered how nice it felt to feel so great, and to know that I was really feeling it, and that it was not induced by something! Or, that I didn't need a pill to feel this good!

I don't need to go out dancing a lot and that night felt so GREAT! I can still go out occasionally and have a good time. It doesn't have to be about the 'partying scene" all the time.

It's wonderful to hear Brad admitting to his choices that he doesn't need the "party drugs" to feel good and have "great time." With this acknowledgment that he doesn't need drugs or be part of the "circuit scene" to feel good when going out dancing; Brad appears to have found a newer perspective with regards to the gay social scene and its excess and is affirming to himself that he doesn't need any substances to feel good about himself. It also appears as if he is truly enjoying his life without anything that could cause him harm or hurt his relationship with Chris.

On the other hand, it seems curious to me that Brad and Chris are being so upfront about their relationship, as if, both men are trying to reassure the other that they are committed to the relationship. But, they also appear to be grappling with their desires to play with others outside of the relationship either sexually or, being a part of the "party scene." But whatever their concerns or questions may be, they clearly appear to be working out all the "kinks" in their relationship.

It used to be that every weekend had to be about going out "partying," and that is not the case anymore. In fact, it felt good not having to participate in that scene anymore like I used to.

At this point we broke for dessert and I stopped the tape but during dessert, Chris confessed that with regards to Brad and his fidelity within the relationship, that he never had a monogamous relationship. That admission of non-monogamy could be a primary reason for their decision to open up their sexual relationship with others and made it work for them.

FIDELITY AND GAY RELATIONSHIPS

So Chris, you just reported to me that you NEVER had a monogamous relationship?

Chris: Right!

So, you gentlemen have had an open relationship for the very beginning of your time together?

Chris: Right.

And you are both comfortable with that? There is no jealousy?

Chris: *(there seems to be some hesitancy in his voice while responding to my question)* Well.... there can be but we try to keep it honest between us. If something happens that concerns the other, we talk about it. *(Chris's voice is getting softer and softer while responding to me suggesting some discomfort with answering the question).*

Are you guys "playing safe" when you're being sexual with other men?

Chris: Well..... we talk about it...... As far as being monogamous, I don't think Brad or I are ever going to make the choice as to whether we're ever going to be completely monogamous. *(quietly laughs)*. I know it may sound strange but, I know that there are other gay couples that have made the same arrangements as we have with regards to having an open relationship. In fact, we have these two friends *(Chris names two friends who will remain anonymous).*

As Chris is hesitantly answering my question, Brad continues to clean up the dishes in the kitchen after the dessert remaining unusually quiet. His silence and involvement in the cleanup while having Chris answer my question himself, causes me to think that perhaps he too was curious as to Chris' responses. Perhaps it was Chris's decision to keep the relationship open and not Brad's? Perhaps, answers will be forthcoming.

When Brad hears Chris mention these two mutual friends who also have a non-monogamous relationship he joins in.

Brad: Well, those two have a very young relationship. So, that's the thing. I remember reading some book on gay relationships when I was with my first boyfriend Neil. *(continuing to make his point)* I had been with Neil for six months when I read this book which said that long-term couples usually open up their relationship around the fifth year.
Chris: The male couples!

Brad: Yes, the male couples; that was it! And I remembered as I was reading this thinking," Oh my God, I couldn't imagine ever wanting to be with anyone other than Neil! *(and displays a very animated expression of shock for effect).*

Couples when they get to that point, often don't stay together or, they make other arrangements to include having sex with other men. Either, because their sex has dramatically calmed down or, they say that they're monogamous and they are NOT monogamous!

And to me, THAT is the WORST offense!

Chris *(who has been helping Brad in his explanation as to why gay men "open up" their relationship to include other sex partners)* - Yes, that to me is also the worse thing gay couples can do, in saying their relationship is monogamous when you know, it is NOT!

Brad: The act of having sex with other men is not nearly as bad as lying about it!

At this point in the interview, I tell the gentlemen of the video on my website: www.drvince.tv which clearly demonstrates how one of the men I am interviewing on the video is trying to convince me in a role play dramatization, that playing with someone in a steam room at the gym does not mean he is cheating on his partner.

Chris: Yes, to many gay men including myself, that playing with someone at the gym does not constitute cheating on one's partner. Playing in the steam room is simply a safe place to "act out" and does not cross boundaries in the relationship.

Of course, many of us who go to the gym and the steam room afterward, often seeing men "fooling around" wearing wedding bands around their ring finger, non-verbally communicating that they are in a committed relationship but available for play. With those thoughts in mind, I decided to ask Brad and Chris a more direct question.

Do you think it is very difficult for gay men to be monogamous?

Chris: I can only speak for myself, but, yes, it is very difficult for me to be monogamous.

Why?

Chris: (*hesitantly*) I just ... well, um....I... I... don't know. For now, I am not feeling as sexual as I usually am. I guess sex drive ebbs and flows for everyone. At present, I am at a low ebb.... I'm not feeling..

What? Sexually attractive?

Chris: Yes, right now I am not. ….

I am positive that there are many gay men who would view you as sexually attractive.

Chris: I know they do, and I am very confident of my sexuality. I just don't equate sex as love. As to why I have a difficult time being monogamous with someone I love, I just don't know.

I think for me, I really have to work at being monogamous because I really do LOVE sex! I love exposing myself that way. If I find myself on a business trip and I have time, I will find a bath house.

You go to a bath house rather than going to a gay bar?

Brad (*interjects*) Why go through all the "rig-a-ma-roll" of trying to pick up someone at a bar.
Chris: Yeah! Brad never wanted to go through the bother of going to a bar and trying to pick up people.

So then, You guys play together?

Brad: (*quickly*) Oh, yeah! I know of boys who have told that they had bad experiences with couples in three-ways. Not us! We've been told we "give good three-way; we'll take good care of you."

I am very amused at this point in the interview listening to Brad and Chris's "pick-up" lines to "hook-up" with other gay men, as if, they are truly enjoying the "hunt" for sex partners, similar to guys (gay or straight) looking for some hot action" for the night.

It is as if they are enjoying getting the opportunity to have "their cake and eating it too!" Enjoying a loving relationship but also, having the freedom to include other men into their relationship for continued sexual pleasure.

But somehow, I do hear some inner conflict with Chris' hesitant responses to the question of monogamy. That perhaps, there is a little voice in his head that creates some guilt over his actions. As if, he knows that he is really doing something wrong despite, his husband's clear willingness to play along. Perhaps, it's that "age-old" Catholic guilt at play here?

Brad (continues) I know for some couples, jealousy becomes an issue. So, I can see how it can become unhealthy for other gay couples but for us, it is really okay! (*giggles*)I mean, we have sexually acted out in many different combinations and permutations possible and have always enjoyed them.

The playing out of "our own thing" for me, is: "if it happens, it happens." I don't really seek it! It's funny, that when I go out of town on business, rather than trying to "hook up" with a guy, I usually bury myself with projects (*laughs*) and become a hermit.

If that is the case, do you wait for Chris to be more of the initiator? I mean, which one would be the more sexually aggressive partner?

Brad: I guess I would say that he is. But, I have my moments.

Chris: Well, I guess that the fact I like to go to bath houses says something.

Brad: We did go to this Pines dance party one summer where we met this hot couple and we took them back to the house, which ended up being a disaster because one of them was drunk and got sick.

Chris: We have also agreed not to be with people who use "party drug" such as Crystal Meth!"

No, PNP? *(meaning: "Party and Play")*

Chris: Correct. That is one thing we choose not to get involved with even though at one point, we did get "sucked up" into that scene. And that scene was clearly steering our lives in the wrong direction but, we "put the brakes" on that!

Yes, the gay male community had a real problem with Crystal Meth addiction and I recall an advertising campaign in the major gay communities to educate the public on the drug. But, with regards to the two of you, other than being more careful with your "party drugs," are there any other changes you have made in your sexual activities?

Chris *(continued):* Yes, I no longer want to be that *"Alpha-male* mentality" in trying to find the hottest guy. That mindset used to mean so much to me. In fact, I remember a time when Brad and I went to the Winter Party in Miami a couple years ago, and I remember acting-out crazily! I was on steroids, along with quite a few "party drugs" which turned me into a "sex crazed beast!"

(Directing my question to Brad) **How did you feel about that?**

Brad: Well, I was mostly there right beside him, benefiting to some degree. But, I saw it in him as a validation of his sexual attraction and let it play itself out. *(sighs)* Eventually, I found it to be a bit exhausting and repetitive.

Chris *(reacting sympathetically to Brad's response)*: Yes, I agree with Brad and after that crazed weekend, I decided to go into a 12-step program for gay men who were addicted to sex and the party drugs that often accompanies compulsive sex.

In the program, I found it to be so wonderful to be able to relate to men in a non-sexual way.

Listening to Brad and Chris discussing their choices to engage in sexual relations with men outside of their relationship and Chris's admission of joining a 12-step program to get help with his addictions, only solidifies my position regarding gay shame and the lengths many gay men go to exorcise their inner demons. But, I am also delighted that he is getting help and interacting with gay men in a more healthy manner..

The reason I attribute gay shame as the cause to Chris and many other gay men's addictive behaviors, is because gay shame creates a deep emptiness of one's soul that to compensate for that emptiness. We seek out external gratification to fill that emptiness be it with sex, drugs, alcohol, or, any obsessive behaviors to compensate temporarily for our lack of self-worth.

The fact that Chris is now "seeing the inner beauty" in knowing his fellow gay brothers in a manner that is no longer primarily sexual but, as fellow human beings with more to give him than just a "hot time in the sack, "perhaps the desire for sex outside of the relationship will lessen or take a different direction?

Chris: In the program, there is a spiritual connection with these men who used to be "partying" but aren't anymore, and sexuality is now out of the equation. We are all there in the rooms to share and connect; and reach out to other people.

This is similar to a memorial Brad and I went to for a lovely woman where there were a lot of handsome gay men in attendance. But instead of viewing the event as an opportunity to "hook up" with any of these men, we connected in a more spiritual and loving way. It was not all about how "hot" you are and more about how kind and generous you are.

In fact, with our friends, we would never have to factor in, how "hot" they are. (*laughs*)

Sounds to me, as if we are playing out some form of adolescence where guys are competing with one another?

Chris: Yes, that kind of thinking does sound as if there is a good deal of adolescent behavior.
Brad: Yes, this reminds me all about high school with all the popular kids.

And this type of thinking with "who's hotter than who" runs rampant in the gay community.

Brad: Absolutely!

At this point in the interview, I decided to tell Brad and Chris about my previous interview with Brian Kent at a gay bar in Chelsea, where the owner of the bar who knew me well, but, was a bit dismissive of me soon after he became a bar owner and more muscular. But, as soon as he saw Brian (a well-known recording artist), he became all sweet and friendly.

The above scene was immediately reminiscent to me, of high school-days where all the popular kids got all the attention, while those who were less attractive or different, were ignored.

Do you fellows agree that once gay men get all pumped up and sexy, a grandiose attitude is shown and their emotional "walls" or "shields" come up, whereupon, they now have the right to "fuck you over?" Meaning, I'm not going to fuck you but, I am going to "fuck you over!" Do you agree with that observation or, am I being too harsh here?

Chris: No, you're very correct! And, I think those walls are quite a bit narcissistic as well with: "I can't look anyone in the eyes because if I do, they'll think I want to fuck them!" (*Immediately, Chris starts impersonating one of these guys and the attitude they may display*).

Chris (*continues with the playacting*) "So, I have to keep them at bay." (*both men laugh*)

What happens if you look them in the eyes, what are you signaling?

(*Brad answers*) Wow, if you do that, they will think you're signaling your interest in them, and will think you are going to want to pursue them! They're also saying to themselves, "If I'm nice to someone, they're going to think I'm coming on to them and then they're going to pursue me and so, I going to keep them at bay!"

The other thing is, that these guys may change on the outside but, they haven't developed on the inside at the same time! So, if you're insecure when you're unattractive, sometimes when you do develop on the outside, you still end up being **even more** insecure than before!

I know it all sounds weird but that's what often happens, because if people are all of a sudden nice to you because you "put some muscle on," and that feels good, in reality, they're not being nice to you for who you are but, because you are now more attractive to them.

So in the end, you feel worse than you did before, because you know that they're only paying attention to you because of your sexy muscles and not for who you are!
So, while there is a wielding of power with this new "hot" look, you have to develop on the inside as well otherwise, you will only judge yourself positively based solely on your outside appearance.

Remember when I talked about those guys at the party in Los Angeles who were sure that if they only put on another ten pounds of muscle, everything would be okay? Well, in fact, when I left LA, I felt "on par" with that group of guys in terms of how developed I was, but when I came back some years later, these friends had become even bigger than before with huge muscles! I mean, these guys used to have sexy, well-built bodies and now, they were huge!

Their mentality remained, "well, all I need to be perfect is to put on another ten pounds of muscle." So, it was never enough muscle for them for in truth, there was very little growth on the inside, which is what they truly needed!

Listening to Brad's analysis of the muscle mentality and how it can become out of control, I continue to see "gay shame' as the primary reason as to why all this weight training becomes an obsession with so many gay men. For, by working out and obsessing about food, it appears to lessen the pain of negative self-worth and loneliness. All of which, is a product of a society that continues to punish those who are different or, demeans those who don't fit the more "normal" lifestyle.

As a result, by working out to excess it become an ineffective attempt to fill up their feeling of emptiness with not only sex, drugs, alcohol, but also, with exercise addiction and eating disorders. In fact, statistics often presented in my Public Speaking classes with my students' presentations on "Eating Disorders and Exercise Addiction" show ever-increasing numbers of men who have been diagnosed with eating disorders especially, gay men.
Brad: And now, we are with a group of men who are choosing to work more of what's on the inside rather than what's on the outside; and that's what so inspiring. Now, being with these men, it's not all about being accepted and having to prove yourself sexually but getting to know them on more a personal and intimate level.

Also, with these men, who are also very sexy and attractive, it's not all about the sex but, the connection on another level!

Chris: This experience with these men and, my time in the rooms, has taught me that we need more outlets to come together in a non-sexual way. Because, there are plenty of other opportunities for us to find ways to be with other gay men such as, a volleyball league rather than, going to a bar.

Hearing Chris and Brad now promoting other activities with gay men rather than sex, and promoting a more spiritual and healthy outlet rather than engaging in the sex outside of their relationship, I decide to confront them with the following question.

But don't you think that sex defines us? I mean, don't some gay men join volleyball leagues not just to play ball but, to find boyfriends?

Chris: I am sure some do but, that's not the purpose for joining a league; it's to play competitive sports and for a healthier form of competition.

Brad: I think there is a wide range of guys who want to play ball, and, there's a wide range of guys who want to have kids and be partnered. We were finding ourselves in a sub-culture that was all about the sex and the parties but, that's not who we are anymore.

Chris: Yes, we are not that anymore, plus, we're finding out that there are all kinds of gay guys out there.

But, wasn't it our sexuality that defined us back in the seventies? That was what many of us fought for after Stonewall and even during the AIDS epidemic when the mayors throughout cities with large gay populations were going to close the bathhouses. In fact, I remember gays shouting in protest: "you can't close the bathhouses, that is how we define ourselves!"

Brad: Right, right. Our sexuality was what defined us, and we glorified in being on the outside of norm of what society deemed acceptable.
That's true, and I would love to have you both on my radio show when the subject is about "Monogamy and Gay Relationships." You would provide some very interesting perspectives.

Brad: (laughing) Yes, you could announce us as: "Here's Brad and Chris, and they are here to share their viewpoints on this week's topic."
Speaking about the media and that you are a successful producer Brad, how do you think the gay culture is going to be viewed now that shows like Will and Grace and Queer as Folk are gone?

Brad: There are still gay characters in television but, they are getting more assimilated within the mainstream. There are more gay characters popping up in television without so much "brouhaha" as there was before.

I personally thought the British version of *Queer as Folk* was really excellent and was a lot better made than the American version. But, I did find that the American version stood out more for its sensationalistic aspect of the culture.

I am personally working on a television series written by this wonderful writer which is about a society of people who are of both genders; male and female. The society is mostly tribal and these people soon begin to separate themselves into male and female roles; some opting to take care of their home and others, choosing to become soldiers to save their tribe.
How do you plan on casting this? I guess you don't plan on casting bodybuilders? (all laugh)

No, I want to cast more gymnastic types who are both beautiful and exotic looking, because these people will have to be convincing as both a man and, as a woman

Well, this seems to be a good opportunity to showcase the transgender community and create some increased sensitivity and compassion for them as a community. I also think the LGBT community would embrace it.

Chis: Yes, you can cast all these beautiful men along with strong athletic women and make everyone happy.

Gentlemen, I want to thank you for taking the time to be interviewed and I wish you the best of luck in your wedding plans and have a fun with the honeymoon trip!

Brad: Thank you Vince, we really enjoyed the opportunity to talk about our life together and our history as well.

Chris: Yes, and even getting the opportunity to talk about the extra-curricular activities *(laughter)*

It's interesting that Chris's last comments make mention of their non-monogamous activities, clearing indicating the importance of being able to discuss that aspect of their relationship. But whatever their sexual choices may be, these men have sustained a very healthy and successful relationship for one another, and I see nothing but a wonderful future for the both of them.

BRAD AND CHRIS ON THE WEDDING DAY AT THE BEACH

END OF INTERVIEW WITH BRAD CARPENTER & CHRIS ARUDA

CHAPTER FIFTEEN-*RAY DUNBAR-SMITH*

"A MAN OF MANY TALENTS AND A GOOD HEART"

JANUARY 15, 2013

I interviewed Ray following a massage at his New Milford, Ct apartment. Ray's apartment is filled with beautiful antiques; passed down from generation to generation from his large extended family who have with strong historical ties to the town. Ray has enjoyed a multi-faceted career as a masseur, professional stage and ballroom dancer, and professional disc jockey. He presently resides with a gay roommate and plays music at the local gay bar in Danbury, Ct..

Ray, I would first like to thank you for volunteering to be a part of this book, <u>Talk it OUT: No More Gay Shame</u>, and on the topic of shame. Could you provide some of your own personal experiences with gay shame by sharing your growing up stories with us and specifically, with how gay shame may have impacted that growing up experience?

Ray: I grew up here in New Milford, Connecticut. I am a former dancer, now, a masseur and play music at Triangles Bar in Danbury. Growing up, I knew I was gay probably around eight years old. But, I didn't choose to come to terms with it until my teenage years, around sixteen.

My first gay experience was at the age of ten with a classmate of mine.

Ten years old, that's pretty young, what happened?

Well, it all started out very innocently, with a little "touchy-feely," and then I kind of suppressed it for a while until I was sixteen and decided to "come out of the closet."

How was that experience for you? After all, sixteen is pretty young to "come out."

It wasn't easy I can tell you, but, I felt that I had to do it because if I didn't "come out," I felt I would be stuck! Also, being the dance world, it helped me in coming to terms with being gay.

So, you were dancing when you "came out?" How old were you when you started dancing?

I was eight.

What forms of dance did you learn?

I would take tap classes, as well as, ballet. After a while, I decided to pursue jazz dance primarily, which became my profession of choice as a performer.

Did your parents encourage your dancing career?

Yes, my mother encouraged me into that career and even pushed me to perform.

Do you have siblings and were they in the performing arts as well?

I have an older brother who became a police officer.

Okay, so let's talk a little about how your first gay experience was like for you?

Well for one, he approached me to do it, and it was pretty great. We went up into the woods of Washing ton, Ct and we explored each other's bodies. It was pretty hot! And this went on for quite a while.

So, you did more than just "touchy-feely?"
Oh yes, we did pretty much everything. Starting off experimenting and then going farther.

Apparently you both knew what to do.

(laughing) Yes, we both knew what to do. Seeing what feels good and what does not feel good

What was he like?

He was Italian boy and knew what he liked to do.

Do you still see him?

I see him around town every once in a while.

Is he gay or, is he living a "straight" lifestyle?

He's "straight," yes. But he still remembers me very well. *(laughing)*

That's typical in this small communities such as New Milford. But, he doesn't sound very "straight" by all the things he liked to do with you!

That's true.

Hearing Ray's very detailed personal stories of his first gay experience and at age ten, I am surprised with his honesty and candor. Clearly having a career in dance and a supportive mother helped in his transition to being gay and becoming a performer.

I also had a friend of my age who was very sexual and we would have oral sex frequently and he too decided to pursue a "straight" lifestyle until his early death at age twenty-one of leukemia. Perhaps if he didn't pass away so early, he may have decided to be more honest with himself and become a gay man. Unfortunately, that was not meant to be and he died with his secrets.

BEING A HIGH SCHOOL OUTCAST

So, Ray. You're sixteen and choosing to "come out of the closet" in your high school; how did that work for you?

I was outcast in a way!

I am so sorry to hear that! What happened to you and why were you outcast? As you know, having these types of traumatic experiences is the basis of how gay shame happens to so many members of the gay community.
Well, I went to Richfield High for one year, where most of my gay friends went, and when I came back to New Milford High School in my junior year, that's when it happened.

What happened? How did you feel outcast?

Well, I had decided one day to tell my best friend in confidence about who I was and instead of keeping it secret, but by the next day, the entire school knew I was gay.

How did you experience that day when everyone knew? What happened?

Well, when I entered the building, I saw a group of my friends and went over to say hello. Instead, they said, "we heard you were gay and we don't want to 'hang out' with you anymore!"

Another sad story of ostracism and shame being perpetuated by a cruel and intolerable society where gay men have to learn how to "steel themselves" from more emotional pain either by avoiding former friends, or, learning to "get through" their day with the least amount of ridicule and scorn as possible. Hopefully, their home was a more supportive place to decompress.

Did they use the word "gay" or "fag?"

Some used the word "fag" yes!

Did you have any sanctuary at that school?

Yes, I had some friends in town who were gay as well.

That was pretty early in age to "come out." What years are we talking about?

I graduated in 1984.

I thought it was okay to be gay in 1984, at least that's what I heard from other guys I interviewed for this book.

Maybe it was easy for them but, it was tough for me.

So, you were gay in 1984 and you were being socially ostracized by friends. So, what did you do then?

I went back to Richfield High, which was a lot more accepting, and where I had friends who comforted me. But, at the end of the school year, I decided to go back to New Milford to graduate.

Why did you go back to New Milford?

I wasn't going to let them run me out of town! And, that is where my parents lived.

What did your parents do during all this?

They were very accepting of it and when I "came out" to my parents, my mother embraced me and told me that she loved me; my father did the same.

I love your parents, they are still so loving and supportive of you, as you are with them.

Thank you, they are very special to me, as is, my brother.

Does your brother have any children?

He has a daughter. He also just recently retired as a police officer in Florida.

Well, that must relieve a little pressure with not having kids.,

My parents never made me feel guilty for not having kids.

So, going back to your story of "coming out "at sixteen. What about the best friend who told everyone you were gay? What happened with him?

He ostracized me too, but, just recently he "friended" me on Facebook. He's a schoolteacher now.

Did he ever apologize to you for what he did?

Yes, and he explained to me why he did it too.

He did? Then what was his reason for exposing you?

He said that he wanted to remain popular.

Typical jerk, he outcasts you so he could remain popular.

You got it!

Ray's story of how his best friend chose to breach Ray's privacy by telling everyone his 'secret' to remain popular, is what causes gay shame to become a reality; as it was for me when my best friend exposed my secret to his sister one day. But unlike Ray's experience, my best friend and I were having sex and due to my own shame, I overlooked his breach of trust to continue having sexual relations with him. He eventually did apologize in time, admitting his own gay shame. Listening to Ray's high school horror story brought back my own painful experiences of feeling different from all the other kids in school and, all alone. Then, when someone exposes your secret, all your fears of being shamed and ostracized quickly becomes a reality.

It is no wonder why so many gay men have moments of depression and suicidal idealization due to shame-inducing memories, as well as, having to "toughen oneself" against discrimination.

Happy are those who have loving friends, parents, and a community of acceptance but, for those who don't, their world must feel very small at times.

So, you graduated from New Milford High School despite all that you went through there? How did that go for you?

It was great! I didn't care about what they said or, how they felt1

You didn't care, or, did you wear a "mask" or fake smile, to get through that day? I say that, because many gay men in this book have told me that they often wore masks to get through the more difficult moments in their life. What was yours like?

It was a mask protecting myself from those who tried to hurt me, in fact, it was more of a protective "bubble" than a mask, that helped me to get through the graduation.

So, you smiled? Do you think that the smile mask shielded you from that tough situations.

Yes, I smiled and it did feel like I shielded myself from them, now that I think about it.

For those who are reading this and thinking literally of wearing some form of Halloween masks, we are not! What I am alluding to here is the "mask" we tend to wear in life with either a pleasant expression or, the fake smiles we wear in life to get through the more difficult moments. As a drama therapist, mask work is a popular technique for working with clients to help facilitate self-expression in discussing painful life moments.

One such moment would be Ray's graduation, surrounded by so many former friends who "wished him ill" at the time. So, instead of walking around in fear or intimidation, Ray walked around with a big smile on his face and would not let anyone "get the best of him" surrounded by his loving family and those few gay friends who stood by and supported him and each other But, just to let you know, I wasn't only gay but, I "hung out" with the "Goths" in school, with whom, I could wear black and be wild. I was really "into" that scene, and it was ironic that those kids who made fun of my friends and I for being gay, ended up copying our style! That irony, told me that they had their own sexuality issues.

Clearly they had their sexuality issues, since they focused so much on you being gay. Also, their actions being young and immature, would account for their uncertainty on how to act or, dress. In retrospect, it must have felt somewhat satisfying to see them following your style of dress after devaluing you for being gay?

Yes, it did.

FINDING ONESELF IN THE WORLD

So, after high school, you went on to college?

Yes, I went to Arizona to attend a two year college for interior design in Tempe, Arizona.

Impressive. You went all the way to Arizona to go to school! Were you allowed to be gay in Arizona?

Arizona was great back then. It was in Arizona where I lived an active gay life; coming to terms with who I was back then, and after Arizona, I moved to New York City to pursue show business.

Before talking about NYC, I would like to hear more about your college years in Arizona. Did you fall in love in Arizona or have a "first crush?"

No, I fell in love later, not, in Arizona.

Well, we're going to hear more about that but what was gay life like in Arizona for you during those college years.

I lived off campus with a college classmate who was also gay.

Did you have a relationship with him?

No, we were just good friends and "hung out" together; we still keep in touch even to this day.

Did you have any memorable college experiences in Arizona?

To tell you the truth, not really. I just did a lot of studying and went out when I had time.

Were there gay bars in Tempe?

Yes, there were gay bars but, I didn't go out as much there, as I did after I graduated college.

What did you do after your received your degree in Interior Design?

I came back to Ct for a while to live with my parents, doing interior display work in various antique stores then later, I decided to go San Diego, California for a while and then, to San Francisco to "find myself."

Wow, you must have had some fun in those two cities. Which one did you enjoy the most.

I loved San Diego more, because that was where I met a lot of wonderful friends who made me feel very welcomed and comfortable.

That sounds wonderful. Did you get to play at the beach much in San Diego?

(smiled) Yes, I did. But, I mostly worked to get by in interior visual display in stores, where I shared an apartment with a friend of mine and kept my expenses low.

Okay, so after San Diego you went to live in San Francisco. That must have been fun?

Yes, it was. I went there to visit a friend and ended up staying there for a while during the late eighties; early nineties. I loved the entire experience of living there. I worked at a "high-end" boutique in the cologne/perfume department and loved it.

When were you in San Francisco?

I was there in 1995.

That had to be a blast back then? Did you have some romance in San Francisco; the west coast "gay mecca?"

It was where I came to terms with myself back then.. I was a little heavy set, and decided to lose the weight. It was also there where I decided to go back to the gym and get muscular.

Well, I have known you for over ten years and you've always been built so, it all began in San Francisco for you.

Yes, it did.

After San Francisco you decided to go to New York or did you come back to Ct?
I went to live in Connecticut again until I decided to follow a career in dance and knew that NYC was the place to do that.

Okay, so you decided to move to NYC and pursue a dance career; and how did that work for you?

MAKING HIS MARK IN SHOWBIZ

Listening to Ray's story I am reminded on my own decision to move to Los Angeles; Hollywood o pursue my acting career and enjoy the freedom to be gay without having my family constantly asking questions as to my dating women.. Thankfully, Ray's family was more accepting and supportive of his being gay so, he didn't seem to face that hardship.

Instead, Ray appeared to be trying to find that love and support for his sense of self within the gay community, both here on the east coast, and in the west.

It was great. I took dance classes there and would go on auditions until one day I found an advertisement for a production of *Chicago* and went to an audition for non- Equity dancers and got the part!

How terrific, so for how long were you in the show and what years are we talking about?

I was in the show from 1997-98 as one of their featured dancers. But, I found myself getting physically exhausted doing eight shows a week and decided to leave and return to Connecticut to open up my own dance studio, teaching jazz and ballroom dance.

How long did you own the studio?

I never owned the studio myself, since I always had several business partners teaching those classes along with me. I still teach classes in Argentine Tango occasionally to this day.

With all these wonderful past experiences, how would you define yourself today in 2013?

Well, I believe we're never complete, because we never stop learning or changing, but, I am more settled with who I am today. For example, I love fitness and bodybuilding.

How has being gay enriched your life or, has it been more of a challenge than a gift?

I believe it is a gift.

How so?

Being a gay man, you find yourself more open to life experiences. Especially for those who live and work in the performing arts world. For me, being gay was something I recognized about myself at a very early age, but, it took years to accept it within myself.

What would you say was the most challenging experience about being gay in your life?

Ignorance from people.

How did that exhibit itself in your life?

When people "turn a cheek" once they realize that you're gay or, give you attitude and won't talk to you.

When has that happened to you and if it did, what would you say to them if you could?

It hasn't happened in quite some time but if it did now, I would speak out and tell them, "you are ignorant and your attitude reflects more upon you, then it does upon me."

What was one of your most rewarding experiences about being gay? Was it a love or a "crush? "Or, was it being with a group of people who comforted and supported you?

I would say it would be my friends, now, and from long ago, who have been like my family.

Was there one friend in particular that was very special to you?

Yes, I have this friend named Peter who has always been there for me. We met in San Diego years ago and I can still consider him like a brother to me. I hold him very dearly. We're sort of like the Wonder Twins, which was a cartoon from the seventies, where these twins would always tease one another and could change their human forms to anything else; sort of like superheroes.

Would you like to be a superhero too?

Well, you know that my nickname is Batman

Yes, I remember that you dressed up as Batman last Halloween. But, instead of being a superhero, how would you define yourself ethnically?

FACING SHAME

(Ray *answered this question immediately with little thought as if he had been asked this question many times before*) I am American Indian; Skateboard, and Cherokee Indian, on my father's side, and, I am Creole, Greek, and French on my mother's side.

Wow, and yet both your parents are both dark-skinned, where does that come from then?

Well, on my father's side, his great-grandfather was American Indian who married a German woman, and my mother's great-grandparents were from the South. He was Caucasian and she was African-American but, I would say she was more Creole than African-American.
So you are of mixed blood but, would you get offended if people identified you as African-American?

I don't usually get that, since most people see me as being either Indian or Spanish, because I don't tend to have Black features or, the "look."

So you would say you are more like Lena Horne, Beyoncé, or Maria Carey, mixed, but a big "melting pot" of a man?

(laughing) Yes, I would.

Listening to Ray's view of himself as almost everything but African-American, I had to wonder if there was any reason as to why he was choosing to emotionally and mentally distance himself from his Black ancestry. So, instead of "gay shame" with regards to Ray's self-identity there may be another form of shame?

Happening to know Ray and his parents well as a long-time friend, I always knew he had some mixture of ethnicity but, there seems to also be a strong denial of any identification as being Black, at least on Ray's part, even though all the members of Ray's family do have some Black "features." In fact, his ancestry traces back to the Civil War and the Underground Railroad.

Ray seems to even be going so far in this interview as to deny being Black, but, as Creole, which appears to suggest a different type of Black than African-American. But then again, that is very true of those of Spanish nationality not identifying themselves with Hispanic or Latin cultures and Italians who refuse to acknowledge Sicilians as Italians. All in all, creating a culture of discrimination and denial and one that continues to promote shame and emotional insecurity.

Have you felt discriminated against in the gay community, as well as, society as a whole?

I don't feel it necessarily but, I see it. For instance, we have the transgender population being discriminated against all the time within the gay community, and that bothers me. I, for one, will talk to anyone; be they wearing a dress or being big and muscular. I, personally, do not discriminate against anyone. What matters to me most, is the person.

I believe that we are all in this together and we are all minorities and as minorities we need to support one other.

Now, instead of responding to my question, Ray seems to be becoming an advocate for peace and acceptance of all diversities within the gay culture. This type of behavior seems to indicate an avoidance strategy on his part that he appears to be unaware of. It is as if he is keeping a deep seated secret to himself, and as a result, will give affirming, but, emotionally detached responses. *In Ray's follow-up interview his secret and emotional detachment will be revealed.
So Ray, I hear that you don't discriminate toward others but, see this discrimination taking place within the gay community?

THE "GAY COMMUNICATION GAME" FOR RAY

Yes, I do. But, only by some and, not by all. That, like with any group, there is always someone who is the "downer" that tries to "put down" others.

What is it about gay people or their behavior that makes you angry?

When people make fun of others and insult them with dismissive remarks.

But, I see guys doing that all the time, especially in the bars with their cliques of friends? So, why do you believe that gay men have a tendency to put others down?

Because they're insecure. Someone who is cocky is only "putting on a show" to try to separate himself from others to make himself feel better about himself. On the other hand, someone who is confident knows who he is, and doesn't have to put others down to make himself feel better.

Also, I don't believe in having a "cocky attitude" either. I am the type of guy who will talk to anyone, and if they don't respond to me, then, I simply walk away.

Ray's statement is very similar to the statements of many others in this book, and why I chose to write on this subject, since, I see this behavior occurring especially, in gay social gatherings.

As you recall with Brad and Chris's interview of Brad's observation of similar non-communication at a Pines Beach party; where he found himself with a group of friends who complained about not meeting anyone new, but, never left the safety of their clique.

What do you believe causes this "cockiness" in gay men?

It has something to do with their background that causes this insecurity; where they will say, "oh, look at the guy" or, "who does she think she is?"

That insecurity comes from living in an insecure world. Fortunately for us, we live in a more permissive and tolerant culture in Connecticut but, there are many who live in states and countries, where it is against the law to be gay, or, even kiss another man in public. With such injustice, it is no wonder why we take it out on one another, rather than, to those responsible!

Yes, I totally agree we need to work together to fight ignorance and those who wish to hurt us.

What would you say to gay men first "coming out" to guide them on the right path?
I would be supportive of them toward coming to terms with being gay and help them in "coming out" to their families or, if not their families, to a trusted friend.

Is there support here in Connecticut. We seem a little more scattered in comparison to cities like San Francisco, Los Angles and New York?

Yes, it is a little more scattered here, and not any many places for gays to go here in Connecticut. And if young gays need to move to the big cities, then they should; I did.

But as far as being gay, we need people to face their fears and take a risk to be honest about who they are. We need to learn from each other and work together as a community.

What is something negative about the gay community that holds us back in life?

Not facing our fears, because if we don't, we will live a shamed existence, such as, trying to be "straight when you are not!".

How did you experience gay shame? Did you ever try to "act straight" any time in your life?

Yes, I did, but, I felt dishonest and couldn't play that game. And, having a supportive family helped me to be honest.

You "came out'" to them when you were sixteen and they were immediately supportive of you and, still are. So, what brings you joy in life?

I enjoy working out and my massage work, and I love to dance and any form of creative self-expression. I love my DJ-ING and playing my music in clubs, such as, what I am doing now at Triangles, our local gay bar?

What would you do if you didn't follow that specific career path?

I would probably do police work like my father and brother did. I love detective work and watch all the crime shows on television. I love solving crimes on these shows, such as homicides.

I didn't know that about you, but, since you didn't follow that career path, what do you see in your future?

I want to be in a loving relationship, which has been a struggle as of late.

Why is it so difficult to find a loving relationship? What is wrong with gay men in their inabilities to commit in general?

It takes work, and I have been fortunate that the men with whom I had relationships with have been monogamous to me? But, as far as most gay men being monogamous, men in general are hunters and are always looking for new prey, but, I do feel that men can be romantic and can commit if they really want to.

Okay then, why do gay men lie so easily?

Because we learned not to trust others, because we were hurt in the past by others we foolishly trusted, such as, my friend in high school. We need to be honest and upfront with one another about how we feel. Be upfront, honest and be who you are.

But why are gay men so quick to reject others? Why can't we be nicer to one another? I for one saw this sweet boy at a bar approach a sexy muscle guy who immediately rejected him and walked away. I felt terrible for the kid and wanted to approach him and tell him something funny and help him feel better such as: "you're cute and that guy is an asshole.'

Why do you think that some gay guys do that to others and act so elitist; responding positively to only men who are like themselves and rarely let another type of guy talk to them or "come on" to them in bars or clubs.

Yeah, there's always a better way of saying, "Thank you, I'm flattered, but, perhaps we can be friends?" To openly reject them for their courage to approach you, is definitely wrong.

So then, why do guys do it to other guys? Why can they only be with men who look like themselves or follow a very limited criteria.

I think it's an "emotional crutch."

What type of "crutch?"

I think it's a "crutch," because they are experiencing a void in their lives and would be showing weakness at allowing the other guy to approach them and give them a chance to "be with them." Instead, they only choose to be with men who "mirror" themselves physically, and that if they allowed the other to seduce them, it could be viewed as a weakness

Why a weakness?

Because they would see themselves as giving up on the chance that a better guy might come along and instead, they allowed the lesser choice to approach them and missed the opportunity for the better choice to seduce them or, vice versa.

Sound s like a sex game similar to the format of the television show <u>Let's Make a Deal</u>, where the contestants have the choice of picking a bigger prize and pass it up for the "sure thing!"

(laughing) Yes, it's Let's Make A Deal for gays! I love that analogy of comparing the gay "cruise scene" to the long-time television show, *Let's Make A Deal*; where gays are afraid of passing up their opportunity to get the bigger prize of the night and fearful of being stuck with their version of the consultation prize.

Yes. But gays are not the only ones who are quick to "shoot down' likely suitors, I remember my days before "coming out," when I went to "straight" bars where I saw average-looking girls "shooting down" handsome men asking them to dance at clubs, and couldn't believe my eyes! I, of course, would have snapped up any of those guys "in a heartbeat" and ignored the girls completely.

(laughing) That's cause you're gay!

So, instead of allowing themselves to meet someone nice, I see gay guys standing all night around the dance floor waiting for someone "hot" to ask them to dance. And as reported recently by one of my guests on my radio show <u>Talk it OUT with Dr. Vince</u>, "I would wait around all night at the Pavilion at the Pines; meeting no one! I felt hot and sexy but, was fearful of getting rejected so, I did nothing instead! Ironically, later that night, some guys from the club told me I looked unapproachable!" As a result, he went home alone and frustrated; feeling less sexy than before.

But, who really wants to feel rejected? I have that fear too, but, I wind up doing it anyway! Then again, what do I have to lose? After all, tomorrow is not promised to you.

That's a very honest saying and, it speaks volumes about life., But, most guys who are doing the rejecting, say "no" to men they're not attracted to, because they don't want sex with them!

Well, you can take it that way, but, it doesn't always lead in that direction. For example, if a guy is looking at me at the bar and I am attracted to him, I will approach him and introduce myself.

So what do you recommend for other gay men in approaching men they are attracted to?

Have a "kindness aura" around you.

How do you do that?

By having a nice smile and act positivity! After all, who wants to be around someone who looks miserable or unfriendly so, take a chance. Have open body language and say, "hi, how are you doing?" Take a chance and if nothing magical happens, you might still end up with a good friend

That sound like great advice but, as far as the GLBT community, where do you see us in fifty years?

I see people being more supportive of one another, and there will be more acceptance of the gay community with universal gay marriage.

I appreciate all your good advice, but in closing, do you have a good story to end this interview with?

Yes, I once met this wonderful guy named Bruce, who was a great love and made me feel "on top of the world."

What happened? Why did you two break up?

We traveled in different worlds and parted on good terms but, I will never forget him.

Thank you for all your wonderful stories and insights for yourself and for other gays..

It was a real pleasure thank you..

END OF FIRST INTERVIEW

In retrospect, I appreciated Ray taking the time to give me this interview but as I reported earlier in this interview, I felt strongly that Ray was withholding something from me and was emotionally disconnected to many of the responses he was making in the interview.

It appeared to me as if Ray was hiding a secret that somehow was affected the tenure of his responses, as if, he was giving me the more correct or "pat" answer to my questions. And, as clearly seen in his responses to my questions, they were mostly one or two sentences in length, which suggests an unwillingness to share honest emotions or give more elaboration.

It wasn't until the following week when we met one another at the local bar where Ray was working as a DJ, that he confessed to me that he was indeed withholding a very big secret that bothered him all week following the interview, and that he wanted to tell me the truth as to why he wasn't being completely honest with me.

FOLLOW-UP INTERVIEW with RAY

Ray, you told me the other night at the bar, that you were raped as a child, and that the rape had a direct effect on your ability to have long-term, loving, relationships with men.

Well, I was six at the time. The person was a very friendly kid who was handicapped, who, one day, grabbed me and pulled me into the garage. He put me over my father's motorcycle and penetrated me, after forcing me to have oral sex on him. Sadly, we continued to have sexual relationships from age six to eight year's old., and then, he stopped.

Did you ever report the rape?

No.

No one knew?

No one knew until I was in my twenties, when I told my parents.

By then, I would guess that there was nothing they could do about it?

No. By then, we had moved away from the area although, I did run into him after I got my driver's license, when I almost ran over him!

Do you think that you seriously thought about running him over when you saw him?

Yes, I did think about it but, I knew that he was mentally ill and couldn't really help himself, so, I got past it.

What type of mental illness did he have?

He was mentally retarded.

Serious retardation, Down's Syndrome or, just "slow."

He was just "slow" but, I learned to "get over it" in time.

But, you do feel as if the rape has had any effect on your relationships with men today. Did you receive professional help for the rape?

No, I cured myself.

As a professional therapist, I know that it is virtually impossible for someone who has suffered trauma as the result of on-going childhood rape being able to "cure himself!" "Also, I strongly believe that Ray is deceiving himself in believing that he was able to get both emotionally and mentally past this "rape" as he calls it without professional intervention.

Similar to my childhood experience with an adult friend of my family, I know that I enjoyed the "playful encounter" as I thought of it as a child but, also felt ashamed when this "friend" told me not to tell anyone about the incident until years later. Unlike Ray, I dealt with this childhood incident with professional therapists and psychologists; mostly gay professionals who continually told me it was "not my fault" and all the fault belonged completely on the perpetrator. I know that Ray would benefit from hearing the same words from others as I did.

But with Ray, I still get the sense that he is somehow "masking" or, being more emotionally detached from the telling of his childhood trauma, with the exception of wanting to "run down'" his molester. After all, it is pretty clear that if he actually did kill his molester, there would be no jury that would convict him once the truth was told about his molester's actions and abuse. But, as a survivor of childhood sexual abuse, it has taken me years to come to terms with my abuse, and the tendency to deny one's feelings, as if, we did something wrong and not just the perpetrator.

You had sex with this man repeatedly for two years, did you sometimes enjoy it?

No, he forced me and told me that he was going to tell my parents about it if I told on him!.

What a disgusting and shameful man. But, I want to thank you for telling me this deep seated secret and I know it must have been difficult to tell me this. I am sure that you felt it was important to have me know the truth, and in doing so, letting others know as well.

Do you see other people hurting one another in the gay community, as this man hurt you? Also, by lying and deceiving others or, are we not hurting ourselves as you were hurt?

Well, I see how gay men are not completely honest with one another online, but then, I have met a lot of wonderful men online such as, my last two boyfriends, Trent and Michael. One lives in San Francisco and the other in Minnesota! But, they have both visited me, and I them, and we have had wonderful relationships while they lasted.

Yes, but Michael deceived you by never telling you about having another relationship while he was seeing you, and Trent broke up with you because he felt the distance was too great, and that you were not paying him back for flying you out to him and vacations you took together.

Yes, Trent and I broke up but, we still keep in touch by phone and online, and Mike and I are still talking of getting back together. Its' all good, and we're all still good friends.

Okay, but in thinking of your relationships with men today, what advice would you give to other gay men about communication and relationships?

I would just emphasize the importance of being honest with one another and be proud of who you are.

Yes, I just interviewed someone who told me he was getting involved with someone who never gave him his personal information other than his Manhunt profile.

But, in going back to what you said about being honest – do you think that gay men are still having difficulty being honest with one another, and in doing so, not being true to themselves?

Yes, I will continue to advocate being true to oneself and don't lie to someone who wants to get close to you. Lying just demeans us as individuals and, as a community.

Again, despite all his good words and concern for others, I still perceive Ray as not being completely honest with himself and continuing to make statements saying all the right words but lacking believability. As if, telling stories about someone other than himself.

Also, there still appears to be some emotional detachment to both his childhood trauma and his most recent relationships. Instead, he is advocating honesty in others and promoting himself as a confident and well-adjusted man and yet, why did he withhold such an important secret in the first interview? It is as if Ray is rehearsing his responses; almost "on automatic" with regards to not allowing himself to be emotionally vulnerable to men and honest with himself in the process.

Clearly, being the victim of on-going childhood rape, it appears as if Ray has suppressed his rage against the man who violated him and denying his true feelings. And, as his good friend and a certified therapist, I worry about Ray and hope that sharing his story here, has given him some level of comfort and support. After all, that's what good friends are for, and Ray deserves good friends, as do we all.

END OF FOLLOW-UP INTERVIEW WITH RAY

CHAPTER SIXTEEN

"ON THE STREET INTERVIEWS"

This chapter is dedicated to "On the Street Interviews" with several gay men on the subject of gay male communication and their impressions on how the gay culture influences that type of communication. The conversations below are representative of those to be included in the final chapter.

INTERVIEW #1

A SPONTANEOUS AND CASUAL CONVERSATION WITH THREE GAY MEN AT GOLD'S GYM IN NYC on the subject of Gay Communication – May 19, 2012:

Ivan, Fred & Jeff (three attractive men who often work out together)

Fred (age 25) – I don't feel that there is a problem communicating with gay men in NYC because there is such a large pool of gay men to choose from.

Jeff (age 36) – to Fred: You don't have a problem because you are very sociable and will talk to almost anyone!

Fred – That's true. But, I can see other gay men having problems communicating with one another especially here at the gym.

Jeff – I tend to have less of a problem approaching men I'm not attracted to as compared to men I am attracted to, because I tend to have more at stake with men I'm attracted to.

Ivan *(age 45, mostly quiet but attentive)* – I am told that I am not easily approachable. Someone told me I should smile more and then I would be less intimidating.

Interviewer: Yes, I noticed you wearing a shirt from NYU, my Alma mater, so, I felt comfortable enough approaching you.

Ivan- Really, why? Did you think I was a bitch before? *(Group laughter)*

Interviewer: Why do you say that? Have people called you a bitch in the past?

Ivan – Yes! One time someone wrote me on an internet site called Gaydar and said I was very unapproachable.

Jeff – That is because they don't know you, I find you to be very approachable but, I know you.
Ivan – (Pause) you know, I think I would love to read a well-written book on gay male communication. Good luck with it because I feel it's a very important topic for people to read.

This group of three were clearly listening to one another and all agreed that gay communication can be a problem when based on superficial first impressions and fear of rejection. It was very interesting to witness how the three men took their time to answer my questions in their effort to understand the potential dynamics of gay male communication in various social settings, and especially, at the gym.

<u>**INTERVIEW #2**</u>
BRETT GLEASON
Interviewed on Valentines' Day – 2/14/2013 at Dish Restaurant in Chelsea, NYC

Let's get right to the point Brett- what exactly do you like about being gay?
Brett: I love that there are no traditional conventions being imposed upon me for my being gay.

I don't want to buy a house and I'm free to be an artist. I don't have to support a family by getting a serious job for the purpose of making money also, gay sex is AWESOME!

Was it tough for you to "come out of the closet?"

Not at all, it was tougher to "come out" as an artist and, be gay as well.

What impression do you believe you give to other gay men?

I just feel it's better to look at everyone than to not look at anyone! But people who don't know me, think I come off as "stuck up!" The truth is, I tend to be more "in my own world" and I am really shy. So, people do mistaken my shyness for being emotionally detached.

What are your impressions of gay male communication?

I believe that men in general are bad communicators especially, insecure men; and many gay men are insecure.

How does that insecurity play out in their communication?

I don't believe gay men are honest about what they want because they fear rejection so, they don't take chances. As a result, many don't go after what they truly want.

Are you dating anyone at present and, do you prefer a specific type?

I haven't dated anyone in a long time but, I tend to like hairy men like myself.

What type do you consider yourself to be?

I am an "otter" (a thin "Bear" type of man)

Sounds sexy to me but as for dating, what type of men are you attracted to?

I like shorter, older men, in creative or artistic fields.

As far as the topic of gay shame and the primary subject of this book, how do you feel gay shame plays out with gay men?

I strongly believe that many gay men suffer with "Bottom Shame" sexually.

Why do you say that?

Because everyone says that they're masculine and "versatile." But every guy that I meet who says that they're "versatile," really only want to take the "bottom" position!

That's a pretty strong opinion but, a good example that strongly exemplifies gay shame. For if someone is not being honest about who we truly are, and feel shame for enjoying the "bottom" position with regards to anal sex, that "speaks volumes" about shame.

Exactly! You got it! Guys that are okay with being gay tend to want to be gay but, masculine gay, not, feminine. These guys don't really want to be viewed as a "bottom" because being viewed as a "bottom" is synonymous with being feminine.

What do you want these guys to do differently?

They should embrace both their masculine and feminine sides; that way, they would have a lot more going for them. They would be able to relate to more people within our own community and, they would be more "comfortable in their own skins."

Brett's comments did motivate me to write an article on that specific topic on "Gay Shame and Sexuality" in my column "Talk it OUT" in Edge Magazine. I, also, support Brett's opinion about gay men and the issues with talking about sex with friends and family outside of the LGBT community

What is your involvement with the gay community today?

I don't really feel a part of the gay community, other than playing my music at gay events such as the ones hosted by my good friend Rob Ordonez and the NYC leather community. Also, I have performed at various charitable events such as: Erin Dinan's One Sandwich at a Time charity. Her charity provides sandwiches and outreach for the homeless population in NYC.

Do you feel that you really don't want to involve yourself in the gay community, and that type of mindset is common with many younger gay men in the community today?

My one connection with a part of the gay male community is through the social site Manhunt, which I happen to believe is not a "hook-up" site but, for men who really want a relationships!

That does not appear the general perception of the site but, if you believe that most gays who log onto that site want relationships and not just sex, then why don't they let that be known?

Because gay men, and men in general, do not want to expose their vulnerability and to me, that is what makes them more adorable. And yet, they won't get those needs met easily, because they pretend to not have those needs.

So, in a sense, they are lying to themselves.

Absolutely true, and that makes me very sad, and more than a little frustrated with my own kind.

Brett's frustration is without dispute, because it is a frustration shared by many human beings, not just gay men. Women, especially, women of a certain age, have expressed unrelenting frustration with men who are unable to share their true desires with them for fear of being viewed as vulnerable. As I stated earlier, men are more task-focused and women, more relational. Gay men seem to have both qualities; hence, the conflict.

So then, what type of men are you looking for as a romantic partner?

I want a man who is balanced, strong, and compassionate. Also, I want a man who has some direction and focus in his life. My type of man has something in his life that they really love to do besides, wanting an active social life. He needs to love the work that he does, and doing that work brings him some level of joy and self-satisfaction; such as, working in the creative arts, either in music, art, or, the theater.

I hear you. So then, what was your most satisfying gay experience?

I lived in Italy for a time, which happened to have a small, but, very gay social scene. Much occurred there, despite the fact that there are only a few gay bars where I lived. But, when I was there, I saw gay men going anywhere they wanted. There were also a few women participating in the scene with their female lovers, which was beautiful to see. Everyone seemed to be having a wonderful time, despite the strong religious attitude that permeates that country.

Sounds beautiful but, what do you dislike about being gay?

Not being able to procreate or combine my genetics with the person I love, which, I feel is very unfair.

Why not use a surrogate as many gay men do?

Of course I would but, I am just thinking in a fantastical way, wishing that gay men could have children with one another.

You actually believe that gay men would want to go through the pain of childbirth?

(laughing) No, I guess not, I am living a fantasy.

So then, there is nothing you really hate about being gay?

Only as I stated earlier, that they are dishonest about communicating their needs, and refuse to being vulnerable with one another.

Well, perhaps this book and its focus on reducing gay shame might help?

I hope so, that's why I wanted to be a part of this.

Thank you. But, on a more positive note, what puts a smile on your face?

Dogs, children, rollerblading, riding bikes in the park, and fast roller coasters.

That's great, I love some of the same things except for the rollerblading. But as far as meeting men, what is your best pick-up line?

Nothing that original, just ask, "who are you? My name is Brett Gleason." Guys need to just be honest and give their full name.

Okay, so what do you see as the differences in my generation with the gay men of today?

I feel that men of the previous generation were more able to simply go up to someone they were attracted to and say hello. Gay men of my generation are not as used to that type of dynamic, being that we are more acclimated to meeting online and not face-to face.

I specifically remember a time when I was working at The Big Cup, a now closed coffeehouse in Chelsea, where while working at the counter, there was this handsome man who cruised me for a long time. When we finally got a chance to talk to one another on my break, instead of giving me his personal information, he asked for my Manhunt profile name!! Needless to say, after I gave him that information, I quickly excused myself to returned back to work.

Did he contact you on the site?

Yes, but he only wanted sex, since he already had a boyfriend.

Brett's story only helped to confirm the need for more gay men to change their communication behavior for their own benefit. Otherwise, we will continue to either stay "in the hunt for sexual conquests" and rarely or, never, leave our computers. Many choosing to find themselves confined to our apartments or bedrooms and not really getting our emotional needs met, choosing only to satisfy the primal sex drive instead.. Of course for many, that idea sounds just fine but, what do you do after the orgasm? Do you go to dinner or a movie afterward or better yet, before. What happened to dating and romance? I for one, choose romance.
Thank you Brett for your wonderful comments and providing a younger, gay male perception of the community and gay men in general,

My pleasure, and please check out my music online and at festivals around the city.

END OF INTERVIEW

Just recently, Brett "came out" in the Huffington Post not only as a gay man but as being bi-polar as well. I was very impressed with this young man's honesty and courage in exposing this. secret part of his life which he has also incorporated into his music.

Brett was also a principal subject in my most recent article in Edge Magazine on the topic of

"Bottom Shame" and its connection to "gay shame;" and why gay men hesitate identifying themselves as preferring the "bottom" position for fear of being viewed as a woman.

INTERVIEW #3 - WITH JEREMY, JESSE, BRENDAN AT DAVID BARTON'S GYM JUNE 19, 2013

The interview began with Jeremy at the gym following my workout. We had Brendan G's permission to use his office, and, who had also agreed to be interviewed along with Jesse Meli, the gym manager. All these men had identified themselves to me to be gay and represented very different body images and lifestyles with Jeremy being more petite; Jesse, a self-identified "muscle bear," and Brendan, of average height and slim.

Jeremy, would you tell us a little something about your background and growing up knowing you were gay?

Jeremy: I am the son of Honduran immigrants who came into this country when they were in their twenties, with all the cultural beliefs that come from living in a Catholic upbringing and an aversion to anything different; especially, with my being gay. So, I wasn't allowed to be gay!

With that rigid belief system, how is your communication with them today?

It is basically "Don't ask, don't tell!" type of relationship and as for today, the only family members I presently speak to are my mother and one cousin but, I don't include them much into my personal life. My family as of today, consists of the friends I have accumulated who have become my chosen family.

Jeremy's opening comments already echo many of the comments made by most of my interviewees for this book; that their families of origin, simply do not provide the comfort and support we all seek in close relationships. Sadly, these important role models are unwilling and unable to give their loved ones those essentials and without that, we will seek that comfort and support from others often, creating another family of new friends to fill in the lack of love.

Does your mother and cousin know you are gay?

My mother does not, my cousin does.

What do you and your mom talk about?

More about work and safe topics; we never talk about anything to do with relationships.

She doesn't ask you about girls or when you're getting married?

No, that subject is never brought up!

Then let's get to the point of the book, and tell me how you feel about being gay today? How do you feel things have changed from my generation of gays?

I feel it's much more acceptable to be gay today. But at the same time, it is all dependent on the city to which you live. We live in New York City, and here, we can be a bit more public about being gay! I see more and more gay men holding hands with another man then I assume, it would be in Central America where my parents are from.

But, I know that with my eccentric style, it's definitely helps with living and socializing in this city, which is much more accepting of us. In fact, I have always lived in a city environment being born and raised in Los Angeles, and then, living both in New York and San Francisco. Also, being in fashion, I am surrounded by the gay culture and those completely accepting of my lifestyle as well.

You are sharing similar feelings to many others I have interviewed for this book, that, New York City and those western cities have become sanctuaries in comparison to other cities.

Yes, and here, you can live your life as it is supposed to be. My sexuality has never played a negative role in my social and work life, especially, being in the fashion world. In fact, here is where I find many straight women customers who seem to prefer a gay man's opinion rather than from another woman!

That is so ironic that you are saying this since I just read an advertisement on a well-known job site, where a female store owner of a fashion boutique in Chelsea was specifically requesting a gay male salesperson to work in their store!

That doesn't surprise me in the least, because that is exactly what I am talking about with the relationship I enjoy with my female customers; they simply prefer to hear advice from a gay man rather than a woman, because they appreciate our sense of style. But, even though they don't want to hear any details about my personal life, they know and accept me for my abilities.

So then, you haven't really dealt with gay shame in your social and work life?

No, I haven't, but I have certainly experienced gay shame with my family of origin. It has never been my friends and even strangers! In fact, I have chosen not to engage with many of my family members today, other than my mother and cousin. Their unwillingness to accept or, even talk about my lifestyle, only presents negativity and it is just too much for me to deal with. Even my mother hasn't fully accepted my sexual orientation, and that makes me sad.

Yes, it is sad, since I see you as such as a warm and effusive young man who clearly enjoys life. But, if they don't accept you as being gay, what is their reaction to your tattoos and the ornate rings you wear on your fingers? Do they ever comments on your appearance?

They are convinced that I am going to Hell! Being that they are very religious people following a devout Catholic lifestyle, my appearance and lifestyle has been a real problem for them, which makes it very difficult for me to get close to them. So, as I stated earlier, I have chosen to create my own family with all the many supportive friends I have in my life. Those friends have now, become closer to me than any member of my own family has ever been!.

Yes, I can hear your pain but, your feelings are not different from many others. Do you feel that your experiences of gay shame for yourself and others have impacted the gay community?

I know that my family's attitude is not right, and has "driven a wedge" in my relationship with them but, I understand where they are coming from, and do not plan to fight or challenge them in their beliefs as devout Catholics.

Yes, but it is really sad that with your family, you have had to emotionally distance yourself from them and they are missing out in knowing such a wonderful young man with a tremendous amount of charm. And if they feel that way about your lifestyle and the way you look, too bad for them.

As I said, they think that I am going to Hell and that tattoos are something only prisoners wear!

(laughter) If you are going to Hell Jeremy, then they are definitely serving cocktails!

At this point in the interview, Jeremy and I have decided to take advantage of an empty office and to continue the interview from there.

Similar to Rob Ordonez, Jeremy too has felt completely unaccepted by his family and now lives his life thousands of miles away from them with limited contact. But unlike Rob, Jeremy was born in America and took it upon himself to move himself away from his family, other than being paid to leave the country as Rob was forced to do.

But in both cases, it is very sad how these delightful young men were pushed away from the love and support of their families only to have to recreate that network of love and support among their friends. Clearly, a sad commentary of our time, although, things are slowly changing with the Obama administration and more states legalizing gay marriages.

(Resuming the interview with Jeremy and we will soon be joined by the gym's manager Jesse)

Jeremy, you were talking about your family of origin and growing up in Honduras with your strict religious upbringing. Do you believe that your upbringing and earlier childhood experiences had contributed to feelings of gay shame for you, such as, with them making statements that: "you're going to hell?"

Most definitely! I think that what I have gone through is similar to what other gay men have experienced in their lives with their families. So, even if my family's opinions have hurt my relationship with them, and I am sad about that, I won't let them "bring me down" and make me feel wrong for being gay.

It is very sad that I had those feelings of gay shame in my early childhood; always feeling wrong for being who I am, which have in turn, not allowed me to "come out" to them.

I know that they know I am gay but, I have still not chosen to "come out" to them, which I know keeps us apart, because I do not discuss this part of my life with them.

Your experiences have indeed been echoed many times not only in this book but, in my radio show and column with <u>Edge Magazine</u>. And it is always discouraging to hear of gay men having to separate themselves from their families, and then, having to create a chosen family of friendships. Here is another example of our families being the source of our gay shame.

Yes, I would agree. Being younger and the opinions I heard at a very early age were very painful. Those feelings stay with you all your life. That is why it is so important to "come out," if not with one's family due to potential rejection, then, at least, in one's social life.

And yet, they continue to make you feel shameful, due to their religion and cultural upbringing.

That's very true, and it continues to be difficult being with them; even with my mother, I simply do not discuss that part of my life, even though I know they know.

I am sure they do and yet, what I am most concerned about is how gay shame has contributed to not only drug addiction and alcoholism, but, to teenage suicide and feelings of depression for many gay men within the community. This book is dedicated to them.

But on a different note, I have observed here at the David Barton Gym, which has a reputation of having gorgeous gay men, where these men frequently exhibit a form of gay elitism; where these gentlemen tend to only talk to other men that are as physically attractive as themselves.

As a result of my observations here and at many other gay social gatherings, I believe that specific behavior exists as a result of the underlying sexual innuendo (wanting sex); that significantly influences communication between gay men? Do you see that behavior occurring here as well?

As someone who has worked here for some time, I feel a bit insecure myself being around these men, and yes, I do see many of these men dating or showing interest in men who are only "mirror images" or, "clones," of themselves.

Many of the men here seem to follow the "Chelsea boy" prototype, and if you do not follow that stereotype, you are not considered seriously by those men pursuing relationships with men similar to themselves. In fact, many of my friends think I must be having this fabulous dating life because I work in a mostly gay gym, but, that is most definitely not true!

In fact, many of these guys in pursuit of that perfect body type often end up becoming exercise addicts, and are never satisfied with themselves. As a result, being with someone who is "hot" gives them a renewed validation of themselves and their own self-worth!

So that is why they only pursue close replicas of themselves?

Yes, that's true but, I don't let that effect my interactions with them, because I know they enjoy me for the "playful elf" I see myself to be while interacting with them. I know that I have to go and find my own "cup of tea" somewhere else. But, honestly, I am not really attracted to that perfect body myself, and tend to like someone similar in type to myself.

As a result, I have absolutely no problem interacting with these men. Of course, I would love to be "hit on" once in a while since I am dressing in my "Sunday best" every day for work and looking for some nice attention. But for right now, I'm perfectly okay with my friendships with these men, because I know that their interactions with only their "mirror selves" are primarily based on their own insecurity!

Are they ever emotionally "cold" to you?

No, not really. They love my personality and I always get along with them knowing who they are and, what they really want.

Jeremy, also known as Cha Cha, has a wonderful insight on himself and his interactions with these sexy and yet unavailable gay men, but there appears to be some sadness and disappointment as well for the role he is forced to play.

Playing the "elfin" or "puck-ish" role may be seen as playful and engaging to others, and yet, he is not being viewed sexually or physically attractive to these men. That the limited view these men have exhibited toward Jeremy, and those similar in type to him, can also be difficult to endure at times. But, I know that Jeremy with his cuteness, ebullient personality, and positive attitude, he will find the love he deserves with someone as special as himself.

It seems at times, that the "straight" trainers at the gym are friendlier than the gay clientele.

The trainers here know their clients and what they need to do to keep them happy.

What do you think that gay men need to do in order to change their social communication?

I think after working in such a gay location all this time, it is really important that they learn to believe in themselves and, in their decisions.

How do they believe in themselves if they can't accept who they are?

Exactly! That's the biggest problem!
Is that something you ever worry about?

I believe it's mainly an insecurity issue. I have always been proud of my ability to "be myself" by placing myself in environments where I am comfortable being myself, such as, in this gym or, in the fashion world.

Also, people need to trust their instincts and even if they are proud of their gayness and who they are, they are still seem to be not fully comfortable with themselves. We just really need to 'break down the walls" they have erected to protect themselves!

Gay Pride is coming up for 2013, what do you see the differences are between gay men of the Stonewall era with the men of today?

In a way, I think people back then were prouder of their gay pride than they are today!

Wow, really?

Absolutely, I think back in the Stonewall era, people were proud of "coming out" and being themselves, and today, it's all about being "hot" and "partying!" People don't appreciate what those men did for us back in the earlier days and should!

As Jeremy and I were talking, the manager of the gym, Jesse Melfi was standing outside the office listening in and was clearly curious as to what was being said between Jeremy and I.

Jeremy spoke to Jesse and invited him to join us in the interview where I gave Jesse a brief synopsis of my work and that I was seeking some quick comments from a diversified group of gay men on gay communication and how it has changed over the years.

END OF INTERVIEW WITH JEREMY

At this point, Jeremy left the area to complete an errand whereupon, I questioned Jesse on how the gay community has changed in the years past Stonewall; for either better of the worse?

JESSI MELI – Manger of David Barton Gym- NYC

INTERVIEW WITH JESSI MELI

Jessie: Oh, we have definitely gotten better!

How so? In what way?

In every way possible if you ask me, and I can give you the perfect example.

Great!

I am first generation European. My generation was not as accepting of gays as the new generation is today. I am from Sicily, where it was more acceptable to murder someone than to be gay! So, it's no surprise to me that many of my friends didn't "come out" until their forties!

I can attest to that! I have several older friends in Connecticut who didn't "come out" until their wives died! They raised families living a "double life" so not to hurt the family, and when

320

their wives passed or they finally got that divorce, then they "came out with a bang" expecting all this hot sex! Unfortunately for them, that was not going to be the case at all!

My nephews, who are just as Sicilian as I am, are in their twenties, and really "cool" with my being gay. My parents were really concerned about how their parents would take my being gay, and everyone was afraid of how my nephews would react! Instead, they were shocked that this generation really didn't think it was any big deal with my being gay!

Also, you're a very muscularly, built man; a formidable presence. How do others react to knowing you as being gay?

They refused to believe I'm gay! "Straight people!" They just couldn't picture me being gay!

It's because you are so big and formidable? I think it's because many of them are more comfortable with the stereotypical view of gays as being ultra-feminine, screaming, "Gurl!"

That's right. In fact, I retired in 2008 from the entertainment business, and a cable network wanted to do a show about me and my family! For a time; they followed me around with cameras. Then, they took highlights of the show and test marketed the show to potential advertisers who ended up wanting me to act gayer; more flamboyant, and do more of *Will and Grace* type of show which, I refused to do; that's just not me!

Why would they do that?

Because they felt threatened with my masculinity, thinking that if I was gay, maybe they could be too!

.

Wow, amazing! That's why we still get television and film characters who are still playing out the century-old "fop" character – screaming all the time and being asexual!

You got it! I was a football player in Wisconsin and had trouble being comfortable in a world where our role models were all hairdressers, and the gay kid who listens all the time to Barbara Streisand! I just wanted people to get that we gays are no different than anyone else; we just like to suck dick!

Jesse's honesty in describing his inner conflict with his gay identity impressed me with his clarity and openness. As a professor of Communication, Jesse is describing his experiences with an aspect of our culture known as "heterosexism," which is very similar to sexism." This type of communication is where the less educated general public equate those men who are big and strong as being "straight", and being "gay," as being effeminate and weak! An example of heterosexism would be to say to a gay man, "no way you're gay, you're so masculine!"

*As Jesse was telling his story, **Brendan G.** (one of the sales reps at the gym) was listening in since we were using his office for the moment. Seeing Brendan listening in, I decided to include* *him in the conversation for the moment by introducing myself to him and getting his name.*

Jesse, Jeremy said earlier, that with Gay Pride, he believes that the Stonewall Generation was more prideful than the gay generation is today. He believed that the gays of today are more interested in looking "hot" and "partying." Do you agree with his view?

(Turning to Brendan) Please feel free to join in anytime in stating your opinion in this as well.

INTERVIEW WITH BRENDAN G. & JESSIE MELFI

Jesse *(quickly responding)*: It's not as political as it was before; now it's more superficial!

The comments I am continuing to hear from many of the men I interviewed, is that there is no real gay community! Do you agree?

Brendan: *(quickly joins in)*: I was personally shocked when I moved to New York from Long Island. I know it's not that far away but, I felt more gay in Long Island!

When I moved here and got this job, I thought I was going to be accepted by everyone, instead, I was shocked at how 'cliquey' gays were here; acting like little girls from high school "talking shit" about one another! These guys were constantly acting like women who hate one another!

Wow, Brendan. That's one of my main points of this book; that many gay men in groups act like teenage girls when talking about guys they think are "hot" but instead, "trash -talk" them; as if, protecting themselves from possible rejection from the object of their desire.

A pleasant feeling of self-justification came upon me as these last interviews affirmed immediately one of my main points of the book; validating my beliefs with regards to gay male communication and its problematic behaviors. Thank you Brendan.

Brendan: Yeah, it's shocking to me and also a little upsetting!

"The Luxury of Being Superficial"

Jesse: First of all, I think my generation had a stronger bond, because we had a tougher time "coming out" then the young kids are having today. I remember hearing stories about how the cops used to raid the bars and your picture or, mug shot, was published in the newspapers! All, for simply being in a gay bar back then; they even included your phone number in the paper so you could receive hate calls from the bigots!

Hearing Jesse's words and remembering stories of those times, I always cringe whenever I hear the older generation whine for the "good ole days!" For us, those were not the "good ole days" when gay men and women were arrested for simply holding hands or standing close to one another at a gay bar. Thank God for those drag queens and angry men who had enough abuse!

Yes, I remember the history. Sadly, it took Judy Garland's death and the funeral near the Stonewall Bar to get all the gays to finally standing up and stopping that bullshit practice!

Jesse: Yes, but those stories still "scared the shit out of me" and kept me from "coming out" earlier than when I actually did! Luckily, the kids of today didn't have to deal with the "crap" we had to, and as a result of it, they are allowed the luxury of being superficial! For us, life was just too real!

Wow, that's a great saying: "the luxury of being superficial!" It speaks volumes about the differences between the gays before Stonewall with those gays of today! But, despite easier times being gay today, we still see acts of violence continuing to be perpetrated toward gays.

In fact, I just wrote an article posted in the <u>Huffington Post</u> and <u>Edge Magazine</u> about the gay man being murdered in the village for no reason other than for being gay!

Jesse: That's because gay guys today walk around with a false sense of security here in the city; thinking that everyone is "cool" with their lifestyles; and that's just not the case!

Jesse and Brendan's honesty and upfront comments about the gays of today and especially, "the luxury of superficiality," are both eloquent and yet, disturbing. Plus, the fact that most gay feel safer and more secure in the big cities, and yet, we still have to be '"on the lookout "for potential danger just around the corner.

Similar to the Stonewall riots, if we as a community stand up together for change; "strength in numbers"' comes into play here. For, the more courageous and determined we are as a community, the more we will achieve with those who oppose us and our right to even exist! We deserve all the rights and freedoms that the majority of our fellow citizens continue to enjoy.

Brendan: I think most gays in the city take it for granted that we are safe here and can do whatever we want; which is not always the case.

Do you remember the shootings at the Ramrod back in the seventies where a gay hater shot up the bar killing quite a few gay men?

Jesse: Yes, I remember the incident but, I was more affected by the serial killer who killed a lot of gay men in NYC back in the seventies and was depicted in the movie *Cruising* with Al Pacino'

Yes, I remember the movie and it scared the hell out of me too! Now that you mention it, I remember that the movie was based on an actual killer.

Jesse: Yeah, he would pick up guys and kill them; stabbing them!

Yes, I remember those days in the city; were you around back then?

Jesse is referring to the alleged "Bag Murderer" Paul Bateson, who was convicted of killing a film critic and once in prison, confessed to murdering a total of six gay men whom he picked up in bars. In fact, Bateson had a small role in William Friedkin's movie The Exorcist and was interviewed by Friedkin in prison, which led to the director making the movie Crusing.

Jesse: Oh, yeah. In fact, the movie *Cruising,* was one of the reasons I hesitated in "coming out of the closet!" I was also too afraid to "come out!"

When did you finally "come out?" How old were you?

I was forty-three!

I can't believe it! You seem like someone who would have been "out" most of his life!

No way! My family are 100% Sicilian, and as I told you earlier, in Sicily, it was more acceptable to murder someone then to be gay!

Amazing, talk about gay shame at work!

You got it! Family pressure and culture played a major part in keeping me from being honest about my sexuality and living a false life; I even got married but, I don't want to talk about it.

(changing the subject) **Then, what do you think the gay community needs to do in order to make a change in this world; especially with regards to reducing gay shame?**

Jesse: They need to stop stereotyping their own community by "putting people in a box!"

What do you mean?

Jesse: By stereotyping ourselves into categories: "Muscle-bears," "pandas," "wolves," "twinks," "gems," etc.

"Gems? I never heard that one? But. why do we do that? Why do we "put people in a box!"

Because people are more comfortable doing that; stereotyping people; safety in numbers! But what's actually happening, is that we are polarizing one another!

I will give you a perfect example of how gays love to type one another. I was in Los Angeles and showed up at a "Bear party" but they wouldn't let me in, telling me: "You can't come in here; you're too muscular! You're a Muscle-bear, and this party is for us!"

I just couldn't believe it! To me, I was being penalized by other gays because I like working out in a gym! I felt prejudiced again, but this time, not for being gay, but, for being too muscular! I couldn't believe I was getting this shit from my own kind! I wasn't there to pick up somebody; I was there just to have a good time!

Yes, I can understand how you feel Jesse, but, "Bears" get a lot of flak for being too fat by many gays as well! So, I guess it was payback in some way for being rejected by guys with muscles.

Jesse: You may be right but, I didn't like it! I wasn't there to pick up somebody, I was just there with a friend to have a good time; and to be turned away because I have muscles instead of fat; that's bullshit! And in truth, I am a Muscle-bear and I like the way I look!

The specific situation that Jesse is describing brings to mind the adolescent type of behavior of rejecting someone before they can reject you; which is all fear based. Also, clearly for the "Bears" Jess is describing, it is all about being around their own type and not having anyone around them that could make them feel inferior. In doing so, it gives this group a certain level of comfort and support; which all humans strive for in relationships and friendships.

On a more clinical note, most people generally put others in groups in order to feel safer and more comfortable within their environment. Once someone feels more comfortable with the other person, then, there is more likelihood of building friendships and stronger relationships.

Stereotyping is not always a negative behavior but something definitely learned from our families of origin. But, when stereotyping is used in a prejudicial or ostracizing manner, then, that behavior indicates insecurities and fear of the other person or group. So, instead, they choose to negate or push others away that are viewed as a threat or, personally unattractive

Jessie: I can understand how they feel, just as I know how that I'm unattractive to some hairless "twenty-something," since I am an older, hairy man with a big belly.

Sometimes when I even walk around this gym and pass some of these young shaven muscle guys, I see them actually cringe when I walked past them, as if, I could give them "cooties" if I touched them! All, because I don't represent anything they could possibly be interested in!

Got it. I can relate as to how some guys act like rude teenage girls in their sad attempts to make themselves feel better at the expense of others.

This book is full of similar examples that exemplify the "Gay Communication Game" of selective and often, dismissive communication within the gay male community. Where, even though the words are not actually spoken, their non-verbal communication is basically saying: "I don't want anything from you so, get the fuck away from me!"

Jesse: Exactly, especially in the clubs! I got the same "crap" at a Xmas event where there were a lot of pretty gay men standing around drinking and when I walked by them, they would move away from me when I walked past them, as if my touching them would contaminate them!

Yes, the annual Toys for Tots event in the city. I see the same thing happening there myself. Lots of "guys with attitude" giving off the "stay away from me" vibe like the 'straight' women in clubs from my college days who would be quick to "shoot down" any guy that approached them; even men who to me, were better looking than the girls!

I remember that these guys were sweet and sexy and I never would have rejected them! But, these bitches were the ones in power, and the ones who could reject without impunity! The same dismissive behavior goes on today in bars, but now, it's our own kind doing this to us!

What about you Brendan? I would suppose that you wouldn't see this type of elitism as much, since you are young and pretty?

Brendan: I wouldn't even bother attending those events for just that reason! I hate the way gay men treat one another in the city and, I see it happening all around me here in the gym!

But Brendan, being from Long Island myself, I saw the same 'cliquey' behavior going on there in the clubs when I came out in the seventies; especially, in Fire Island!

Brendan: I understand but, I just don't see that shit going on with my friends and the people I "hang-out" with. I just don't!"

I do see a lot of this behavior going on during Gay Pride events around the city where everyone is "showing off" with their shirts off! Those guys view the Gay Pride Parade as an opportunity to show off all their muscles and make out with one another!

So, they're using the occasion to "party" and have sex rather than truly celebrating Gay Pride?

Yes, that's only my opinion but, I believe they've lost the truth behind the Gay Pride movement and instead, are only there to party!

Ironically, Brendan's comments would echo that of an organizational movement ironically called "Gay Shame," which rose up in defiance to commercialized gay events that said they were celebrating Gay Pride. Their organization professes that many gays have lost the true ideology behind the gay movement and have followed the "party mentality" and moved away from what Gay Pride was originally all about; gay freedom and gay pride.

It sounds as if you are saying that with many of the gays today, they are only interested in finding another opportunity to party and have sex?

Jesse: Yeah! They are only out there to show of the muscles they worked on for the past six months at the gym!

Ironically, Jesse and Brendan work in a gym, who's aim is to help men build muscles but, their frustration and anger is not about bodybuilding PER SE, but, with how gay men tend to use their new-found physiques to separate themselves from those they view as lesser than themselves.

And yet, isn't that type of behavior common with most human beings who have attained either increased physical beauty or success in our culture; to separate themselves from others who do not have what they have, as if with their new found beauty or success, they have become more superior to the rest of us?

If that is true, it reflects poorly both on our community and our culture. In fact, those individuals who misuse their new found power, seem to enjoy becoming cruel, or, even abusive, to purposefully hurt others. More importantly, that specific type of behavior is based on insecurity and shame; a weak foundation to build any house upon, especially, a community.

With regards to Jesse and Brendan's personal experiences, the abusive behavior of cringing or openly devaluing others, results in laying the groundwork for division and hate among members of their own community and contributes little to nothing.

Jesse *(continuing on the same point):* Interestingly enough, I saw this type of superior behavior more frequently in California than in New York, since there were more men building their bodies up for the beach in California then, in New York. But, I see the ways in which other gays ignore men who are not their type, simply because they want nothing from them!

Sexually speaking or romantically?

Jesse: Either way!

Brendan: I see these big muscle guys who would probably ignore me because I don't have big muscles! As a result, I would never approach them at a club!

So how do we end this behavior? How do we live our lives in pride so we don't hurt others?

Jesse: I am going to live my life as I am. I am not just a gay guy but, as a man in my fifties. I don't have "an ax to grind" with the younger generation because I feel they don't appreciate what we older gays went through, so that, they could live a freer and more open life then we could.

I know for a fact, that there are men older gays who resent the younger ones for not thanking them for paving the way to an easier life but, I am not one of them. I simply live my life comfortably with pride and "don't give a shit" as to what others outside of my community think of me!

What about those gay guys who cringe when you walk by them? What do you want to say to them?

Jesse: Go fuck yourselves and lighten up!

Interestingly enough,, my philosophy in response to guys who are not interested in me or, are even dismissive of me, is that "if you are not interested in me, I am not interested in you!"

Jesse: It "speaks volumes" for who they really are. Because if those guys are going to "cringe" when I walk past them, what are they going to do when someone with a physical handicap walks by them? Are they going to be so wrong as to "cringe" when they walk by them as well?

But Jesse, you are not handicapped in any way! You are a sexy man with an amazing build, do you put yourself in that category because you walk with a cane? If that is the case, you should not do that to yourself or allow them to do that to you?

Jesse's anger at both the Bear group that refused to allow him entry to the party and the pretty boys cringing when he walks by because he walks with a cane, are synonymous to how society and our families shame of us for loving or desiring someone of our own sex. The only way that this shameful pattern is stopped, is when someone "takes the bull by the horns" and stops the shame inducing behavior by acting prideful and more respectful of those deserving of their respect and refuse to associate with those who don't!.

Writing this book and hearing so many stories of a similar nature, has shown me to be more mindful of my own actions, and to know whenever I am ever quick to "put someone else down," it is in reality, "putting myself down" in the process. Because, I am the one who ends up looking bad by hurting someone else to make myself feel better.

Jesse: The one thing I want to say with regards to the way the younger gay generation treats their gay elders, is that they should be more appreciative of what that older generation did for them in making their lives easier. I know that it is still tough to be gay today, don't get me wrong, but, it's a lot easier than what I went through. And I can't emphasize it enough, that with what I went through a lot to get to where I am today, I don't see the younger gays having to go through that in any way. They get to live their lives freer and more open than I did. These guys are not ostracized from the world as I was, or, have to walk around in fear for their lives!

I know how you feel. My boyfriend and I were physically attacked by a gang because we were gay, and I have had beer bottles thrown at me while waiting for a friend on the street; both of those incidents happening in Los Angeles, not, New York City.

But other than the threat of physical violence for being gay from hateful others, what about the increase in bare-backing among the younger generation? Their refusal to wear condoms and the increase in Crystal Meth and the like? What do you think that behavior says of the younger generation of today?

Jesse: They're committing suicide.

Yes, that behavior is also indicative of gay shame and the lack of self-care and preservation. They think that all I have to do if I get infected with the HIV virus is to take a pill.

Jesse: I say, get over your daddy issues. Go to therapy and stop acting out for daddy's attention.

That's great. I love it. "Stop looking for daddy's love in the worse way possible!"

Thank you Jesse, you should be on my radio show sharing your comments about the gay culture and the pursuit of muscles

I would love it, just let me know when?

Jesse leaves to go back to his office but Brendan stays in his office, and we continue to talk for a few more minutes.

Well, Brendan, do you agree with what Jesse said about the younger generation being unappreciative of what the older generation did for them?

I want to say that we should work harder at treating one another better. Stop acting as if you are better than everyone else. After all, if we don't unite, then what is the world going to say about us? We're always going to have our differences but, try to work out those differences rather than compete with one another!

Yes, many of my interviewees say the same thing about the games being played with one another.

I see it happening all the time! For instance, when I sign someone up for membership, they are always so excited about being in a popular gym hoping to meet new friends and getting the physique they always wanted to be. But, as soon as they start building up, they change. They become a totally different person than who they were before?

What do they become?

Someone completely different from the person I first met when I signed them up.

Is it New York or is it the gay community?

I can only speak for the gay community in New York, but I am sure it happens everywhere!

What is the problem? Do you think they become jaded, angry, egotistical, elitist?

They become "snooty." They're always trying to "up" somebody else, even the next person they meet or encounter.

Do you think that some guys "look right through" other people as if they are invisible?

Absolutely! I see some people in here looking right through other people walking by, as if to say, "OH, why bother?"

Wow, what did these people do to cause that kind of reaction? Such as, what Jesse said about those guys who "cringe" when he walked by them.

I can see that happening, yes! But sometimes, I would see some of these guys in here actually look at some guy walking by and turn their face, as if, trying to avoid looking at them; then, walk away!

One time I observed this really cute boy walking up to this very sexy, "muscle-head" who put his hand out to stop him from approaching him then walked away! I felt terrible for that kid!

Guys like him are disgusting and should "get over themselves" real quick!

At this point in the interview Brendan had to leave his office to join Jesse in a meeting and I ended the interview. But, hearing Brendan's comments only reinforced my efforts to complete this book and to address this egotism and its origins.

END OF INTERVIEW WITH BRENDAN AND JESSI

INTERVIEW WITH MATTHEW GRIFFIN
JUNE 26, 2013 AT DAVID BARTON GYM, CHELSEA, NY

We began the interview in the front of the gym after one of Matt's training appointments at six in the evening.

Matt, can you tell us a little something about yourself, such as, how long you have been in New York and where you grew up?

Matt: I've been in New York for two and a half years coming from Virginia Beach, Virginia.

What was it like for you growing up in Virginia Beach?

It's the South for sure, close to the border of North Carolina. A real "beach town."

What was it like growing up gay in that beach town, which sounds pretty "straight?"

There really weren't a lot of options for us there but, there was one gay bar named the Rainbow Cafe where everybody knew one another. It was amazing!

Why was it amazing?

They had some really talented drag queens, and I was very popular there.

I am sure you were very popular.. But, rather than being in a small town with one gay bar, what is it like for you to be here in the city where you are one of many?

I don't necessarily find myself worrying about what I am wearing or how I look when I walk outside, in comparison to how I felt while living in a small town in the South.

You mean you had to be more careful of being viewed as "too gay?"

Yes, and here you don't! I really don't worry about it here. I can just be myself and not think about it!

I hear what you are saying but here at your workplace, the David Barton Gym in Chelsea, you do think about how you look, especially, being a trainer and someone who is very fit.

Of course I do.

Did you want to be one of the "A Gays?" Meaning, being on the "A List" of popular men in the city? I mention this, because that was the primary focus of my conversations with Jeremy, Brendan, and Jessie, your workmates. They felt that many gays tend to ostracize others that don't fit their "hotness" criteria! Do you agree with that?

Before I moved here, I kind of became a part of "the scene" here, having been a trapeze artist at Cirque De Soliel. Here in NYC, it was such a different world from the small hometown scene from where I came from, and I got a "little lost" within the social scene; with all these beautiful men with the amazing physiques who "played hard."

What happened to you?

I just wasn't being truly honest with what I wanted to be and found myself conforming to the norm of the group. I was seduced with so much stimulation out there, which resulted in my not being truthful as to who I really was.

What did you do that made you feel dishonest with yourself?

I quit the circus and started just hanging out with the "in crowd" and stopped doing what was really important to me.

Matt is a very attractive and extremely well built young man who came from a quieter gay scene with fewer options, to a scene with beautiful men desiring him. Who wouldn't be changed by all that attention and stimulation? It is no wonder he was seduced by such desire; most gay men would have been seduced as well. The only thing that truly concerned me about his story, was that he quit doing something he loved so he would have more time to play with the boys.

Matthew's experience brings back my own memories of the days before AIDS, when open sexuality and promiscuity was more rampant and compulsive, and Matthew's experience with the "in crowd," may have led him on the same potentially self-destructive path.

Matt, you have to admit that you're pretty much a "hottie," and in the gay world, that gives you plenty of attention from the guys that many of us desire, is that true?

Yes, I know what you're saying but, I wasn't really comfortable with whom I was becoming. I lost whom I inspired to be, by playing the game everyone else was playing.

What was this game, and how did you lose yourself in it? This is important because it is the main crux of this book – playing a game and being inauthentic to yourself!

Hearing Matt admit to playing the "gay game," as so many other interviewees did, gave me further proof that this perspective of the gay world was true. That for many of us, we are often seeking that only that '"quick fix" to satiate ourselves; similar to a sexual orgasm – "hot" for just that moment but, not sustaining.

If we all truly seeking self-fulfillment and self-actualization of for our successes, both career-wise and in love, than being distracted by our more those more immediate and transient desires will not serve our long term goals. Although I have nothing against those "quick fixes," I know they don't serve anything other than what they are; a quick fix and nothing more!

Matt, when do you see gay men playing the game and following others "down the wrong path" and not being true to themselves?

Well, for one, at the gym, I see people who are trying to attain something that simply isn't attainable, such as having a chiseled body or an impressive physique; which simply is not going to happen! So, instead of training in the correct manner, they go to unnatural techniques to obtain that body.

As a trainer, I try to help people get comfortable with what they have, and make the best of how they look by working out and eating right to get into the best shape naturally.

Okay, so let's talk about the gay game with the point mentioned earlier by your manager Jessie, who stated of seeing a group of young gay men "cringing" when he walked past them. That situation angered him and caused him to view these gays as dismissive and devaluing, because he wasn't attractive to them.

Fortunately for Jessie, he knows he is "hot" to many other gay men who like powerfully built men, and viewed the actions of that group as indicative of those who seek to hurt others to feel

better about themselves. Is that something you have seen at the gym or other places?

I call guys like that the "Mean Girls of the Gay World."

Exactly! Thanks for that, and because there are, we need to stop that behavior whenever we can!

Good luck with that, but, when I see somebody like that, I will simply walk away from them. Maybe they'll get the message that they're being a jerk and stop it, or, maybe not.

So how does the gay community in New York embrace you being that you are someone that many of us would want to know. Have you felt anyone acting in a dismissive manner with you in here?

No, everyone here at the gym have been really nice to me but, I can "spot an asshole a mile away" so, I will tend to avoid them if I can. If I come across someone who is acting rude to me, I can feel my "walls coming up" and I will get quiet and try not to engage them if at all possible.

Lucky for you, not everyone else has that ability or choice, after all, it's all about rejection and no one wants to be rejected. Otherwise, we as gay men go to great lengths not to be rejected, since many of us have experienced an initial rejection from our families when we made the conscious choice to "come out of the closet."

I can appreciate that and fortunately, I never experienced that kind of rejection, because I have a supportive family. Also, I wouldn't be friends with anyone who doesn't know I'm gay and is okay with that.

But for many, gay shame has had a detrimental effect on their self-concept and has often led to self-destructive behavior and poor self-esteem. Do you recall ever have a problem with gay shame in your life?

Yes, I remember the time when I "came out. I didn't feel it was anything but normal, so, when my mother asked me where I was going on a date and with whom, I told her it was with my friend Fletcher. Her immediate response was a quiet "oh, okay," and that was all she said at the time.

Later, she confessed of being shocked at my admission but, loved me just the same. Of course, she was a little disappointed at the possibility of my not having children but, came around to accept me for who I was. We agree to disagree whenever she shares her concerns over my lifestyle. Still, I consider myself very fortunate, other friends of mine were not as fortunate.

Yes, I can understand. But, how about your father? How did he take the news?

My father had not been around for some time when I "came out" and my mother remarried, My stepfather felt similarly to my mother; and he too eventually came around to accepting my lifestyle and helped my mother toward accepting my lifestyle as just a part of the "real world."

I recall your friend Jeremy's comments about his mother never being able to accept his sexual orientation, and how painful it was for him not to be able to tell her who he was. But, you clearly didn't have a problem with telling your mother of your true sexual orientation?

Not at all! I would never want the type of unspoken truth that exists between Jeremy and his mom and, as his best friend, I try to be there for him whenever I can.

That's really wonderful of you. But, Jeremy's situation with his mom, and his inability to tell her who he truly is, only perpetuates gay shame. What would you say to gay men like Jeremy about gay shame and its effects on our self-esteem?

Also, do you feel that we in the LGBT community help one another with these shameful feelings by supporting one another in times of crisis, especially, with the spate of young people still committing suicide or, following down self-destructive paths.

I can see that everything is being talked about in the media today, and people are much less fearful of "coming out" and admitting to being gay than they used to be. There also seems to be more of us living more comfortably being gay, and living our lives as normally as anyone else.

Are you living comfortably living today as a gay man?

Yes, I am.

Great! But as I stated earlier, most gay men are not as fortunate as you and are still struggling with living openly and honestly as gay men. So, what do you think we could to help one another in living more honest and authentic lives?

I remember when I was living back home in Virginia, I used to dream about the type of men I would see working out here at the gym and being around them. These men were my fantasy, and now, to know that I have become a part of this world makes me feel great. So, it was easy to understand how I was seduced by being a part of it.

On the other hand, I love helping other men, gay or straight, in reaching their workout goals and as a result, they get to feel better about themselves in the process; that makes me feel really good. *That's certainly one way to help reduce low self-esteem by encouraging others to be the best that they can be; and in the process, feel sexier and more attractive about themselves.*

Exactly. I love the work that I do and especially, helping my clients toward feeling better about themselves. That is what makes me truly happy.

Wonderful, but what about you? Where do you see yourself in another ten years?

Right now, there are a great many things I want to do with my life but, I realize that I could never completely satisfy another person if I am not satisfied with myself. If something romantic comes along with that connection with another person, I would still consider it, but at present, I am focusing on myself.

What about going back to the circus?

I have considered that, but at present, I am focused on transitioning to a job path that is in the more creative, conceptual, design fields, but at present, I really like my work at the gym.

DON'T BE RUDE TO THE WAITER!

What about a boyfriend? I know that you are not really looking for a relationship but, what if the right guy does come along?

I would love to have a boyfriend but if it really doesn't happen, I am okay with that. It will happen when it happens.

I am still curious as to whether the potential boyfriend would be like one of these men at the gym, since I can assume that many of these men fall within your physical type? Or, like many other gay men in this book have said, that's it's not just the physical it's so much more.

It's funny that you're asking me that, because there are so many men in here that I am attracted to but, when I meet with them on the outside, I see how they truly are.

Such as what? What would be a real deal-breaker for you; a total turn-off? Guys, really need to hear this!

If he's not genuine. Or, a more specific turn-off for me, is if he is rude to the waiter.

Wow, that's a good one!

Yes, forget about it! I feel that if he is rude to the waiter then, it says a lot about who he truly is. Because if he rude to them, then he has the potential of being rude or, cruel, to me as well. *That's a really good point. That type of dismissive behavior with someone who is performing a service does indicate a propensity to be that way with those they are intimate with as well.*

Yes, it does say a lot to me and I don't like it!

On the subject of this book, what do you feel that gay men need to do in order to feel better about themselves so they won't take their anger and frustration on the waiter? What do they need to "talk it out, "and in the process, feel better about themselves and reduce gay shame for instance?

You need to find what you love to do. It doesn't have to be complicated. It doesn't have to be hard to find. And if it is hard, then maybe you're not doing the right thing.

What do you believe that gay men are doing to themselves that is the wrong thing other than being rude to the waiter? For instance, what about the way they interact with each other?

I see many guys "talking shit" about one another at the bars but when I meet them in here, they are so sweet and genuine. It's really weird how different they are. So, we all need to make more of an effort to be nice to everyone; not only with those with whom you are physically attracted to.

Thank you Matt, that was a great line to end this interview with.

You're welcome, I had fun, thank you.

END OF INTERVIEW WITH MATT

"THE SWEET GENIUS" – RON BEN-ISRAEL

Interviewed on July 17, 2013 in his office on Greene St. NYC

On my annual attendance to the Garden Party sponsored by the NYC LGBT Community Center in June of this year, I enjoyed all the delicious food and open bar. But, on a special note during this specific occasion ,was my meeting Ron Ben-Israel, the celebrity chef from the Food Network show Sweet Genius for the second time.

Only this time, I was a little more assertive than the first time we met, and asked Ron if we would be a guest on my weekly radio show on WRHU: 88.7 FM, for which, he gladly accepted! We continued to exchange pleasantries and I was secretly flattered that he remembered me from first time we met.

Ron emailed me within the week with his schedule, and a time to meet was arranged. We were set to meet at his SOHO office and kitchens on Greene Street two weeks later for a preliminary interview for the show.

My first impression of the celebrity chef did not change when he graciously invited me into his office and gave me a tour of his kitchen, introducing me to his hard working staff busily making intricate flowers and leaves made of sugar for his high profile clientele.

Our hour-long interview began with Ron quickly sharing on his early childhood memories being gay in his home city, Tel Aviv; which the chef viewed as "gay friendly." He talked openly about his dancing career and his mandatory military service in Israel, in addition to, his gay life and cooking career.

Ron: Living in Israel as a gay boy, I quickly developed a "thick skin," being that I always demanded upon myself that I would act outwardly gay and proud, both as a dancer and in my personal life.

And yet, I was still very sensitive to ridicule by insensitive peers, mainly in the military, where instead of ignoring comments as many often do, I would quickly "get in your face" when confronted by someone who would attempt to intimidate me!

As the interview progressed, I could see both sadness and anger in the chef's body language; especially in his eyes. He continued to relate his childhood history and the choices he made in his career. Interestingly enough, he purposefully chose to be in professions where his artistic talents and creativity would be appreciated and accepted.

I attended mostly performing arts schools because they were less restrictive, and being that I loved to dance and was really good at it, I got to dance with two Israeli Dance Companies and toured internationally.

My dance career continued when I decided to leave Israel for Toronto and finally getting the opportunity to live and work in New York. After all, many of my fellow Israelis love New York! Who doesn't?

Unfortunately, when I came to New York, I found myself with little to no income once my dancing career ended in the late eighties; early nineties. So, I would walk dogs, sell my paintings, and bake cakes!

But it wasn't until I marched in Gay Pride parades in Queens, New York in the early nineties, where I was inspired by the work of Keith Haring, the color purple, and pink triangles; which I chose to incorporate in my cake designs. Ironically, it was those specific sources which helped me to find another successful forum for my creativity and passion.

Soon my cakes designs were gaining a large audience of fans and I found myself making cakes for showrooms such as Swarovski Crystal among others. It was in such a public forum where I was fortunate enough to gain the attention and appreciation of Martha Stewart, who invited me on her television show and promoted my work!

Ron's story was clearly an example of the importance of affirming one's special talents and not allowing self-doubt to stop one from following one's passions, also, in knowing how to make something people need and cherish beautiful, didn't hurt.

After my television appearances with Martha, other television appearances soon followed along with winning culinary competitions in fancy food shows throughout the country; attracting the attention of the Food Network and the offer to do my own cooking show.

Sweet Genius enjoyed three seasons on the Food Network but at present, there is no offer on the table for a fourth season. Fortunately, many of my fans have since wrote to the network demanding that my show be put back on the air; so who knows what the future will be?

For now, I am very happy with running my successful bakery and doing my philanthropic work with such charitable gay organizations as City Harvest. Callen-Lorded, Lambda Legal Defense, and of course, the New York City Gay Community Center, where we got to meet at its annual fundraiser.

My next question for Ron was on how he viewed his own gay identity resulting in his strongest reaction thus far in the interview.

I identify as an Israeli, Jewish, and now a gay American who is passionate on the subject of human suffering, which further fuels my desire to help those most in need, especially, gay youth!"

On the subject of gay shame, his response was equally vociferous.

I view gay shame as another word for "internalized homophobia," where we instinctively as younger gay men, feel bad about being. Even today, I see and hear kids calling each other "faggots;" not even knowing half the time what the word means!

Fortunately we live in a more accepting and permissive culture, imagine living as a gay man or woman in Russia where its forbidden for even the media to talk about gays, and where gay men and women are persecuted daily, and individualism is suppressed.

When I asked about famous celebrities in film and television who continue to refuse to "come out of the closet" and reveal their true identity, Ron's response was even more virulent.

If someone does not step up and speak about who they truly are, then they are murderers! For their inaction is not helping to prevent young gay people struggling with their true natures from committing suicide! We see it happening everywhere, not only in this country!"

While living in Toronto, Canada, Ron wrote for the gay monthly magazine <u>Body </u>Politic, which remained in publication from 1971 to 1987and helped spearhead that gay community's activism in Toronto.

Ron: While writing for *Body Politic,* I learned that our bodies speak for us so, how can we not take an action when it is necessary to do so? Also, how could I live my life without helping others when the need is so great?"

As a result of experiences learned in his social activism, Ron felt it was imperative that we all live our lives "out of the closet" and advocated being honest with those who are important in our lives.

Ron: "The more people who get to know the gay people in their lives, the less ignorant our culture will be! So "come out of your closet" if you are still locked inside it, because being gay is not only about sex but, it is simply who we are!

In closing our interview, Ron emphasized the care needed in "coming out" to family and friends and should not be done impulsively if possible but, with care and consideration.

"After all, we don't have to shove it down their throats!

We don't have to wear leather or be in "drag," to show others our gayness, even though I have done both! Just be yourself and live honestly, and tell your story whenever the opportunity presents itself, as I am doing here with you.

The interview ended with Ron bringing out a sampling of his wedding cakes, much to my enjoyment. I was also very grateful for having such a kind and caring man with amazing talents and verve in our community participate in this book. In addition to being interviewed for this book, he also volunteered to be interviewed on my talk show at Hofstra University.

END OF INTERVIEW WITH RON

CHAPTER SEVENTEEN

"CLOSING COMMENTS"

After extensive investigation of the communication within the gay community, it is clear that "gay shame" 'has clearly had its effects on the communication between gay men within a variety of social situations. Hopefully, hearing the stories of myself and my friends will precipitate some changes in the more negative and devaluing communication within our culture.

The following observations and comments are primarily based on my interviewees' own words, as well as, my own analysis based on my training and experience as a therapist and professor of communication.

BOD DOBSON & TIM ROGERS - *"GAY SHAME" clearly had a detrimental effect on both Bob and Tim, resulting in their mutual drug addictions and troubles with the law for both men. These addictions have tragically led to Bob's death and upon a recent phone interview with Tim on June 17, 2013, the suicide of another lover following Bob's death who according to Tim, was jealous of Tim's devotion to Bob's memory. These deaths led to Tim falling into a "downward spiral" which he just recently pulled himself out of.*

"It took me a long time to deal with both deaths and for today, I am just trying to manage my day to day living, or, according to the 12 Step program, living one day at a time."

According to Tim, Bob's death was directly the result of gay shame, because Bob and he both loved being gay but like many gay men, Bob was having a "really tough time with aging and not looking old; always trying to keep up with the image of being beautiful and desired.

"As far as Bob's drug problem, he didn't think he was being self-destructive because he viewed himself as indestructible!"

This statement is a form of self-denial for Bob who clearly had a problem with drugs (prescription medication) which contributed to his early death. As far as gay shame holds on Tim today:

"I had a lot of trouble accepting being gay when I first came onto the gay scene but for today, the gay world has changed. Gay people are much more open, and things are really different than it used to be. Being gay appears more "mainstream" as well, especially, with so many states passing Gay Marriage initiatives. So for me today, being gay is just not as important as it used to be. Even my HIV status doesn't play a big part in my regular life as it once did."

At present, neither myself or our mutual friend Frank, have been able to contact Tim and I worry about his present situation.
WAYNE SCHERZER *"GAY SHAME" - in a recent interview with Wayne, he felt that shame came into his life through his fear of being raped or victimized by gay men; viewing gay men as*

the predators that society at the time (early 70s) perpetrated through ignorance and non-acceptance.

In a phone interview with Wayne on June 14, 2012, he went even further with the predator description of gay men when he went to the gay bars and clubs with his cast mates back in the early seventies. "

I felt so sure that gay guys were going to victimize and corrupt me that I recall my hands shaking when I entered the bars with my friends."

As far as gay shame is concerned, Wayne felt similar to Tim's statements, in that, the shame for being gay is more pervasive with older gay men than with the younger generation of gays:

"Gay shame is more prevalent with the older gays based on the mindset of their day. Today's generation is clearly being embolden by the support they are receiving from statements made by President Obama and his administration. I was personally affected hearing our President speak of the importance of gay rights in his Inaugural Address, and that he made purposeful mention of our rights three times! That speech brought tears to my eyes, as it did for many gays throughout this county."

Wayne went further on the subject of gay shame to add historical and theatrical references:

"The days of Oscar Wilde, as depicted in the play *Gross Indecency,* when homosexuals could be imprisoned simply for being sexual or intimate with one another, even in their own homes, have indeed changed, and thank God for that!"

DAVID PEVSNER - *"GAY SHAME" - David reported that for him, gay shame appeared most evident through the selective communication of gay men in only choosing to talk to men that they were primarily physically attracted to. Also, David made mention of how gay men, often while "cruising for sex," would often scowl as they "were on the hunt;" thinking that facial expression made them look "hotter" and sexier to other men but it truth, made them more unapproachable.*

At present, David is still living in Los Angles and pursuing his theatrical career; acting in films, television, plays, and writing plays. He is also very involved in gay politics and activism.

AARON TANNER - *"'GAY SHAME" - for Aaron, I strongly believe had a significant impact on his decision to follow a career in pornography and engaging in unsafe sex and yet, still hoping to meet "Mr. Wonderful" for a happy and healthy relationship. Although being in the porn industry does not mean he won't find that healthy and happy relationship; in interviews with several porn stars for my weekly radio show, the chances are lessened due to feelings of jealousy and insecurity. *As of late, I have been unable to reach Aaron for further comments on gay shame and I am very concerned that I have been unable to reach him as are his friends here.*

ROB ORDONEZ- "Gay shame" for me has to deal with the shame my family tried to make me feel for being gay and not worthy to being a part of the family. I am glad that my father paid me to leave my family behind in Mexico to create a much better life here in New York City. My life now is much happier and I am doing the kind of work I love as a party promoter, performance artist and photographer. I love the family I created for myself in New York and I thank my father for providing me the opportunity to pursue my real life. I am the winner here, not him!

BRIAN KENT – *Brian continues to be actively involved in his singing career and has been performing all over the world. Tragically, "gay shame" seems to have contributed to the deaths of several of his friends as posted on Facebook, either through apparent suicide or substance abuse, including the grandson of screen legend, Rita Hayworth. As for Brian, he seems to be doing wonderfully and looks fantastic in recent photos also posted on Facebook...*

Most recently, Brian responded to me on Facebook about his work with suicide prevention following the deaths of his young friends. He is also in a very healthy relationship with a wonderful man and is performing throughout the world in mostly gay music festivals and concerts. His latest cd is coming out soon and he is very proud of it.

IRA SMITH – "My brother is a classic "homophobe" and so we haven't spoken in years. I recently lost my lover to cancer and don't give a fuck about what others think of me anymore!"

Following the death of his lover who was suffering with cancer for year, Ira continued to work in his lover's leather store at the Ramrod bar in Ft. Lauderdale and has slimmed down and seems to be happy and more at peace. He is seen frequently posing for new pictures on his Facebook profile.

BRAD CARPENTER & CHRIS ARUDA: *Both men are doing very well and are thrilled with their married life. Brad most recently appeared on my radio show; Talk it OUT with Dr. Vince with his good friend George Jagatic on the subject of "Flag Dancing and Circuit Parties." Both men were active participants in Flag Dancing and loved performing at circuit parties and gay festivals throughout the country. The men even volunteered to be videotaped on YouTube performing their Flag Dancing routine for my listeners. Brad continues to produce television shows including Nurse Jackie and Boardwalk Empire. Both men continue to vacation at the Fire Island Pines but are spending less time there than in their past.*

JEREMY LOPEZ (CHA-CHA) – As of June 30, 2014, Jeremy still calls himself, "very single" and continues to have a difficult relationship with his mother and the rest of his family. As far as dating in the gay world, he continues to view other gays as: "dating clones" and not willing to consider someone smaller or more petite. And yet, his family's rejection has only served to make him stronger and more focused on being a success in his career and in finding love. *Jessie Meli, Brendan G. and Matthew Griffin* still continue to work at the David Barton Gym and are all doing amazingly well. In my frequent visits to the gym, all ask me about the status of my book.

BRENDAN GLEASON – Brendan is performing and promoting his music and is in healthy gay relationship for the first time. His present concern for the gay community is that we don't treat our gay elders with the care and consideration they deserve. He just recently performed and produced his first full length studio record of his song "Imposter" which can be downloaded on YouTube.com. He continues to teach gymnastics and piano and loves life and his new lover.

DR. VINCE'S PROFESSIONAL EXPERIENCE

Having attained a doctorate in May of 1992 following the publication of his dissertation which investigated the need for supportive therapy for health professionals working with AIDS patients, Dr. Pellegrino continued to work for several years in psychiatric units and hospices filled with PWAs (People with AIDS). In working with this population, he observed a high degree of worker "burn-out" in both settings; which also occurs in many other high stress professions.

His dissertation asserted the need for supportive group therapy for health professionals working within the AIDS milieu. Research conducted by Dr. Pellegrino proved the necessity of having a "safe place" for health professionals within the workplace that provided easily accessible therapeutic sessions during the worker's schedule when needed.

At present, Dr. Pellegrino teaches classes in Interpersonal Communication, Public Speaking and Oral Communication at Hofstra University and Nassau Community College in addition to hosting a weekly radio show *Talk it OUT with Dr. Vince* on WRHU 88.7 FM. In addition to completing this book on gay male communication, he had been writing articles for *The Huffington Post* and has been a long time columnist for *Edge Magazine*.

APPENDIX

*The following are questions specifically designed for my interviewees, please review and answer these questions for yourself as if you are also subjects for this book.

I. QUESTIONS FOR THE GAY MALE INTERVIEWEES

*All the following questions were subject to some change.

1. Give us some background about yourself, specifically, your childhood experiences of being gay or simply different from the other children around you.

2. How and when did you "come out of the closet?"

3. How did you see yourself as a child? Isolated, out-going, talkative, creative, scared?

4. How would you best use your communication skills as you traveled through life; in childhood/ adolescence/ as a young adult/ an adult?

5. For today, do you experience a more positive gay, self-image or does it still feel mostly negative? Why? How does your self-image reflect in your communication?

6. How do you feel speaking one on one in social situations? Are you honest about yourself? Are the majority of your conversations mostly superficial? When do you begin to feel safe enough to self-disclose more?

7. How do you think gay men relate to one another? Mostly honestly, deeply, superficially, dramatically, or fill in the blank?

8. In either one-on-one or group communication, are you a leader or a follower? Why?

9. The term, "gay-mob psychology?" Define it for yourself?

10. Being "odd man out" or "picked on?" Has that happened often to you? If it did, for what reasons do you believe caused that to happen and how did that bullying affect your communication with others?

10a. If bullying was never a problem for you, then happened to cause you to avoid being bullied? Did physical appearance play any part in the possible outcome?

11. Give us details as to your most satisfying gay experience? Was it during a gay event or was it during a more private moment?

12. When do you feel shame with regards to your gay identity? When do you experience guilt,

and how do both these feelings affect your behavior?

13. What do you perceive are the origins or history of your feelings of shame and guilt with regards to your gay identity?

14. Do you perceive that feelings of shame or guilt have or have had an adverse effect on how you interact or relate to other gay men? Specifically, do you see attitudes of superiority and, or indifference to other gay men being a result of that shame and guilt about being gay?

15. Do you perceive those feelings of shame and guilt has also had an adverse effect upon how you interact or relate to heterosexual men and women?

16. As with myself, did you feel that "coming out" to your family and friends as a gay man, was an important step toward your acceptance of being gay?

17. Who was the most significant person in your life at the time you "came out of the closet?" What did they do that propelled you to take that step? Was your experience of that person positive or negative?

18. What is your best technique in meeting other gay men in either a gay bar or social event for future interactions?"

19. What physical attributes do you find attractive in other gay men? What non-physical attributes do you find attractive? What attitudes do you find unattractive?

20. What do you envision a potential future for yourself with regards to you gay life? What goals do you hope to accomplish in your lifetime and how does your acceptance of your gay identity aid you toward achieving your life plans?

II. *QUESTIONS SPECIFICALLY ABOUT GAY COMMUNICATION*

1. Do you perceive social communication with other gay men to be affected by an implied "class system" based primarily, on physical attractiveness?

2. Regarding the "game analogy" and gay male communication, do you feel that analogy fits? Yes or no? Why or why not?

3. What are your personal feelings about gay communication? Does it seem "normal" to you? Do you share any of the author's views on the subject? Why?

4. How would you rate your communication skills today? How do you communicate with friends/ lovers/family/acquaintances? How does your communication differ with each situation?

5. How does your communication differ today from when you recall occurring when you first

began interacting with gay men? How did your communication change as you began to assimilate into a more gay-friendly or focused culture?

III. *QUESTIONS FOR LESBIAN INTERVIEWEES*

1. How do your experiences as a gay woman or a lesbian, differ from what you perceive to be the experiences of gay men you either know or have observed?

2. Do you prefer being called a lesbian or a gay woman? If you prefer being recognized as a gay woman, is it because you feel closer to gay men and don't want another term to describe yourself? How do you feel about the term lesbian?

3. What advice would you give gay men as to how they interact and relate with one another? Do you feel there is serious room for improvement?

4. What do you perceive the feelings of shame and guilt affect how gay men interact and relate to one another?

5. Do you feel that gay women suffer from the same lack of a positive gay identity as do many gay men to whom this book is devoted to?

6. What future to do envision for the gay community if gay men and gay women can learn to deal more effectively with their shame and guilt?

7. Do you agree that feelings of shame and guilt contribute toward gay men mistreating or disrespecting one another?

8. Specifically, how do you perceive gay men mistreating or disrespecting one another? Is it evident in their behavior toward one another individually or within groups or cliques?

9. What is your memory of "coming out of the closet?" Was it an important step toward your acceptance of your own gay identity?

10. What advice would you like to give to other gay men and women who may be reading this book with regards to how they communicate with one another?

REFERENCES

1. <u>Collins Gem English Dictionary</u>, Revised edition, Great Britain: Wm. Collins and Sons, 1989.

2. Johnson, David R. "Shame Dynamics among Creative Arts Therapists." <u>Dramascope</u>, N.A.D.T. Newsletter, Vol. XVI, (Winter/Spring 1996), 6-7.

3. Marcus, Eric. <u>The Male Couple's Guide</u>, Revised edition, New York: Harper Collins Publishers Inc., 1992.

4. McKinley, Jesse. "Dirty Dancing." <u>OUT</u>, (May, 1998), 90-95.

5. "Sex in America; A Definitive Survey," July 24, 2012

6. Trenholm, Sarah. <u>Thinking through Communication</u>, Boston: Allen and Bacon, 1995.

7.. Zeuschner, Raymond. <u>Communicating Today</u>. 2nd ed. Boston: Allyn and Bacon, 1997.

<u>INTERVIEWS</u>

1. Anonymous Gay Man, Brooklyn, NY (now living in) Rome, Italy, July 30, 2006.
2. Anonymous Gay Woman, Brooklyn, NY, October 27, 2007.
3. Barton, Rick., Tulsa, Oklahoma June, 20, 1998.
4. Danz, Cassandra., New York. N.Y., May 19, 1998.
5. Dobson, Bob & Tim Rogers, Yarmouth, Massachusetts, June 16, 1999.
6. Dunbar-Smith, New Milford, Ct, January 15, 2013.
6. Gleason, Brent, New York City, NY, February 14, 2013.
7. Kent, Brian, New York City, NY, May 4, 2007.
8. Ordonez, Rob, Queens, NY, June 22, 2007.
9. Oruda, Chris & Brad Carpenter, New York City, NY in 2009.
9. Scherzer, Wayne, NYC, NY. August 9, 2006.
10. Tanner, Aaron & Eric, NYC, NY, May 4, 2007.
11. Three Gay Men from Gold's Gym, NYC, NY, May 9, 2011.
12. Interview with Cha Cha Lopez, Jesse Meli, Brendan G., and Matthew Griffin at Chelsea David Barton Gym on July 2013
13. Interview with Ron Ben-Israel, *The Sweet Genius* on July 17, 2013

Vince Pellegrino

www.ingramcontent.com/pod-product-compliance
Lightning Source LLC
Chambersburg PA
CBHW082350270326
41935CB00013B/1575